Organization, Policy, and Practice in the Human Services

Organization, Policy, and Practice in the Human Services

Bernard Neugeboren

School of Social Work
Rutgers University

Longman
New York & London

This book is dedicated to my wife, Ramona L. Neugeboren, whose day-to-day experiences as a "good bureaucrat" in the public services enhanced my interest in applying these concepts to *real* problems in human service organizations.

Longman Inc., 95 Church Street, White Plains, N.Y. 10601
Associated companies, branches, and representatives throughout the world.

Developmental Editor: Irving E. Rockwood
Editorial and Design Supervisor: Barbara A. Lombardo
Production Supervisor: Ferne Y. Kawahara
Composition: David E. Seham Associates, Inc.
Printing and Binding: The Alpine Press

Library of Congress Cataloging in Publication Data

Neugeboren, Bernard.
   Organization, policy, and practice in the human services.

   Bibliography: p.
   Includes index.
   1. Social work administration—United States.
2. Social service—United States.   3. Organization.
I. Title.   [DNLM: 1. Social Work, Psychiatric.   WM 30.5
N4840]
HV91.N445   1984   361.3′068   84-14383
ISBN 0-582-28507-0

Manufactured in the United States of America
Printing: 9 8 7 6 5 4 3   Year: 92 91 90 89 88 87

84464 TABLE OF CONTENTS

FOREWORD

Social work, like most professions, encompasses a range of functions, settings, and modes of practice. At a given point in time, one or another subset of functions and intervention strategies may predominate and the profession as a whole comes to be identified with one of its parts. Currently, for example, social workers concerned with providing counseling services to individuals and families experiencing difficulties in psychological and social functioning have attained a position of sufficient influence to enable them to shape the direction of the profession as a whole. This is reflected in the curricula of schools and departments of social work and the preference of professional social workers for employment with counseling agencies, particularly those under voluntary auspices or, when possible, to enter into private practice.

In the present volume, Professor Neugeboren directs our attention to other dimensions of social work practice that, while they reflect the bulk of the actual responsibilities of social workers, both historically and currently, have been neglected by educators and practitioners. Social work is, and has been since its beginnings in the Charities Organization Societies of the last century, an *organizational* profession. Most social work practice takes place within bureaucratically structured and controlled organizations, whether in the public or private sectors. For social services to be effectively provided, practitioners must be knowledgeable about the nature of these organizations, and skillful in operating within them.

As Professor Neugeboren makes clear, administrators are not the only social workers who require tutoring in the complexities and vagaries of organizational life; this is needed by all who have a part in providing services through the medium of the modern social service organization. The present volume performs an important educational service by making available to social work students knowledge of the complex organization's behavior, along with insights into how that knowledge can be applied to organizational problems that impede service goals.

In addition to offering a basic orientation to the structure and operations of social service organizations, the present text provides the reader with an understanding of some of the latest explorations in organizational theory, particularly the application of political models of analysis to organizational behavior. Historically, the study of social service organizations and their proper management relied heavily on theories of economic organizations and the management practices developed for them. As a result, most social service organizations and social administrators were seen as "poor copies" of the business firm and the business manager.

In addition to directing attention to the organizations where social work is practiced, Professor Neugeboren reassesses the kinds of practice appropriate for contemporary conditions. In his emphasis on "social care," Professor Neugeboren highlights a central feature of modern life—the transformation of social problems from episodic "crises" to more-or-less permanent "conditions." Advances in the biomedical sciences, for example, lower infant mortality rates while extending life expectancies, thus increasing the demand for long-term care for both infants (and later, children and adults) with physical and mental defects and for an increasing number of elderly. Lack of advances in race relations, on the other hand, exacerbate the social and psychological fallout of the racism that has tainted American society since the 17th century and that continues to produce intractable social problems for significant proportions of our non-white populations.

These situations are exacerbated by the breakdown in the care-giving capacity of the American family. Between 1960 and 1979, the proportion of married women in the labor force with children under six years of age more than doubled; over nearly the same interval, divorce rates rose 112 percent. By 1980, 18 percent of families with children were headed by a single parent, typically a woman, with little or no support from the other parent. Simultaneously, the proportion of the elderly who live with their children declined by approximately 50 percent, while the number of Americans over 65 increased by a similar percentage. For these, and many other groups, the social services have to provide on-going care and assistance for conditions which are not likely to go away.

Emile Durkheim once remarked that "the categorical imperative of the moral conscience is assuming the following form: *Make yourself usefully fulfill a determinate function.* The extraordinary rate of change in modern society requires continuous monitoring of how successful we are in heeding this advice. The social work profession has been undergoing something of an identity crisis over the past decade as we try to identify the functions that we can successfully fulfill. The present volume points to two problems that society needs to solve. The first concerns the successful operation of complex institutions. Ours is truly an "organizational society" and will become more so. A major need in such a society is for people knowledgeable about the nature of this complexity, and skillful in making institutions work for people.

A second problem has to do with the reexamination of what is meant by the word "dependency," and a rethinking of the best ways for dealing with the social and personal problems confronting people in the last quarter of the twentieth century. New approaches to social services are needed, as well as new ways of organizing and providing them. Both of these problems are addressed in this book, which can be expected to make a significant contribution to assisting tomorrow's social workers to deal more effectively with the world they will face. After all, "the future," as Karl Weick so aptly puts it, "is not what it used to be."

Burton Gummer
School of Social Welfare
Rockefeller College of Public Affairs and Policy
State University of New York at Albany

PREFACE

THE NEED FOR HUMAN SERVICE ORGANIZATIONS

The commitment of human service practitioners—whether administrators, supervisors, or direct service personnel—is to assist others to live a better life. As society becomes more fragmented and such institutions as the family can no longer perform their traditional functions, the human service professions must fill the resulting gap. The task of providing effective service is made more difficult by the fact that many human problems are complex and require a variety of institutional responses. Although the individual professional may be eager to meet these needs, in many instances complex problems cannot be solved by individual effort alone.

Human service organizations have been established to provide a structure to meet these multifaceted needs—whether of a proverty-stricken single parent overwhelmed with child care responsibilities, or a chronically ill schizophrenic recently discharged after many years in an institution, an ex-convict on parole, or an elderly disabled widow who cannot be taken care of by her children. Human service organizations allow for the coordination of the wide variety of resources needed; they allow for the organization and delivery of services. Thus, it has become crucial that different human service practitioners work together cooperatively within large multifunction agencies.

BUREAUCRATIC EXPERTISE

The need to work effectively within an organizational context means that human service practitioners must not only master skills related to their particular specialization, but must also acquire a certain level of "bureaucratic expertise" (Pruger 1973). Although technical professional skill is essential, whether such skill actually benefits clients depends greatly on how it is delivered within an organizational context. The present book is intended to instruct human service practitioners in this bureaucratic knowledge and skill—to enable them to navigate more effectively through the bureaucratic maze characteristic of complex organizations. This understanding should facilitate appreciation of the organizational opportunities and constraints on practice. By understanding which pathways in the organizational maze are available for use—and which are not—the practitioner can conserve energy and avoid the occupational burnout so characteristic of work within human service fields. Above all, bureaucratic expertise helps the practitioner achieve the ultimate goal of the profession—client benefit.

As indicated, this book is directed to practitioners in human service organizations. "Practitioners" here refers to *both* direct service personnel and the supervisory and administrative staff. The organizational concepts contained in this book can therefore help individuals at all levels of the organization understand how the "system" may constrain or facilitate their particular roles. (Rein and White 1981:2). "Bureaucratic expertise" is required of all organizational members if they are to maximize their performance of assigned tasks. In different ways, such expertise is needed by the caseworker, line supervisor, program developer, manager, and executive in the human service organization.

As indicated, "bureaucratic expertise" is based on the understanding of both the organizational opportunities and constraints on practice—how the system constrains as well as facilitates practitioner role and function. Practitioners are usually well aware of how the agency constrains their efforts—how the rules and regulations limit what they are able to do. These constraints operate on all levels. Direct service workers often assume that policies only constrain their decision making. They tend not to realize that administrators and supervisors also have their constraints. This lack of awareness stems from the fact that one can only perceive what is happening in an agency from the position one occupies. We "stand where we sit." Our perspective and goals are influenced by events that impact on us because we occupy a particular position in the organization. A direct service worker doing discharge planning is influenced by the pressures associated with service to clients (pressures from the clients themselves, from direct service personnel in other agencies, the community, etc.). In contrast, the administrator is influenced both by superiors and subordinates and by such pressures as demands for accountability from funding authorities.

To focus on constraints *only* would be counterproductive. A more constructive approach is to understand and appreciate the opportunities the organization provides. This may appear somewhat Pollyannaish. *How can a bureaucratic organization be helpful?* Line workers often wonder how "those bureaucrats on the upper levels can manage to make things so complicated with their rules and policies." It is often true that administrators who make policies are not fully aware of the realities of day-to-day practice. This is intrinsic to life in a bureaucracy. It is the nature of complex organizations to have many barriers to communication. In a large system with many people, who are on different levels and have different functions and roles, one cannot communicate as one does in primary groups such as the family. By gaining bureaucratic expertise, however, we can accept the inevitable strains and exploit the opportunities. We can appreciate the fact that work in a large complex organization requires a unique set of skills, different from those involved in serving clients. We understand also that as rules are general there is some room for interpretation and discretion. This is because bureaucratic expertise crucially involves the idea that rules are means and not ends in themselves. The "good bureaucrat" does not lose sight of the primary purpose of his or her efforts—client benefit.

Bureaucratic expertise also helps us understand the difference between problems caused by individual versus organizational dysfunction. In the human services many are trained to understand individual problems in order to provide direct service to clients. Although this individual focus is important to the direct service role and function, it can also be a handicap in working in complex organizations. There are many problems in agencies which stem from inappropriate agency policies and procedures. By focusing on the individual, be it direct service worker, supervisor, or administrator, we in a sense are *blaming the victim*. Bureaucratic expertise can help us distinguish between individual incompetence and organizational incompetence. It is sometimes difficult to separate the two, especially because they often interact. Yet distinguishing the source of the problem is important if we are to reach the appropriate solution. It should also be noted that individual incompetence itself often has its origins in institutional problems. Individual incompetence involves a gap between what was taught in school and what the job requires. Often this gap lies not in the area of technical skills, but rather in the ability to appreciate the influence of agency contextual factors—organizational opportunities and constraints on practice.

An assumption made throughout this book is that human service organizations for the most part are structured in a traditional bureaucratic manner, with official power and authority centralized at the upper levels (Tannenbaum 1974). It is crucial that human service practitioners be fully aware of how this inherently autocratic power structure influences their daily practice and shapes opportunities and constraints. Professional commitment to advocacy needs to be moderated by an understanding of how the hierarchical power structure limits the feasibility of conflict strategies by lower-level employees. This does not mean that lower-level staff must be powerless in their relationships with the upper levels; it simply means that in order to maximize their effectiveness, they must be "good bureaucrats," with an understanding of structural constraints on action. Such structural constraints are counterbalanced by the opportunities derived from wide areas of discretion (see Chapter 6). This perspective is presented as a corrective for the notion that practitioners can openly confront the power structure in human service organizations, a notion which has all too often resulted in their inability to manipulate the system for themselves and their clients. Ultimately, this notion derives from the incorrect assumption that all practitioners have power similar to that of the "full professional" (e.g., doctors, lawyers, and professors), who have freedom and autonomy to act related to their status and practice in nonhierarchical settings. The "semiprofessionals" (e.g., teachers, nurses, and social workers), because they work in hierarchical systems, do not have the kind of authority and power available to the "full professionals" (Etzioni 1964).

STRATEGIES USED IN THE BOOK

This book makes use of several strategies to help the reader grasp organizational concepts and their relevance. Because the state of our understanding is still limited, organizational concepts are presented in *issue* terms. That is, such concepts as organizational goals, structures, leadership, decision making, change, ideologies, and technologies are presented as the basic knowledge human service practitioners need to understand the day-to-day problems confronted in their practice. The different points of view on how these concepts are relevant for human service practice are introduced, to enable the reader to examine the pros and cons of various approaches to the analysis of human service organizations. These different viewpoints can thus be related to the practitioner's own experience working in complex organizations. Even the beginning worker in the human service field has had exposure to life in large complex bureaucratic organizations. Whether from being educated in large schools or from receiving medical care in a general hospital, we have all been exposed to the difficulties inherent in complex organizations. Therefore, the first strategy used in exploring human service agencies is to view these organizations in issue terms, keeping in mind there are few absolutes that hold in this field.

A second strategy is to integrate organizational knowledge with the general goal of client benefit. In particular, three key goals of human service programs will be emphasized: social care, social control, and rehabilitation. Throughout the book an effort will be made to assess whether organizational structures and administrative actions are conducive to achieving these goals. These three goals will also be related to such substantive areas of human service as child welfare, mental health, health, corrections, and gerontology. Again, the purpose of integrating the understanding of the goals of specific fields of practice with organizational knowledge is to prevent the latter emphasis from displacing the former. No matter what degree of bureaucratic expertise we may develop it should always be clear that this expertise has one purpose— to help alleviate human difficulties.

A final strategy used to insure that readers will fully appreciate the relevance of organizational and administrative concepts is the application of these concepts to real case situations. Thus, at the end of each chapter the concepts and principles that were introduced are applied to one of the three cases in the appendix.

Two of the cases, "From Psychological Work To Social Work" and "Mental Health Rules and Regulations," illustrate attempts made at major organizational and policy changes in the child welfare and mental health sectors. "From Psychological Work To Social Work" depicts a human service administrator introducing modifications in the goals, structures, ideologies and technologies of a county child welfare agency mandated to provide protective services to children. The administrator attempts to use a socially oriented service delivery approach and demonstrates the obstacles encountered and the strategies used in the process.

"Mental Health Rules and Regulations" provides case material of major policy change on a state level. The case describes the problems and issues associated with the attempt to shift emphasis in mental health programs to servicing the chronically mentally ill.

The third case "Disciplinary Action" is a brief narrative of a personnel problem involving the sanctioning of an employee for nonperformance of work and inappropriate behavior. Issues related to management philosophies, bureausis, burnout, authority, control, and power are illustrated through this case situation.

These cases provide not only a vehicle for illustrating organizational concepts but also enable their linking with policy and practice in the human services. This integration of knowledge on bureaucratic organization with content from human service programs should enable a more comprehensive understanding of how the human service organization works in practice.

FRAMEWORK AND CONTENTS OF THE BOOK

The framework and contents of this book are based on three areas of knowledge: (a) goals of human service programs, (b) theoretical foundations, and (c) knowledge relevant for professional action. Accordingly, the book is divided into three major sections. The two chapters of the first section focus on the goals of human service programs. This initial stress on the goals is intended to alert the reader to the importance of differentiating between the program means and ends. Such differentiation is important if goal displacement—a common tendency in the field—is to be avoided. Goal displacement in the human services is the phenomenon whereby organizational means displace the ends of consumer benefit.

Chapter 1, "Social Care, Social Control, and Rehabilitation," analyzes three major goals of human service programs. Chapter 2, "Organizational Goals," elaborates on the goals of human service agencies by examining the concept of organizational goals, including the functions they perform.

The second section, Chapters 3–7, provides the theoretical foundations needed for understanding human service organizations. It utilizes two polar approaches to the analysis of human service agencies—individual versus systemic. Together, these two views explain the causes, and therefore the possible solutions, of organizational problems.

Chapter 3, "Management Models," discusses three different approaches to the organization and administration of human service organizations: the classical, human relations, and structuralist approaches. These three management models stress to varying degrees the importance of individuals versus organizational factors in the operation of human service agencies. Together, they provide the practitioner with a comprehensive approach to understanding why and how human service agencies function. A systems model that integrates the three basic management models is also presented in Chapter 3.

A more specific understanding of the structural aspects of human service agencies is given in Chapters 4 and 5. In Chapter 4, "Organizational Structure," the focus is on how the structure can provide opportunities as well as limit human service practice. As will be emphasized throughout, appreciation of the purpose of organizational structure can enable the human service practitioner to act more appropriately and effectively in the pursuit of the ultimate goal of client benefit. Chapter 5, "Organizational Subsystems," presents a more detailed model for organizational structure, including subsystem functions, dynamics, and mechanisms. This comprehensive subsystems model provides a diagnostic tool for analyzing and solving human service organizational problems.

Chapter 6, "Bureaucracy, Bureaupathology, Bureausis, and the Good Bureaucrat," examines the two basic causes of human service agency difficulties, the individual and the system. First, bureaucracy is presented in functional terms, with a discussion of the inevitable strains present in this form of organizational structure. The discussion then turns to bureausis—individual dysfunction—and bureaupathology—defective organization. The good bureaucrat is presented as a solution to the inherent difficulties of working in a complex organizational environment. The good bureaucrat is one who has the skill to maximize opportunities and minimize the constraints on his or her practice.

One potential consequence of the strain of working in a bureaucratic system is occupational burnout, the focus of Chapter 7. Like agency difficulties, burnout can be caused by the individual and/or the system. Chapter 7 discusses occupational burnout on both the direct service and administrative levels and proposes different solutions for each.

The concluding section, Chapters 8–14, is devoted to the more specific knowledge required for professional action within the organizational context. Included in this section are topics such as authority, leadership, decision making, organizational change, interorganizational relations, professional ideologies, and technologies. Although this material is particularly relevant for administrative and supervisory staff, it can also be useful for direct service practitioners.

Chapter 8 on "Authority, Control, and Power," moves the analysis to an area that poses much ambivalence for the practitioner. The chapter tackles the reasons for the difficulties in the use of authority and control in relationship to clients, colleagues, superiors, and subordinates. It explains the need for authority and control to integrate the individual and organizational goals, and it considers the use of personnel selection, training, rewards, and structure to achieve this integration.

Chapters 9 and 10—"Leadership" and "Decision Making"—focus on the role of the individual in assuming leadership and decision-making responsibilities. Leadership is viewed as dependent not only on the ability of the person, but also on situational factors. Different levels of leadership are related to varying organizational positions and leadership needs. The analysis of administrative decision making in Chapter 10 also combines the individual and situational aspects of the decision-making process. A decision-making model is presented, including both rational and nonrational elements.

Chapter 11, "Organizational Change," analyzes the goals and methods involved in achieving change, as well as the various sources of resistance to change. Strategies discussed include the two alternative targets for change— the individual and the organization—and the tactics of power and consensus.

Chapter 12, "Interorganizational Relations," presents a model of coordination between organizations which assumes two basic requirements: shared goals and resource exchange. The barriers to coordination are analyzed and strategies for overcoming them are presented. The distinction between coordination and integration is also discussed.

Chapter 13 explores the area of professional ideologies, showing how they function as important determinants of the behavior of human service practitioners. After analyzing the ideological basis for conflicts within agencies, the chapter suggests strategies for avoiding this type of conflict.

The final chapter of the book, Chapter 14, deals with human service technologies. It directs attention to two alternative service delivery approaches:

changing people or changing situations. The extent to which human service technologies are determinate or indeterminate is discussed and linked to the three goals of human service programs: social care, social control, and rehabilitation. Public versus voluntary organizational auspice is also related to two service delivery technologies: extensive versus intensive.

CASE APPLICATIONS

Throughout the fourteen chapters a variety of situations in the human service field are used as examples. In addition, three cases, which are included in the Appendix, are used to illustrate how the organizational principles and concepts introduced in each chapter can apply to real human service problems.·

As indicated earlier, the purpose of this book is to facilitate the practice of the human service worker by providing knowledge on the influences of the agency context. The case applications are a crucial means to this goal. They can facilitate either a depth or breadth of understanding. The case applications of a single concept area at the end of each chapter provide an example of a depth approach. This approach can help the reader achieve a detailed understanding of specific aspects of one concept area. For example, the need to understand the issues and tasks associated with interagency relations can be met by application of the concepts in Chapter 12 ("Interorganizational Relations") to several case stituations. A breadth approach strives to accomplish a comprehensive understanding of an organizational situation through the application of several concepts to a single case. For example, the concepts on organizational change, ideologies and technologies (Chapters 11, 13, and 14) could be applied to one of the cases in the book. This approach facilitates the appreciation of the interrelationships among the different areas.

These two approaches, depth and breadth. can be used in structuring formal training programs. Whether the book is used in a university or in an in-service agency setting, assignments can be structured to accomplish the depth and/or breadth objectives. For example, student presentations can focus on application of a single concept area, whereas a comprehensive final paper can include the application of all the concepts to a case situation.

I would like to acknowledge the financial support provided by a grant (#2C199-201) from the Office of Human Development Services of the United States Department of Health and Human Services. I am especially appreciative of the assistance given by staff member Ms. Estelle Haperling, Child Welfare Services Specialist.

I wish to acknowledge the assistance given by Lori Schlosser, who was responsible for the preparation of the initial drafts of the cases in this book. I am also appreciative to the following human service administrators, who provided the material for these cases: Karen Albert, Thomas Blatner, and Dr. Michael Rotov. The cartoons in this book were done by Dorothy W. Avis, a former student, who by her portrayal of the contradictions in organizational life substantiates the adage that a "picture is worth a thousand words."

Dr. Harold Demone, Dean of the Rutgers University School of Social Work, provided support and encouragement. The educational leave granted by Rutgers, The State University, enabled me to write the initial drafts of this book. I would also like to acknowledge the assistance given by Mrs. Sylvia Forman and Mrs. Barbara Molnar, who typed the manuscript as well as my secretary, Jane Knauss. The assistance provided by the staff at Longman—Randee Falk, Barbara Lombardo, and Irving Rockwood—is most appreciated. Finally, I would like to acknowledge the important influence that the writings of Robert Morris had on my thinking and writing in the area of social care.

ACKNOWLEDGMENTS

Excerpts from *Human Service Organization* by Yaheskel Hasenfeld © 1974 by Prentice-Hall, Inc., Englewood Cliffs, NJ. Reprinted by permission of the publisher.

Excerpts from *Supervision in Social Work* by Alfred Kadushin © 1975 Columbia University Press, New York, NY. Reprinted by permission of the publisher.

Excerpts from *Child Welfare Services* by Alfred Kadushin © 1974 Macmillan Publishing Company, New York, NY. Reprinted by permission of the publisher.

Excerpts from *The Bureaucratic Experience, Second Edition* by Ralph Hummel © 1982 by St. Martin's Press, Inc. Reprinted by permission of the publisher.

Excerpt from *People-Processing* by Jeffrey Manditch Prottas (Lexington Books, D.C. Heath and Company) © 1979 by D.C. Heath and Company. Reprinted by permission of the publisher.

Excerpts from "Skills and Tactics in Hospital Practice" by Allison Murdach from *Social Work*, Vol. 28 No. 4 (July-August 1983) © 1983 National Association of Social Workers, Inc. Reprinted by permission of the publisher.

SOCIAL CARE,
SOCIAL CONTROL,
AND REHABILITATION

HUMAN SERVICE PROGRAM GOALS AND MEANS

1

OUTLINE

I. Issues
   A. Policy—A Philosophy for Practice—Goals versus Means
   B. Social Care, Social Control, and Rehabilitation
      1. Individual and Situation Are Correlated
         a. Changing the Individual will Result in Situational Change
         b. Changing the Situation will Result in Individual Change
         c. Interaction between Individual and Situational Change
      2. Individual and Situation Are Not Correlated
      3. Inverse Relationships between Care, Control, and Rehabilitation
         a. Rehabilitation and Control
         b. Rehabilitation and Care
         c. Care and Control
   C. Policy Implications of Conflicting or Congruent Goals
   D. Prevention as a Goal of Human Service Programs

II. Definition
   A. Social Care
   B. Social Control
   C. Rehabilitation
   D. Program Goals—Means versus Ends
   E. Program Goals—A Continuum

III. Implication of Analysis of Social Program Goals for Human Service Administration
   A. Policy Formulation
   B. Program Design
   C. Program Monitoring and Control

IV. Summary

V. Application to Case "From Psychological Work to Social Work"

ISSUES

Policy—A Philosophy for Practice—Means versus Ends

Human service practitioners, whether administrators or direct service staff, need more than technical skills. They need a *philosophy* of service delivery—a framework that is related to the goals and purposes of human service programs and that will facilitate choice among different service delivery models. Administrators need a rationale that will assist them in allocating resources, establishing criteria for recruitment, developing staff reward systems, and evaluating the accomplishment of their programs. Technical knowledge of fiscal, personnel, and service modalities cannot provide the broad-based knowledge that is required in setting priorities and delivering services that are relevant and effectively meet consumer needs. This knowledge comes from the integration of the goals and purposes of human service programs with the understanding of administrative structures, processes, and skills (Demone and Harshbarger 1974:4). Direct service practitioners also require an understanding of the relationships of their efforts to the policies and purposes of the programs within which they work. This philosophy for practice provides a service rationale linked to the causes and solutions of social problems. This chapter explicates this philosophy for practice by identifying it with three major purposes of human services programs: social care, social control, and rehabilitation.

The need to integrate social welfare policy content with administrative and organizational knowledge and skill (Richan 1983, Saari 1977:47) becomes increasingly evident as the social welfare industry gives greater attention to the efficiency and effectiveness of organizations. Thus, Kahn (1976:39) has noted a tendency to underplay service *content* issues in favor of structural and organizational questions. He cites as an example how service integration efforts to correct inefficiency seldom specified case-level outcome criteria. Similarly, Street, Martin, and Gordon (1979) have characterized managers of human services as having an "ideology [which] focuses less on effects of agency operations than on a civil service conception of the organizational mission as extending and administering authorized programs in as fair and judicious a manner as is reasonable [p. 27]."

More efficient use of scarce resources is also being emphasized, especially as economic constraints force administrators to be concerned with costs in making decisions among alternative policies and programs. The pressure for better utilization of existing resources has thus raised the issue of the relative importance of, and the relationship between, *efficiency* and *effectiveness* of social programs. Should management focus its efforts on cutting costs, or should more attention be given to insuring that programs achieve their intended purposes? Are efficiency and effectiveness mutually exclusive or can they be complementary? Might not the emphasis on efficiency and productivity have a negative impact on the effectiveness of social welfare programs, that is, on the extent to which agencies can serve client needs? An approach is suggested here that may help avoid the substitution of efficiency for effectiveness by emphasizing social policy goals as an integral part of human service practice.

This issue of the degree of emphasis on efficiency versus effectiveness of social programs has also led to the question of who should manage human service programs, a manager or a professional. Is it preferable to have a nonprofessional, educated in business or public administration with technical administrative expertise, or is it more desirable to have a person trained in a human service discipline, who by this training should have a better understanding of the goals and purposes of social programs? It has been suggested (Etzioni 1964:83–84) that professionals should direct nonprofit organizations, in order to avoid goal displacement. The nonprofessional manager may emphasize efficiency or means of achieving program goals at the expense of the ends or primary purposes of the program. In contrast, a person trained in a particular professional field (e.g., medicine, nursing, or social work) should be able to direct the organization to achieve the primary goal of service to clients, with efficiency remaining the secondary goal. The introduction of specialized training in management in the various professions including hospital administration, nursing administration, educational administration, and social work administration (see Neugeboren 1971:34–47) is an attempt to integrate knowledge of a specialized profession with technical knowledge of administration.

Social administration has been defined as "the study of the social services whose object is the improvement of the conditions of life of the individual." It is concerned with "the machinery of administration which organizes and dispenses various forms of social assistance" (Titmus 1958:14). However, much of the writing on social administration is directed at issues of social welfare policy, with less attention given to the organizational problems involved in service delivery. A more directed effort at integration of policy and administration is Donnison and Chapman's *Social Policy and Administration* (1965). Specifically, this very important book attempts to integrate knowledge of organizational task, structure, and process with policy analysis of service delivery in substantive areas such as housing, child welfare, family welfare, and education.

Returning to the discussion of which profession is best equipped to manage human service organizations, it is of interest to note that in Great Britain the study of social administration was first introduced as training for social workers (Donnison and Chapman 1965:26). However, regardless of who the manager is, it will be necessary also to integrate substantive knowledge of social policy with knowledge of practice to avoid the overemphasis on *means* to the detriment of the goal of client benefit (Neugeboren 1979).

That is, social policy analysis based on understanding of goals of social programs in relationship to social problems such as poverty, corrections, mental illness, and ill health needs to be integrated with knowledge of organizational opportunities and constraints on human service practice. This integration will be explicated in the chapters that follow through the analysis of goals and purposes of human service programs within three major areas: social care, social control, and rehabilitation.

Social Care, Social Control, and Rehabilitation

The goals of social programs—social care, social control, and rehabilitation—need to be differentiated from the overall mission—client benefit. That is, client benefit is the end to be achieved through the alternative or combined means of social care, social control, and rehabilitation. Clarity as to the means–ends relationship is needed to insure that client benefit remains the primary purpose of human service programs. The overall mission of human service programs is the improvement of the quality of life of persons who are in distress and suffer from such problems as mental illness, poverty, mental retardation, ill health, problems of old age, crime, child abuse and neglect, inadequate housing, etc. In short, the ultimate mission is to benefit people who are in difficulty and require assistance.

In a discussion of medical care organizations Mechanic, noting that bureaucratically designed institutions treat clients in an impersonal and dehumanizing way, concludes that: "our society desperately needs experiments in new forms of social organization that provide renewed bases for personal commitment, that contribute to the deprofessionalization of the expert, and that encourage a higher level of caring. . . . *Medicine without caring is technics run wild* [1976:3; emphasis added]." We can equate policy with clarity regarding the effect of programs on client benefit. Therefore, an understanding of how the goals of human service programs are influenced by administrative means can facilitate the "caring" that Mechanic advocates and thereby facilitate the mission of client benefit.

In this analysis of purposes of human service programs we will be referring to the *operative* goals. The operative goals are the *actual* goals, which may or may not differ from the *official* goals (see Chapter 2). These operative goals are determined by the *activities* and *results* achieved by the human service program.

The distinction among these three goals of human service programs (care, control, and rehabilitation) rests on the focus of intervention of these programs. Social care, social control, and rehabilitation have as their targets of intervention either the individual or the situation surrounding the individual.

Social care is concerned primarily with changing the situation or environment for clients. *Rehabilitation,* in contrast, is directed at changing the individual. *Social control* is concerned with containment of the individual's deviant behavior. This threefold classification is being used here in order to make explicit the primary purposes of human service programs. Although most programs will have multiple goals, administrators and practitioners should be aware of the major emphasis of their programs. An awareness of where the resources and efforts of staff are directed should facilitate more effective and efficient service delivery.

The above typology of program goals may be viewed by some as based on a false dichotomy (see W. Schwartz 1969:22–43). There are those who believe that separating interventions into categories of individual versus situational change denies the need for change in both areas at the same time. Thus, the stress in social work on "psychosocial" intervention assumes the need to direct efforts at changing situations *and* individuals.

The distinction between changing persons versus policies has led to the proposal of dividing social work practice into two areas: one providing direct service to people with problems in social functioning, and the other dealing with programs and policies. Those who propose this division hold that the knowledge and skills required in the two areas are critically different: "The interactional skills of the indirect services tend to focus more on the sociopolitical variables in relationships than on social-psychological variables (Gilbert, Miller, and Specht 1980:37)." They feel that the generalist approach to practice "ascends to conceptual levels that obscure real and important differences [Gilbert, Miller, and Specht 1980:36]."

We, too, will make the assumption that there is a distinction between changing people and changing policies and programs, associated with the distinction between direct and indirect practice. However, we also assume that direct practice can include not only people change (rehabilitation), but also modification of their situations (social' care), which requires sociopolitical skills.

It is possible that if one were to examine the daily activities of persons employed by human service programs one would determine that individual or situation change is given more emphasis and priority. This priority is probably influenced by the ideologies and technologies available to the persons working in the organizations. Mechanic (1974) suggests that in the health field the distribution of care reflects ideological preferences and medical knowledge, as well as the system of power. (See Chapters 13 and 14 for discussion of ideologies and technologies.) Regardless of how one feels about dichotomizing and typologizing program goals, what human service organizations give priority to in actuality is basically an empirical question. And regardless of the answers to this empirical question, one can raise the issue of what the goals of human service programs *should* be. Given the kinds of problems presented by the consumers of human service programs, which is the more appropriate goal: care, control, or rehabilitation? Under what circumstance is change of the individual more valid than modification of the situation? Should a juvenile delinquent be treated (rehabilitation), given a job (care), or punished (control) or a combination of all three? Are care, control, and treatment congruent or conflicting goals? The criticisms of combining treatment and punishment, "coerced cure" (N. Morris, 1974), suggest that rehabilitation and punishment are not compatible. In light of the limitation in resources which should be given priority? This decision may be made by the direct service worker based on his or her particular philosophy and skills. From a policy point of view it would seem important that administrators be clear as to which goal is most appropriate for meeting the needs of particular client groups.

The above can be illustrated by the debate in the health field over the degree to which specialization is required. Underlying the issue of division of labor between general practitioners and specialists is the question of the functions to be performed by these two types of practitioners—care versus treatment. Overelaboration of medical specialties is believed to result in a fragmented pattern of service (Mechanic 1974:49). The effort to establish the role of the general practitioner by the development of the specialization of family medicine has been questioned on the grounds that certain problems prevalent in general practice, such as alcoholism and drug abuse, require knowledge not presently available in the education for family practice (Mechanic 1974:50). A more critical question would be whether the nature of the problems brought to medical practitioners are in fact "medical" problems requiring "treatment." If problems such as alcoholism and drug abuse are defined as "social" problems, then the provision of rehabilitation and treatment may be less appropriate than a social *care* type of intervention directed at environmental modification.

> Epidemiological investigations of the occurrence of illness and seeking of medical care suggest that much of the motivation for contact with the health care system results from environmental stress. . . . The technological structure, which characterizes modern medicine, . . . is a good deal less than perfectly responsive to the forces bringing patients into the health care system [Mechanic 1976:11].

Another factor that should influence these policy choices regarding the goals of human services is that of the relative effectiveness of these three types of intervention. Given the knowledge of service effectiveness, how realistic is it to expect individual or situational change? Research studies have questioned the effectiveness of social casework (Meyer, Borgatta, and Jones 1965; G. E. Brown 1968; Mullen, Chazin, and Feldstein 1970; Fischer 1973), especially in "situations of social and economic deprivation which require practical assistance [Goldberg and Warburton 1979:2]." Justifications for interventions to change people are often based on the unavailability of material resources.

The question of whether we are any more effective in changing situations is also unanswered. There is evidence, however, in the health field that changing policies is more feasible than changing attitudes: "Barriers to medical and health care that are a product of the way health professionals and health care services function are more amenable to change than client attitudes and behavior . . . when cost and other barriers are removed from access to medical care, and a valuable service is offered, differential utilization of medical services by social class largely disappears [Mechanic 1974:12]."

Are human service practitioners able to modify environments that are dysfunctional for people? Even with good intentions can we anticipate negative consequences of our efforts? When Dorothea Dix crusaded for the establishment of public mental hospitals it was hoped that they would provide a more benevolent environment for the mentally ill than was available in the jails and almshouses. With rapid population growth in the United States, however, these hospitals became overcrowded and benevolent care was replaced by inhuman and dehumanizing conditions (Joint Commission of Mental Illness and Health 1961:62).

If we are uncertain as to the effectiveness of social care and rehabilitation, is social control a legitimate goal for human service programs? Should deviant behavior be treated or punished? Are deviant persons sick and therefore in need of treatment, or are they responsible for their actions and therefore to be controlled through sanctions? These issues and questions will be discussed at various points throughout the book and treated intensively in the sections on ideology and technology (see Chapters 13 and 14).

The question also arises as to whether individual and situational change are related or unrelated. That is, one can assume that changing the person and changing the situation are associated phenomena (Coulton 1981:30). On the other hand, it may also be the case that the two factors are independent. An understanding of whether individual and situational change are or are not correlated should foster more rational organization and delivery of human services. In what follows we look at each of the possibilities in turn.

Individual and Situation Are Correlated

If changing the individual and changing the situation are related, then one can hypothesize three different kinds of relationships: 1. Changing the individual will result in the individual's changing his or her situation. 2. Changing the situation will result in individual change. 3. There is an interaction between individual and situational change, so that one has to influence both simultaneously (Pincus and Minahan 1973:9).

Change of Individual Will Result in Individual Changing His Situation. Much of the literature on therapy and counseling assumes that maladaptive behavior results in the individual's inability to cope and modify his or her situation. Consequently, this literature focuses on the use of "inner resources," on helping the client to "discover and actualize his creative powers, to realize his capacities and strengths for personality change and growth . . . helping people to surmount obstacles, relieve stress, resolve problems, and accomplish life tasks [Siporin 1975:299; see also Hashimi 1981]."

Changing the Situation Will Result in Individual Change. Situational change is directed at external material or social resources required by clients, in the belief that such change stimulates "hope, relieves tension, strengthens motivation, and reinforces the commitment of the client [Siporin 1975:309]." The assumption that social stress is the cause of maladaptive behavior seems to imply that reduction in this stress would result in less difficulty for the individual. Thus, the social provision of basic resources in situations of child abuse is viewed as the first step toward enabling the client to achieve personal growth and change (Wolock and Horowitz 1979). Maslow's hierarchy of needs (1970) assumes that only after basic survival needs are met can the individual be capable of meeting such higher levels as self-actualization.

An illustration of how social stress can have deleterious effects can be drawn from Wing's (1978) study of the relationship between family environment and relapse in schizophrenia. Wing found that living with relatives who are critical and hostile resulted in a return of psychotic symptoms. It is of interest to note that drugs remedied symptoms only in the negative family environments; in the noncritical home, they were less important. Thus, in this example, change of the situation had a direct influence on individual performance, whereas change of the individual via drugs had little impact in certain situations. This suggests the possibility that individual and situation can be unrelated.

Interaction between Individual and Situational Change. Many of the contemporary practice theories in the human service field embrace the interactional approach, which assumes that one cannot separate individual from situational change (e.g., Germain and Gitterman 1980). This approach holds that maximum benefit for the client can be achieved by modifying both person and situation ("Working Statement on Purpose of Social Work" 1981:6). The assumption behind this approach is that it is impossible to separate the individual from the situation, as there is continuous interaction between the two. Whether it is possible to have the resources to direct efforts at *both* the individual *and* the situation is debatable. However, the basic assumption remains that attention needs to be directed at both.

The dual focus of interactional models notwithstanding, in practice the first task is usually the engagement of the client in order to motivate him or her to become involved with the service. This is especially the case in programs that serve recalcitrant or involuntary clients, such as child protective services (Neugeboren, McGuire, and Neugeboren 1981). Therefore, in daily practice the interactional model may revert to the model discussed earlier which is based on the assumption that changing the individual must precede change of the situation. '

Individual and Situation Are Not Correlated

The second basic assumption possible is that individual functioning is independent of the environmental and situational influences. If this assumption is made, then the task of helping persons with problems may involve changing *either* the person *or* the situation. Both strategies are valid, as each factor is simply *irrelevant* for the other. For example, individual psychopathology may be unrelated to role performance. This was the situation in the Lodge experiment where, although schizophrenic patients continued to have symptoms (hallucinations), they were able to perform on a job (Fairweather 1969). Assuming the variables are unrelated, we can justify allocation of resources, for example, to find better housing for clients on the basis that it fulfills an unmet need regardless of the question of whether this will affect the client's individual functioning. Similarly, we can justify providing a person with counseling to alleviate personal distress without having to assume that this will necessarily affect how this person will adapt to his or her situation.

The discussion of the relationships between the individual and situation assumed positive associations. It is also possible that an inverse relationship could exist, in that these goals may be in conflict. This possibility will be discussed next in regard to the relationships among care, control, and rehabilitation.

Inverse Relationships among Social Care, Social Control, and Rehabilitation

Rehabilitation and Control. Earlier in the chapter, reference was made to the inverse relationship between control and rehabilitation. The criticism of efforts to rehabilitate persons in correctional institutions is based on the conclusion that treatment cannot be "coerced." If it is assumed that rehabilitation requires the *voluntary* participation of the client, those settings in which involuntary placement occurs (e.g., prisons and mental hospitals) are by definition inappropriate for this kind of service. A person who has committed a crime and been told that he or she is "bad" cannot then be expected to assume the role of being "mad" and respond to a therapeutic relationship that tries to deal with feeings of guilt and low esteem.

Rehabilitation and Care. If the purpose of rehabilitation is to help *individuals change their environment,* then efforts to change it for them may be considered to be counterproductive (Johnson and Rubin 1983:54). The treatment goal of enabling the patient to overcome intrapsychic barriers to successful role performance assumes that the experience of gaining mastery over the environment will in itself be therapeutic. Therefore, actively changing the environment for the person will create "dependency" and detract from the therapeutic goal.

Care and Control. The successful provision of social care (creating positive social environments) can also be defeated in settings that are coercive. Here we need to be clear that we are referring to the negative aspects of control. For example, a mental hospital that uses shock treatment as a tool for control cannot very well provide a positive social environment.

Policy Implications of Conflicting or Congruent Goals

The extent to which care, control, and rehabilitation are conflicting or complementary has implications for the design of service delivery programs. An assumption behind "integrated" and "comprehensive" program designs is that it is desirable to have under one authority human service programs with multiple goals. The pressure for more effective coordination of autonomous programs also assumes that human service agency goals are shared (see Chapter 12, "Interorganizational Relations"). Yet these goals have been found to be, in some situations, incompatible: Rehabilitation is not possible in a coercive setting; care for chronically mentally ill is not possible in acute psychiatric treatment services in general medical hospitals *(Better Services for the Mentally Ill* 1975:14; Neugeboren 1970a:162–163).

The chronic nature of such social problems as child abuse and neglect, addiction, mental illness, mental retardation, difficulties associated with old age, crime, poverty, etc., suggests that human service intervention needs to be on an ongoing basis, with emphasis on providing more supportive environments rather than changing or "curing" the individual (DeWeaver 1983:436). It has been suggested that the cure may be worse than the disease since antipsychotic medications are less appropriate for the chronically mentally disabled in contrast to the acutely ill (Gerhart and Brooks 1983: 154 Gardos and Cole 1976:32). The kinds of ideologies and technologies appropriate for service to "chronics" are different from those required for short-term crisis or transitional problems. The human service professionals who deliver these chronic services need an orientation and philosophy that enables them to persist in their efforts despite only limited gains by those being served. As this example illustrates, the explication of the goals of care, control, and rehabilitation is a basic requirement for human service administrators, planners, and practitioners if they are to effectively design and implement social programs.

The issue of shared versus conflicting goals is also relevant in light of the current impetus toward universal rather than selective service programs (see Kahn 1979:76–81). This impetus stems in part from earlier experiences in England with comprehensive and universal services *(Report of the Committee on Local Authority and Allied Personal Social Services* 1968). The difficulties in establishing such programs in the United States have been documented (D. Austin 1978) and have been explained in terms of the general antipathy toward centralization in this country. Another possible factor, which has not been recognized, is that basic conflicts in goals among human service programs in this country may preclude cooperation. In England the primary emphasis of statutory-based human service programs has been on social care, in contrast with the psychological and social emphasis present in the United States. It may therefore be the case that the difficulties in establishing universal human service programs in the United States relate in part to a lack of shared goals (for further discussion see Chapter 11).

Having discussed the issues associated with the goals of care, control, and rehabilitation, we now proceed to analyze the issues related to prevention as a viable goal in the human service field.

Prevention as a Goal of Human Service Programs

The preceding discussion of goals gave primary emphasis to the remediation of social problems through changing either people or their environments. Ideally, it would seem desirable to strive for a situation where social problems could be avoided or prevented. If actions could be taken to deal with the basic causes of social problems, then we could expect to prevent their occurrence in the first place.

The validity of preventive intervention was initially demonstrated in the field of public health. Eradication of communicable illnesses was achieved through modern methods of sanitation and through immunization. In view of its success, attempts were made to apply this preventive disease model to social and emotional problems as well (Chafetz and Demone 1962:175–237; Wittman 1977:1051).

The preventive disease model involved several questionable assumptions, however:

1. The basic assumption underlying the disease model is that an illness, if untreated, can be expected to worsen. Yet it has been found that physical as well as emotional symptoms can be self-limiting and transitory.

2. A related assumption is that treatment can only be beneficial. The possibility that treatment can have negative consequences (Illich 1976) is generally not recognized by the advocates of preventive intervention. Yet the wholesale use of X-ray screening for tuberculosis has been challenged because of its potential for causing cancer. The annual medical check-up has also been questioned.

Although the value of preventive intervention in such specific areas as neonatal care to avoid mental retardation is generally recognized, the widespread advocacy of preventive programs in the mental health field (Caplan 1964; President's Commission on Mental Health 1978: Vol. 1, pp. 51–53) has come under question (Panzetta 1971:110–119; Wagenfeld 1972; Gilbert 1982). Mechanic (1980) criticizes the assumption that psychiatry should engage in prevention by attempting to influence policymakers and the mass media: "The concepts implicit in preventive psychiatry are unfortunate not only because they are grandiose, naive, and an obvious projection of political values, but also because they continue to divert attention from making many of the remedial efforts more consistent with existing knowledge and expertise [Mechanic 1980:162]." He also criticizes Caplan's advocacy of crisis intervention to prevent social breakdowns, on the grounds that there is little evidence that reducing stress will have any real "impact on the occurrence of mental illness or [be] directed at those who are likely to become mentally ill if untreated [Mechanic 1980:163]." Nuehring (1979) characterizes primary prevention in the mental health field as "a nonrational technology [p. 452]."

The basic issue regarding the role of prevention in human service practice relates to the allocation of scarce resources (Nuehring 1979:465). Should priority be given to such preventive programs as crisis consultation and mental health education or should funds be channeled into remediation efforts to meet specific and pressing needs? Until more substantial evidence is available to support the claims for prevention, it would seem advisable to give priority to people's more pressing needs.

DEFINITION

Social Care

Social care is directed at changing situations for people. The primary purpose of social care is the creation of positive social environments (R. Morris 1977). It includes efforts to make available concrete resources such as medical care, money, housing and jobs (Torczyner and Paré 1979; Ewalt and Honeyfield 1981). Social care also encompasses "resource provision" (Gilbert and Specht 1974:28–105). In addition, it is associated with the emphasis on providing the "least restrictive environment" for persons who are disabled, as well as with the concept of "habilitation." Habilitation is concerned with providing the resources and supports to enable persons to utilize their maximum potential (in contrast to rehabilitation, which is directed at increasing potential). Social care also includes the principle of "normalization." The movement toward provision of environments that approximate normal environments has been a major emphasis in the field of mental retardation (Wolfsenberger 1972). A related effort was the stress in poverty programs on the goal of "opening up opportunities" (B. Neugeboren 1970b). The concept of the opportunity structure (Cloward and Ohlin 1960) and the need to open up this structure to provide access for lower-class persons is another example of efforts to focus intervention on the environment. An area that has been receiving increased attention is that of "community support systems" (Turner 1976). The movement toward deinstitutionalization of the chronically mentally ill, mentally retarded, and the elderly has led to the development of programs of community support, which provide these chronically disabled persons with the kinds of environmental conditions that are conducive to their maximum functioning. Another area that can be related to the concept of social care is that of "people-processing organizations" (Hasenfeld 1974). The purpose of people-processing organizations is to "attempt to change their clients *not* by altering basic personal attributes, but by conferring upon them a public status and relocating them in a new set of social circumstances [Hasenfeld and English 1974:5]."

"People-sustaining technologies," as discussed by Hasenfeld (1983), have some similarities to—and differences from—social care.

> Technologies for people-sustaining aim to prevent, arrest, or delay the deterioration of a person's well-being or social status. They do so by removing or minimizing the effects of conditions that threaten a person's well-being, or by compensating for the deficits in personal resources that cause deterioration.... The underlying assumption of people-sustaining technologies is that the clients have little, if any, potential for change.... These assumptions ... are based on a social and moral evaluation of such persons that casts them into socially marginal categories.... The core activities in this technology are custodial care.... There is a high potential for neglect, abuse and exploitation of clients.... Staff view clients as objects rather than subjects and can foster dehumanization [pp. 137–140].

Hence, the emphasis of people-sustaining programs is on *custodial* care, which corresponds with the negative end of the dimension of social care. Whereas people-sustaining programs are assumed to have primarily negative consequences for client benefit, social care aspires to provide environments that will enhance social functioning.

As already suggested, the increased attention given to social care and the development of supportive environments has been stimulated in part by the movement of deinstitutionalization of the chronically mentally ill and the mentally retarded. The need for formal systems of social care can also be attributed to changes in the family structure: For example, with the increased participation of all family members in the work force, the family can no longer assume its traditional function of providing care for handicapped members.

Although social care has traditionally been particularly relevant for service to the "chronics" (e.g., the mentally ill, retarded, physically handicapped, and elderly), conceptually it can apply to any problem group. Its relevance depends on one's determination of the cause of a problem. For example, a person who has difficulty in a job situation may resolve this difficulty by changing jobs, on the assumption that the problem lies within the job environment rather than within himself (see Chapter 7, on occupational burnout). For an extended discussion of social care see Chapter 14, "Technology."

Social Control

Social control is defined as activities concerned with controlling behaviors that deviate from societal norms. Thus, the goals of social control programs are to publicly identify, control, and stop social deviance. Often this is accomplished by transferring the deviant from the community to a closed institution. Although traditional social control programs such as prisons and correctional institutions clearly fall within this category, it is also evident that social control is often a "hidden agenda" of many human service programs. For example, efforts at diversion of juveniles from the correctional system may lead to their incarceration in treatment institutions to accomplish the primary purpose of removing them from the community for social control purposes (Lerman 1975). In this instance, rehabilitation becomes the *means* for achieving social control goals (see the section on "Means versus Ends" in what follows). The proposition that society uses social programs to "regulate the poor" (Piven and Cloward 1971) when the poor become discontented and threaten stability of the community is another example of how human services can be the means for achieving social control (Hasenfeld 1983:40).

The distinction must be made between social control as a goal for the human services and the use of technologies to control and change client behavior. Intrinsic to efforts to influence clients are the use of various positive and negative sanctions. Clients can be controlled by such means as stripping them of their personal identity, controlling resources available to them, and restricting their mobility (Hasenfeld 1980:123). Although this method of client constraint could be used to achieve the goal of social control, social control in the human services differs in that it is primarily a response to community pressure to control deviant behavior. Typically, control technologies are part of rehabilitation efforts to change client behavior, whereas social control interventions are usually directed at removing the deviant client from the community, for example, by institutionalization.

Rehabilitation

Rehabilitation is defined as changing the individual. This could mean changing the individual's attitudes and/or behavior. The individual change goal is assumed under the medical and clinical models of intervention. The kinds of technology that may be used in rehabilitation include the psychological therapies (psychotherapy, behavior modification, clinical social work, counseling, etc.), physiological treatments (e.g., chemotherapy), and educational modalities (Vinter 1963). The purpose of people-changing organizations is to use rehabilitation to "alter directly the attributes or behavior of their clients through the application of various modifications and treatment technologies [Hasenfeld and English 1974:5]." It is contended that human service organizations in the United States have rehabilitation as their primary goal.

Program Goals—Means versus Ends

As indicated earlier, the three goals of programs may be understood as means as well as ends. Thus, rehabilitation may be a means for achieving social control (Perrow 1978:198), as when a criminal is treated to prevent him from committing future crimes. The reverse is also possible, in that control may be a condition for rehabilitation. For example, a violently mentally ill person may receive drugs to control his behavior in order to facilitate psychotherapeutic treatment. Social care may also be a means, as when the provision of basic survival needs is assumed to be a prerequisite for the treatment of psychological problems. (As previously indicated Maslow makes this assumption in his hierarchy of needs.)

This clarification of the various means—ends relationships can affect how we design human service programs. Making explicit these relationships should, for example, aid administrators in selecting staff with the different kinds of technological skills appropriate to the different kinds of organizational goals.

Program Goals—A Continuum

Social care, control, and rehabilitation may also be conceptualized as continuums. That is, their consequences for client benefit may be either positive or negative to different degrees.

Thus, "iatrogenic" or negative effects have been found in conjunction with various kinds of rehabilitation. In the medical field, iatrogenic illness can be induced by medical treatment (Mechanic 1978:348; Illich 1976; Bosk 1979; Fuchs 1974, Spitzer 1980). Studies of the effectiveness of casework (e.g., Fischer 1973) have also found that although there are positive effects there are also some negative effects (one third of the clients improve; one third don't change; one third get worse). For example, rehabilitation of schizophrenics through use of group therapy can lead to recurrence of delusions and hallucinations that were dormant for years (Wing 1978:251).

When we look at social care as a single dimension having positive or negative effects on people, we see at the negative end the warehousing of the mentally ill in asylums (Goffman 1959). As indicated earlier, people-sustaining organizations (Hasenfeld 1983:137–138) also stress the custodial function of social care. Community care for the mentally ill can be viewed as the functional equivalent to institutional care (Lerman 1982). Moos (1974) has done research evaluating the positive and negative effects of various treatment environments.

The potentially positive or negative effects of social control are also apparent. Structured situations that compel adherence to specific norms may be constructive for some people by facilitating the development of their own controls. For example, an institution that has high expectations for patients who are emotionally disturbed may help them develop skills for daily living by structuring their environment to make it conducive to such development. The negative effects of coercive environments are demonstrated in such institutions as prisons and mental hospitals, where use of punishment results in alienation (Etzioni 1964:60).

Social care, social control, and rehabilitation may also be viewed as continuums in relationship to each other. Thus, social care and rehabilitation may be conceived of as a single continuum, as illustrated by a medical day-care setting for the elderly where patients move through different levels of care, for example, from social care to rehabilitation services (Kurland 1982:55).

IMPLICATION OF ANALYSIS OF SOCIAL PROGRAM GOALS FOR HUMAN SERVICE ADMINISTRATION

The foregoing analysis is relevant to human service administration because it makes explicit existing program goals and hence enables a more efficient and effective management of human service programs. More specifically, the process of making explicit existing program goals can help administrators in three areas: (a) policy formulation, (b) program design, and (c) program monitoring and control.

Policy Formulation

The explication of program goals can assist in the formulation of policy through the process of goal clarification. Goal clarification consists of the identifying and clarifying the relationship between means and ends of programs to avoid goal displacement (i.e., the situation in which means become ends). For example, the clarification that treatment is a means for achieving control or that care is a means for achieving treatment should help administrators understand whether, in fact, the organization's purposes are being achieved or whether its intended and official goals are being displaced and subverted.

Program Design

More appropriate design of human service programs may also be accomplished by clarifying program purposes. Clarification makes possible a more appropriate selection of technologies for achieving the organization's purposes. For example, if social care is the primary purpose of the organization, then technologies directed at creating positive environments would be appropriate. The better understanding of the different means for achieving these different program goals would facilitate the selection of staff as well as their training.

Program Monitoring and Control

From what has been said it follows that the specification of program goals will facilitate monitoring and administrative control. The content of management information systems required to monitor programs will be enhanced by the specification of program goals and means. The acquisition of more appropriate data will be facilitated by the understanding gained from this analysis of goals and means. This data should help administrators detect the barriers to effective goal achievement, thus enabling them to take steps to correct problems.

The ultimate purpose of this three-part model for goal specification in human service organizations is to insure that the overall mission of client benefit will be achieved. If this mission is not achieved, this model should help the administrator understand why the program has not been effective and what kinds of constraints may be operating. This knowledge may facilitate plans for changing the organization's goals to make it more responsive to clients' needs.

SUMMARY

This chapter on the goals of human service programs highlights three primary goals—social care, social control, and rehabilitation. These goals are viewed as a means for accomplishing the mission of human service programs—client benefit. Social care, social control and rehabilitation are considered different approaches to the solution of human problems. Social care is concerned with creating positive environments for the consumers of human service programs. Social control is directed at controlling deviancy while rehabilitation is concerned with the direct change of client attitudes and behavior. Although these three goals are seen as discrete, each may be considered as means or ends. In addition, they may be viewed as continuums—having potentially positive as well as negative consequences for client benefit.

The purpose of emphasizing the goals of human service organizations is to stress the importance of a service philosophy for practitioners to use as a foundation for their practice. The three goals mentioned above can provide a framework to guide decision making and action for both administrators and direct practice staff. Specification of organizational purposes facilitates the differentiation between technical means and the outcomes of client benefit. A clear definition of the goals of human service programs can make a more efficient and effective practice through better policy formulation, program design, monitoring and control.

In subsequent chapters, the goals of human service organizations will be linked to the discussion of issues associated with the human service organizational environment. This discussion should facilitate integration of program goals with the various organizational structures and processes established to achieve these goals.

APPLICATION OF CONCEPTS ON SOCIAL CARE, SOCIAL CONTROL, AND REHABILITATION TO CASE "FROM PSYCHOLOGICAL WORK TO SOCIAL WORK"

The case "From Psychological Work to Social Work," which is given in full in the Appendix, can serve to illustrate how concepts on the goals of social care, social control, and rehabilitation operate in practice.

In this case situation, the administrator of a public child welfare office in an urban city is proposing a change in the goals of the agency from rehabilitation to social care. His activities indicate an *integration of social policy and administration,* with attention paid to the distinction between the program's means and ends. The administrator has a philosophy for the delivery of child welfare services, according to which the agency's mission is to provide child protection services appropriate for lower-class clients. He attempts to integrate this philosophy with a service delivery model and administrative structure that concentrate on the provision of concrete resources to relieve some of the environmental stresses on the clients. This caseload management approach to service delivery included cooperative working relationships with other community agencies.

In addition to this social care goal, the administrator stresses that the staff needs to develop more expertise to fulfill a social control investigatory role in child abuse situations. For example, the staff must become familiar with the proper legal procedures for collecting and presenting evidence in judicial hearings, to insure that the legal rights of the child, parents, and the community are protected.

The *goals of social care, social control, and rehabilitation* are illustrated in this case situation. As mentioned, this agency had traditionally favored the people-changing goal of *rehabilitation*. Its focus was on helping parents become more aware of their interpersonal difficulties with their children in order to develop better "parenting skills." The assumption made was that *changing clients' attitudes would lead to changes in their behavior toward their children*. Not only would clients be able to cope better in terms of family relationships, but they would also be able to be more successful in influencing their social situation. That is, the enhancement of their coping abilities would enable them to change their situation, whether by obtaining a job or finding better housing.

Although rehabilitation was the *official* goal, the pressures of the job situation precluded it from being the *operative* goal. High caseloads, constant emergencies, and pressures from other community agencies prevented the workers from having the time to do the intensive counseling required for the goal of rehabilitation.

The statutory mandate of this public child welfare agency also established *social control* as the official goal. The child abuse legislation prescribed an investigatory role and function to protect children and, if necessary, to prosecute parents who abused their children. The workers were obligated to prepare reports on child abuse cases and present evidence in court. Therefore, social control was both an *official* and *actual* function of this child welfare agency.

Social care, the changing of the client's environmental situation, was the goal advocated by the administrator. His assumption was that as the clients were generally from the lower classes, they needed basic resources to survive. The administrator was also cognizant of the *social control* function of the agency. Although he understood and accepted this as a legitimate goal, he wanted to be certain that it was pursued within a context in which clients' rights were protected. He did, however, view the obligation of carrying out the societal function of controlling deviant behavior as part of the agency's mandate.

In contrast, the staff had difficulty recognizing their legal role and social control functions. They viewed social control as a goal that was in conflict with rehabilitation. Their investigatory function was laden with role conflict. Thus, from the staff viewpoint the *correlation between rehabilitation and social control* was an *inverse* one.

Although the staff understood the need for environmental change (social care) for the clients, they assumed that rehabilitation could be the means for accomplishing this. From the staff viewpoint, there was a *direct correlation between rehabilitation and social care*.

The issue of whether *rehabilitation and social care goals are complementary* or *conflicting* is evident in this case: The staff favored rehabilitation and disagreed with the position that environmental change should be the primary goal for the agency. The administrator in effect assumed that the two goals were also in conflict. The kinds of ideologies and technologies advocated by the proponents of the rehabilitation and social care goals were obviously different and were not acceptable to both parties.

The explication of the differences among the goals of social care, social control, and rehabilitation in this case had *administrative implications.* Through such an explication, the administrator could more readily *formulate the policy* of the agency, including the goals and the major strategies for achieving these goals. Clarifying the agency's social control goal was particularly critical as a first step toward remedying worker role conflict and burnout.

Program design also was facilitated by the clarification of this agency's goals. The need for a particular service delivery model and the selection and training of staff with appropriate technologies was clarified and expedited. Finally, the *system of monitoring and control* was also facilitated by the specification of program goals of social care, social control, and rehabilitation.

ORGANIZATIONAL GOALS

OUTLINE

I. Issues
    A. Concept of Organizational Goals
    B. Means versus Ends
    C. Concern for Accountability
    D. Organizational Literature Reinforces Resistance

II. Definition

III. Goal Displacement

IV. Efficiency and Effectiveness

V. Goal versus Systems Models of Organizational Effectiveness

VI. Multiplicity of Goals and Goal Conflict

VII. Functions of Organizational Goals

VIII. Task Environment

IX. Conclusions

X. Application to Case "Mental Health Rules and Regulations"

ISSUES

Human service agencies, like any organized human activity, require some end toward which to strive. This objective or purpose is needed to guide activities of members and to gain acceptance and support from the community. Although this statement of the purpose of organizational goal may appear self-evident, the concept is more easily understood in the abstract than it is accepted in operational terms. If one were to ask executives of human service agencies to state the goal of their organization, they probably would not be able to do so in clear and unambiguous terms. If one then asked direct service workers the same question, in all likelihood the answers would differ significantly from those given by the executives.

This lack of concern on the part of human service practitioners regarding the goals and purposes of their organizations is a serious constraint on effective organizational performance. The problem can be traced to four factors: (a) failure to appreciate the importance of the concept of organizational goal for the functioning of human service organizations; (b) lack of understanding of the difference between means and ends of organizational activity; (c) an implicit concern by staff regarding accountability for the service results; and (d) an overemphasis in the literature of the difficulties of conceptualizing and operationalizing organizational goals in human service programs.

Concept of Organizational Goal

The failure to understand the concept of organizational goal is associated with the difficulty that human service personnel who work primarily on a one-to-one basis have in visualizing the organization as a unit. Although they can readily understand that individuals have purposes and objectives, they have difficulty comprehending that organizations can also have a specific objective or goal. Their orientation to the direct service level gives them a perspective that precludes their thinking on a "systems" level. This is illustrated by the difficulty that personnel have in organizing, planning, and evaluating their daily work activities. Decisions are made on a case basis, which precludes the aggregation of experiences to facilitate planning, evaluation, and modification of overall effort. Although personnel are concerned with achieving success in a particular case outcome, they have difficulty comparing efforts and results between cases and/or staff members.

Lacking understanding of the concept of organizational goal, the human service practitioner naturally tends to minimize its importance. This tendency is illustrated by the frequent statement that one cannot measure the results of human service programs. Practitioners' reluctance to quantify their efforts and accomplishments, based on their conviction that "quality" cannot be "counted," reinforces their dismissal of the need to have an organizational goal as a measuring rod to evaluate their day-to-day activities.

Means versus Ends

Failure to understand the concept of organizational goal also results in the confusion of means with ends. When the executive states that the goal of the organization is to "obtain resources to provide service," several assumptions are being made. First, it is assumed that having more resources will be beneficial to the organization, that "more is better." A related assumption is that having more resources will be beneficial to the consumer receiving the services. In other words, it is assumed that the availability of resources, which are means, will *inevitably* lead to consumer or client benefit, which is the organizational end or goal. Such assumptions are to be expected in a field that has unverified knowledge. The "indeterminacy" of professional practice (see Chapter 14 on technologies) requires strong convictions (see Chapter 13 on ideologies) to allow decisions to be made and action taken.

The confusion of means with ends is also evident in the emphasis placed on the *process* of interaction between human service worker and client. This emphasis on process (means) can result in a minimization of the importance of the purpose (ends) of the intervention. It should be noted that all specialties and professions tend to place a high value on methodology, as so much of the training they require focuses on techniques and procedures. But, in the human service field where interventions stress people changing, the details and intricacies of the interactions between worker and client can overshadow the concern for outcome. This minimization of outcome relates to another factor: the concern for accountability.

Concern for Accountability

Practitioners' deemphasis of the concept of organizational goals may in part be related to an implicit fear of being held accountable (Weatherly *et al.* 1980). The results of evaluative research on the accomplishments of human service programs give the administrator and practitioner ample reason to be concerned with lack of success. Although this research is often ignored (again, because of the conviction that quality cannot be measured), there is probably an underlying uneasiness that efforts are not achieving desired results. Practitioners are justified in their criticism that evaluation tends to emphasize such productivity measurements as interview counts, but all too often they do not participate in formulating more relevant criteria for service accomplishment. As the movement for greater accountability gains momentum through the implementation of periodic internal and external reviews, the pressure on practitioners to justify their efforts increases, leading to additional concerns and anxieties.

Organizational Literature Reinforces Resistance

A final key factor contributing to the tendency to downplay the importance of organizational goals is the emphasis taken in much of the organizational literature (Hasenfeld 1983:89–92; Hall 1982:294–302). This literature has tended to stress the "indeterminacy" of human service goals and technologies. From the fact that human service organizations can have multiple and conflicting goals, the conclusion is drawn that it is difficult to arrive at an agreement as to what the goal should be in any particular human service organization.

We will see in what follows that contrary to the literature, it is possible to specify organizational goals in human service programs and also to develop procedures for evaluating their achievement.

DEFINITION

Organizational goals have been defined as "desired and intended ends to be achieved [Etzioni 1964:6]." Organizational goals can be viewed as a means–ends chain. The ultimate purpose or goal of human service organizations is by definition some form of benefit for the persons being served. For example, in mental health, the goal is the successful adjustment of the mentally ill in the community; in child welfare, the goal is the normal development of the child. The means–ends chain refers to the existence of various means or subgoals that are intended to achieve the ultimate purpose of human service organizations. Therefore, all activities performed by persons in human service organizations, including service delivery as well as management, have as their ultimate purpose some end state of client benefit. This distinction between means and ends has been made by Meringoff (1980) in his differentiation between maintenance management and service management. This distinction is useful in highlighting the importance of a service *outcome* to human service organizations and the activities that managers must engage in to achieve that outcome.

The importance of a clear goal definition for persons working in human service organizations relates to the need for some standard by which to measure the success of the worker and the organization. That is, effective performance, on whatever level one operates, must be related to some standard of evaluation. Often these measures of performance are based on the means rather than the goals of the organization. Thus, measures of the kinds of service given are considered adequate criteria of success, on the assumption that these means will achieve the desired ends of client benefit. However, as evaluative research (e.g., Fischer 1973) has not demonstrated effectiveness of human service programs, we must be constantly aware of the importance of goal clarification. That is, specification of the client benefit that will be used as the outcome criteria is necessary if goal displacement is to be avoided.

GOAL DISPLACEMENT

Goal displacement has been defined as the situation where the means of an organization's activities become its ends. Thus, the activities that the organization engages in (interviewing clients, supervising staff, managerial tasks such as budgeting and personnel selection, etc.) are used as criteria to judge the success of the organization. This displacement of goals, whereby the means become the end, often occurs because goals were not made operational. Operationality of goals refers to the extent to which goals are defined in specific terms so that one can know whether they have been achieved (Patti 1983:84). When an organization has been evaluating success in terms of such general and vague criteria as "client well-being" or "client adjustment," it then will tend to seek more operational measures. Thus it may turn to measures of some of the activities engaged in by staff (means), foregoing the measurement of the ultimate client benefit (ends).

As indicated in the section on issues, the question of whether the goals of human service organizations can be made operational has been answered in different ways. The contention here is that there is no conceptual or analytical barrier to defining goals in such a way as to make them operational and, therefore, measurable. Outcome studies have been doing this for years. Although there may not be complete consensus as to the adequacy and validity of the criteria, to expect such unaninimity would be unrealistic. For example, as a measure of outcome for a mental hospital program, one can use the amount of time the mentally ill person remains in the community (Ullman 1967:3–9). The validity of this criterion may be questioned, as we know that community tenure is a function of community tolerance (Freeman and Simmons 1963:6). An alternative criterion could be based on a measure of patient functioning in the community (e.g., holding a job, attending school, etc.) (Weiner 1982:363–364). Either criterion could be legitimately used as a measure of organizational effectiveness, although the one evaluating patient performance would be more relevant. The point is that the human service administrator can develop valid measures to evaluate the progress the organization is making.

The use of organizational survival as a criterion for goal accomplishment is another example of a possible goal displacement. Although survival is by definition a precondition for any goal accomplishment, focusing efforts on survival will detract from the primary purpose of client benefit.

EFFICIENCY AND EFFECTIVENESS

Effectiveness can be defined as how well an organization achieves the goal of some intended client benefit. Efficiency is the measure of cost in terms of resources expended to achieve a specific goal—in other words, how much input is required to achieve a fixed goal (Etzioni 1964:8–10). Efficiency is therefore a means for goal accomplishment, and stressing efficiency over effectiveness is another form of goal displacement. However, efficiency has to be taken into account because of its relationship to outcome. That is, given that certain means costing a specific amount of resources will accomplish specific goals, the ability to be more efficient will result in increased goal accomplishment. In other words, if outcome is fixed, the ability to be more efficient on the input will result in greater maximization of the outcome. This relationship between efficiency and effectiveness is frequently overlooked by human service staff who complain that efficiency is stressed at the expense of effectiveness. Although this may occur, it does not preclude the possibility that greater efficiency can lead to an increase in effectiveness. For example, two different kinds of interventions having different costs may produce similar results. In the area of psychological treatment, for example, if drug treatment is as effective as psychotherapy (Eysenck 1965) and costs less, then shifting resources to drugs, the more efficient therapy, will enable more patients to be served, an overall increase in goal achievement.

GOAL VERSUS SYSTEMS MODELS OF ORGANIZATIONAL EFFECTIVENESS

The *goal model* of organizational effectiveness involves the measurement of goals in very specific and simple terms. The assumption here is that there is a fixed relation between the means and the ends and that more means will result in more ends (Etzioni 1964:16–19).

The *systems model,* in contrast, suggests that organizational success is relative. That is, organizational accomplishment cannot be viewed in fixed terms, but rather in relationship to other organizations. The reason for this is that most measures of success by their very nature are relative. Success will vary with the goal established. For example, objectives such as helping the mentally ill to adjust in the community or insuring that a criminal will not return to crime are quite complicated and difficult and are affected by many factors outside the control of the human service organization. Thus, a success rate of 5% may be realistic. However, one can measure the performance of a human service organization by comparing it with similar organizations, under the assumption that the external factors are somewhat constant.

The systems model makes no assumption regarding the efficiency of various means. In contrast to the goal model, it takes into account the possibility that overallocation of resources may lead to less effective performance. That is, more does not necessarily mean better. This view is supported by the finding that short-term casework is somewhat more effective than extended casework (Reid and Shyne 1969). A further contrast between the two models is that the goal model assumes that there are single goals in human service organizations. This is again an oversimplification, as organizations can in fact have multiple goals, some of which may be in conflict.

MULTIPLICITY OF GOALS AND GOAL CONFLICT

In Chapter 1 the three major goals of human service programs were discussed: social care, social control, and rehabilitation. Some authors have suggested that social control and rehabilitation are intrinsically incompatible. Thus, in the field of corrections "coerced cure" is by definition unattainable (Morris 1974:12–20). In the field of public assistance it was determined that financial aid and service provision were noncomplementary goals and, therefore, efforts were made to separate these two services.

Although multiplicity of goals may be problematic in some instances, in other situations it may actually be functional. Thus, it has been suggested that multipurpose organizations are more effective than single-purpose organizations (Etzioni 1964:14). The explanation given is that the diversity of multipurpose organizations leads to more competition and more stimulating interaction, resulting in greater effectiveness.

Multiplicity of goals may also be understood in terms of the distinction between *official* and *operative goals* (Perrow 1961). Official goals are those goals that are stated in the charter of an organization and represented to the public. Operative goals, in contrast, are the actual goals of the organization, that is, what the organization is actually trying to accomplish. The official–operative goal distinction is reflected in the different perceptions that people at different levels of an organization have of the organization's goals: People at the top levels often view their organization's goals in official terms, whereas lower-level staff are more familiar with the operative or actual goals. A problem that administrators and practitioners have to deal with is how to determine the actual goals of a human service organization. Management information systems provide an important mechanism for determining what actually is going on in an organization and what is being accomplished. Another method for determining operative goals involves analyzing the allocations of resources, that is, the operating budget: Where money is being spent is a good indicator of the direction in which the organization is going.

FUNCTIONS OF ORGANIZATIONAL GOALS

The distinction between organizational goals and functions needs to be made. Whereas goals are intended end states, organizational *functions* are any consequences that actions have, whether intended or not. Organizational functions have been associated with the accomplishment of purposes different from the official goal. Environmentalists view much of organizational activity as being directed at accomplishing purposes that are important for external groups sometimes to the detriment of the organization's own purposes. The performances of social control functions for the community is an example of how human service agencies are compelled to accomplish purposes that may be in conflict with their own (Perrow 1978:107–108) Other functions that human service agencies perform for the environment include absorbing part of the work force and providing resources for other organizations (Perrow 1978:109–112). Similarly, certain functions that human service organizations perform for their employees may also detract from the official goals. Systems analysts (see Chapter 5) take such organizational functions into account. The critical question, however, is the extent to which these functions facilitate or detract from the official goal. In contrast with the previous discussion of organizational functions we will focus on the functions or purposes of organizational goals.

Organizational goals themselves have three functions. They serve as a guide to activity, a measuring rod, and a means of legitimation. These functions have the potential to *facilitate* the positive performance of human service agencies.

1. *Guide to Activity.* Organizational goals establish a framework for activity. That is, the goal determines what tasks need to be performed, what kind of division of labor may be necessary, and what technologies are required. In this way, the goal helps guide the day-to-day activities of administrators and practitioners. A nursing home that establishes as a goal increased longevity of patients would need to determine what kinds of activities (means) would be appropriate for achieving this goal. Should stress be given to more and better nursing care, or should there be an increase in efforts to encourage more social interaction among the patients?

2. *Measuring Rod.* As discussed earlier, goals provide a standard for evaluating organizational performance. That is, the efficiency and effectiveness of organizations is determined by measuring staff activity in terms of the goal criteria. For example, if the goal of the organization is social care, then the criterion used to determine whether this goal has been achieved (effectiveness)

would be the extent to which staff has accomplished environmental change for clients. The extent to which the organization was efficient in achieving this goal would relate to the amount of resources used (cost).

3. *Legitimation.* Organizational goals are used by the community to assess the organization's contribution to society. Thus, the community's view of the organization is influenced by what the organization's goal represents to the community. This legitimating function of goals is very important because it will determine the amount of support the organization will receive from the community. That is, the amount of resources given to an organization is often determined by its degree of legitimation. In the human service field one can judge the relative legitimacy of different types of organizations in terms of general goals. The following is a rank ordering based on decreasing degree of legitimacy: public education, health, mental health, child welfare, public assistance, and corrections. In our society, in other words, education is viewed as a much more legitimate function than welfare or corrections. The importance of legitimation has led to several changes in the human service field. For example, the interest in developing more universal programs is in part an attempt to overcome the stigma and illegitimacy associated with certain of the more selective programs. Some of these programs have also tried to change their public image by changing their names. Thus, county welfare boards have become "boards of social services," and state public mental hospitals are now termed "psychiatric centers."

The issue of legitimation has arisen in the area of mental health services. Pressure to have community mental health centers provide more service to the chronically mentally ill has created concern that such service will drive away the middle-class neurotic patients who have traditionally been the clientele of these centers. As these mental health centers become more "comprehensive" they also may become less legitimate.

The issue of legitimation makes clear that organizations are a part of the larger society and very much influenced by that society: This perspective has been summarized in the concept of task environment.

TASK ENVIRONMENT

Task environment has been defined as: "a specific set of organizations and groups with which the organization exchanges resources and services and with whom it establishes specific modes of interactions [Hasenfeld 1983:51]." It has been suggested (Hasenfeld and English 1974:10) that the reason that goal definition in human service organizations is problematic is that goals are established in response to pressures from the various external groups—parents, politicians, agencies, and professionals—comprising the task environment. Because these groups are diverse, their demands and expectations are diverse and even conflicting. This fact can be appreciated by analyzing the task environment into the following sectors (Hasenfeld 1983: 61-62): (a) providers of fiscal resources, (b) providers of legitimation and authority (c) providers of clients, (d) providers of complementary services, (e) consumers and recipients, and (f) competing organizations. Thus, the organization's development of multiple goals and strategies is in part an effort to appeal to these multiple interest groups in order to enhance its legitimation. In this way, goal setting is related to the organization's adaptation to and manipulation of its environment (Thompson and McEwen 1958:23–31). It should be noted that the adaptation of organizations to the demands of the task environment will vary depending on the degree of consensus present in the environment for a particular kind of organization; for example, there is more consensus in the community on the functions of a medical hospital than a psychiatric hospital.

SUMMARY

This chapter on organizational goals stresses the utility of this concept for practitioners in the human services, be they administrators or direct service personnel. Practitioner difficulties in accepting and utilizing organizational goals as a guide in the performance of tasks was associated with inability to conceptualize an organization's aggregate goals and purposes as distinguished from goals established for individual clients. Goal displacement was also highlighted and was attributed to confusion of technical means with the ends of client benefit. Goal displacement was also evident in the lack of differentiation between organizational efficiency and effectiveness. Further confusion occurs because organizations often have multiple and conflicting goals as well as official and operative goals. The three functions of goals (guide to activity, measuring rod, and legitimation) were presented as a rational approach to insuring more efficient and effective organizational performance.

Although the concept of organizational goals is a complex one, its understanding is basic for those working within formal organizations. Pure and unambiguous goal definition is not always possible in human service organizations. Nonetheless, administrators and practitioners must make constant efforts to define organizational purposes, in order to avoid goal displacement and to enhance professional and organizational functioning to achieve consumer benefit. The difficulties in arriving at a consensus on organizational goals should be viewed as a political problem rather than as a difficulty intrinsic to the task of goal formulation. The fact that various subunits of an organization will have different goals (Gummer 1978) does not relieve the leaders of the organization from being accountable for achieving the *official* goal of client benefit. Granted that power struggles will influence the *actual* goals, the professional administrator, who has a commitment to meeting client needs, should use this goal as the basic criterion for organizational decision making. One method for determining the achievement of client benefit is the use of systematic procedures for obtaining consumer feedback (Warfel, Maloney, and Base 1981).

APPLICATION OF CONCEPTS ON ORGANIZATIONAL GOALS TO CASE "MENTAL HEALTH RULES AND REGULATIONS"

The case "Mental Health Rules and Regulations" illustrates how concepts related to organizational goals can operate in practice. In this case situation, the Department of Mental Health has, in its new rules and regulations, established as the goal for community mental health programs the successful adjustment of the chronically mentally ill in the community. It operationalized this goal by specifying that the target service population should be those persons who were hospitalized in a mental institution for a minimum of 6 months.

The case illustrates the difficulty the provider agencies had in *understanding the concept of organizational goal.* The idea of establishing priorities and thereby giving preferential service to one group was unacceptable to these agencies. In order to be able to accept the principle of priorities one needs to understand that it is legitimate for an organization to establish a specific goal (e.g., a target population) and allocate resources to this goal. The agencies' failure to understand the principle of organizational goals was also illustrated by the difficulty they had in using statistics to evaluate their efforts.

A related problem was the agencies' *confusion of means with ends.* The stress they placed on the "process" of therapy intervention prevented them from differentiating it from outcomes of their efforts. For this reason, they resented attempts to base evaluation on measures of results.

The confusion of means with ends had resulted in *goal displacement* in the mental health programs. The Department of Mental Health specified that the end goal was successful community adjustment. The service providers, however, placed emphasis on the "process" of patient–therapist relationships. Their assumption was that the input (process) would be effective in achieving desired outcomes.

A confusion between *efficiency* and *effectiveness* was also evident. It was commonly assumed that quality was equivalent to intensity of intervention. Agencies failed to consider the possibility that reductions in the costs of the programs (efficiency) could, by freeing resources, facilitate effectiveness.

The concept of multiplicity of goals was also operating in this case. The new rules and regulations advocated the inclusion of community social care for the chronically ill. This goal was different from the traditional one of rehabilitation of the emotionally disturbed. The difficulty that the service providers had in setting explicit priorities may stem from their perception of the goals as being in conflict.

The distinction between *operative* and *official* goals was also illustrated in the case. The official stated goals of most mental health programs is to "serve the community" as a whole. In actuality, these programs served primarily the lesser disturbed middle-class persons because of their referral sources and intake criteria (e.g., admit only the "motivated").

In this case, *organizational goals* fulfilled the *functions* of *guide to activity* and *measuring rod*. Thus, using the criteria of target population and community tenure, the Department of Mental Health could establish a monitoring system to determine whether the community programs were accomplishing the goal.

If the *goal model for organizational effectiveness* is used, the department would have to establish some absolute standards against which to compare results. Such standards might be, for example, a minimum percentage of the patients served coming from the target groups or an average amount of time these patients are able to remain in the community. These standards could be related to the proportion of the budget funded by the state. For example, if the state funds 50% of the community program, then the department could require that one-half of those served belong to the target group (or that one-half of the total staff activity be devoted to that group). This standard might be lowered to 25% on the grounds that state funds are also provided for service to the nonchronics.

If a *systems model for organizational effectiveness* is used, a standard could be derived from the data collected. Thus the average proportion of the target population of the total served could be used. For example, if there are 50 community programs which vary in the proportion of the target population served from 0 to 75%, the median (possibly 50%) could be used as the standard. Thus, those services less than 50% would risk loss of funding. A formula for funding might be developed so that community programs would be rewarded if they served more patients from the target groups. It may be important to include as part of the goal standards not only the numbers of individuals served but also the amount of service they received. This measure would prevent the community programs from discriminating against the chronics by providing only minimal service.

Like the Department of Mental Health, the individual could use this specific goal definition as a guide for activity and as a measuring rod. Performance expectations for departments and individual staff members could be tied to the standard of the proportion of clients belonging to the target population and the amount of time devoted to serving these clients.

The third function of organizational goals—that of *legitimation*—was also evident. In this instance, the goal of serving the chronics was perceived as *reducing* the legitimacy of the community programs. This situation is not uncommon with human service programs that have as their goal service to disadvantaged groups.

MANAGEMENT MODELS

OUTLINE

I. Issues
 A. Single versus Multiple Ideologies
 B. Ideologies Conflict

II. Definition

III. Classical Model
 A. Scientific Management School
 B. Public Administration
 C. Bureaucracy
  1. System of Rules
  2. Sphere of Competence
  3. Hierarchy
  4. Knowledge Base
  5. Exclusive of Personal Consideration
 D. Critique of the Classical Model

IV. Human Relations Model
 A. Definition
 B. Characteristics of the Human Relations Model
 C. Critque of the Human Relations Model

V. Structuralist Model
 A. Definition
 B. Characteristics of the Structuralist Model
 C. Critique of the Structuralist Model

VI. Systems Model
 A. Definition
 B. Characteristics

VII. Summary

VIII. Application to Case "Disciplinary Action"

ISSUES

Organizations, like people, are complex phenomena. Although scholars have studied organizations extensively, there persist different points of view as to how organizations function and should be administered. These management models or ideologies provide contrasting explanations of what factors motivate people to participate in and contribute to organizational life. Management ideologies can have an important influence on how human service agencies organize their policies and programs, on the bases established for decision making, the kinds of reward systems used, and the way in which staff roles are structured and supervised. It is important for the human service administrator or practitioner to be aware of these different management models in order to appreciate how they can facilitate or constrain practice.

Single versus Multiple Ideologies

A basic issue associated with management ideologies is whether it is more desirable to adhere to one ideology or to be eclectic and draw upon several. Belief in a single management philosophy simplifies action in contrast with the multiple ideology approach. Integrated management models are difficult to implement since they contain a combination of several contradictory belief systems. Stress on one ideology may not be effective as it may set too narrow a boundary on available solutions available to organizational problems. However, given the nature of ideology, it is possible that most people will emphasize one or another management approach in their definition of organizational problems and selection of solutions. Nevertheless, familiarity with the range of options for the resolution of organizational problems is still the most functional approach in management.

Ideological Conflict

Given their diversity, ideologies of management are a possible source of conflict within an organization. Thus, administrators and practitioners need to keep in mind the possibility that conflict between organizational units can occur on the basis of ideological differences (Weissman 1973, 113–125). As ideologies are like religions (see Chapter 13), people with different organizational ideologies often hold to them with strong emotional conviction. As a result, differences of opinion among staff members on various organizational problems may become irreconcilable. Understanding the ideological factor involved in such conflicts can help those concerned to separate the value differences from the factual differences. Differences based on inadequate knowledge of facts can be dealt with more objectively than differences in values. Indeed because such conflicts tend to be very difficult to resolve, it is an important function of effective leadership to maintain an awareness in this area (see Chapter 9).

DEFINITION

As already indicated, management models are philosophies of management based on assumptions concerning the way in which organizations function and the proper role for administrators. Like other ideologies, management philosophies consist of a series of logically related postulates that are internally consistent but have never been empirically proven. Management models are needed to provide administrators with a rationale for taking action and making decisions, given the lack of proven solutions to specific organizational problems. Thus, they facilitate action in indeterminate situations, where clear-cut cause-and-effect relationships do not exist.

There are three basic management models or philosophies: the classical, the human relations, and the structuralist models (Etzioni 1964:20–49). Although some authors (e.g., Perrow 1972:145–204) have suggested other models, such as the institutional school and the neo-Weberian model, these can be included under the structuralist model. The three basic models have distinct characteristics, based on different assumptions regarding the critical factors that influence behavior in organizations. These models reflect different views on the issue of whether the goals of individuals within an organization can be congruent with organizational goals. They also reflect different views on the role of conflict and rationality in organizations. Thus, these models provide significantly different frameworks for formulating policies to motivate staff to participate in and contribute to organizational life. They suggest different strategies for dealing with such organizational problems as low morale, low productivity, turnover, and conflict.

Although these management ideologies may appear mutually exclusive, they can in fact be integrated within an eclectic *systems model*. The systems model assumes that the three basic approaches may each be valid, depending on the nature of the organizational task involved. The following sections discuss in turn each of these four models of management.

CLASSICAL MODEL

A basic assumption of the classical management model is that the organizational members are primarily economically motivated. Individuals will strive and work for the organization's goals provided they are given economic incentives. Thus, it is possible for the individual's goals and the organization's goals to be congruent, provided that the organization is able to compensate the individual in economic terms.

The classical management model borrows assumptions from the scientific management, public administration, and bureaucratic theory schools. A key assumption it makes is that organizations are rational systems and can be planned and blueprinted much like a machine. For this reason, it has also been termed "machine theory" (Katz and Kahn 1978: 259–263). This "prescriptive" model is based on prediction of what an ideal organization should be rather than on a study of organizations and their actual functioning. Although the classical model has been considered inappropriate for human service organizations (Litwak 1961), it remains the dominant model in the field. Therefore, it is important that human service administrators and practitioners be familiar with its specific principles and concepts.

Scientific Management School

The scientific management school (Taylor 1923) stressed the importance of the physical capabilities of people in organizations and therefore focused on the time and motion required for individuals to perform tasks. It attempted to establish various criteria for division of labor, in order to maximize the contribution that an individual could make given the limits on his or her physical capabilities. Once the division of labor or specialization was established, the pay could be related to the performance of the specific task.

The applicability of these concepts to human service administration lies mainly in the area of work load and task analysis (M. Austin 1981:90–98). For example, in public agencies where the workloads are excessive, it may be fruitful to examine staff capabilities, task expectations, and compensation systems. In some public agencies "combat pay" has been introduced because of the hazardous nature of the work in low-income areas. In a public child welfare agency, a group grievance was filed on the part of beginning-level direct service workers who claimed that their role (and pay level) should not require them to prepare and present cases for court hearings. Psychiatric aides have also protested against being used as "therapists" without additional compensation. In general, the importance of monetary remuneration has been underestimated in the human service field (see Chapter 8).

Public Administration School

The public administration school (Gulick and Urwich 1937) also stressed the concept of *division of labor* and the breakdown of tasks into the simplest form. In addition, it stressed *unity of control*. That is, assuming that a task needed to be broken down into small units, there was some need for some centralized control to supervise and coordinate performance. Unity of control established a limit on the number of employees who could be supervised by one superior, a limit referred to as the *span of control.*

The public administration school assumed that there should be person-to-person responsibility down the line, in other words, that there should be *one* superior to whom the subordinate is accountable (Katz and Kahn 1978:260). This assumption has been challenged by those who advocate a matrix organizational structure (e.g., Gates 1980:196–199), in which there is a "multiple subordination of authority." However, a matrix structure can lead to problems. Multiple lines of authority can result in role conflict for a subordinate who receives conflicting expectations from his or her superiors. If this organizationally generated conflict is blamed on the subordinate, he or she becomes the victim of a structural problem. An example of this structure is seen in such organizations as mental hospitals, where line workers are supervised by a unit director as well as by the head of a specialty department (e.g., social work, psychology, psychiatry). The bureaucratic model in which each subordinate is accountable to one boss avoids this problem.

A third concept stressed by the public administration school was that of *specialization* among organizational units. Rationales were developed for specialization according to such criteria as purpose, process, clientele, and geographic area.

The various concepts associated with the public administration school are relevant to human service administration in different ways. The relevance of the concept of unity of control depends on the need for coordination, which in turn depends on the extent to which staff tasks are *different* and *interdependent.* Differentiation in tasks is associated with specialization. The issue of specialists versus generalists has been a perennial one in the human service field (E. Schwartz 1977; Yessian and Broskowski 1977). There have been periodic swings from one extreme to the other.

As mentioned, the need for coordination and control via the supervisory structure depends not only on tasks of staff members being different, but also on their being interdependent. Although there has been criticism of the excessive fragmentation of services, it is debatable whether there is in fact much interdependence in service delivery. A study of a social service unit in a poverty program (Perlman 1975:26) found that a large proportion of consumers sought help for *one* problem, a finding contrary to what might have been expected in this population group. In short, much of direct service may require efforts of only a single provider, and therefore coordination may not be needed.

The concept of span of control relates to the issue of how much supervision is required. Large span of control (i.e., high ratio of subordinates to supervisor) results in less close supervision. In public welfare agencies close supervision results in low productivity and discourages initiative and creates dependency on superiors (Blau and Scott 1962:149). The stress on close supervision in therapeutic human service organizations may, therefore, not be functional for independent worker performances.

Specialization of organizational units by purpose, process, clientele, and geography has varied with the times and emphasis of funding sources. The organization of services by geographic areas (e.g., catchment areas), which was stressed in the 1960s, seems to be on the decline, as the emphasis has shifted to specific clientele (the elderly, mentally ill, etc.). Specialization by purpose or goal has not been used, except in the very general sense of having agencies responsible for "human services" as opposed to services for business or industry. It might be possible to divide services into such goal categories as care, control, and rehabilitation. This kind of division of labor would have the advantage of grouping together personnel and programs with similar objectives, ideologies, and technologies. It would also enable a more clear-cut system for accountability as the purposes could be made operational. The objection to this type of division would come from those who advocate a more "generic" approach.

Bureaucratic Model

The Weberian model (Weber 1947) stresses the relationship between legitimated authority and control. The relationship between legitimation and control is derived from the assumption that people in superior positions who have *authority* also have *ability*. The subordinates view superiors as legitimate because they recognize their abilities, and consequently, they are willing to follow their directions. The subordinate views legitimate power as representing the "legal" authority of the organization, whose laws are just and fair. The norms and values established by the organization are in agreement with those held by the participants in the organization.

The Weberian model also includes the following principles:

1. *System of rules.* The purpose of rules in organizations is to standardize behavior so that "programmed" solutions for problems become possible. Programmed solutions in turn lead to equality in treatment of persons served.

In the human service field, where there is much uncertainty and unpredictability in decision making, attempts to standardize procedures and establish rules are met with resistance. This has led to the charge that human service practitioners have too much discretion and often use it to coerce clients (Handler 1973). Underlying this resistance to standardization of procedure is the reluctance of human service staff to be "programmed." Professionals pride themselves on their ability to use judgment; if their decisions have to conform to preestablished rules, then they feel that they are not needed and that "clerks" could do the job. This either-or viewpoint distracts from the more basic issue of the need for equality of treatment. Thus, understanding this function of rules in formal organizations is essential for the human service practitioner.

2. *Sphere of competence.* The concept of sphere of competence assumes the need for division of labor and also the accompanying authority to carry out the particular functions. Here there is an emphasis on the concept of role in the organization, that is, on the expected behavior associated with a particular position (see Chapter 4).

These principles of sphere of competence and legitimated roles have relevance for administration and practice in human service agencies, which have often been characterized by an inability to link authority with responsibility. Part of the reason for this has been the difficulty human service administrators sometimes have in delegating authority (M. Austin 1980:157–162). At a deeper level, the problem is related to a failure to appreciate the concepts of organizational role and structures. All too often, personality has been a key determinant of role performance, which has also hindered the establishment of a legalistically based system of rules, rights, authority, and power.

3. *Hierarchy.* The basic assumption behind the Weberian model is the need for control and supervision and the establishment of a hierarchy of authority in order to meet this need. The hierarchy attains compliance by checking and reinforcing the appropriate behavior of the subordinate.

The use of authority and control in the administration of human service programs is problematic because of the role of professionals in these organizations. Professionals' need for autonomy leads them to resist supervision and control by administrators. As our society moves away from the private practice entrepreneurial model of professional practice, the need for accountability and hierarchical control will become more legitimate (see Chapter 8).

4. *Knowledge base.* Another characteristic of the Weberian model is the emphasis on technical skill as a basis of legitimation. This principle of expertise is widely accepted in the human service field. As the knowledge base expands there will continue to be a lag between the development of the newer skills areas and their legitimation by the "old guard." For example, if practitioners and administrators view the emphasis on social care for deinstitutionalized populations as requiring less knowledge and skill, then the persons assigned to these roles will have lower status and legitimation.

5. *Exclusion of personal considerations.* A final characteristic is the separation of personal interests from organizational interests, that is, impersonal behavior on the part of organizational members, so that all persons served will be treated in a fair and equitable manner (Weiner 1982:562–565).

Most human service practitioners would readily accept the principle of exclusion of personal considerations in providing service to clients. The dispensing of favors to friends or relatives or the use of influence to gain special privileges is probably severely limited in most human service programs. Inequitable treatment of clients, however, can result from inappropriate application of procedures and rules. Middle-class clients, in general, probably receive better service than do lower-class clients (Hollingshead and Redlich 1958). Inequitable treatment of staff probably also occurs not infrequently in the human service field, where lack of structure provides the environment for subjective decision making.

Critique of the Classical Model

The ideological nature of the Weberian model's stress on hierarchy has been discussed by V. Thompson (1961:114–139). Thompson views the basic belief in hierarchical structures in organizations as an authoritarian ideology which rests on the assumption that ability and authority are equal. He believes that conflict is inevitable in organizations because there is in fact an interplay between specialization based on expertise and hierarchy based on power. He also concludes that democracy in hierarchically arranged organizations is impossible and is incompatible with control exerted through the pyramidal structure.

The incompatibility of specialization and administrative control presents a dilemma for human service agencies that have been moving toward increased specialization. As the number of specialists increases, administrators lose ability to know what to monitor in terms of workload and task performance. As suggested earlier, the amount of specialization required in the delivery of human service is an open question. In making decisions regarding specializations we should be clear as to whether they are justified in terms of the knowledge gained and the benefits (versus the costs) for service outcome.

There have been a number of other criticisms of the classical school in addition to the one put forth by Thompson. March and Simon (1958) point out that the classical model is deficient because it fails to recognize the importance of environmental forces that impact on the organization. Moreover, it does not take into account the human factor or the importance of subsystems and informal systems in organizations.

Merton (1957) also pointed out deficiencies in the classical model, suggesting that the stress on rule enforcement and control leads to rigidity and limits staff spontaneity and creativity. Gouldner (1954) has a similar criticism related to control, which he feels has the dysfunctional consequence of lowering levels of participant performance. These criticisms are consistent with the findings alluded to earlier on close supervision. It should be noted that these potential negative consequences associated with administrative control are linked with monitoring of means and methods rather than ends and results. Management by objectives (M. Austin 1981:125–156), which exerts control through monitoring the results of efforts, avoids some of the negatives described here.

HUMAN RELATIONS MODEL

Definition

The human relations model developed in reaction to the classical model, and it emphasizes the importance of the human element in organizations. The stress is on the unplanned and nonrational elements in organization due to the influence of staff needs. Despite the differences, however, the human relations model resembles the classical model in making the basic assumption that if human needs are met, individuals will work for the organization's goals. Organizational and individual goals can be congruent if attention is given to staff needs.

Characteristics of Human Relations Model

There are four basic characteristics associated with the human relations model. These are as follows:

1. *Productivity is socially determined.* The assumption here is that individual performance is determined more by "social" norms than by the individual capacity of workers. This assumption was in part derived from the Hawthorne studies (Roethlisberger and Dickson 1939) where increased productivity of workers was related to the increase in attention that they received rather than to the change in the physical circumstances (lighting). Productivity norms are set by the group, which sanctions those who work above or below these norms. The phenomenon of social influence on performance is fairly common in human service agencies. The use of supervisory leadership to influence group norms would be one way to raise performance standards.
2. *Social and noneconomic rewards.* Individuals are motivated more by social approval, recognition, and status than by economic rewards. Stress here is on the importance of symbolic rewards for worker satisfaction. Human service agencies have stressed symbolic rewards in theory but not always in practice. Supervisors in public welfare agencies have been found to be less supportive than those in industrial organizations (Granvold 1977).
3. *High specialization is dysfunctional.* In contrast to the classical model, the human relations model stresses the dysfunctional aspect of specialization. Excessive specialization tends to make individuals feel like robots and machines; it does not take into account the human

need to gain satisfaction from performing an integrated task. This stress, then, would argue for a more generic approach in human service agencies. The question that again needs to be answered is, what are the consequences for client benefit of generic versus specialized service? How does one reconcile the need to master an ever-increasing store of knowledge with the desire for integrated approaches?

4. *Importance of communication and leadership.* The assumption made by the human relations model is that because organizations are social units, influences occur though processes of communication and participation of organizational members. Therefore, stress is placed on the role of the leader in encouraging participation and facilitating communication. Problems are solved through group efforts to achieve consensus. Group problem solving and participation is widely accepted in human service agencies. Poor communication is perceived as cause of staff dissatisfaction (Olmstead and Christensen 1973:13). The success at achieving consensus through group meetings needs to be evaluated as much staff time is devoted to this.

Critique of the Human Relations Model

Criticisms of the human relations model are similar to those of the classical model in that they emphasize the lack of attention given to the effect of the environment on the organization. A more important criticism, however, is that the model fails to recognize the inevitable strains produced by incompatibilities between individual and organizational goals. The basic question raised about the human relations model concerns its lack of attention to the issue of power (Hasenfeld 1983:28) and hierarchy in organizations and to the very difficult goal of attempting to have a democracy within an authoritarian structure (Thompson 1961).

A more serious criticism of the human relations model is the charge that it has often been used to manipulate lower-level employees into believing that they are participating in organizational decision making when in reality this is not the case (Hasenfeld 1983:28). The human relations model has been directed at providing opportunities for staff to participate but in relatively unimportant areas of decision making. It has therefore provided them with a false sense of participation and autonomy. Thompson (1961) has referred to the human relations model as "the contented cow" school, which by providing satisfaction to employees through human relations programs, distracts them from more basic issues such as greater economic rewards or greater power and control in organizations. These criticisms are applicable to human service agencies that use extended staff meetings to "cool" discontent (Weatherly 1983:48). The emphasis on rational persuasion in the effort to achieve consensus ignores real differences in interests and beliefs (Weissman 1973:93).

STRUCTURALIST MODEL

Definition

The structuralist model differs from the human relations and classical models in that it does not make the assumption that individual and organization goals can be congruent. Rather it assumes conflict is inevitable in organizations. Moreover, this model highlights the importance of the environment in influencing the activities and purposes of organizations. It is descriptive rather than being prescriptive, inasmuch as its conclusions are derived from empirical studies, many of which are of human service organizations.

Characteristics of the Structuralist Model

There are two basic characteristics of the structuralist model. These are as follows:

1. *Importance of conflict.* In contrast to the first two models discussed, the structuralist model views conflict as functional rather than dysfunctional. Conflict can accomplish social functions by making problems visible and thereby promoting solutions (Coser 1956). Differences between management and worker are inevitable and can only be negotiated or mediated through some conflict resolution mechanism. Unions, grievance machinery, and other adjudication procedures arose in recognition of the inevitability of conflict in organizations.

In the human service field there is widespread discomfort with the use of conflict as a constructive strategy for the analysis and solution of problems. In contrast to such professions as law and politics, human service practitioners usually view conflict in personal terms or even as a symptom of personality problems. This perception is related to the reluctance to use power and control because they view this as "unprofessional." (see Chapter 8).

2. *Importance of environment.* The importance of the environment's impact on the organization is also highlighted by the structuralists. The changing and turbulent environment characteristic of our society must be dealt with if the organization is to function and survive. In contrast to human relations and classical models, the structuralist model advocates various kinds of administrative and organizational roles related to the external environment. Thus the role of *institutional leadership* (Selznick 1957) requires the executive to be active in influencing the environment.

This emphasis on the environment is becoming increasingly important for human service organizations. Recent years have seen growing pressure from the various sectors of society for their share of government budgets. Moreover, the legitimacy of the human service sector, called into question during the Nixon administration, has under the Reagan administration come under renewed attack. It would seem crucial that human service administrators and practitioners be aware of these environmental factors, in order to be able to act to influence them.

Critique of Structuralist Model

The basic criticisms of the structuralist model come from the human relations school, which claims that the model does not give sufficient attention to the human factors and which asserts that although conflict occurs in organizations, it can best be resolved through open communication and trust.

The following chart summarizes the three management models in terms of the assumptions made regarding: (1) congruency or noncongruency between staff and organizational goals (2) the source for staff motivations and, (3) the dynamic underlying each management philosophy.

Management Model	Goal Conguency	Staff Motivation	Dynamic
Classical	congruent	economic reward	control
Human Relations	congruent	symbolic reward	meet human needs
Structuralist	not congruent	self-interest	conflict can be constructive
			importance of environment

SYSTEMS MODEL

Definition

As suggested earlier, the systems model is based on the assumption that the three basic models can be integrated as each may be relevant depending on the particular tasks that the organization needs to perform. The systems model looks at organizations as being complex, with a number of subsystems which perform specific functions based on various dynamics and mechanisms (Katz and Kahn 1978:69–120).

Characteristics of the Systems Model

The systems model includes the following five subsystems: (a) production, (b) maintenance, (c) boundary, (d) adaptive, and (e) managerial. In what follows, each subsystem will be defined briefly, with note made of which of the basic models it includes. (For a more complete discussion see Chapter 5.)

Production Subsystem

All organizations have to perform tasks that are related to a product to be produced. These tasks are accomplished in the production subsystem. In human service organizations the production subsystem performs service delivery tasks. The dynamic associated with the production subsystem is that of proficiency achieved through such mechanisms as division of labor and specification of job standards and roles.

As can be seen, the basic characteristics of the production subsystem are based on the assumptions of the classical model. They stress the importance of proficiency and rationality in the design of organizational roles and tasks.

Maintenance Subsystem

The function of the maintenance subsystem is to mediate between the task demands and the human needs of the individuals in the organization. The dynamic of the maintenance subsystem is the achievement of a stable state for the organization. The mechanisms used for this end are formalization of activities, establishment of systems of rewards, socialization of new members, and staff selection and training. The basic philosophy of the maintenance subsystem derives from the human relations model in the emphasis placed on the integration of the individual's needs with the organization's needs.

Boundary Subsystem

The boundary subsystem includes production support and institutional systems. The production support aspect of the boundary subsystem is concerned with the relations with other organizations, through negotiation, manipulation, etc. The institutional systems aspect is concerned with obtaining support and legitimation from the environment. As can be noted, the boundary subsystem is based on assumptions related to the structuralist model. The emphasis is on the environment and the need to establish mechanisms for influencing it.

Adaptive Subsystem

The adaptive subsystem performs the function of research and planning. It assists in organizational adaptation through the evaluation of organizational performance and the monitoring of the external environment in order to suggest changes in the organization. The basic dynamic of the adaptive system is for change through recommendations to the management. The adaptive subsystem's emphasis on environment borrows from the structuralist model. Its emphasis on research and planning is related to the stress given in the classical model on rationality and proficiency.

Managerial Subsystem

The managerial subsystem cuts across the other four subsystems and has as its main task their integration. This integration is accomplished through several mechanisms:

1. *Conflict resolution.* Conflicts arise between different hierarchical levels and subsystems. These conflicts are resolved through the use of control and authority.
2. *Coordination.* Coordination is required because of the different purposes and values of subsystems within the organization. It is accomplished through compromise by means of adjudication machinery.
3. *External coordination.* Coordination with the external environment is necessary if the organization is to obtain resources and insure its long-term survival. Such coordination needs to be integrated with the plans for restructuring the organization in relationship to environmental changes.

As can be noted, the managerial subsystem shares some characteristics with each of the three models. Thus, it resembles the classical model in its emphasis on control, the structuralist model in its emphasis on external coordination, and the human relations model in its emphasis on compromise.

SUMMARY

This chapter reviews three basic management models: scientific management, human relations, structuralist, and a fourth integrative approach— a systems model. Management models offer a philosophical framework for understanding how organizations function. The models can provide human service practitioners with knowledge that facilitates their functioning in complex agencies. These different management approaches are based on assumptions of what factors motivate staff to identify with organizational goals. While the scientific management model focuses on economic incentives, the human relations model emphasizes social and humanistic bases for motivation. The scientific management and human relations models assume that individual and organizational goals can be congruent. The structuralist model accepts the inevitability of conflict and views this conflict as being functional. The importance of environmental influences is emphasized in this model. The fourth model, the systems model, assumes that each of the approaches— scientific, human relations, and structuralist—can be integrated within the organization's subsystems.

APPLICATION OF CONCEPTS ON MANAGEMENT MODELS TO CASE "DISCIPLINARY ACTON"

In the case situation "Disciplinary Action" the question arises as to the cause of the malperformance of a supervisor, who oversees five direct service workers with a total of 250 child welfare cases. The various management models would offer different explanations for the problem as well as suggest different solutions.

The director of the child welfare agency seemed to favor the *human relations* model. She responded to the supervisor's difficulties by giving him reassurance and support. She also recognized his abilities in the film-making area. Consistent with the human relations philosophy she viewed his problem as resulting from a lack of adequate *communication* between him and his colleagues and subordinates. The director made the implicit assumption that individual staff interests could be congruent with the agency's goals. Thus, she failed to consider the possibility that there existed a conflict between the supervisor and the administration. Her response to the supervisor's difficulties on the job reflected a view of conflict as having only negative consequences.

An administrator who advocated a *classical* approach would have defined the difficulties in quite different terms. The classical model, with its stress on role definition and specialization, would suggest investigating whether the role of supervisor was sufficiently clear. The *span of control* concept would lead to an examination of whether the number of workers and cases that a supervisor was expected to oversee was reasonable or excessive. The workload would be analyzed in terms of what would be realistic to expect given the time and abilities of the individual involved. Instead of assuming that the unit should be working together, the classical approach would first analyze the tasks performed in order to determine whether they were in fact interdependent.

The classical model's stress on authority and *control* through the *hierarchy* would have led the administrator to be more forthright in confronting the supervisor with his inadequate performance. Emphasis would be placed on the value of *rules* and procedures as guidelines for action. The supervisor would be held responsible for following rules relating to absenteeism and lateness.

The stress on *sphere of competence* in the classical model would have led to an examination of the skills of this staff member in relation to those required by the job. If they were found incongruent then reassignment would have been recommended. In the actual case situation (see Appendix) this was what was actually done as a consequence of the grievance hearing.

The *exclusion of personal considerations* is another aspect of the classical model which could have led to a different approach in this case situation. This criterion of impersonality would have cautioned the administrator from considering the staff member's personal problems as potentially germane to his job performance.

The *structuralist* model would have suggested a different approach to this problem situation. The value placed on *conflict* as a constructive means for clarifying issues would have led the administrator to confront the supervisor directly with his inadequate performance. Such a confrontation could have led to a clarification of the issue of lack of clear role definition and performance expectations. The use of the disciplinary hearing (see case) is an example of how a conflict resolution mechanism can clarify issues and lead to constructive solutions.

The sensitivity to *external environmental factors* in the structuralist approach could also have led the administrator to see a different dimension of this problem. In this child welfare agency much of the work pressure came from other organizations such as the courts and schools. The structuralist approach would have investigated the relevance of this environmental factor on the work of the staff, looking into the kinds of techniques and skills required to constructively respond to these outside pressures. For example, some formal working agreements between this agency and the school system might be needed to obtain better coordination and cooperation (see Chapter 12 on interorganizational relations).

Finally, an integrated approach to the analysis and resolution of this administrative problem could have been obtained by using the *systems* model of management. The systems approach would employ the production subsystem's stress on rationality and efficiency in analyzing the service delivery subsystem (classical model). Included in such an analysis would be efforts to clarify the roles of the supervisor. The maintenance subsystem's concern for integrating individual needs and organizational purposes (human relations model) could provide training for the supervisor. The *boundary* subsystem would be concerned with the environmental pressures exerted by other agencies that affected the supervisor and how this might be modified. Such sensitivity to environment is associated with the *structuralist model*. The *adaptive* subsystem, with its function of research and planning, could direct efforts at a study of causes and solutions of burnout. This rational approach is related to the *classical model*. Finally, the *managerial* subsystem would be responsible for making the changes needed to remedy system dysfunctions that were found to be the cause of occupational burnout. As change engenders conflict, the managerial subsystem would have to negotiate and mediate this conflict. The use of conflict as a constructive means for problem resolution is part of the *structuralist model*.

ORGANIZATIONAL STRUCTURE

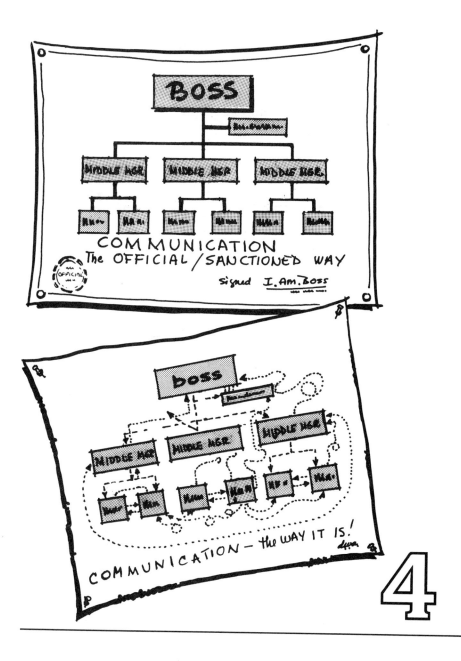

4

OUTLINE

I. Issues
    A. Opportunities and Constraints on Practice
    B. Structural versus People Problems
    C. Professional Freedom Control

II. Definition

III. Purpose of Organizational Structure

IV. Individual and Structure

V. Official versus Operative Structure

VI. Bureaucratic Structure

VII. Centralized vs. Decentralized Structure

VIII. Organizational Size and Structure

IX. Summary

X. Application to Case "From Psychological Work to Social Work"

ISSUES

Organizational structure is important for administrators and practitioners in human service organizations because it can constrain and/or facilitate practice. By understanding the concept of organizational structure, administrators and direct service personnel can achieve more effective and efficient delivery of human services.

Before discussing the issues involved in organizational structure, we need to be clear as to the meaning of the term. Organizational structure refers to the *pattern of activities* of staff in their performance of their roles and tasks on the job. It is the *behavior* of staff in implementing official policies of the organization. *Operative policies* and *structure* will be used interchangeably as they both correspond to the pattern of staff behavior. There are five types of organizational structures: authority, communication, role, reward, and organization–environment relations.

Organizational structure influences administrative and practitioner practice because it provides the context for this practice. The rules and procedures that prescribe organizational behavior provide constraints as well as opportunities for task performance. How this occurs is the first issue to be discussed.

Opportunities and Constraints on Practice

In the human service field it is often felt that complex rules and regulations constrain the administrator and practitioner to the extent of depriving them of the flexibility needed to make appropriate decisions (Kurzman 1977). The prescriptions established by funding authority guidelines or agency manuals are viewed as "red tape" and unwarranted intrusions on the autonomy of the staff member (Kadushin 1974:71), who has the knowledge and expertise to make independent decisions. From the organization's point of view, however, independent action on the part of the staff can subvert the purpose of organizational structure, which is to obtain uniformity in decisions so as to insure equitable and effective treatment of staff and clients. If administrators and practitioners understand the *purpose* of structure and accept it as valid, then they will be able to make better *use* of structure.

Organizational structure has been compared to a maze whose walls are fixed and cannot be moved (constraints). However, there are choices (opportunities) in the different pathways available for one to navigate through this maze. The difficulties of moving through the pathways in complex organizations may be better appreciated by understanding how organizational rules function to affect practice.

Although rules limit independent actions, because their nature is such that they can only prescribe practice in fairly general categories they do provide the *opportunity* for discretion. The administrator in following the guidelines set up by the board or funding authorities can often find ways of "bending" these rules to *facilitate* his practice. For example, budget categories are general and therefore leave room for interpretation. Similarly, the direct service worker has discretion in interpreting the service delivery manual to provide the resources needed by the client. In short, organizational structure constrains practice less if the staff member is aware of the opportunities available to interpret rules. Usually the less experienced staff will learn this fact from those who have worked in the organization longer and, as a result, are very familiar with the existing structure. *Only by knowing the system is one able to use it effectively.* Not understanding how the organizational structure *has* to influence practice will lead to frustration and burnout (see Chapters 6 and 7).

Structural versus People Problems

A second issue that bears on how organizational structure influences practice is the issue of whether structure is the same as or different from the individuals in the organization. Given that structure is defined as behavior of people should we not conclude that structural problems are people problems (Perrow 1970:2–8)?

Consider a unit of a public welfare office where the morale is low and turnover is high. The personnel are very critical of the supervisor because he does not provide them with the opportunity to communicate their complaints and dissatisfactions. The supervisor is described as insensitive and incompetent because he is only concerned with statistics on productivity and is not interested in staff needs. The direct service workers are overwhelmed with paperwork and do not have time to develop meaningful relationships with clients in order to counsel them on overcoming their problems. The supervisor is not available to train the workers to be more effective with clients. The question can be raised as to whether the problem this unit faces is a structural one, requiring a change in policies and procedures, or primarily a person problem, requiring that the supervisor be replaced. To clarify this issue it is necessary to answer the following questions:

1. Is there a clearly stated definition of the role of the supervisor?
2. Is there a clear statement as to the role of the direct service worker?
3. Is there clarity as to the goals that this agency is supposed to achieve?

If the answers to these questions are negative, then the problem may lie not in the individual supervisor but in the lack of clear policies regarding organizational goals and roles. Replacing the individual supervisor will not change the policies. Only after the policies are changed can we be in a position to determine the level of competence of the supervisor.

The tendency to attribute organizational problems to individuals is common in the human service field (as it is in society in general). Firing the director or replacing the president is not sufficient to change basic policies, however. An understanding of the concept of organizational structure will help administrators and practitioners in human service organizations avoid "blaming the victim." If human service administrators and practitioners are to provide better service for clients they need to differentiate between people and structural problems.

Professional Freedom and Control

A third issue associated with organizational structure concerns the way in which it influences administrative control and staff autonomy. Earlier in the chapter we discussed how structure can be viewed as a constraint and/ or as an opportunity. Here our concern is with the somewhat general feeling on the part of staff members of human service agencies that structure limits professional action. Although this may be true, another view is that structure can facilitate staff freedom. The *lack* of structure can be more restraining than clear-cut boundaries for staff roles and functions. It has been found that lack of rules and regulations opens the door for more subjective and *personal control* by supervisory staff (Rosengren 1967). Where structure is lacking, the evaluation of staff performance may depend on whether the superior likes or dislikes an individual; judgment can be made on the basis of personality rather than on the objective job performance. Rules that specify role expectations can be a *protection* against arbitrary demands and preferences of supervisors: "The rules offer a worker the serenity of unambiguous guidelines as to how the agency expects him to respond in defining clearly the minimum set of behaviors which are prescribed and proscribed. The rules mitigate conflicts to which workers might otherwise be exposed [Kadushin 1976:72]." Thus, although structure does establish limits, the lack of structure can have constraining effects which may be more pervasive because they are not self-evident (see Chapter 8 on authority and control).

From the administrative point of view, organizational structure does provide the opportunity for more systematic procedures for accountability and control. Clear role expectations and job descriptions provide the supervisor with an objective basis for evaluating subordinate performance. It is interesting to note that with the introduction of unions in the human service field there has been a much greater specification of the rights and duties of personnel. This has been a natural outcome of union–management grievance hearings, which highlighted the ambiguities in agency performance expectations. Thus, more elaborated structures evolved as a protection of the rights of staff.

DEFINITION

In order to fully understand the concept of organizational structure, it is necessary to first define the term "organization." Blau and Scott (1962) have defined an organization as "having an identity of its own which makes it independent of people who have founded it or are its current membership." They also describe it as characterized by "observed regularities in the behavior of people that are due to the social conditions in which they find themselves rather than their physiological or psychological characteristics as individuals."

Social conditions are defined in terms of the structure of social relations and in terms of shared beliefs and orientations. The structure of social relations itself contains three elements: *(a)* patterns of social interaction, *(b)* members' sentiments toward one another, and *(c)* a status structure. The area of shared beliefs and orientations also contains three elements: *(a)* common values, *(b)* social norms, and *(c)* role expectations [p. 2].

Organizational structure may therefore be defined as the patterns of behavior of employees in an organization that reflect the structure of their relationships and their shared beliefs and values. These patterned activities of staff may be categorized in terms of the five types of structures: communication structure, authority structure, role structure, reward structure, and organizational relations with the environment (Indik and Berrien 1968: 7–8).

Communication structure is the pattern of behavior of people in the process of communicating information within the organization. One determines the communication structure by observing how information is transmitted and who transmits what to whom. *Authority* structure is the patterned behavior in the area of decision making and the exertion of influence and power. The *role* structure of an organization is the specification of tasks according to various positions in the organization. Here again, what is of interest is the behavior of staff members in their performance of various tasks assigned to them. The *reward* structure refers to those activities in the organization that are concerned with the distribution of rewards and sanctions. That is, it includes the behavior patterns associated with such things as promotions and disciplinary actions. *Relations between the organization and its external environment* can be viewed as a continuum of patterns, ranging from open interaction, extensive influence, and interdependence to a more constrained and restricted pattern of interorganizational relations.

In summary, organization structure has been defined as the actual behavior patterns of the staff in relationship to the functions performed by the organization and to the ways in which communications are transmitted, decisions are made, tasks performed, and staff motivated.

PURPOSE OF ORGANIZATIONAL STRUCTURE

A basic purpose of organizational structure is to minimize the influence that individual variations have on organizational activities. That is, organizational structure provides some uniformity in the carrying out of organizational tasks, by limiting the amount of discretion available to individuals in the organization. Organizational structure insures that the individual behavior will conform to the organization's purpose. It is therefore a mechanism for achieving organizational control, which is required in order to integrate the individual staff member with the organization's goals. However, it should be realized that, although structure does provide for *formal* control, it also has the function of limiting the use of *personal* control. As discussed earlier, prescribed roles and job specifications generally entail more objective evaluations, whereas low amounts of structure permit more discretion by superiors.

In the human service field, organizational structure is the *means* for achieving organizational goals of client benefit. Understanding the concept of organizational structure makes it possible to perceive structure as the means rather than the ends of human service programs. It makes it possible to avoid an exclusive emphasis on organizational structure, which could lead to goal displacement (see Chapter 2). The administrator must also be concerned with whether the organizational structure in existence is functional or dysfunctional for client benefit. Organizational structure must be evaluated on an ongoing basis and altered when necessary.

In summary, the purpose of organizational structure is to provide continuity in organizations as well as the means for achieving organizational goals. Clarity regarding the relationship between organizational structure and organizational goals is crucial, inasmuch as lack of clarity may result in less effective achievement of goals.

INDIVIDUAL AND STRUCTURE

As indicated earlier, the structure is more than the sum total of individuals' attitudes and behaviors. Organizational structure is the composite of officially prescribed rules and evolving practices. However, a basic issue is that of the relationship between changes in individual behavior and changes in structure. Do individuals shape the situation or do situations determine individual behavior? The structuralists (e.g., Perrow 1970) argue that the structure (system) is the more powerful force and that major change can occur only if policy (structure) is modified. We have already argued that changing individuals—for example, replacing the director—is insufficient in itself to deal with policies that are defective. The question that remains is whether changing people is a task that is different from changing structure or policies.

Continuing with the structuralist imperative, one can propose that the attitudes and behaviors of individuals will be strongly influenced by the policies and structure of the organization. For example, an individual at the top level of the organization will tend to think differently from an individual who is at a lower level. Katz and Kahn (1978:503) refer to this phenomenon as "system centrism." Our perceptions are influenced by the kinds of tasks and roles that we perform; our values are shaped by our functions. A person performing a line service delivery function will be influenced by contact with clients and by having to respond to clients' needs. The attitudes and values of an executive will be influenced by the expectation that he or she will insure the survival of the organization by obtaining resources and negotiating with funding authorities.

Another perspective is to view the individual and the structure as interacting variables. This point of view, which will be discussed in more detail in Chapter 9, suggests that the structure and policies are important influences but that the individual can have a role in changing these policies. The premise of this book is that individual practitioners, whether administrators or direct service staff, can influence agency policies and structures if they have adequate understanding of the "system."

The relative importance accorded to individual versus structural factors has important implications. If one defines problems in individual terms, then the solutions will have to involve changing people. However, if one views problems in structural terms then the solutions sought will be structural (i.e., the redefinition and reformulation of policies). In human service organizations, this issue of where to place responsibility for problems is one that continually arises. For example, individual lack of performance can be viewed as being caused either by individual incompetence or by inappropriate procedures and policies which constrained the individual from functioning. Thus, an individual could be involved in a conflict situation either because of his personality or because of a lack of clear role specification (i.e., role conflict). The solution to this problem of conflict will then depend on how one locates its source in the individual or in the structure.

OFFICIAL VERSUS OPERATIVE STRUCTURE

In Chapter 2 the distinction was made between official and operative goals. In a similar fashion, one can distinguish between official and operative structures. Thus far, our discussion has dealt with organizational structure defined in behavioral terms, or operative structure.

Official Structure

The *official structure* of an organization refers to the formal structure as laid out in the organization's official documents, such as the organizational chart and the written rules and regulations. These rules and regulations can prescribe the criteria for service provision, the personnel practices (including criteria for hiring, firing, promotions, disciplinary actions, and staff benefits), and other policies governing the ways in which staff members are to make decisions and carry out their tasks. The organizational chart specifies the official authority and communication structures. Job descriptions provide information on the official role structure. Personnel practices manuals, including the union contracts and civil service regulations, specify the official reward structure.

Operative Structure

The *operative structure* refers to the actual activities engaged in by staff in the course of carrying out their duties. These patterned activities may or may not coincide with the officially prescribed rules and regulations. For example, the official structure, as reflected in the organizational chart, may indicate that the power and the decision-making authority rest exclusively in the upper levels of the organization. In reality, lower-level employees, such as clerks and secretaries, may exert considerable influence and power (Mechanic 1962; see also the discussion of power in Chapter 8). Although roles are specified in rules, there is usually considerable opportunity for discretion. This situation holds in general. As we have seen, rules by definition allow for discretion, which may result in behavior quite different from that which is officially prescribed. The concept of the *informal system* (Blau and Scott 1962:6–7), which was emphasized in the human relations model (see Chapter 3), highlights the unplanned aspects of organizational life—the patterns of relations which have evolved on the basis of human interaction and diverge from the "blueprint" of the classical model.

The distinction between official and operative structures is important in the day-to-day functioning on both administrative and practitioner levels. Understanding this distinction can help one to "understand the system" and appreciate opportunities for action. Both kinds of structure must be taken into account. The knowledge that a secretary or chief clerk has considerable power can be instrumental in facilitating one's functioning in an organization. Similarly, understanding the official rules and regulations permits one to make decisions from a base of legitimacy and authority. As has been suggested repeatedly, structure can be a facilitating factor in organizational life if one understands its purpose and develops the skills of "using the structure."

BUREAUCRATIC STRUCTURE

Any discussion of organizational structure must touch upon the principles underlying the type of structure that exists today in most human service organizations namely, the bureaucratic structure. The bureaucratic structure, which was originally described by Weber, has been discussed here under management models (see Chapter 3). Weber's definition of bureaucratic structure involved the following criteria: *(a)* system of rules, *(b)* sphere of competence, *(c)* hierarchy, *(d)* knowledge base, and *(e)* exclusion of personal considerations.

The bureaucratic model was advocated by Weber as an efficient and rational form of organizational structure. It was assumed that the system of rules would result in continuity, efficiency, and equity in treatment. The criterion of sphere of competence, which is equivalent to division of labor, was to lead to the appointment of individuals to specialized positions on the basis of their abilities and particular expertise. The hierarchical concept assumed that responsibility and authority would be present in the same person and that the superior would be able to insure compliance of subordinates through this hierarchical control structure. The knowledge base provided that technical skill would be the basis for the legitimation of the individual in the organization, that is, ability and authority would be equivalent. Exclusion of personal considerations, the final factor, was thought to be functional in that it separated personal from organizational interest.

The critical question for us is the extent to which the bureaucratic form of organizational structure is functional in the human service field. As suggested earlier, aspects of the bureaucratic model are functional but dysfunctional aspects exist as well; including the unanticipated negative consequence of use of control and the false assumption that ability and authority are always equal. Given the predominance of the bureaucratic structure in the human services, it is important that administrators and practitioners be fully aware of both its functional and dysfunctional aspects.

CENTRALIZED VERSUS DECENTRALIZED STRUCTURES

The relative merits of centralized versus decentralized organizational structures have been the subject of ongoing debate. Over time the pattern has been one of cyclical swings, in which efforts to decentralize are followed by a return to greater centralization of authority.

In essence, centralization versus decentralization of structure refers to the decision-making authority structure, which may be either centralized on the top levels of organization or delegated to the lower levels.

An indicated previously, the human relations model stressed the importance of a decentralized structure in permitting the participation of lower-level employees in the decision-making process. Research supports the contention that centralized structures have less experimentation and flexibility than decentralized structures, where there is more opportunity for innovation (Etzioni 1964:29).

A key question concerning centralization versus decentralization of authority structures is that of which functions need to be centralized or decentralized. For example, policy decisions may need to be made at the top, whereas decisions regarding the implementation of these policies can be made by lower-level staff. The issue of expertise and specialization is relevant here. Given the trend toward increased specialization, it is logical to delegate various kinds of specialized tasks, rather than concentrate them in the hands of upper-level management. Parsons (1960) recognized this in his distinction among three major levels in organizations—the institutional, managerial, and technical levels. Parsons' assumption was that each level performs different functions and requires specialized knowledge and expertise. For example, the institutional level needs the expertise to deal with the external environment and to obtain community support and legitimation. The managerial function of coordination and integration of the various subunits inside the organization requires a different kind of expertise and skill. The technical level, which is concerned with service delivery, requires yet another knowledge base.

Parsons' model implies a system of decentralized functions, with each level performing its own tasks and having the expertise to complete these tasks. However, an overriding question remains: Who has the final authority in an organization and who is accountable for the organization? The need to have accountability clearly placed would seem to require some hierarchical arrangements.

ORGANIZATIONAL SIZE AND STRUCTURE

Organizational size has been extensively studied as a key structural variable influencing many other variables in the organization (Hall 1977:101–129; Indik 1964). Organizational size, as measured in terms of the number of employees, has been contrasted with organizational complexity, that is, the number of functions performed. It may be the case that organizational complexity is a more critical variable than organizational size (Hall 1977:130–151).

In any event, organizational size has been found to have numerous implications. Large organizations tend to be correlated with less discretion, less individual satisfaction, increased stress, and decreased productivity. The impact of organizational size is especially evident when professionally trained employees are involved. Thus, the need for professional autonomy and flexibility becomes a more critical problem for professionals in large organizations.

The problems posed by large organizations seem to be mitigated somewhat by the common practice of establishing small work groups within the organization. Small work groups in a sense diminish the impact of size and complexity on the individual. Decentralization is another means for dealing with the negative consequences of large and complex organizations.

As with the other aspects of organizational structure discussed, size can have an important impact on organizational functioning and hence must be taken into account in the design of organizations and the implementation of programs.

SUMMARY

Organizational structure is a critical factor that will facilitate or constrain professional practice in the human service field. Organizational structure can be functional or dysfunctional for professional activities. In order to insure that structure is functional in terms of achieving the goals of client benefit, practitioners must be cognizant of the impact of structure. They must be able to take advantage of structural opportunities and avoid being overwhelmed by structural constraints. The distinction is made between structural versus people problems to highlight the value of differentiating between problems whose solutions lie in changing individuals versus changing policies. Lack of structure is identified with organizational constraints on practice since it can allow subjective control by superiors. Structure can be functional in that it can provide clear boundaries for professional action yet permit areas for discretion.

APPLICATION OF CONCEPTS ON ORGANIZATIONAL STRUCTURE TO CASE "FROM PSYCHOLOGICAL WORK TO SOCIAL WORK"

The case "From Psychological Work to Social Work" illustrates how organizational *structure can either constrain or provide opportunities* for discretion. In this case, the administrator turned a structural constraint into an opportunity for action, when he used external pressure from a citizen review board to initiate a systematic procedure for monitoring the work of the staff. The review board's need for case information provided the administrator with an opportunity to accomplish his own objective of getting the staff to accept a new management information system, which he could use to assess staff productivity and effectiveness. In contrast, other administrators in similar positions in the state viewed the external review board's demands for accountability as an encroachment on their authority and autonomy—a *constraint.*

The administrator in this case, when confronted with staff dysfunction, decided to focus his efforts on *changing the structure* rather than on *changing the staff members' attitudes and behavior* directly. This strategy is illustrated by his actions with regard to the hiring officer and the manager of administrative support operations, both of whom were leaders in the staff resistance to change. The hiring officer exercised his power through his use of personal influence in informal relationships with staff. The administrator was able to curb this unofficial power by establishing a clear-cut job description for his position, thereby limiting his opportunity to interact with a wide variety of staff. The administrator therefore used existing structure to constrain the hiring officer's areas of discretion. These constraints eventually motivated the hiring officer to leave the agency. Thus, changing the structure resulted in changing the individual. Similarly, in dealing with the manager of administrative support operations, the administrator insisted that he fulfill his job functions, which included keeping the clerical department fully staffed. The establishment of clearer job expectations and insistence on accountability reduced the manager's power and led to his early retirement.

The *effect that structure can have on staff freedom for action* is also evident in this case. The initial lack of clear-cut job descriptions and performance expectations gave the supervisors much *personal control* over subordinates. The result was a reward system based on personal prejudice and favoritism. In situations of this kind there is usually little variation in the official evaluations of staff performance (everyone gets "outstanding" performance ratings). These *official* performance evaluations, therefore, have little relationship with the *actual* reward system of promotions, which is influenced by personal and political considerations. This type of reward system results in low staff morale and lack of motivation to perform beyond minimum expectations.

The difference between the official and actual structure was also evident in this case, inasmuch as the *actual* authority structure departed significantly from the *official* structure. Power and influence had become concentrated in the hands of the manager of administrative support operations and the hiring officer. One of the major tasks of the administrator was to change this *authority structure* by reducing the power of these two staff persons. In other words, he used his understanding of the difference between official and actual structure to modify the pattern of staff behavior. By *knowing the system,* he was able to change it.

The preceding points were made with respect to one aspect of organizational structure—the authority structure. In order to change systems one also needs to be aware of other types of structure—the communication, role, reward, and interorganizational relations structures.

The administrator in this case also changed the *communication structure* and the *role structure*. As will be recalled, the lack of definitive job descriptions gave the hiring officer the opportunity to talk to and influence any staff member—even those outside his official jurisdiction. This was one source of his power in the agency. By establishing a more definitive role structure, the administrator simultaneously changed the pattern of communication.

The lack of role structure had other repercussions for staff performance. First, the absence of clear job expectations contributed to burnout. Second, it had a direct influence on the reward structure. The *reward structure* determines how staff are promoted and disciplined. A just reward system requires objective criteria for evaluating job performance. In this agency, given the absence of clear-cut criteria for job performance, the reward system was influenced by nonobjective criteria, such as personal favoritism. The administrator changed the reward structure by introducing an objective system for performance appraisal, which enabled him to be more rational in the use of promotions and sanctions.

Finally, the administrator modified the pattern of relations between his organization and other agencies. This *interorganizational relations structure* had previously consisted of very limited interagency cooperation and coordination. The introduction of new roles such as resource coordinator led to the development of affiliation agreements between the agency and other community services such as the mental health center and juvenile court. The interorganizational relations and structure was thus changed from a closed to an open system pattern.

Organizational structure should be a means for achieving the goals of the agency. However, there is always the risk that organizational structure will become an end in itself, displacing the primary goal of client benefit. In this case situation, the administrator focused on case outcomes (client benefit) as the criterion for staff performance. He did so by establishing clear job expectations, with a reward system linked to case outcome. Therefore, the structural changes in this case situation facilitated the achievement of organizational purposes. The issue of *centralized versus decentralized* structure is also evident in this case. When the administrator entered the agency the situation was one of *decentralization*, in which decision-making power and authority was dispersed. In his efforts to introduce major change, the administrator was compelled to centralize power and authority.

ORGANIZATIONAL SUBSYSTEMS

OUTLINE

I. Issues
   A. Centralization versus Decentralization
   B. Equilibrium versus Independence versus Conflict
   C. How to Evaluate Organizational Success: Input versus Outcome

II. Definition

III. Subsystem Functions, Dynamics, and Mechanisms
   A. Using the Subsystems Model to Diagnose and Solve Organizational Problems
   B. Production Subsystem
   C. Maintenance Subsystem
   D. Boundary Subsystem
      1. Production—supportive
      2. Institutional
   E. Adaptive Subsystem
   F. Managerial Subsystem

IV. Stages of Organizational Evolution
   A. Primitive Stage
   B. Stable Stage
   C. Advanced Stage

V. Summary

VI. Application To Case "From Psychological Work To Social Work

ISSUES

In Chapter 3 on management models, the systems model (Katz and Kahn 1978:69–120) was briefly discussed. This integrated approach to understanding human service organizations assumes that to be effective administration must view the organization from a perspective that combines the approaches of the classical, human relations, and structuralist schools of management. As will be seen in what follows, this systems model, with its multifaceted view of organizations, provides a comprehensive tool for diagnosing agency problems. Before proceeding, however, we discuss three issues that emerge in relation to the systems model: *(a)* centralization versus decentralization, *(b)* equilibrium versus independence versus conflict, and *(c)* input versus outcome as measures of success.

Centralization versus decentralization

The costs and benefits of centralized versus decentralized structures have been discussed in Chapter 4. The issue is relevant here because the systems model assumes a *decentralized* structure. In contrast to a hierarchical model, the systems model does not assume that ability equals authority (V. Thompson 1961). It recognizes that the complexity of modern organizations and the need for extensive specialization and expertise make it impossible for the upper levels of administration to have the knowledge to control all decision making. Thus, the model provides for a division of labor according to organizational subfunctions. For example, the production subsystem, which has the expertise in the service delivery area, must also have the authority to make policies and decisions in that area. A similar situation obtains for the maintenance, boundary, and adaptive subsystems. The integration of subunits, which is needed to insure that the organization's primary goal is served, rests with the managerial subsystem. Although this subsystem has overall responsibility and authority, it uses it selectively in relation to its function of resolving conflicts between hierarchical levels and between functional subunits. The systems model, therefore, accepts the need for power and authority, but in circumscribed areas.

This subsystems model may be contrasted with a "power politics" model (Gummer 1978; Hasenfeld 1980), which assumes that competition for control of resources is the basic dynamic of organization and self-interest the basis for action. Although Gummer believes this dynamic is neglected in a systems model, it can in fact be included in the model, as is the case here. The role of power in determining goals and structure is also granted in the model presented here, in that power struggles between different subunits are assumed to be inevitable. The area that the power politics model tends to underplay is that of the power held by upper-level officials. Granted that often official power is constrained by power struggles between subunits, it can be and has been exerted by leaders who are cognizant of the constraints and opportunities in the system.

Equilibrium versus Independence versus Conflict

A second issue is whether in reality all parts of a system are interrelated and interdependent (Gummer 1978). Observation of organizations reveals that some units can be fairly autonomous and that this situation can be functional for the organization. The adaptive subsystem perhaps best fits the criteria for an autonomous unit. Nonetheless, the competition for the limited resources in a system will require different groups to interact in an attempt either to defeat one another or to work out some compromise on resource distribution.

The question of whether interdependence or independence of subunits is preferable needs to be answered on the basis of consequences for goal achievement. The stress on communication in the human service field may necessitate collaboration and efforts to achieve "equilibrium." Nonetheless, the value of autonomy for the individual or groups needs also to be recognized. The balance between independence, interdependence, and conflict should be based on what is functional for the organization in terms of client and staff benefit.

How to Evaluate Organizational Success: Input versus Outcome

Another valid criticism that has been made of the systems model is that the stress on subunit goals makes it difficult to have a standard for the overall system. As a result, measures of organizational success fall back on inputs (resources) (Yuchtman and Seashore 1967). This problem is discussed in what follows in terms of the responsibility of the managerial subsystem to be clear about the overall goals of consumer benefit. Recognizing the potential in a systems model for goal displacement, where subunit goals become dominant, the model suggested here views subsystem objectives as the *means* for achieving overall organizational goals. As pointed out in the previous chapter, organizational structure is by definition a means for achieving organizational goals. In human service organizations, the fundamental standard for evaluation of agency success has to be consumer benefits and not the structural input.

DEFINITION

The systems model assumes that organizations are made up of five sub-systems which have different purposes (functions). The subsystems are pro-duction (service delivery); maintenance (personnel-staff development); boundary, which is divided into production-supportive (interorganizational relations) and institutional (board of directors) components; adaptive (research and planning); and managerial (coordination, both internal and external). These subsystems have distinct rationales (dynamics), as well as distinct methods and procedures (mechanisms) for accomplishing their different purposes. They are interrelated, so that a change in one subsystem will have an effect on the other subsystems (Katz and Kahn 1978:69–120). The systems model is therefore an "organic" model, similar to that for any living structure that has different elements (e.g., heart, lungs, etc.) which perform separate and interdependent functions.

Slavin's framework for social administration is similar to the systems model (Slavin 1980:3–21). He includes three elements: client, practitioner, and agency. The administrator's task is "orchestrating these diverse constit-uencies, with their different, and often conflicting, interests and needs. How-ever, this role must be guided by a primacy of orientation toward the client/consumer [p. 3]."

The political economy model (Hasenfeld 1983:43–49) also attempts a comprehensive approach to human service organizations. This model focuses on "the interaction between the political and economic forces within and without the organization that shapes its basic structure and process," including the "exchange relations established between the different interest groups that comprise the organization [pp. 83, 44]." Although the political economy model is as comprehensive in scope as the subsystems model; it is less specific and therefore less useful as a tool for organizational diagnosis and action.

A systems model for organizations assumes that subsystems are in con-stant movement because of the dynamics of competition for survival and enhancement. The assumption that conflict among subsystems is inevitable contrasts with the view that rational planning can produce organizational de-signs in which subunits are complementary rather than competitive. This later view is exemplified by Glisson's (1981:22–27) "contingency" model, which suggests, for example, that the goals subsystem should influence the technology subsystem, which in turn should determine the structure sub-system. Although the model presented here also aspires toward rationality, it simultaneously stresses basic contradictions among the functions of the different subsystems. For example, the production subsystem (service deliv-ery) is responsible for meeting client needs. This purpose may come into conflict with the maintenance subsystem (e.g., the personnel department), which is concerned with responding to staff needs. The boundary subsystem's purpose is to relate to the external environment, including other community agencies. Staff in the service delivery system, however, may feel that clients are not being adequately served by these other agencies. Thus, the boundary subsystem's goal of obtaining community support and legitimation may conflict with the production subsystem's goal of service delivery.

Subsystem differences also result from differences in their contact with and pressure from the external environment. Thus, the boundary subsystem by definition has greatest contact with external forces and will be most responsive to their demands. The service delivery subsystem receives input from the outside through clients served. In contrast, the maintenance subsystem is more inward looking and is somewhat protected from external pressures. As with other differences among subsystems, these differences may lead to conflicts, which may need to be reconciled by the managerial subsystem.

This systems model assumes that in order for an organization to function optimally it must have all subsystems functioning according to their purpose. To achieve this the managerial subsystem has the task of integrating and coordinating the other four subsystems. The following diagram illustrates this system model.

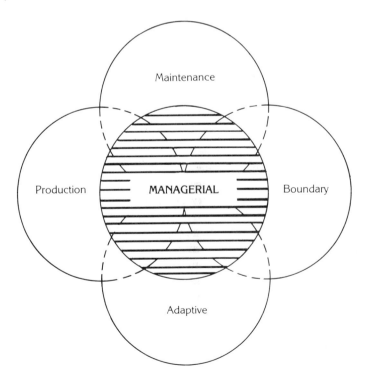

SUBSYSTEM FUNCTIONS, DYNAMICS, AND MECHANISMS

Using the Subsystems Model to Diagnose and Solve Organizational Problems

The subsystems model provides administrators with a method for analyzing and diagnosing organizational problems. This diagnostic tool can be used to pinpoint which part of an organization is malfunctioning, thus enabling corrective action. It accomplishes this by making available a normative model specifying which functions, dynamics, and mechanisms are associated with particular organizational units (subsystems). The organization can then be evaluated by comparing the performance of these units with this standard. For example, the production subsystem, which performs the service delivery function, uses the mechanism of job specifications. An administrator confronted with the problem of a high staff turnover can explore the possibility that there is an inadequate specification of roles among the service delivery staff in relation to the objectives to be achieved. It may be that an agency with a social care goal needs a division of labor among service delivery staff to insure adequate cooperation with other agencies in order to provide services needed by their clients. An analysis based on the standard for a properly functioning production subsystem might find that the turnover problem is related to inadequacies in this subsystem. In a similar fashion, malfunctioning could be identified in the maintenance, boundary, adaptive, and managerial subsystems.

Production Subsystem

The production subsystem of human service organizations is concerned with service delivery to clients. This task is accomplished through the establishment of job specifications and a division of labor. The dynamics of this subsystem stress proficiency and technical skill. The rationales for specialization are of particular concern in this subsystem. In the human service field there have been shifts to different types of specialization and division of labor, in order to achieve more effective service delivery.

Specialization can be organized around four areas: purpose, process, person, or place. If *purpose* is the basis for specialization, service delivery is designed around the kind of problem being addressed. Thus, an organization has specialists dealing with mental health, legal, housing, marital, work, etc., problems. This type of specialization seems to be on the increase, as more emphasis is being given to the unique needs of various social problem groups in our society. Administration education has recognized this shift by developing various specialized programs in fields such as health, gerontology, corrections, and public welfare.

A more traditional division of labor uses a *process* rationale. Here the emphasis is on methodological skills such as casework, groupwork, and community organization in social work or the various professional specializations in the mental health field, such as psychiatry, psychology, and nursing. The advocates of a generic method (e.g., Siporin 1975; Pincus and Minahan 1973) view the various process subspecialties as too narrow and advocate a combined generic process method.

A division of labor utilizing *person* as the rationale would organize programs around demographic characteristics of people. For example, service might be geared to different age groups: children, adolescents, the elderly. Alternatively, special programs might be designed for specific ethnic groups: Hispanics, blacks, Asian Americans, etc.

Specialization by *place* or geography was emphasized in the poverty programs of the 1960s. Local neighborhood services were established in order to facilitate client access. The catchment area rationale for community mental health centers also exemplifies division of labor by place. The assumption here is that human services should be responsive to the needs of the particular community and hence can increase effectiveness by establishing units within the community.

A problem in the production subsystem is the potential overemphasis on technique. This can have negative consequences, if skills displace consumer needs. For example, in the health field there is criticism that too much unnecessary surgery is being done (Illich 1976). Statistics reveal that there is a relationship between the amount of surgery performed and the numbers of surgeons practicing. The "law of the instrument" applies here. This law states that if you give a hammer to a child he will solve all problems with this hammer. Similarly for specialists in the human service field (see Chapter 14 cartoon).

Maintenance Subsystem

The goal of the maintenance subsystem of human service organizations is to facilitate integration of the individual staff members' goals with those of the organization. The interests and abilities of staff members will not coincide completely with the requirements associated with organizational tasks. Moreover, their loyalties are divided because of the demands placed on them from outside of the organization (e.g., professional and personal pressures). The maintenance subsystem attempts to facilitate identification with organizational goals by formalizing and standardizing procedures and establishing systems to select new members and train and reward staff. The dynamics of this subsystem stress the maintenance of stability and predictability.

The formalization of rules and procedures achieves uniformity and hence insures that services will be predictable and equitable. Regulatory mechanisms are established to monitor staff activities to make sure that they are in accordance with organizational objectives. In the human service field, agency manuals provide this kind of control over routine decision making.

Systematic monitoring of staff activities has received increased attention with the development of computerized management information systems. The ease with which large amounts of information can be processed has been somewhat of a mixed blessing. As these systems become more sophisticated and centralized, it is evident that their practical usefulness for administrators and practitioners is limited. This is attributable to two factors: First, these computerized systems do not allow for flexibility, in that they cannot provide operating staff with information not planned for (programmed) in advance. Yet such a need often arises, for example, with basic client demographic information. Second, these overly complex systems preclude quick retrieval of information which staff may need for decision-making purposes.

Another problem impeding efficient and effective program monitoring is the failure to specify what information is required for decision making. In part, this failure may stem from the lack of participation of line staff in the design of management information systems (Weissman 1977). I have found (Neugeboren 1967) that it is possible to design a relatively simple management information system that serves several purposes, including provision of ongoing and current information on client characteristics, staff activity, and case outcome, as well as provision of a case-recording system.

The integration of staff into the organization is further accomplished through *selection procedures.* Industry has developed systematic procedures recruiting and selecting employees whose personal goals will be congruent with the organizational goals. These procedures have included tests and even interviews with wives to determine whether they will "fit in." In human service agencies recruitment and selection have not been as highly developed. Civil service procedures have attempted to standardize recruitment and selection. However, civil service tests have been criticized because although they may measure certain cognitive skills, these skills do not necessarily correlate with performance ability (Steiner 1977:39). Moreover, the primary selection tool used in the human service field—the interview—has been found to be a somewhat biased and invalid technique (Walden 1979). Yet despite evidence that the personality factor biases objective appraisal, the belief persists that performance can be predicted on the basis of an interview.

An alternative that could be used more is situational testing. That is, an instrument containing problem situations characteristic of a particular job can provide information on how an individual may be expected to function in that job. An extension of this idea of situational testing is the probationary period (e.g., 6 months) established to test whether the individual is performing up to standard.

The limitations of recruitment and selection procedures require that organizations establish methods for training and socializing new members. In-service training programs have flourished in recent years, particularly in the public social welfare sector. Staff development departments, with funds from the federal government, have instituted a variety of in-service as well as extramural institutionally based training and educational programs. Educational leave programs have become a basic benefit for workers in the public human service sector. Efforts to socialize new members must confront the problem of designing training programs that are relevant for the tasks to be performed on the job. Staff development departments which are divorced from the line operation may not be familiar with the changing needs of the direct service personnel. An example of lack of congruity between training and job requirements is the practice of sending public agency personnel to graduate schools of social work for education in the direct service area (casework) and then, upon their return to the agency, moving them into supervisory and administrative positions. A common consequence is that these staff who receive inappropriate education develop a trained incapacity to perform on the job, resulting in high turnover (B. Neugeboren 1977; Sullivan 1976). In-service training in new service methods may also be resisted if it is perceived as questionable by staff (Reid and Beard 1980:81).

Another mechanism that the maintenance subsystem uses to facilitate integration of the individual into the organization is the establishment of reward systems. Thus, for example, promotions are used as positive sanctions and disciplinary actions as negative sanctions. The equitable distribution of rewards is crucial in motivitating the individual to participate and perform, and in turn depends upon the establishment of systematic procedures. A lack of such procedures for job specification and performance evaluations opens the door to subjective and inequitable treatment of employees. As is discussed in Chapter 11, this type of organizational dysfunction can be detrimental to staff morale and performance. It is this kind of problem with which the maintenance subsystem should be concerned. Therefore, the establishment of clear job expectations (production subsystem) is a basic condition for the setting up of fair or equitable reward (and sanctioning) systems. This is also an example of the interdependency between two subsystems.

Equitable reward systems are influenced by methods used in performance appraisal. Human service agencies tend not to use results-oriented appraisals, favoring instead such methods as essays and rating scales (Wiehe 1980:6–7). A method that emphasized objectively measured results would in all likelihood increase the potential for a fair and equitable reward system.

Given that its primary purpose is to foster integration of individual and organizational goals, the maintenance subsystem will of necessity be involved in combating policies that are prejudicial and discriminatory. As indicated, inequitable reward systems can have negative consequences for staff morale and productivity. This problem is especially deleterious if it results in racism and sexism in the selection, promotion, and other forms of rewards for staff.

Organizational racism and sexism can take the form of institutional policies and/or individual behaviors (M. Austin 1981:165). *Institutionally based discrimination* refers to organizational policies and procedures that result in the inequitable distribution of rewards with negative consequences for particular groups (e.g., minorities). *Discriminatory behavior* consists of discounting an individual's capacities because of a belief that the particular group that individual belongs to is in some way inferior to others. The maintenance subsystem is equipped to counteract both types of discrimination.

On the *institutional*, or policy, *level* the maintenance subsystem can counteract racism and sexism by insuring that recruitment and selection procedures are equitable. Through affirmative action policies, efforts can be made to recruit from particular groups by developing specialized channels or networks to reach persons from those groups who are qualified for the positions available. The use of situational testing, which is a valid and unbiased selection procedure, can also help insure equality of access by those groups discriminated against. The recruitment and selection of minority staff is important for the human service field given the high proportion of minority clients. There is a need for staff who understand the culturally based values of particular groups (see Chapter 13). Nondiscrimination in the distribution of rewards and sanctions requires objective staff performance appraisal systems. As emphasized earlier, vague and poorly defined job performance expectations allow for excessive discretion on the part of supervisory staff and hence may lead to discrimination.

Discrimination on the behavioral level can be counteracted through sensitivity training programs. For example, in-service training that promotes cultural awareness of racial and ethnic differences can help counteract racist behaviors.

The issue arises as to whether priority attention should be given to institutional or behavioral discrimination. This is related to the larger question, discussed earlier, of whether problems lie within the individual or the system. As was indicated earlier, attributing problems to individuals when the real difficulty is in the policies is a form of victim blaming. A relevant example concerns explanations for the failure of women to move into management positions in the human service field (Chernesky 1979). The emphasis placed on individual characteristics of women (e.g., on assertiveness training to compensate for childhood socialization experiences) (Weil 1983) can distract attention from possible discriminatory policies. The question of whether to focus on changing the individual or the policy can also be answered by deciding which course of action might have a greater impact on the problem of discrimination. As changing policy can have the consequence of modifying individual attitudes and behavior, then that option may have greater potential. Modifying individual behavior without changing discriminatory policies cannot be a long-range solution to racism and sexism in the human service field.

As indicated, the maintenance subsystem has as its purpose the achievement of a steady state. This can be interpreted as maintaining the status quo, and, indeed, the term maintenance has been given the connotation of conservativeness. If this subsystem becomes the defender of the staff's needs *at the expense* of the consumer, then it will be dysfunctional for the organization. Here one should be aware that studies of the relationships between employee satisfaction and productivity indicate no clear association. That is, happy employees are not necessarily effective ones. Integrating staff needs with organizational purposes can be an *ideal* toward which the organization strives. However, it must be kept in mind that the ultimate goal is consumer needs and that employee interests are a *means* to that goal.

The maintenance subsystem because of its functions tends to look inward into the organization. This, in part, may be the reason for its basic conservativeness. A subsystem is directed outward in the boundary subsystem. This will be discussed next.

Boundary Subsystem

The basic purpose of the boundary susbsystem in the human service organization is to influence the external environment of the agency. The subsystem's rationale is that a human service agency in order to survive and thrive needs to be constantly aware of, and able to respond to, changes occurring in the external environment (Hasenfeld and English 1974:98–101). This need has become particularly critical today, as the human service field finds itself under increasing pressure from the political and economic environment. The Reagan administration, with its budget cuts in social programs, exemplifies the impact the external environment can have on the human service organization. The human service agency responds to the external environment through the two components of the boundary subsystem: the production-supportive and institutional systems.

Production-supportive System

The production-supportive unit is concerned with those activities needed to provide backup and support to the service delivery system. Its basic function is to transact exchanges with other organizations on which the agency depends. In the human service field there is increased awareness of the interdependencies among agencies. Cooperation and coordination are essential so that consumer needs may be adequately met (see Chapter 12). The purpose of the production-support unit is thus to develop linkages with other agencies through affiliation agreements and other coordinating procedures. For example, agreements might be established between a child protection agency and a local hospital to insure that child abuse clients are adequately served. Traditionally, there have been problems in achieving coordination among human service agencies, in part because of a lack of shared goals and a lack of awareness of the need for exchange of resources. Thus, it is important that the production-supportive system of an agency have the knowledge and skill needed to facilitate interorganizational cooperation and coordination.

Institutional System

The purpose of the institutional system in human service agencies is to insure that the organization obtains community support and legitimation. This is usually the task of board of directors under the direction of the executive. The institutional unit needs to publicize the agency (public relations) and, in general, interpret to the community the organization's mission and accomplishments (Schneider and Sharon 1982). In the process it develops *constituencies* that it can turn to in times of need. For example, it might seek support from other agencies if funding authorities attempt to reduce the services it provides. This institutional subunit manipulates the environment by influencing other organizations like united funds, the state legislature, and citizens. It also organizes persons who received service to help put pressure on funding authorities. For example, parents of children in Head Start programs are a very active constituency for the program. The need for legitimation and community support has become critically evident with recent budget cuts in social programs. The programs that seem to be least effected are those with strong constituency support (e.g., child welfare and Medicare).

As mentioned, the board of directors of human service agencies are part of the institutional subsystem. The board, which is composed of representatives from the community, can perform the important function of legitimizing the agency in the community. Its members may represent various constituencies whose support the agency needs (Slavin 1980:8). When difficulties arise in the relationships between the agency and other external groups (e.g., funding agencies), the members of the board can take on responsibility of interpreting agency policy and, in general, acting as a buffer.

Traditionally, agency boards have been most active in the voluntary sector of the human service field (Rosenthal and Young 1980:88). Their *official* functions are formulating fiscal and personnel policies and holding the director accountable for the functioning of the organization (Rosenthal and Young 1980:90). Their *actual* functions, however, are more in the areas of obtaining social support and legitimation. Given their part-time, volunteer status, board members are not in a position to assume a great deal of responsibility and, therefore, are heavily dependent on the paid, full-time executive. For this reason, the policy formulation and accountability functions are primarily advisory and supportive in nature. A skillful executive will "manage" the board in such a way as to achieve his or her own objectives for the organization (Weissman 1973:73; Slavin 1978:112). However, one area in which the board makes critical decisions is that of hiring and firing the executive. Dismissal usually occurs in response to extreme pressure from sources outside the agency, for example from funding authorities or other community groups.

Adaptive Subsystem

The adaptive subsystem in human service organizations is concerned with research, development, and planning. It is the intelligence arm of the organization. It performs an adaptive function in that it must recognize the need to change the organization in response to changing environmental needs and make the appropriate recommendations to management. Its basic tools are systematic study and evaluation.

In contrast to industry, human service agencies have, in general, been reluctant to allocate resources for research and planning. When budgets are cut usually the first area to be affected is research and planning. However, in the 1960s and 1970s the availability of grant funds has stimulated research-related activities in human service agencies.

Internal program evaluation has also become more legitimate in the human service field. As pressures for accountability increase, human service agencies are being forced to systematically monitor and evaluate the efficiency and effectiveness of their programs. The use of computerized management information systems has facilitated the collection, storage, and retrieval of data for ongoing programs evaluation.

One of the issues associated with the establishment of an effective adaptive subsystem is the tendency for internal evaluation to be coopted by the system and thereby lose some of its objectivity. It has been suggested that outside experts are needed in order to insure objective evaluation. However, one way of lessening the possibility of the organization coopting the adaptive subsystem is to place the latter high in the organizational structure and divorce it from daily operations. In other words, the adaptive subsystem should be an arm of the top executives and should make recommendations directly to them.

MANAGERIAL SUBSYSTEM

The purpose of the managerial subsytem in human service organizations is to provide the leadership to coordinate and integrate the other four sub-systems. Its basic functions are *(a)* resolving conflicts between hierarchical levels through use of authority, *(b)* coordinating subsystems through compromise and adjudication, and *(c)* coordinating with the external environment to increase resources and, if necessary, to restructure the organization.

As indicated earlier, the managerial subsystem cuts across the other subsystems and is the overall controlling and decision-making unit of the organization. This subsystem requires the knowledge and skills to deal constructively with conflict and negotiate its resolution. The managers need to have a system perspective in order to understand how the different subsystems can be coordinated and integrated (see Chapter 11). Given the basic differences between subsystems in terms of their ideologies, the managers have to be alert to the potential for ideological conflict. Furthermore, the differences in the tasks performed by the different subsystems require that managers understand the problems associated with contradictory structures (Litwak 1978:143). Routinized and nonroutinized tasks require bureaucratic and human relations structures respectively. To coordinate these two types of structures, it is necessary to understand how their differences may lead to conflicts. For example, the coordination of income maintenance (routinized) and adoption (nonroutinized) programs must take into account how their interdependencies can be used to facilitate cooperation within the constraints of contradictory structures. Finally, the staff of the managerial subsystem needs to utilize information obtained from the adaptive and other subsystems to change the organization if needed (see Chapter 11). With the aid of the adaptive subsystem the managerial subsystem needs to anticipate changes in the environment that will require the organization to change in order to survive and thrive.

Because each subsystem strives to enhance its own position, it is the responsibility of the managerial subsystem to direct attention to the primary purpose of the human service organization, the welfare of the consumer. This is necessary to avoid emphasis on maintenance management rather than service management (Meringoff 1980:9).

STAGES OF ORGANIZATIONAL EVOLUTION

Now that the five subsystems have been discussed, it is possible to analyze their relation to the general evolution of organizations (Katz and Kahn 1978: 70–74). It is useful to classify human service organizations in terms of their stage of development, inasmuch as each stage—primitive, stable, and advanced—is associated with a particular set of problems. Just as understanding child development helps us accept and deal with a child's problems and crises, so by understanding organizational evolution can we deal with the developmental difficulties of an organization. This does not mean that all problems are necessarily related to developmental phases. As with people, it is possible for an organization to become arrested at an early stage in its development.

Primitive Stage

Organizations when they are first started are said to be in the primitive stage of development. At this stage the organization is primarily concerned with its own survival. It will be particularly interested in performing its primary task and meeting expectations from the environment. The threat to survival binds the individuals together, insuring cooperation and commitment. The production system receives the most attention. However, structure is not required to control staff, as their commitment to the common cause insures their identification with organizational purposes.

Human service agencies that fall into this category are usually small community development agencies such as community action organizations. As the role structure is not developed at this stage, there is little division of labor and everyone is expected to do any task that is required (answering phones, typing, etc.). Work in an organization that is at this stage can be difficult for those who are not fully identified with its mission (e.g., graduate students in placement).

Although the primitive stage of development is most common in new organizations, some organizations never progress beyond this stage. Thus, organizations that are dependent on grants that are allocated annually may not be able to obtain the financial security to move beyond the primitive stage of development. Working in and managing an agency in the primitive stage of development requires certain types of understanding and skills. The smallness of these agencies makes them like families, with a high amount of personal and social involvement. This can make it difficult to separate personal and organizational goals. The lack of structure and of status differences can prove especially problematic for professionally oriented staff. Administrators must understand these different sources of tension. Leadership skills based on expert and referent power are probably especially critical for organizations at this stage (see Chapter 9).

Stable Stage

The next developmental stage in the evolution of organizations is the stable stage. As the organization becomes more secure, the problem of integrating individual and organizational goals becomes more evident. This problem necessitates the development of more adequate structure in the maintenance (reward), managerial (control), and production (division of labor) subsystems. The further development of these subsystems allows for the greater reliability and predictability that has become necessary. Many human service agencies remain at the stable stage, without much movement toward further development. Their financial support guaranteed, they are satisfied to remain stationary.

Advanced Stage

In the advanced stage of organizational development, an agency must be responsive to environmental oportunities and demands. It must therefore develop boundary and adaptive subsystems. Human service agencies at the advanced stage actively seek to expand and analyze opportunities in the external environment that can be exploited for this purpose. As noted earlier, more and more human service agencies are developing the capabilities of planning and research as well as performing boundary functions. This may, in part, be a response to a changing and turbulent environment. It may also be related to the increasing numbers of administrators whose education has prepared them to appreciate the need for boundary functions and roles in organizations.

SUMMARY

The systems model for human service organizations presented here is an ideal model which can be useful in diagnosing organizational problems. It offers a comprehensive view of organizations, by blending other models such as the scientific management, human relations, and structuralist models. It is a dynamic model containing five interrelated subsystems which have different functions, dynamics, and mechanisms. The subsystems are: production (service delivery); maintenance (personnel); boundary (public relations-interorganizational relations); adaptive (research and planning) and, managerial (coordination and control). Organizational problems can be analyzed and solved by the determination of which subsystems are or are not fulfilling their expected functions. This subsystem model is a decentralized one with each subsystem having authority in its respective area.

APPLICATION OF CONCEPTS ON ORGANIZATIONAL SUBSYSTEMS TO CASE "FROM PSYCHOLOGICAL WORK TO SOCIAL WORK"

In the case situation "From Psychological Work to Social Work," the administrator, in order to change the goals of his county-level child abuse agency, had to modify organizational subsystems in a number of ways.

The *production* subsystem, which is concerned with service delivery, was a major target for change. It will be recalled that prior to this administrator's assuming his position there had been a lack of clear-cut role definitions and job specifications. Also, the roles performed had been directed at client-changing objectives through clinical interventions. The legal investigatory role had been not clearly identified, even though the agency functioned under statutory mandate to implement the child abuse law.

With the change to a social care goal the job specifications were modified accordingly. Workers were now expected to promote the delivery of concrete resources to clients. Also, they were required to establish closer linkages with other community agencies. New positions were created, such as resource coordinator, to facilitate achievement of social care objectives.

In keeping with the legally mandated investigatory role, workers' reports shifted away from an emphasis on feelings and attitudes to an emphasis on behavioral facts related to child abuse. This factual reporting facilitated the role of workers in their testimony in court procedures and insured greater protection of the legal rights of clients. Another aspect of the production subsystem was also modified—the specialized units. These specialized units had had lower workloads than the generic units. As overload was a basic problem, the administrator attempted to reduce workloads by equalizing them through the abolishment of the specialized units. The emphasis on generic service delivery units was also justified as being more appropriate for accomplishing social care objectives.

Related to the modification of the production subsystem were changes in the *maintenance* subsystem. In order to change the service delivery goals, the administrator implemented a more rigorous system of performance evaluation. Under previous administrations, this state-required system had been in effect but had not been operationalized. By clarifying job specifications and standards, the administrator was able to establish tighter control and a more systematic method for rewarding and sanctioning employees. Therefore, changing the production subsystem enabled also the modification and improvement of the *maintenance* subsystem.

Associated with the shift in agency goals and the establishment of more clear-cut criteria for job performance was the development of two other aspects of the maintenance subsystem—employee selection and training. The social care goal required the service delivery technologies of social provision and community linkages. In order to recruit staff with this "social" orientation a change was needed in the procedures used for staff selection. New situational tests were devised which measured a "macro" orientation to direct service practice. These tests were used both for selection of new employees and for promotion of existing staff. Training programs were developed to help staff make the shift to a social care goal.

The administrator's changes in the *boundary* subsystem affected both the production-support and institutional subunits. In the *production-support* area new relationships were developed with other community agencies to enhance linkage. Affiliation agreements were established with the juvenile court, education, mental health, and public welfare systems. Regular meetings were held with the executives of these other organizations in order to achieve effective coordination. The administrator had to be clear as to how this child welfare agency could have shared goals and an exchange of resources with other human service organizations. For example, coordination between this public child welfare agency and the community mental health center required the understanding that the CMHC's goal of rehabilitation would complement the child welfare agency's goal of social care. Resource exchange enabled the CMHC to obtain help with such concrete services as transportation, day care, and homemaker service, while the child welfare agency obtained the diagnostic and therapeutic services needed by its clients. The administrator's attempt to coordinate service with the public assistance agency was less successful. The competition between the goals of these two agencies precluded cooperation.

Another method for promoting interorganizational cooperation and coordination was the use of "cross-training." This consisted of mutual exchange of staff from the other organizations to participate in the regular in-service training being conducted in the agency.

The *institutional* subunit, responsible for obtaining agency legitimation and community support, was greatly in need of modification. At the time the new administrator assumed his position, the agency's public image was somewhat tarnished. The administrator's efforts to change this public image involved the use of all of his staff in a speakers' bureau, coordinated by a staff member. Any community group that wished a speaker on child welfare could contact the agency and arrange for one free of charge. In addition, a number of staff were made responsible for representing the agency in a variety of committees on the local and state level. As word spread, requests were made for agency participation on national-level committees as well.

The administrator himself participated actively on committees in the central office at the state capitol. As this statewide agency moved more in the direction of social care, the administrator was asked to share with other county offices the work done in his office. This served to increase the legitimation and support received from the top-level administrators in the central and regional offices. Consequently, more resources were made available to this county agency.

Under pressure from a citizen's review board, the administrator introduced more systematic procedures for evaluation of program input and outcome. Therefore, the *adaptive* subsystem also was changed. An ongoing data collection system was devised to provide the administrator with information on staff productivity. This data was fed back to supervisory personnel for control and training purposes. Norms were established for number of client contacts and length of time that cases were active. As a consequence of this objective system of monitoring, the policy of giving priority to severe child abuse cases was successfully implemented. Associated with this more focused, time-limited intervention was a decrease in caseload size. Together, the more appropriate method of intervention and the reduced caseloads resulted in less job pressure and hence less staff turnover and burnout.

Throughout this application of the concepts on organizational subsystems to the case "From Psychological Work to Social Work" reference has been made to the role of the director of this county public child welfare agency. As indicated, he was very active in instituting the change in goals from rehabilitation to social care. He therefore performed an important function of the *managerial* subsystem, namely, the introduction of change. Another function performed by the managerial subsystem is the coordination and integration of other subsystems. In the case discussed here, it was crucial that the changes in the production subsystem be coordinated with changes in the maintenance and boundary subsystems. It was imperative that these subunits' effort be integrated toward the primary goal—social care service to child abuse clients.

BUREAUCRACY, BUREAUPATHOLOGY, BUREAUSIS, AND THE GOOD BUREAUCRAT

OUTLINE

I. Issues
   A. Individual versus Organizational Dysfunction
   B. Are Bureaucracies Unfit for Human Habitation?

II. Definition

III. Bureaucracy
   A. Imbalance between Ability and Authority
   B. Inversion of Ends and Means
   C. Formalistic Impersonality
   D. Resistance to Change

IV. Bureausis
   A. Personalizing the World
   B. Present Time Orientation
   C. Love without a Price
   D. Resisting Interrogation

V. Bureaupathology

VI. The Good Bureaucrat
   A. Staying Power
   B. Vitality of Action
   C. Use of Discretion
   D. Conservation of Energy
   E. Organizational Skill
   F. Ability to Exploit the Rules
   H. The Good Bureaucrat versus the Bureautic

VII. Summary

VIII. Application to Case "Disciplinary Action"

ISSUES

The distinction between people- and system-caused difficulties will be elaborated in this chapter through the analysis of the differences between bureaucracy, bureaupathology, and bureausis. The concluding section will integrate the individual and organizational emphases through a description of the role of the "good bureaucrat"—one who has the bureaucratic expertise needed for effective functioning in complex human service organizations.

Individual versus Organizational Dysfunction

Human service administrators when confronted with ineffective perform-ance in the organization need to determine whether the problem lies in in-dividual incompetence or inappropriate policies. Does the solution for poor morale of direct service staff reside in changing the reward system or in replacing the workers because they have unrealistic job expectations or in-appropriate skills? To what extent is poor individual performance a result of lack of "fit" between individual and organizational needs? (Performance problems are particularly evident in public human service agencies, where there is very low morale and high turnover; when turnover rates exceed 50% per year (Galm 1972:33) one can infer that there is something wrong with the organization.) Should staff complaints of excessive paperwork and in-sufficient time to do intensive counseling be understood as lack of proper job expectations and/or inadequate selection procedures and/or poor allo-cation of job responsibilities by administration? Is occupational burnout due to dysfunctional policies and structures or to unrealistic expectations stem-ming from ignorance of the kinds of personal satisfaction possible from work in complex, formal organizations? These questions will be addressed through the discussion of the differences between the dysfunctional organization (bureaupathology) and the malfunctioning individual (bureausis).

Are Bureaucracies Unfit for Human Habitation?

Critics of life in complex organizations claim that the environment is basically antihuman. If this "alien" environment is inevitable, however, what should one do? How is it possible for the individual to obtain gratification working in an impersonal, bureaucratically organized system?

Bureaucratic organizations have been described as environments char-acterized by low interpersonal trust and openness (e.g., Argyris 1972:vii). Thus, the situation of employees in formal organizations has been described in the following terms:

(1) they have little or no control over their workaday world
(2) they are expected to be passive, dependent and subordinate

(3) they are expected to have a short time perspective
(4) job specialization asks them to perfect and value only a few of their simplest abilities
(5) they are asked to produce under conditions (imposed by the priniciple of unity of direction) ideal for psychological failure [Argyris 1970:25]

Other criticisms of bureaucratic organizations are that:

(1) It does not allow for personal growth
(2) It develops conformity and "group think"
(3) It will modify the personality structure such that man will become and reflect the dull, gray, conditioned "organization man" [Bennis 1966:6]

Max Weber, the father of the theory of bureaucracy, is quoted as saying: "It is horrible to think that the world could one day be filled with nothing but those little cogs, little men clinging to little jobs and striving toward bigger ones ... [Bendix 1960:455–456)."

Hummel (1977) summarizes Weber's view as follows:

Bureaucracy gives birth to a new species of inhuman beings. Man's social relations are being converted into control relations. His norms and beliefs concerning human ends are torn from him and replaced with skills affirming the ascendancy of technical means, whether administration or production. Psychologically, the new personality type is that of the rationalistic expert, incapable of emotion and devoid of will. Language, once the means for bringing people into communication, becomes the secretive tool of one-way commands [p. 2].

Hummel himself advises those who have to work or interact with the bureaucracy to be aware that they have to make a major adjustment in their orientations and behaviors because life in a "bureaucracy is radically different from life in society [1977:3]."

Another author (Prottas 1979) offers the following characterization of bureaucrats:

"Poof! You're a Client"—This is a story about magicians. But it is not a story about old crones in secluded hovels turning princes into frogs. It is about modern, mundane magicians, with powers more relevant to urban crises than to sleeping princesses. ... What is called for in modern magic is mass marketing—the capacity to change a great number of citizens into a limited number of creatures economically and efficiently ... these modern magicians are organization men and women. They work for welfare departments, police departments, hospitals, housing authorities, courts, and so forth, and if they can't change a citizen into a frog they can certainly do a goat and will generally try for a sheep. These practitioners of modern magic are frequently called bureaucrats—street level bureaucrats ... their occult task is to turn ordinary citizens into "clients" (or "suspects", "patients", or any other trade name for client) [p. 1].

Regardless of whether these critics are correct in their appraisal of bureaucracies, the fact remains that organizational life is problematic from the perspective of the individual. Often workers turn to ridicule as a means of coping. "Ridicule, however, even if it does help make bureaucracy more bearable, is not good enough." Jokes about bureaucracy by human service personnel are indicative of a more basic problem—the inability of these workers to "take seriously the organizational environment that surrounds them." They confuse "a superficial anti-bureaucracy ideological rhetoric for the complex body of insights and skills that are needed to manage a personally and socially productive organizational career [Pruger n.d.:Chapter 1, p. 2,4,7]."

Accepting bureaucratic life as a "given," the question becomes how to maximize the integration of the individual into the organization. If the bureaucratic organizational environment *cannot* be responsive to human needs, then what kinds of skills and knowledge are required by the individual to enable adaptation to this "alien" environment? Is the lack of these skills evidence of individual maladjustment? If it is, can this defect be remedied?

DEFINITION OF BUREAUCRACY, BUREAUSIS, BUREAUPATHOLOGY, AND THE GOOD BUREACRAT

The terms bureaucracy, bureausis, bureaupathology, and the good bureaucrat will be defined briefly here and later given more complete elaboration. *Bureaucracy* is a form of organization characterized by specific characteristics including a hierarchy of authority, specialization, impartiality, and fixed rules and regulations. *Bureausis* refers to the pathological behavior of individuals who cannot function within a large complex organization because of unreal expectations that their personal needs can be met within the organizational situation. *Bureaupathology* refers to the dysfunctional organization which is ineffective because its structures are inappropriate for its goals. The *good bureaucrat* is an individual who has the organizational expertise to successfully use organizational structure to achieve the goals of client benefit. Thus, bureaucracy is defined in functional terms as conceived in the Weberian model. Bureaupathology refers to the "sick" organization whose "pathology" is related to inadequate policies and structures. Bureausis, in contrast, is a problem related to individual deficiencies associated with inappropriate behavior in a large, formal organization. The good bureaucrat functions effectively in a bureaucracy because of his or her understanding of the opportunities and constraints of the system.

BUREAUCRACY

The bureaucratic structure, as defined in the preceding section, has evolved not only from ideological convictions (see Chapter 3), but also from the organizational imperatives for efficiency in accomplishing complex tasks involving many people (Hall 1972:116). That is, bureaucratic structure makes it possible to organize and coordinate work efforts of many people in order to achieve organizational purposes.

Intrinsic to bureaucratic structure are several sources of strain which one needs to understand in order to function within this organizational context. These sources of strain include (a) imbalance between ability and authority, (b) inversion of ends and means, (c) formalistic impersonality, and (d) resistance to change (V. Thompson 1961:14–21).

Imbalance between Ability and Authority

A basic dilemma of the bureaucratic form of organizational structure is the conflict between specialization and hierarchy. As knowledge has developed and expanded, it has become impossible for persons in positions of authority to be sufficiently knowlegeable to make the required administrative decisions. Superiors therefore lost to experts the *ability* to make decisions although they were given the *right* as part of their role. This dilemma is evident in the human service field, where professionally trained experts are confronted by administrative personnel who have authority to supervise and direct them but lack the requisite knowledge. Thus human service practitioners and administrators need to understand this constraint associated with the bureaucratic structure, so that they can cope with it and thus prevent it from interfering with the accomplishment of the goals of client benefit. Administrators who understand their inability to "know all" will define their responsibility in more realistic terms, that is, as organizational coordinator or integrator (see the discussion in Chapter 5 of the management subsystem). Practitioners also need to reconcile this imbalance between ability and authority insofar as it has repercussions for their daily activities.

Inversion of Ends and Means

The elaboration of organizational substructures in large complex bureaucracies is also a consequence of the increased specialization derived from the knowledge explosion. Concomitant with this trend is a focus on means or subgoals, sometimes to the detriment of the ultimate goal of client benefit. For example, in the child welfare field the specialists in foster home care are concerned with selection of foster parents, an emphasis that could detract from the more basic goal of returning the child to a permanent situation with the natural parents. Inasmuch as this inversion of ends and means is a structural constraint associated with bureaucratic organizations' emphasis on specialization, human service practitioners and administrators need to take it into account. That is, rather than seeing this only as a limit on practice, they need to develop ways of adapting to it. An awareness of the distinction between means and ends can help avoid their inversion. Such an awareness is crucial for specialists who have a high investment in their particular techniques. Administrators, also, while being sensitive to the professionals' investment in their specialties, should be ready to remind staff of the ultimate purpose of these means, which is client benefit.

Formalistic Impersonality

Another characteristic of life in bureaucratic organizations is the impersonality required in the performance of organizational roles. Relationships, whether with colleagues or clients, are "secondary" rather than "primary." As has been mentioned, a purpose of this impersonality is to insure fairness in treatment to subordinate and client. It requires bureaucratic classification in order to accomplish "evenhanded justice." Human service personnel have difficulty understanding this need for bureaucratic classification (see the segment above "Poof—You're a Client" quoted earlier) because it hinders *individualized* treatment.

Impersonality in relations with colleagues, subordinates, and superiors is itself an organizational constraint that human service practitioners find problematic. The definition of "secondary relationship" is pertinent here. It is associated with organizational role, which can be characterized as the "public personality" of the staff member. It entails not only specific behavior expectations (e.g., completion of specific tasks) but also general characteristics, such as being universalistic and affect free (V. Thompson 1975). The universalistic quality insures that any person occupying a position will be treated like others in the same or similar position. The affect-free quality means that there is "no fear or delight in interdependence, no pleasure in giving rewards, no hatred in receiving punishment [Katz and Kahn 1978:552]."

Human relations advocates attempt to counteract impersonality in a bureaucracy by personalizing relationships. Because of its basic inconsistency with the assumption underlying bureaucratic structures, this attempt can lead to frustration and further alienation. Hummel (1977) describes the problem as follows:

> Managers who "humanize" or "personalize" some of their relationships with their hierarchy (they obviously cannot personalize *all* relationships given the size of most bureaucracies) are not simply stepping on toes of some people who will be jealous of such relationships from which they are excluded. They are, in fact, subverting the basic structure of modern organization: they are opening up to question the taken-for-granted values system that provides most functionaries with guidelines for success, attacking the identity of functionaries as organizationally defined and thus frightening the excluded to their very core, and factually and legally engaging in "corruption" in the true sense of the word by propagating emotional relationships that threaten death to rationalistically legitimated ones [p. 16].

Human service administrators and practitioners need to understand this formalistic impersonality characteristic of life in bureaucratic organizations. They need to adapt to it in such a way as to not be alienated by it. Formalistic impersonality does *not* preclude relationships characterized by warmth and mutual appreciation. It does establish limits on the extent that primary relationship needs can be met in bureaucratic organizations.

Resistance to Change

Another characteristic of bureaucracies that human service professionals find difficult to understand is their slowness to act or change. Part of the source of this resistance to quick action is the reliance on expertise and complex knowledge, which requires the processing of large amounts of information. The difficulties of coordinating and obtaining cooperation among different specialists within a hierarchical structure create a natural source of inertia and hence resistance to innovation and change.

This basic constraint on change in bureaucratic systems provides a challenge to human service professionals who see the need for system change in order to maximize client benefit. Accepting that in a bureaucracy change requires time can be the first step to coping successfully with the problem. Understanding the source of resistance to change can help the administrator and practitioner develop strategies to minimize this resistance. Thus, circumventing tradition-oriented specialists may be one strategy that could facilitate change.

BUREAUSIS

Although the analysis of bureaucracy given in the preceding section may appear self-evident, many people have difficulty in accepting, and hence dealing with, the characteristics of organizational life. They have difficulty with fixed (rigid!) rules which prescribe behavior, roles which establish boundaries for individual action (constraints), hierarchy which gives great power to superiors (authoritarinism), and division of labor which "atomizes" the individual. This difficulty stems, in part, from the socialization process. People are socialized initially in the family, where the emphasis is on primary relationships and meeting emotional needs. Although they are then exposed to large bureaucracies as they proceed through public education, there is very little formal education directed at understanding the basic nature of large complex systems and their limits in meeting the primary needs of people for support, recognition, and appreciation. This gap in socialization may eventually contribute to what is known as "bureausis."

Thompson (1961) has defined bureautics as those "individuals who find the rationalism, orderliness, impartiality and impersonality of bureaucratic organizations intolerable [p. 24]." Bureautics attempt to use the formal organization as a means for meeting their *primary* relationship needs. They view the requirements for secondary relations as conflicting with their needs for support, attention, and recognition. They view formal aspects of organizations, such as written memos, as being inhibiting and as interfering with the more "natural" interpersonal methods of communication. Rules are viewed as "red tape." As their basic frame of reference is the family unit, bureautics consider any practice that is impersonal as being "dehumanizing." Thus, filling out forms, reporting statistics, obeying "orders" from superiors are all denials of their identity, freedom, and privacy (see case "From Psychological Work to Social Work").

Although Thompson associates bureausis with a personality defect in which a childish behavior pattern persists into adult life, the explanation presented here rests more with the individual's unreal and inappropriate expectations of the work environment in complex organizations. As a result of inadequate education and socialization, the individual fails to understand the purpose of bureaucratic structure, and the result is bureausis. Although there is some similarity between immaturity and bureausis, it is suggested that the solutions are different: Whereas immaturity would require a therapeutic solution, the resolution of bureausis lies in education. Nonetheless, the similarity between immature behavior and bureausis *is* sufficient so that, if we keep the differences in mind, we can validly examine the latter in terms of the former. The bureautic may thus be associated with the following characteristics: (*a*) personalizing the world, (*b*) present time orientation, (*c*) love without a price, and (*d*) resisting interrogation (V. Thompson 1961:170–177).

Personalizing the World

The bureautic, like the immature person, imputes human motives to all events. All decisions are viewed as being made on subjective basis and that one needs "pull" or "connections" to succeed. Rules are viewed as unnecessary red tape and one cannot understand why an exception can't be made in his or her case. Not making the exception is considered ritualistic application and disinterest. The bureautic is incapable of viewing the politics of organizational life as a "game" with specific rules. Instead, it is looked at as a conspiracy, in which there are only groups of friends or enemies. He or she cannot enter successfully into an impersonal, functional, bureaucratic relationship because only personal relations are important. Unable to put himself or herself in another person's place, the bureaucrat expects others to feel the way he or she does.

Present Time Orientation

The bureautic's present time orientation is associated with a number of other characteristics. For example, the bureatic's difficulty in waiting exacerbates his reaction to "red tape," and his inability to understand the rationale behind rules and regulations in turn aggravates his impatience. Like the child, he cannot understand why others cannot accept his word for the need for immediate action. He views planning ahead—for example, establishing schedules and priorities—as tedious, ultimately unnecessary, and not "professional." Thus, from his/her perspective, the use of statistics for planning is also inappropriate, as intuitive feelings are the best basis for decisions.

Love without a Price

Infants are unconditionally loved by their parents. As children grow older, however, expectations are placed on them and demands made, or else they become "spoiled." The bureautic, like the spoiled child, reacts negatively to the impersonal bureaucracy because it does not respond unconditionally to his desires. He or she craves support, recognition, and tender loving care, and takes any criticism personally. A supervisor who writes a negative evaluation is viewed as "insensitive." This need for interpersonal support and "trust" can be manipulated by supervisiors who, under the guise of "helping" the subordinate, can convince the individual that he or she is unfit for the job. The employee is then "counseled out," that is, convinced that he or she should resign. (See Chapter 8 on authority and control.)

Resisting Interrogation

The bureautic resists attempts to obtain information on his or her activities, viewing them as calling into question the person's honesty and worth, as invasion of privacy and violation of civil rights. The bureautic will refuse to keep records or make reports because these are all unnecessary "red tape." He or she views interrogation as not legitimate because it comes from superiors, who don't know "practice."

This phenomena of the bureautic in large human service organizations is further complicated by the strains created for professionals whose value system is in conflict with the bureaucratic structure. The need of professionals for autonomy and freedom from control creates similar symptoms as seen in the bureautics. Thus, professionals' criticism of the impersonality and "rigidity" of formal structures may help reinforce the conviction of the bureautic that the organizational environment is unfit for human existence. The criticism of organizational situations requires further clarification of the concept of bureaupathology—a dysfunctional organization.

BUREAUPATHOLOGY

Thompson (1961:23) defined bureaupathology as individual insecurity and dysfunctional behavior which result from an imbalance between ability and authority. Thus, he views bureaupathology as the response of the individual to the dysfunctions associated with hierarchically structured organizations. Critics have analyzed some of these dysfunctions as relating to factors such as excessive stress on control and as resulting in rigid staff behavior (Merton 1957) and performance on a minimal level (Gouldner 1954).

In contrast to the definition used by Thompson which focused on the individual, here we shall stress the pathology of the organization, which requires solutions that address structural rather than individual factors. Pathological organizational conditions may be identified with dysfunctional role, authority, communication, or reward structures. Throughout this book examples are given of how organizational structure may not be appropriate for achieving the goal of consumer benefit. Inequitable systems for selecting and rewarding personnel and lack of appropriate planning, service delivery, control, or coordination are other examples of dysfunctions that are symptomatic of bureaupathology.

As has already been stressed, it can be difficult to determine whether a particular situation involves an individual or organizational dysfunction. How do we determine whether an individual is malfunctioning as a result of inappropriate expectations and inadequate understanding of organizational life or as a response to malfunctioning policy? Although there are no clear-cut criteria to use in answering this question, we can obtain some insight by examining the characteristics of the "good bureaucrat."

THE GOOD BUREAUCRAT

Pruger (1979), in his discussion of the bureaucratic career, states:

> No one loves a bureaucrat. Even bureaucrats don't love bureaucrats. Given the slightest opportunity to do so, they will describe themselves in other terms: "I am a teacher;" "I am a social worker." "I am a program analyst," "I am a therapist." "I am an administrator." But, "I am a bureaucrat" appears to be an unspeakable phrase. It may be impossible even as a private unguarded thought. And when told "you are a bureaucrat," it is most likely to be taken as an indictment or accusation, even when that meaning was never intended [p. 1].

This reluctance to recognize the unique skills required to function effectively in a bureaucracy is remarkable considering that most people spend much of their working lives in bureaucracies. The literature on the "good bureaucrat" attempts to analyze the set of skills involved. As Pruger has indicated, knowing the system implies an element of "beating the system" (n.d.:Chapter 1, p. 10). The responsibility of the good bureaucrat in the human service field is also to improve the system. At a general level, the good bureaucrat can be defined as an individual who successfully "negotiates the opportunities and constraints of organizational life [Pruger 1973]." This ability can be broken down into a number of characteristics, which are discussed in the following sections.

Staying Power

Staying power refers to the ability of the individual to persist in attempting to accomplish professional goals in spite of the resistances encountered and the general difficulty of achieving change in a short period of time. To have staying power, an individual must have the long-term perspective needed to understand that change requires persistent effort over an extended period of time. Staying power is also derived from the appreciation that organizations are not static but are in constant movement (Pruger 1978:162). The opportunities for and constraints on innovation are also changing, and by having staying power one can be in a position to capitalize on any favorable circumstances that arise.

Vitality of Action

Vitality of action is based on the ability to maintain independence of thought and not become completely embedded in one's officially prescribed role. Vitality of action requires an understanding of the fact that rules and regulations allow considerable discretion.

In addition, vitality of action depends on the understanding that one must rely on one's own resources and not expect active interest and support from others. In the many instances where the proposed action or change will not impinge on others' "turfs," one can expect an indifferent reaction. Individuals usually have a certain freedom of action while working within their own domain. Recognizing that others in the organization are likely to be apathetic to doing more than the minimum should not limit one's own desire for the self-directed action needed to accomplish one's professional goals.

Vitality of action assumes that the individual accepts organizational barriers and constraints as an intrinsic part of the job. The individual addresses these as problems and uses his or her energies and skills to find solutions. Pruger (1979) illustrates this problem-solving perspective in discussing "getting started in the organization," which he distinguishes from receiving "orientation":

The former emphasizes what the individual does or might do to influence his progression from newcomer to organizational regular. From this point of view the organization is the problem and he is the problem solver. Orientation, on the other hand, refers to what the organization does, formally and informally, to shape and integrate the new recruit [p. 2].

Use of Discretion

Discretion is defined as the ability of the individual to have decision-making options in the performance of organizational tasks. Use of discretion in day-to-day organizational activities enhances the ability to be self-directed, which is a major resource available to human service personnel (Pruger 1979:8). The accumulation of this resource occurs at various stages of a practitioner's bureaucratic career. Discretionary power can be enhanced or diminished, depending on the individual's awareness of its potential. For example, when an employee begins the job, he or she will receive a variety of messages from the "old-timers" as to the different constraints (lack of discretion) present in the system. By too quickly accepting this information as the "truth," the new employee can foreclose the possibility of discovering how to see beyond these constraints to potential opportunities for action (Pruger 1979:9).

The way discretionary opportunities operate in human service organizations can also be illustrated with reference to the official job description. Job descriptions, like all written procedures and rules, are by nature fairly general. Thus the individual potentially has wide discretion as to the tasks he or she will perform. Evidence of discretion was found in a study of significant decisions made by public welfare workers. Two-thirds of these decisions were made independent of higher authority (Kettner 1973). The importance of the use of discretion has been shown for direct service practice in hospitals (Murdach 1983):

> The gaining of a satisfactory level of control over the work environment thus becomes an important goal for the hospital social worker, because being able to regulate the pace and demands of the work environment keeps workers from feeling that they are pushed around, constantly at the beck and call of surrounding pressures. Practitioners can then become better able to exercise autonomy (flexibility in the way an action is performed) and discretion (flexibility of judgement when deciding which action to take) in their daily work, which constitutes a significant hedge against unpredictability in their environment [p. 279].

As has been discussed, the ability to make one's own decisions is not unconstrained. Job descriptions, as well as the different formal and informal expectations of colleagues and supervisors, do establish boundaries for action by the individual. Within these boundaries, however, a variety of options are possible (Lipsky 1980). Take the example of supervisors. As indicated, supervisors can establish limits on discretionary ability. Supervisors who emphasize control can in fact heavily constrain their subordinates' freedom to act. However, given the pressures existing in most human service agencies, supervisors, like other personnel, do not seek extra work. The subordinate who is able to be clear as to the supervisor's expectations can usually treat them as setting the boundaries within which there is opportunity for discretion.

In summary, the good bureaucrat has discretion because rules by definition have to be somewhat general, leaving open wide areas of discretionary action (Gummer 1979a:217; Hasenfeld 1983:150). In order to be able to use discretion constructively to achieve professional purposes one first has to understand thoroughly the basic rules of the game. For example, it is necessary to understand that there are limits on organizational authority and rule enforcement, in part because of the inability of the upper levels to observe and to be aware of all rule breaking (Kadushin 1976:107; Gummer 1979a:220). Complete control would require an all-pervasive surveillance system, and this would be too costly and have negative consequences for morale.

Conservation of Energy

Conservation of energy refers to the ability of the individual to understand the opportunities and the constraints of the system and hence avoid wasting time and effort trying to overcome constraints that cannot be modified (Pruger 1973). Conservation of energy is based also on the realization that personal recognition is very difficult to obtain within large formal organizations. The very competitive nature of these organizations precludes recognition and rewards for a job well done, and political factors can hinder equity in such formal rewards as promotions. In short, personal support and praise are not readily available from superiors or colleagues. The good bureaucrat must therefore seek gratification and personal satisfaction from accomplishing tasks, rather than from formal recognition. In human service agencies, helping to accomplish client benefit should be the main source of staff satisfaction and gratification.

Organizational Skill

In addition to possessing the characteristics discussed thus far, the good bureaucrat must also have organizational and administrative skills. Such skills include formulating grant proposals, analyzing organizational problems, working with the community, budgeting, and personnel management. That is, the good bureaucrat not only has to understand how to work within the system and use the existing structure, but also has to have specific skills that will benefit the organization.

Ability to Exploit the Rules

The good bureaucrat needs to distinguish between the organization's mission and the means for achieving that mission, in order to be the master rather than the servant of administrative rules. By continually evaluating the relationship between means and ends, it becomes possible to avoid expending an inordinate amount of energy on the means at the expense of the basic purposes of the organization. Katz and Kahn (1978) refer to a similar characteristic when, in their description of upper-level leadership in organizations, they discuss how a person must "use the structure rather than be used by it [p. 554]." Similarly, in reference to the area of discharge planning in hospital social work, Murdach (1983) states:

> It is essential that workers seeking to develop their roles always be responsive to, but never completely bound by, the needs of the hospital. This legitimates workers' efforts to perform work tasks in new and creative ways. Thus, serving but not being subservient to organizational needs is a prime requisite for any attempt at redefinition and development of the work role [p. 280].

Political Skill

The above characteristics of the good bureaucrat all imply a basic understanding of the *political* environment of the human service agency. What exactly does such an understanding entail? In Webster (1973) *politic* is defined as "shrewdness in managing, contriving or dealing; sagaciousness in promoting a policy; shrewdly tactful; expedient."* Gould and Kolb (1964) define political skill as "art of persuasion, negotiation and compromise . . . skill in manipulating people and opinions [p. 515]." Underlying these definitions is the idea that political skill requires a basic understanding of individual and group self-interests. Political skill enables the individual to influence behavior by appealing to the self-interests of the parties involved.

The importance of political skill to workers within a bureaucratic organization is readily apparent. Although the literature has not devoted much attention to politics within organizations, practitioners quickly recognize the constant "wheeling and dealing" that goes on within their agency. Some authors are beginning to specify the strategies needed for more effective practice in the human services. Murdach (1983) views practice building and implementing skills as "quasi-political." Practice building skills include developing work and gaining influence while practice implementing skills include task management and creating power. Task management involves task claiming, task preferring, task discovery, and task stripping. Creating power requires understanding the sources of power (information, people, instrumentalities) and knowing such tactics as monitoring territory, making alli-

---

*By permission. From Webster's Ninth New Collegiate Dictionary © 1984 by Merriam-Webster Inc., publisher of the Merrian Webster ® Dictionaries.

ances, compromising, being aware of the importance of timing, and managing one's image. Kennedy in *Office Politics* (1980) attributes much of the job failure in industrial organizations to *political* ineptitude rather than a lack of technical competence. The following discussion of political skills draws on the material contained in *Office Politics,* on the assumption that it is equally relevant for human service organizations.

Human service practitioners tend to view office politics as a nasty game and "unprofessional" (Lee 1983:302). Kennedy examines negative reactions to organizational politics in two ways: (*a*) "Most people see themselves as victims. They see no way of controlling events," and (*b*) "The majority of people see office politics as a war game between good and evil [p. 45]." She indicates that viewing office politics as a moral issue relieves the individual of the need to participate. In actuality, office politics may be used for positive or negative purposes. In the human services this political process can and should be used to enhance the accomplishment of the mission of client benefit.

Kennedy also discusses the "myth of political savvy," that is, the idea that politicians are born—not made. She contends that political skills can be learned. The basic knowledge underlying such skills is an understanding of the *informal* organizational structure; for example, an understanding of where the actual power resides. Kennedy also presents specific political tools, including (a) the process of personal distancing, and (b) the politics of mentoring.

Personal distancing is a technique used to protect oneself from the personal barbs of the political process. It is based on the principle of separating the personal self (ego) from the public self (role), of viewing conflict in organizational rather than personal terms. Personal distancing "allows you to disengage your ego and therefore makes you less vulnerable. The result is greater productivity and less pain. . . . It means that you look at the event as a factor in the dynamics of the office [p. 80]." The "bureautic" discussed earlier is one who has not learned to develop this skill of personal distancing. Although discussions on being a good organizational politician often stress personal payoffs to the individual, the skill is viewed here primarily as a means of enhancing professional effectiveness in order to achieve better service for clients.

The politics of mentoring (pp. 187–209) refers to the process of making use of individuals whose experience in the organization has given them knowledge and influence. Kennedy describes five types of mentors: the information mentor, peer mentor, retiree mentor, competitive mentor, and godfather mentor. By fostering relationships with these different mentors, the individual can obtain important information on the informal system, information that can facilitate more effective job performance.

The difficulty that young staff members have in understanding the political nature of organizational life is summarized in the following unrealistic attitudes and actions: "(1) Expecting promotions on about the same schedule that schools keep; (2) Subjecting *every* management decision to a test of rightness and fairness; (3) Looking for the definitive answer and refusing to compromise short of victory; (4) The constant brokering of decisions does not fit the decision models learned in school; and (5)Letting the cruelty of some decisions and the cannibalization of some people perceived as innocent having a lasting effect on themselves [pp. 227–232]." Although these points were made with regard to the politically naive, they can also apply to older staff who, through either lack of experience or simple misunderstanding of organizational life, are unaware of the political nature of the world of work.

A driving force underlying the political processes in organizations is the rewards sought by staff, both economic and symbolic. In the human service field, where economic rewards are limited, personnel often focus on symbolic rewards such as status and power. Much of the control exerted by the hierarchy is through the allocation and withholding of such rewards. A potential problem thus arises when a staff member has professional incentives—that is, being able to achieve client benefit—as the primary basis for motivation. This staff member, who places *professional* reward ahead of *personal* reward, may be viewed as politically dangerous because he or she cannot be controlled by traditional economic and symbolic incentives. However, we suggested earlier that achievement of professional purpose *should* be the main source of gratification for the human service practitioner. If this is the case, then administrators should deal with the potential problem of control by understanding this motivational source. Responding to professional self-interest may pose less of a threat than coping with the competition that can be generated by personal self-interest.

The Good Bureaucrat versus the Bureautic

The characteristics of the good bureaucrat may be considered as an antidote for bureausis. For example, as was indicated, staff in human service organizations sometimes feel that they are victims of the system and have little control over their destiny. This fatalism leads to apathy and feeling of helplessness. In contrast, the good bureaucrat has a more assertive approach to organizational constraints, based on the conviction that there are always *opportunities* available for influencing the organizational situation. Not only does this optimistic orientation facilitate an active search for alternative solutions to problems, in contrast to the passive and complaining response of the bureautic, but it is also a preventive for occupational burnout.

SUMMARY

This chapter emphasizes the need for practitioners to understand the inherent strains of bureaucratic organizations and offers knowledge that facilitates the development of bureaucratic expertise. The "good bureaucrat" maximizes organizational opportunities and minimizes constraints, offering an antidote for the inevitable frustrations associated with bureaucratic systems. The inability to understand the strains inherent in complex organizations leads to "bureausis." The bureautic is the individual who has unrealistic expectations of work in a bureaucracy based on the assumption that personal needs can be met in these impersonal organizations. Individual dysfunction (bureausis) is contrasted with organizational dysfunction (bureaupathology). Bureaupathology can be seen in an organization whose structure is so inappropriate that it cannot achieve its goals. Being able to distinguish between the problems of bureaupathology and bureausis is the key to finding solutions. Human service practitioners, whether they be administrators or direct service staff, must understand this distinction in order to function effectively in the bureaucratic system.

APPLICATION OF CONCEPTS ON BUREAUCRACY, BUREAUSIS, BUREAUPATHOLOGY, AND THE GOOD BUREAUCRAT TO CASE "DISCIPLINARY ACTION"

In the case "Disciplinary Action" the issue arises as to whether the problem behavior of the supervisor is attributable to *individual or organizational dysfunction*. Was his inappropriate and explosive outburst a sign of mental disturbance or a natural reaction to an overdemanding and dysfunctional work environment? If the problem is with the individual, does it stem from a personality defect, lack of skill and ability to do the job, lack of appreciation of the limitations that the bureaucratic structure imposes on the staff, or a combination of these? If the problem is with the organization, which of its policies are dysfunctional? Again there are a number of possibilities. For example, if the goals of this child welfare agency are inappropriate for the problems of child abuse, then the excessive pressures this produces for staff may be the root of the problem.

The issue of whether *bureaucracies are unfit for human habitation* also arises in conjuction with this case. Is the bureaucratic structure of this agency demeaning and destructive of individual worth and self-actualization? If this supervisor reacted so violently because he felt alienated and demeaned by the impersonality of the work situation, then perhaps efforts should be made to "humanize" the work environment through participatory management techniques. If staff are encouraged to present their points of view more, will this remedy problems rooted in excessive job pressures?

The public child welfare agency in this case situation was bureaucratically organized. To what extent was the supervisor's problem related to the basic strains and contradictions present in bureaucratic structures? One contradiction of bureaucratic structures is the *imbalance between ability and authority*. Did the superior in this case situation have ability as well as authority? It may be possible that the subordinate had skills in certain areas that surpassed those of his superior. The fact that the superior was not able to establish clear performance expectations suggests the possibility that she lacked some basic supervisory skills. A second contradiction present in bureaucratic structures is the potential for *inversion of ends and means*. Was the emotional upset of this supervisor a result of his sensitivity to the fact that much of the activity he was involved with had little apparent connection with the purpose of client benefit? Was he overwhelmed by the realization that the productivity of his workers, as measured by such criteria as being up-to-date on paperwork, was considered more important than the number of times children moved from one foster home to another?

Another contradiction associated with bureaucratic structures is strain created by the need for *formalistic impersonality*. It seemed evident in this case that the superior had difficulty distinguishing between primary and secondary relations. Her efforts to provide psychological support and counseling to the supervisor may have helped blur the distinction between formal and informal superior–subordinate relations, which in turn may have accentuated the subordinate's emotional upset.

Having explored the possibility that the problem in this case situation resulted from the strains and contradictions present in bureaucratic structures, we can turn to the alternative possibility that the supervisor was suffering from *bureausis*. It is possible that he had unrealistic expectations about the kind of support and recognition that could be obtained in a bureaucracy. Perhaps he was confused about the differences between primary and secondary relations in formal organizations. Thus, his emotional outburst may have stemmed from frustration at not receiving the attention and recognition he would obtain in primary relationships.

A third possibility is that this staff member's problem resulted from *bureaupathology*. That is, agency policies might have been inadequate and dysfunctional. Specifically, in this case situation the lack of clear role definition and staff performance expectations may have been symptoms of bureaupathology. If so, the solution arrived at in the disciplinary hearing—that is, to punish the employee and have him transferred—would not be appropriate to the problem.

Throughout this case analysis various possible solutions, based on different explanations of the problem, have been suggested. The characteristics of the *good bureaucrat* give insight into other potential ways that administrators could resolve this type of problem. Note that these characteristics are applicable to any organizational position, to the administrator as well as supervisor in the case.

The characteristic of *staying power* and persistence is a quality that could have helped the supervisor in this case situation. Had he understood that change in bureaucratic organizations takes time, he might have been able to control his frustration at the slow pace at which problems were resolved. Had he had the patience to persist, he might have become aware of new opportunities to improve his situation.

Related to staying power are the characteristics of *vitality of action* and *use of discretion*. Implicit in the supervisor's actions was the assumption that superiors have complete control and that subordinates are helpless and defenseless. He failed to appreciate that in a bureaucracy there are always areas for discretion and freedom to act through selective interpretation of rules. This understanding that vitality of action and independence of thought is possible would have reduced his feeling of helplessness.

Underlying these other characteristics of the good bureaucrat is the general principle that in bureaucratic system one needs to *conserve energy,* that is, understand the opportunities and constraints of the system and thereby not waste time and effort trying to overcome limitations instead of taking advantage of opportunities. The supervisor in this case situation may have expended energies unnecessarily in trying to overcome limits imposed by upper-level policies. His "psychiatric breakdown" may have been a consequence of his inability to conserve his personal resources. Recognition that frustration is endemic in large complex organizations could have helped him develop the "thick skin" necessary to conserve his energy so that it would be available for more constructive use.

In this case situation, both the administrator and the supervisor would have benefited from *organizational skills,* as each lacked some of the specific skills that their particular position required. Administrative knowledge and skill would have helped the superior to understand the problems inherent in "psychiatric supervision." Knowledge and skill in caseload management might have helped the subordinate cope more adequately with the pressures of supervising 5 workers and 250 cases. He also could have benefited from *political skills.* Personal distancing would have enabled him to be less vulnerable to the stresses placed upon him in this situation. He would have been able to view the conflict with his superior in organizational rather than personal terms.

OCCUPATIONAL BURNOUT

7

OUTLINE

ISSUES

As pressures mount to develop more effective and efficient human service programs, the tensions created for administrators and practitioners also increase. Concerns about quality, quantity, relevance, and equity in the delivery of human services impact on the staff of these programs, fostering an atmosphere of doubt as to whether their performance is adequate and appropriate. The emphasis on economy and accountability reinforces these pressures and tensions on the staff. As turnover increases and evidence is accumulated on the negative effects of the work situation on the physical and emotional well-being of staff, efforts are being made to understand the cause and consequence of this "occupational burnout."

Individual versus System Cause

Examinations of the roots of occupational burnout focus on whether the cause lies in the individual or the system. Much of the literature on burnout emphasizes individual stress and breakdown, proposing ways to relieve the person of these anxieties. Various types of tension-reducing techniques have been proposed, including physical exercise and meditation. Emphasis also has been placed on encouraging peer support as well as support from superiors (Pines and Kafry 1978; Katz and Kahn 1978). The organizational literature has found that peer support is useful for job performance (Blau and Scott 1962:95). Questions can be raised, however, as to whether peer support and "therapy in the work place" are adequate solutions to work situations that are basically problematic. One can help the individual feel more comfortable in an inadequate work situation, but the stress caused by the job will remain unless efforts are made to redesign the job. In fact, support and "therapy" given to persons suffering from occupational burnout may aggravate the burnout by making the individual more aware of the difficulties and pressures present in the job situation.

The contrast between the levels of worker alienation in the United States and Great Britain, on the one hand, and in continental Europe and Japan, on the other, highlights the distinction between the two alternative causes of occupational burnout—the individual and the system. The greater worker alienation in Anglo-Saxon economies can be attributed to the rigid class distinction between manager and employee in the United States and Britain. In Europe and Japan, where business leaders rose from the factory floor, there has been a basic acceptance of the need for job security and for worker participation in decision making. It has in fact been claimed that the "basis of Japan's industrial success lies not in management styles but in the reality of the economic and social position of the Japanese worker [Gummer 1982:92]." This contrast, then, leads to the suggestion that it is systemic factors that are critical in causing work alienation and occupational burnout in the United States (Karger 1981; Dressel 1982).

It should be noted that the term burnout can be used as a way of justifying incompetence: "We have stumbled upon a worthy and thoroughly modern concept with which to label our discontent.... Burnout—the visual image of which is a pile of cold ashes—covers our personal failures much better than ordinary forms of irresponsibility to ourselves and others [Quinnett 1981:A-23]." However, such incompetence may itself stem from problems in the work situation. If so, rather than placing blame on the individual, efforts might be made to redesign the work situation in such a way as to diminish the pressures (Cherniss 1980:79–112). In the public social service agency, for example, the problem of very high caseloads could be dealt with through a system of priorities and clarification of agency goals.

DEFINITION

Occupational burnout has been described in the following way:

> When work demands exceed one's endurance and ability to cope, when one can no longer tolerate the occupational pressures and feels totally overwhelmed by work stresses, one is likely to reach a breaking point and experience a cluster of symptoms termed "tedium".... The experience is characterized by feelings of strain and "burnout", by emotional as well as physical depletion, and by negation of oneself and one's environment. It is the experience of distress and discontent with one's work and way of life, the sense of failure, and the feeling that one cannot take it anymore [Pines and Kafry 1978:499].

Burnout has been associated with work overload, which may be either quantitative or qualitative. Quantitative overload is having too much work to do; qualitative overload is having work that is too difficult to do (Katz and Kahn 1978:598).

Occupational burnout occurs at all organizational levels. At the administrative level, a manager may experience difficulties in coping with internal and external pressures and hence may develop various kinds of defenses, including physical and emotional problems or negative characteristics associated with the "bureaucrat" stereotype (Daley 1979:375). At the direct service level occupational burnout may occur when workers are unable to cope with the multiple pressures placed on them from clients, the organization, and their professional colleagues.

Regardless of the level on which it occurs, occupational burnout is the result of lack of congruence between the individual's skills, abilities, and job expectations and the demands of the position in which the individual is placed. Thus occupational burnout can be diagnosed by looking at the individual's capacities in relationship to the demands of the job situation. It can then be dealt with by either changing the individual to adapt to the job situation or redesigning the job situation to permit the individual to function.

Occupational burnout has for some time been studied in the industrial organizational field (e.g., Kahn *et al.* 1964). More recently, it has become a focus in the human service organizational area as well. Studies have shown that burnout is associated with the pressures of working with involuntary clients and having to deal with never-ending emergency situations. "Overwhelmed by the cumulative impact, perhaps the cumulative terror, of a large number of cases—are the human suffering, deprivation, disorder, ignorance, hostility, and cruelty—he must face as part of his everyday work situation [Wasserman 1970:96]."

Kadushin (1974a) explains occupational stress in the child welfare field as follows:

> Many situations encountered by child welfare workers have all the essential elements of the classic Greek tragedies. They involve conflicting but legitimate interests and needs. There may be conflict between the justifiable needs of the parents as they conflict with the justifiable needs of children; it may be a conflict between the rights and privileges of a foster parent and the rights and privileges of a natural parent. The child welfare worker has to act so as to recognize and understand the conflicting needs of all parties in the situations. . . . The professional commitment is to individualize the client: bureaucratic efficiency requires that the client be categorized, and his eligibility judged according to uniform regulations. Regulations and procedures restrict the professional exercise of autonomous judgment and decisions [pp. 720–722].

On the administrative level, stress has been related to six sources: (*a*) the job itself (e.g., work overload), (*b*) assigned role (e.g., lack of authority), (*c*) relationships with superiors, subordinates, or colleagues, (*d*) lack of career opportunities, (*e*) agency climate (e.g. office politics), and (*f*) outside sources (Cooper and Marshall 1978).

Democratization of the work place has been advocated as a solution to occupational stress and burnout (Bernstein 1976). However, there are limitations on democracy in organizations, given the need for accountability to both client and community (M. Austin 1981:295). The conflicting pushes and pulls of organizational life create inevitable stresses and strains. Thus, while "centralization reflects dehumanizing work environments . . . decentralization can also, however, reflect anarchy [M. Austin 1981:297]." In short, single solutions such as democratization fail to take into account the complexities of organizational life.

Having defined and briefly discussed occupational burnout, we can now attempt to answer the following specific questions:

1. Is occupational burnout more prevalent in the public sector than in the voluntary human service sector?

2. What form does occupational burnout take on the administrative and direct service levels?
3. Is occupational burnout primarily attributable to staff's lack of appropriate training and skills or to defective policies and structures?
4. How does the bureaucratic context of human service practice influence occupational burnout?

BURNOUT IN PUBLIC AND VOLUNTARY HUMAN SERVICE AGENCIES

Job pressures vary depending on whether a human service agency is under public or voluntary auspices (Kupers 1981:224). This is because the two kinds of organizations differ in their ability to control the demands for services. Such public agencies as welfare boards, correctional institutions, and mental hospitals have high client–staff member ratios. They are required to provide human services on a "wholesale" basis, in contrast to the voluntary sponsored organizations, which are permitted to give more intensive "retail" type service (B. Neugeboren 1970:166). Publicly sponsored agencies, because they are in a "public fishbowl," are also more vulnerable to political pressures (Cupaivolo and Dowling 1983:16). Evidence of inefficiency and/or ineffectiveness can be used by politicians to gain visibility with the electorate. Consequently, the administrators and practitioners are subject to continual monitoring and pressure to respond to such critics as the public advocate, legislators, and citizen and professional groups.

In addition, public human service agencies are constrained by various rules and regulations imposed from higher levels of government, for example, by civil service regulations. Such constraints may limit the freedom of administrators and practitioners in human service agencies to operate and make decisions. Hence the staff may feel that they cannot control their work situation and are bound by whims and wishes of others.

Concomitant with the pressure stemming from the excessive demands of high workloads and elaborate rules is the additional stress of working with clients who are socially deviant and pathological. The emergencies and crises that such clients may create add to the burden of practitioners and administrators in the public human service agencies. Moreover, whether the practitioner is working in a prison or a slum neighborhood, the personal threat of mugging, rape, robbery, etc., is very real (Kadushin 1976:85); it has even been suggested that extra "combat pay" be provided to these practitioners.

In view of the various pressures discussed here, administrators and practitioners in public agencies are as a rule more susceptible to burnout than are their counterparts in private agencies.

BURNOUT ON ADMINISTRATIVE AND DIRECT SERVICE LEVELS

Because administrators and practitioners have different tasks and re-sponsibilities, the demands placed on them are also different.

Top-level administrators in human service agencies are subjected to pressure from groups external to the agency, and in recent times such pres-sure has been increasing. External monitoring groups such as granting au-thorities, official accrediting bodies, and citizens review boards are establishing standards that they expect administrators to meet. Client advocate groups are turning to the courts and using legal pressure to hold human service administrators personally liable. As a result, the stress and strain on top ex-ecutives can be considerable, as is reflected by the relatively short tenure of their jobs. For example, deans of schools of social work have an average tenure of five years (B. Neugeboren 1977:9).

There is evidence that job strain is particularly acute in those positions in which the individual is responsible for others. Physicians and airport traffic controllers have been found to have especially high rates of peptic ulcers (Kahn 1978:62). This suggests that people in different fields who have re-sponsibility for the performance of others may suffer from similar kinds of stress. Certainly direct service workers who work in child abuse areas must feel stress from taking responsibility for the lives of children.

As has been discussed, at the direct service level, stress and occupational burnout can result from the need to cope with multiple and conflicting de-mands from clients, supervisors, and the community (Daley 1979:377). The complexities inherent in the task of assisting persons with social and psy-chological difficulties can lead to frustration, as hoped-for results may simply not be attainable. A partial remedy might be to shorten the amount of time that staff are involved with clients, by using part-time staff and by including other types of responsibilities as part of their jobs. Another source of relief can be the greater use of outside supports such as other formal agencies and informal networks (Kahn 1978:63).

BURNOUT DUE TO INDIVIDUAL OR SYSTEM DEFICIENCY

When low morale, job dissatisfaction, and turnover are evidenced on a large scale, one is inclined to assume that there is something wrong in the system. However, individual deficiency may also be a factor; individual job skills may not be relevant to the task at hand. Although individual performance and organizational structure are closely interwoven, for the purpose of analysis it is possible to separate the two, in order to be clear where to apply the remedy.

Individual Deficiency

Practitioner Burnout

Occupational burnout on the direct service level can stem from inappropriate practitioner ideologies and service technologies (see Chapters 13 and 14). Value differences between practitioner and consumer can result in ineffective service outcomes, causing the worker frustration and feelings of failure. Middle-class practitioners' lack of understanding of lower-class attitudes and values (R. Neugeboren, C. McGuire and B. Neugeboren 1981) can result in withdrawals from service. Areas in which there are potential value differences abound. For example, in the child welfare field the middle-class worker and the lower-class client may have different values regarding child-rearing practices. The client may have a more traditional value orientation toward child rearing which includes the use of physical punishment, whereas the middle-class worker educated in the use of psychological approaches would find physical punishment unacceptable.

An attempt has been made to resolve this problem of value differences by selecting staff members whose culture and class background was similar to that of clients. However, it has been found that this strategy raised other problems (R. Neugeboren, C. McGuire, B. Neugeboren 1981). That is, the conflict between the staff with the traditional values and the middle-class staff creates additional tensions and pressures, particularly on the staff recruited from the lower classes. This situation, in turn, can result in burnout of these nonprofessional staff members. However, other studies (Pines and Kafry 1978; Reisman, Cohen, and Pearl 1964) have found that the lower-class and less-educated staff members suffered from less burnout than the more-educated, middle-class caseworkers when performing similar tasks.

Professionally trained, clinically educated human service practitioners may not have appropriate service delivery technologies for case management service delivery tasks. Consequently, these tasks are usually assigned to non-professionals (R. Neugeboren, 1976).

Thus, in the public social service sector demands of the job require a "wholesale" (extensive) rather than "retail" (intensive) approach to service (B. Neugeboren 1970a:166). Use of intensive people-changing strategies and skills are especially likely to lead to frustration and burnout when applied to such chronic social problems as poverty, mental illness, old age and crime. Furthermore, training that stresses primarily the clinical role does not prepare the human service practitioner to cope with the large amount of paperwork required. In protective service agencies it has been estimated that 75% of time is devoted to such tasks as transporting clients, filling out forms, keeping case records, and attending staff meetings (Daley 1979:377). Inappropriate training may also be a factor in role conflict and ambiguity, which can lead to burnout (Harrison 1980). In the child protection field, for example, workers are required to perform an investigating and social control function, which conflicts with their expectation of being therapeutic agents (R. Neugeboren, C. McGuire, and B. Neugeboren 1981; Harrison 1980:32). Similar role conflicts occur in the areas of corrections and mental health.

Administrative Burnout

The literature on burnout in the human service field has generally stressed the direct service area; however, many of the factors found apply also at the administrative level (Vash 1979; Veninga 1976). Thus, administrative burnout caused by individual deficiency can also be attributed to inappropriate education and skills. Most administrators in the human service field received their education in the direct service areas and then moved up into administrative and supervisory positions. Not only do they lack specialized administrative skills, but their direct service training may act as a hindrance in performance on the administrative level (Sullivan 1976). They may, in fact, have a "trained incapacity" to perform (B. Neugeboren 1971:37). Use of clinical skills to solve organizational problems can result in frustration, burnout, and turnover. A study of staff turnover in a public child welfare agency supports the dysfunctions of clinical training for administrative positions: Clinically educated social workers who later moved into supervisory positions were found to have a much higher turnover than those educated in social work administration (B. Neugeboren 1978). Solving organizational problems through the "treatment" of the individual staff member is dysfunctional for the agency because it is impractical in view of the many day-to-day organizational problems that must be dealt with. More generally, problems are caused by the discontinuities between attitudes of direct service personnel and the requirements of administrative roles (Patti et al. 1979). Differences in orientation to authority (expert versus position), relationship orientation (expressive versus instrumental); decision making (optimizing versus satisfying), orientation to effectiveness (process versus impact), and collegial relationship (mutuality versus competitiveness) make transition from direct service to administration problematic (Patti and Austin 1977:267–280; Patti 1983:209–221). Considerable role conflict may be engendered when human service administrators who entered the profession with primarily humanistic and people-oriented values are placed in positions of authority and power. Professional education may have accentuated this problem (Patti 1979:42). The importance of quantitative skills (e.g., statistics) for administrators also creates strain for management personnel in the human service field who tend to lack these particular abilities or interests.

These individual deficiencies of human service administrators can also have consequences for burnout on the lower levels. For example, it has been found that role conflict and burnout on the practitioner level in child protective services is associated with dissatisfaction with supervisors (Harrison 1980:41). Therefore, inability of supervisor to structure and clarify subordinate role and responsibilities has a direct link to direct service stress, strain, and burnout (Davis and Barrett 1981).

The various individual deficiencies in both practitioners' and administrators' skills can be remedied by more appropriate recruitment, selection, and training policies. This suggests a strategy that focuses on system deficiency rather than on individual staff deficiency.

System Deficiency

Occupational burnout can be viewed in terms of "bad apples or bad barrels" (Bramhall and Ezell 1981:24). As mentioned earlier, many suggestions made for burnout in the human service field involve individual remedies, using such stress management techniques as deep breathing, transcendental meditation, yoga, and physical exercise (Daley 1979:379). Such strategies do not take into account the dysfunctional policies that may be at the root of occupational burnout. Staff recruitment policies that select staff with inappropriate skills and service philosophies need to be examined and modified. Training policies also need to be evaluated. In-service training programs that perpetuate the discrepancy between skills taught and skills required maintain staff frustration and burnout. Educational leave programs that encourage direct service education for staff who will be assuming supervisory and administrative positions also perpetuate and reinforce burnout in the human service field (B. Neugeboren 1977:20).

Dysfunctional organizational structures may contribute to burnout by exacerbating the problem of conflicting role expectations. Organizationally induced stress is associated with the multiple roles performed by direct service staff members in human service agencies. These roles are in response to the pressure from three references groups: the profession, the bureaucracy, and the client. Studies of role performance of social workers have found that, in general, workers responded more to the demands of the bureaucracy than to the demands of the profession or the client (Rothman 1974:83). Therefore, it is suggested that occupational burnout in human service organizations may in part be the result of the role conflict associated with differential expectations imposed on staff by different constituencies. The organization can help lessen the problem through the establishment of clear role definitions as well as priorities for staff decision making.

A second way in which dysfunctional organizational structures can lead to burnout is by producing excessive case loads. This problem can be dealt with by establishing priorities for service. In child protection service, for example, a policy decision could be made to give priority to child abuse and secondarily give attention to child neglect. In mental health services priorities should be established between service to the chronically mentally ill versus service to neurotics. More rational human service organizational environments can be structured so that the allocation of resources is in line with actual goals. (See cases "From Psychological Work to Social Work" and "Mental Health Rules and Regulations.")

Davis and Barrett (1981:58–61) pinpoint the role the supervisor can perform in alleviating burnout caused by organization- and client-related stress. They apply the three functions of supervision (administrative, educational, and supportive) to the task of reducing work stress. Some of the administrative tasks of the supervisor include establishing clear work expectations, representing workers' interests to the administration, and establishing policies and guidelines for services. The educational tasks include helping workers understand and manipulate the system and helping workers understand the need for organizational changes. Finally, the supportive tasks include helping workers accept the inevitable stress associated with case failures; workers learning to live with "tough decisions," and providing time off for "R & R."

BUREAUCRATIC WORK CONTEXT AND STAFF BURNOUT

Occupational burnout may also be related to the bureaucratic work context of the human service agency. This bureaucratic work context (see Chapter 6), which includes formalized procedures, hierarchy of authority, and impersonal and formal relations, may be difficult for staff members to adapt to if their socialization and education have not prepared them for it. The "bureautic" (see Chapter 6) is the individual who is unable to adapt to the formal bureaucratic job situation because he or she does not understand the inability of the organization to provide the sorts of satisfactions derived from primary relationships. Occupational burnout may, therefore, be related to the lack of understanding that some people may have of the nature of bureaucratic systems. The "good bureaucrat" (see Chapter 6) has been defined as an individual who does understand the constraints and opportunities of working in a bureaucratic system and can therefore function in a more effective way. Understanding the purpose of organizational structure (see Chapter 4) and the dynamics of subsystems (see Chapter 5) should help the individual to "conserve energy" (Pruger 1973). It is believed that many of the frustrations and feelings of helplessness experienced by staff in human service programs are related to the lack of understanding of the nature of "life in a bureaucracy."

SUMMARY

Occupational burnout in human service organizations has been related to public agency auspices, individual staff deficiencies, system dysfunction, and the bureaucratic work environment. Low morale and high absentee and turnover rates for employees of human service agencies attest to this burnout syndrome. Solution of this problem requires evaluation of staff selection and training policies, as well as of organizational structures that impact negatively on employees. Appropriate modification of policies can result in a better integration of the individual into the human service organization, which should reduce burnout and in turn enhance client benefit.

APPLICATION OF CONCEPTS ON OCCUPATIONAL BURNOUT TO CASE "DISCIPLINARY ACTION"

The issue of whether the *cause of occupational burnout lies in the individual or the system* is evident in the case situation "Disciplinary Action." The apparent breakdown of the supervisor was viewed as caused by intrapsychic difficulties, as it was recommended that he receive psychiatric treatment. His emotional outbursts were obviously inappropriate and indicated extreme stress. Although therapeutic aid could provide support and tension relief, the question remains as to whether the basic cause may have been in a *dysfunctional job situation*. It was evident that the work situation had excessive job pressures related to the nature of child protection work. Constant emergencies and crises and very difficult social problems created a very stressful work environment. Therapeutic aid for the individual could help him adapt but would not modify this difficult work environment.

This high-pressure work environment is not unusual in the *public* human service agency. A public child welfare agency, with its statutory mandates to investigate and assist in prosecution of child abuse situations, creates role conflicts in social workers who have difficulty accepting their investigatory and social control responsibilities. Additional pressures in a public agency relate to the excessive demands for service made by the community and to extensive rules and regulations which require much paperwork. The staff in this agency, who were oriented to the counseling of clients (intensive "retail" approach), increased the pressures on service delivery because of their inability to respond to service needs. Such pressures confront the line workers directly and their supervisors indirectly. Occupational *burnout on supervisory levels* can be related to pressures from above as well as below. This supervisor's responsibility for the work on 250 cases might have proved an unbearable burden.

The other possibility is that this supervisor's difficulties may have been caused by his own *individual deficiency*. His stress may have resulted from a lack of the abilities and skills needed to perform the role and functions of a supervisor. For example, he may not have had the skills to establish clearcut performance expectations for the line workers in order to monitor and evaluate their work. The task of monitoring work on 250 cases requires quantitative skills, which are often absent in individuals with a clinical orientation and training.

The "trained incapacity" of the administrator in her use of clinical supervision is another example of individual deficiency that can cause job stress and burnout in subordinates. This administrator's difficulties may be attributed to the role discontinuities present for persons who move from direct service to administration positions. Attempting to resolve administrative problems by treatment of individual difficulties often compounds the problems, for the manager as well as the staff.

That *deficiencies in the system* could cause burnout was also evident in this case. The basic lack of role structure prevented the establishment of clear job performance standards, illustrating how a system deficiency can cause strain on staff. Recruitment and selection procedures were not possible in the absence of firm criteria for job expectations. Agency policies that establish inappropriate goals and technologies can also be a cause of strain and tension on staff. In this public child welfare agency, social care may have been a more appropriate goal than rehabilitation, the goal that was actually pursued. Similarly, environmental-change technologies may have been more relevant than the people-change methods used. High caseloads suggest the lack of clearly established service priorities, which is another example of a system deficiency that could produce burnout.

Cultural differences between clients and staff could have added to the frustrations of this supervisor. Clients from lower socioeconomic classes may have had child-rearing values that were in conflict with the psychologically oriented philosophy of the middle-class staff. Lack of understanding of such differences can contribute to *practitioner burnout.* High turnover of line workers creates added burdens on supervisors, who have to be continually involved in selection and training of new personnel. This system-induced problem could be remedied by in-service training designed to give staff an understanding of the cultural values of clients.

Evidence that the burnout of this supervisor was a result of a lack of fit between the individual and the particular system was provided when he was able to function after being transferred to another system. The fact that he performed adequately on his previous job also suggests that the defect may have been more in the particular job situation rather than in the individual.

The influence that the *bureaucratic work context* has on occupational burnout is also evident. The hierarchical authority structure and the impersonality in staff relations in a bureaucracy seem to have been difficult both for the supervisor and the administrator. The supervisor may have had unrealistic expectations as to the type and amount of support possible in a large bureaucratic system. He may also have been uncomfortable with the subordinate status he had to assume within the hierarchical organizational structure. These frustrations with the bureaucratic work situation can be described as bureausis. The combination of the use of hierarchical authority with psychiatric supervision seem to have placed the supervisor in a double-bind situation which may have contributed to his burnout.

AUTHORITY, CONTROL, AND POWER

OUTLINE

ISSUES

Human service practitioners often feel ambivalent about using authority, control, and power (Patti and Austin 1977:269–270). This discomfort is evident in relations with clients, colleagues, subordinates, and superiors. The underlying issue is how and when to use authority, control, and power with the conviction that their use is legitimate, functional, and appropriate to one's role and status. In particular, the concern is that their use will be viewed as coercive and hence result in alienation and resentment (Vinter 1959:262–263). How can administrators and practitioners arrive at a shared understanding of the opportunities and constraints in the appropriate use of authority, control, and power, so that the resulting cooperative relations can facilitate the accomplishment of the goal of consumer benefit?

Use of Authority in Relations with Clients

The obvious fact that in the relations with clients the practitioner is in a superordinate position often is not recognized (Palmer 1983:120) or is vociferously denied (Wolfensberger 1972:1–2). The powerlessness of clients and their dependency on practitioners is not made visible until an advocate comes forth to equalize the relationship. Equality in relations between client and practitioner has been viewed as essential for success in motivating clients to accomplish the desired change effort (Hasenfeld and English 1974:469). Human service practitioners justify the equality "presumed" in their relations with clients by using such phrases as "starting where the client is." They vigorously deny the unilateral nature of decisions by insisting that their role is merely to "enable" clients to reach their own decisions (Gummer 1979a:15). The right of "client self-determination" collides with the assumption that the professional's expertise means that he or she knows what is best for the client. This "cognitive dissonance" produces discomfort and anxiety in the professional, resulting in a denial that the problem exists.

Use of Authority in Collegial Relations

In collegial relations the discomfort is with admitting that power struggles over resources are a common phenomenon (Gummer 1978). The belief in group process and participatory decision making often obscures the fact that there is much behind-the-scenes bargaining or even that majority decisions themselves are by definition the imposition of the will of one group over another. The fact that power and influence varies among individuals is denied and covered up with the justification that the democratic process is possible among equals. The unwillingness to recognize status differences among staff results ultimately in difficulties in implementing "teamwork" (see Chapter 14 on human service technologies).

Dilemmas associated with the use of authority, control and power are seen in the role of client advocate which is promoted in the human service field. (Ad Hoc Committee on Advocacy 1969, Gerhart and Brooks 1983, Richan 1980, Rules and Regulations 1980, Willetts 1980). The use of conflict strategies underlying the advocate role presumes the power to influence colleagues or superiors to change their behavior and policies (Sosin and Caulum 1983:13). However, the lack of legitimated authority and power from direct service staff makes them vulnerable to possible sanctions. In contrast to the legal advocate, the human service advocate does not have the power of the judicial system as a basis for confrontational tactics and strategies (Mailich and Ashley 1981).

The problem of using authority and power is evident in the areas of case management and discharge planning (see Chapter 14). These two functions entail the linking of clients to resource systems which requires authority and power to influence staff in agencies autonomous to the worker's organization (Johnson and Rubin 1983: 49). The issue of case managers not having the authority or power to influence external systems was recognized in the Channeling Program by the inclusion of a financial control case management model (Baxter et al. 1983: 25–28). In this model funds are provided for the case managers to purchase services needed by the client. The case managers power is thereby enhanced by using economic rewards to influence external agencies. Another mechanism for providing the authority needed for service coordination is through agency affiliation agreements (see Chapter 1 case— "From Psychological Work to Social Work"). For example, discharge planning of elderly disabled patients from general hospitals may require interagency agreements to facilitate placement in nursing homes. A greater recognition of the need for power and authority in case management and discharge planning areas would facilitate more realistic expectations of case coordination services.

Use of Authority in Superior–Subordinate Relations

The assumption that professionals must be autonomous in order to function at optimal levels leads to resentment of efforts by those in superior positions to assert authority and control. Authority is equated with "authoritarianism" and attempts to monitor as "gestapo" tactics and evidence of a lack of trust. This discomfort with the use of authority and power is also felt by those in supervisory roles. Hence supervisors will often attempt to screen their control efforts by using interpersonal strategies. Such attempts are generally unsuccessful, however, because subordinates soon grasp the fact that these startegies are quite controlling. Although attempts to explain ensuing conflict in personality terms and the resort to the final solution of "counseling out" by the supervisor may be accepted by the subordinate, there is a residue of tension and doubt as to whether these conflicts could have been resolved in a more constructive manner.

Tension in superior–subordinate relations relates also to lack of understanding that authority, control, and power are interwoven with the factor of bilateral dependency. Although it is readily recognized that subordinates are dependent on superiors for various kinds of material and symbolic rewards (e.g., promotions and recognition), it is less obvious that superiors are also dependent on subordinates. Lower-level employees can make life difficult for superiors by their unwillingness or reluctance to perform in their job (Mechanic 1962). Even working according to the "rule book" can be used as a strategy to resist upper-level authority; rigid overcompliance can effectively sabotage and undermine agency authority (Kadushin 1976:106).

In addition, people in positions of authority have personal needs that make them dependent on subordinates. Being human, they need support and expressions of appreciation from their workers. The loyalty of subordinates has been found to be an important source of emotional support for supervisors (Blau and Scott 1962:162). Fear of losing this loyalty can have a significant constraining influence on a superior's actions. Moreover, subordinates can manipulate their superior's dependence by "apple polishing" and calculated deference. In short, the dependency relationship is a mutual one, and failure to recognize this can interfere with the effective use of authority, control, and power.

A further constraining factor is agency size. That is, small agencies, where physical proximity results in frequent social interactions among subordinates and superiors, have a constraining influence on the overt use of authority, control, and power.

DEFINITION

The terms authority, control, and power relate to the concept of legitimation. The connection between legitimation and control was enunciated by Max Weber (1947). He stressed that the superior's ability to control was based on the willingness of subordinates to obey and comply because they felt the superior was legitimate. This legitimacy was assumed to be based on expertise.

Hence authority, power, and legitimation may be distinguished as follows: *Power* is the ability to obtain involuntary compliance. *Legitimation* is the voluntary acceptance of the use of authority because it fits one's values.

A problem with Weber's conception of authority is his assumption that ability equals authority (see discussion in Chapter 3). As we have seen, given the extensive specialization present in human service organizations, it is unrealistic to expect that persons in top-level positions will possess the knowledge required to deal with the range of decision-making situations that arise.

Weber also stressed that legitimation was related to subordinates' belief that rules were just and therefore should be followed. In a society, laws are obeyed because they are assumed to be rational and just. When a law is believed unjust (e.g., prohibition of alcohol or marijuana) widespread violations occur. In the organization, given that it is impossible for top-level officials to "know all," the primary basis of their legitimacy has to be not expertise but the belief that they stand for justice. Thus, in the human service field, as in other areas, legitimated authority rests on the perception that top-level officials are fair and "even-handed" in making decisions and allocating rewards.

Another basis for achieving legitimacy of authority in human service organizations can be the mutual agreement between staff and administration on the "common good." "When the agency and the supervisees are committed to the same objectives, the supervisee will more freely grant the right to be controlled. The common goal becomes the common good which justifies acceptance of authority [Kadushin 1976:93]."

As legitimated authority is based on voluntary compliance of subordinates, it requires the use of methods that are acceptable, involves objectives that are shared, and must be exercised within the limits legally established by the rules of the agency.

> Authority needs to be used with a recognition that supervisees, as adults, tend to resent the dependence, submissiveness, and contravention of individual autonomy implied in accepting authority. Authority is best exercised if it is depersonalized ... supervisor is acting as an agent of the organization rather than out of a sense of personal superiority. ... If it is not to be resented, authority has to be impartially exercised. ... The supervisor needs a sensitive awareness that her authority is limited and job related [Kadushin 1976:112–113].

In contrast to the association of organizational control with authority, Levy relates staff compliance to agency demands to occupational ethics.

> As much as social organizations control and coordinate non-administrative personnel ... it is part and parcel of the ethical responsibility of those personnel to *be* controlled and coordinated. They are organizational men and women not only in the sociological sense and in the sociopsychological sense explicated by William Whyte in *The Organization Man* (1956), but also in the ethical sense. As employees of social organizations, non-administrative as well as administrative personnel owe ethical duties to those social organizations [Levy 1982:43–44].

NEED FOR AUTHORITY AND CONTROL

The need for authority and control in organizations is related to the lack of congruity between staff goals and organizational goals (Etzioni 1964:58). The organization's requirements for efficiency and effectiveness may not always be compatible with the employees' needs for satisfaction. If it were possible to create a situation in which the organization and individuals were completely compatible, then a system of control would be unnecessary. However, individual loyalties tend to be divided, with personal and professional pressures going counter to organizational demands. Although highly professionalized organizations (e.g., hospitals and universities) are thought to approximate congruency of professional and organizational goals, there is evidence that professional self-interest may conflict with the consumers' interests (Friedson 1970).

The degree of congruence between individual and organizational goals varies according to the individual's level in the organization. In general, the higher the level, the greater the congruence. In human service organizations, where consumer benefit is the goal, it may be that the lower-level direct service employee's goals are also congruent with the official goals, provided that there is not an overemphasis on the technical aspects of the task. Nevertheless, one can assume that in the Western culture the perfect "organization man" is probably rare (although in the Japanese paternalistic organizations there appears to be much more congruence between staff and organizational goals).

Appreciation of the importance of integrating human and organizational goals has been lacking in the human service field. Industrial organizations have moved toward a greater acceptance of the importance of human factors in planning and administration. But, whereas business administration has incorporated the human relations model to balance its primary emphasis on organizational goals, the human service field has been slow in achieving a similar balance by recognition of organizational needs. It is this lack of an organizational perspective that has resulted in the tendency to view organizational problems in terms of individual personality difficulties (Kadushin 1976:115).

The inevitable differences between organizational and individual interests will necessarily result in conflict, requiring mediation and control. Those who view conflict as legitimate and functional can accept the use of authority and control as a method for conflict resolution. In contrast, those who believe that conflict can have only negative consequences will fail to perceive the need for authority and control. Their emphasis is exclusively on consensus and the democratic process. Thus reactions to the use of authority and control are influenced by underlying attitudes toward organizational conflict.

To summarize, the need for authority and control derives from the need to integrate individual and organizational goals. Various specific mechanisms may be used to obtain staff compliance. These are (a) selection and recruitment, (b) socialization and training, (c) reward systems, (d) role structure, (e) psychological versus impersonal control. The sections that follow will discuss each of these mechanisms in turn.

PERSONNEL RECRUITMENT AND SELECTION

The success of personnel recruitment and selection depends on two conditions: (a) the ability of the organization to be clear as to its objectives, and (b) the kinds of individual characteristics required of prospective employees in order for them to perform the tasks appropriate for achieving these organizational goals.

In the human service field it can sometimes be difficult to arrive at a clear specification of organizational goals (see Chapter 2) and to determine what means are appropriate for achieving these goals. Nevertheless, there are situations in which there is obviously a lack of fit between an organization's goals and the kinds of employees it has hired to achieve these goals. For example, a people-processing organization that engages in extensive interorganizational coordination requires personnel who understand the community as a system and who possess the techniques needed to facilitate interorganizational cooperation. Selecting people who are interested primarily in people-changing goals through clinical intervention will result in a lack of fit.

Even if the organizational goals are clear there remains the problem of inadequate selection tools. The interview, which is the most commonly used tool, can be readily manipulated by applicants who know the kind of person an organization is seeking. Interviews are also heavily biased by personality factors, favoring the verbal and expressive individual, who might not be the most qualified applicant for a position (Walden 1979:53). As discussed in Chapter 5, the use of situational testing can help objectify the selection process.

There is evidence (e.g., Hardcastle 1971; Pearl and Reisman 1965) arguing for the selection of employees who possess individual characteristics similar to those of the consumer population. Given the influence that culture and class have on social problems (Pelton 1981) it has been suggested that staff recruited from similar groups would be better able to understand the need of the particular client group. Self-help groups for alcoholics, drug addicts, rape victims, etc., are based on this premise. The use of indigenous nonprofessionals recruited from client groups in poverty programs is another example (B. Neugeboren 1970b).

TRAINING

As recruitment and selection cannot be expected to accomplish a complete fit between individual and organizational goals, training becomes crucial for this purpose. Training employees to understand organizational purposes and the particular techniques that these require is a function of supervisory and staff development personnel. It is an important function, as training can to some extent lessen the need for control: "Training prepares the organization member to reach satisfactory decisions himself without the need for the constant exercise of authority.... Training procedures are alternatives to the exercise of authority or advice as a means of control over the subordinate's decision [Simon 1957:15–16]."

Training is aimed at changing attitudes and behavior of staff. It can be accomplished through didactic educational efforts, for example, through individual and group discussions. It also can be achieved indirectly, by structuring the work situation to facilitate change of employee behavior through task performance.

Training can occur either within the agency or extramurally. They may involve anything from short courses to education culminating in a professional degree. Professional education compared to in-service training has a great impact on the individual's thinking and behavior, facilitating more autonomous activity. Studies of the relationships of bureaucratization and professionalism found them to be inversely related. Higher levels of professionalization are associated with lower levels of bureaucratization. Therefore, professionally trained staff will generally require less supervision (Hage and Aiken 1967:90). This reduced need for supervision holds only if the goals and skills of the particular professional specialization are congruent with those of the agency. Professionals who are educated in rehabilitation goals and techniques (psychiatrists, psychologists, and social workers) may not be congruent with agencies that have social care or control purposes. In such cases, greater administrative controls may be required to remedy the incongruency (see case "Mental Health Rules and Regulations").

The success of direct attempts to change attitudes will depend on how deeply ingrained these attitudes are. Changing belief systems (see Chapter 13 on ideologies) can be very difficult, as these involve strongly held convictions. The goal of developing new techniques and skills may be more feasible, provided these new approaches do not require that individuals give up technologies in which they invested much time learning and practicing. A similarly feasible strategy is to change people indirectly by structuring their work situation. The rationale here is that if the work situation is changed, people are compelled to change in order to function in the new situation. For example, a poverty program that had the goal of opening opportunities for community residents (B. Neugeboren 1970b) achieved an environmental-changing orientation by compelling staff to cope directly with poverty-related problems (poor housing, lack of money, poor health, etc.). This direct exposure to the harsh reality of poverty was achieved by establishing social service offices in the poverty areas and requiring the staff to provide outreach services in the streets and in the homes. Many of the staff selected for this program intially came with a people-changing philosophy. In response to the change in their work situation most modified their attitudes; they discovered for themselves that changing clients was not an appropriate method for resolving poverty-related problems. Other staff who could not change found the job too stressful and felt compelled to leave.

As indicated earlier, the function of training employees rests with supervisory personnel. This educational function of supervision (Kadushin 1976:125–197) has been traditional in human service organizations. A limitation on that function resides in its potential conflict with the administrative function of the supervisor. The administrative tasks of monitoring, evaluation, and task direction may detract from a supervisee's willingness to admit mistakes that often precedes seeking aid and advice. This problem of supervisor role conflict does not affect the supervisor's ability to use the alternative strategy of changing the supervisee by structuring the task that is required. Thus, for the supervisor, changing behavior by changing the work situation remains a viable strategy.

Another constraint on the educational function of supervision is the lack of time available for this activity. Especially in the public sector of human services, pressures of day-to-day administrative tasks of monitoring and coordinating work limit the time available for educational supervision. On the line-supervisory level, where caseloads may start at 50 clients per worker, a supervisor is required to oversee about 250 cases. The various pressures associated with emergencies and crises in these cases, and the resulting pressures from higher-level administrators and other community agencies, are the kinds of demands made upon the supervisor that preclude the performance of the educational function.

The potential conflict between the administrative and educational functions of supervision has led to the establishment of special departments for staff development and training. The success of staff development departments will depend on their knowledge of the reality of the tasks that need to be performed "on the line." The fact that personnel in staff development departments are separated from line operations may lessen their understanding of the demands confronting line workers. One consequence in some human service agencies is that staff-training programs serve mainly as an opportunity for staff to verbalize their complaints and frustrations. Although this allows cathartic relief, it does not deal directly with problems.

As mentioned, training may also be provided by giving staff opportunities for formal education outside of the agency. Special seminars in management are conducted in universities and, for public sector agencies, under the auspices of the civil service. Educational leave programs often allow selected staff to take time off to obtain advanced degrees. As was already discussed, the issue of congruence arises here. For example, public human service agencies have sometimes sent supervisory and administrative staff for education in direct service practice. This lack of congruence has led to turnover, as the staff developed a trained incapacity to function in supervisory and administrative roles (B. Neugeboren 1971:37).

Another strategy for educating and socializing staff involves the process of *delegation* (M. Austin 1981:157). Through delegation, supervisors can enhance the skills of subordinates by enabling them to assume different responsibilities which increase the scope of their work experience. For example, if a supervisor plans to be away from the office, he or she may delegate to a subordinate the responsibility for overseeing a unit of line workers, thus giving the subordinate an opportunity to develop new skills in directing and decision making.

Human service administrators have been noted to have difficulty in delegating responsibility and authority (M. Austin 1981:158). Part of the problem may be the discomfort in use of authority to hold accountable the subordinate since this authority is required when monitoring the subordinate's effort.

Educational supervision, in-service and extramural training, and delegation of work are formal devices for training personnel. However, it has often been observed that much training occurs informally on the peer level. Frequently, new employees learn how to do their jobs from colleagues rather than from superiors. The influence of peer group norms can be substantial, given the hierarchical barriers to communication (Blau and Scott 1962:87–115, 121–124). Such group norms may either help or hinder the training process. For example, a new employee who is placed in a work group that is antagonistic to the agency's goals and expectations will become discouraged from using learning if it conflicts with the norms and expectations of work group peers. Therefore, any agency strategy for training needs to take into account peer group norms, which may either support or undermine educational objectives (see case "From Psychological Work to Social Work").

REWARD SYSTEMS

The system of rewards and sanctions has been termed the compliance structure of an organization. It has been found (Etzioni 1964:59–61) that organizations may be classified according to three types of compliance structures: physical, material, and symbolic. Each of these three approaches to obtaining compliance to organizational requirements has different consequences for alienation and commitment of members: most alienation occurs in organizations that use physical power and most commitment in organizations that use symbolic power.

1. *Physical*—Coercive power is involved when the threat of force is the main method for obtaining compliance. Such organizations as prisons, mental hospitals, and correctional institutions use coercive power.

2. *Material*—Utilitarian power refers to the use of material means to obtain compliance. Factories and industrial organizations use utilitarian power as their predominant mode of obtaining compliance.

3. *Symbolic*—Normative or social power refers to the use of such rewards as prestige, esteem, love, and social acceptance to obtain compliance. Normative power is used in human service organizations like social agencies, schools, and therapeutic organizations.

This compliance model suggests that for most human-service organizations a symbolic, or normative, structure would be appropriate. However, studies of human service organizations do not reveal a consistent relationship between satisfaction and productivity (see Chapter 9). The tendency in human service agencies to undervalue monetary rewards and overutilize symbolic ones may be a source of problems. Where lower-level employees are concerned, economic rewards may be especially critical. The attempt to utilize such symbolic rewards as allowing mental hospital attendants or prison guards to participate in therapy has led to resentment, as well as to the intervention of unions on grounds that these lower-level employees are not being adequately compensated. Alienation also has resulted from the inequities in compensation in the mental health field, where psychiatrists receive much higher salaries than psychologists and social workers while performing essentially the same duties. The increasing unionization of such human service employees as social workers, nurses, and teachers evidences the importance of economic rewards. All this is not to deny that symbolic rewards can motivate individuals and that for the human service practitioner receiving recognition for successfully helping clients is extremely important. It is only to say that rewards that provide *both* material and symbolic recognition would seem to have the greatest potential for motivating employees in the human service field, as elsewhere.

Implicit in this discussion has been the assumption that it is possible to link staff rewards to performance. In the literature, selection and socialization have been contrasted with evaluation as alternative mechanisns for controlling and motivating staff. It has been suggested that an approach emphasizing evaluation of task performance is the more appropriate basis for control of professionals (Yankey and Coulton 1979:53). This assumes, however, that the professionals agree to the criteria for performance appraisal.

ROLE STRUCTURE

The preceding section discussed the reward structure as a vehicle for influencing members of the organization to comply with its expectations. Here attention will be directed at how role structure can be used to assert control.

A basic purpose of structuring organizational roles is to insure that members' activities will be predictable and have some uniformity (see Chapter 4 on organizational structure). By defining boundaries for behavior of staff, the formal division of labor acts as a type of control. Practitioners in human service organizations often view role prescriptions as confining and equate them with the "red tape" that reduces their ability to be autonomous and creative. Their plea is for fewer rules that prescribe their roles. The common-sense assumption is that fewer rules equals less control. However, there are indications (e.g., Rosengren 1967) that the absence of rules opens the door to much more *personal* control by superiors (see Chapter 4). If rules are not available to define expectations for employee performance, then the supervisor's power to use subjective evaluation criteria is enhanced. Given the opportunities for discretion available because rules by definition need to be general, then structured role expectations may facilitate freedom (see the discussion of the good bureaucrat in Chapter 6).

PSYCHOLOGICAL VERSUS IMPERSONAL CONTROL MECHANISMS

We have seen that the lack of role expectations opens the door to greater personal control by superiors. A common form this takes in human service organizations is what may be termed "psychiatric supervision"—the use of psychology as a mechanism for control (Blau and Scott 1962:188–191). This therapeutically oriented approach to control attributes poor performance to intrapsychic problems. As these difficulties are assumed to be on an "unconscious level" the subordinate is not held fully responsible. The subordinate's primary responsibility, then, is to try to understand and obtain "insight" into his or her difficulties. This psychological form of control makes the supervisor somewhat of an omniscient power, who stands in the role of therapist to the subordinate. Conflict between supervisor and subordinate is blamed on "resistance of subordinate due to unresolved problems with authority figures." Therefore, the use of the psychological control mechanism can be quite manipulative and even border on the invasion of the privacy and civil rights of employees.

Another form of psychological control present in agencies is the use of group participation of staff as a means of achieving administrative control. The human relations model (see Chapter 3) which emphasizes "participatory management" may "substitute one form of control for another, less out of humanitarian concern for employees . . . than out of concern about the successful management—or control—of organizations [Levy 1982:44]."

In contrast to the extreme form of personal control represented by psychiatric supervision are impersonal mechanisms for control, which involve the use of nonhuman devices for controlling employee behavior (Blau and Scott 1962:176–183). Performance records are an example. By posting comparative data on staff performance—interview counts, number of field visits, student evaluation of courses, etc.—it becomes possible to put considerable pressure on the underachievers. A supervisor in this situation does not have to intervene personally. A problem with this type of impersonal mechanism for control as currently used, however, is that data usually measures input and not outcome (Hasenfeld 1983:167; Wiehe 1980:6). If the *results* of efforts were used as the criteria, then more freedom and discretion would be available to staff as to the kinds of means that could be used.

PROFESSIONAL VERSUS ADMINISTRATIVE AUTHORITY

The literature often assumes that professionals and administrators are implacable enemies, who are destined to everlasting conflict because of the professional's need to maintain autonomy and the administrator's need for control. The fact that in the human service field most professionals are bureaucrats (Pruger 1973; Finch 1976) tends to break down the differences between professionals and administrators. Similarities between professionals and administrators do exist. Thus, both groups tend to make decisions based on universal standards, expertise, affective neutrality, and clients' interests (Blau and Scott 1962:60–62). The basic source of conflict between administrators and professionals centers around the area of control. Professionals value autonomy (who doesn't!) and resent and resist control from people outside their professional circle (Davidson 1978: 48–50). A crucial question is that of what areas are shared and hence potential bases for cooperation. Here we return to the fact that the basic purpose of human service organizations is client benefit. Assuming that client benefit is also the primary concern of the professional, here, then, lies the basis for mutual cooperation. The problem, however, is that professionals are often concerned with clients on an individual basis. They want to maximize benefits to the client with whom they are working (Patti and Austin 1967:270–271). Administrators are responsible for the aggregate of clients. It would seem that the professional should also share responsibility for the total client group. Inasmuch as this is not possible, given the different role responsibilities of professional and administrator, perhaps some *appreciation* of their shared concerns could help bridge the gap between professional and administrator. This does not mean the conflict will disappear. Administrators will have authority and must exercise it if they think it is required to accomplish organizational purposes. Professionals have to work within this context, with the understanding that authority can be legitimate.

The basic conflict between administrator and professional can also be moderated through the use of leadership. Leadership entails the ability to exert influence to obtain *voluntary* compliance (see Chapter 9). The supervisor who attempts to influence the professional by creating a participative structure facilitating autonomous practice will thereby minimize the conflict. But, although this use of leadership can moderate the friction between professional and manager, the basic paradox remains of trying to motivate people to do what they are mandated to do. Unless the superior can delegate complete power to the subordinate, democracy cannot exist in the true sense. The "bottom line" has to be the achievement of the goals of consumer benefit. The professional can be given ample freedom to decide on the *means* that are to be used. However, the administration must be able to hold the professional accountable for meeting the goals.

POWER OF LOWER-LEVEL EMPLOYEES

Authority was discussed as legitimated power. What about the power exerted by lower-level employees such as clerks and secretaries—power that is not legitimated? This power derives from the access that these employees have to information, persons, and facilities (Mechanic 1962). Upper-level employees depend on them because of their knowledge of the system and of how to "get things done." They may be in "buffer" positions that enable them to "protect" professionals from system pressures. For example, in a mental hospital ward attendants act as a buffer for psychiatrists, protecting them from being overwhelmed by large numbers of patients. In prisons a similar relationship exists between inmate leaders and guards.

Professionals in human service organizations are often upset at the power of lower-level employees to exert control over their daily activities. Refusal to recognize this power, however, can severely constrain a professional's ability to do his or her job. As in any power struggle, the practitioner must recognize the costs and benefits of direct confrontation versus compromise. Administrators need to evaluate the problems associated with this type of power concentration to determine whether they are severe enough as to warrant action.

SUMMARY

The use of authority, control, and power has been discussed in relation to practice in human service organizations.

Despite the ambivalence that human service practitioners feel in using and responding to authority, there is a basis for legitimated authority in human service organizations: it rests on equity and sharing of the common goals of client benefit. As practitioners become more cognizant of the purpose of hierarchical structures and administrators more sensitive to professionals' value systems, then authority and control can be used more constructively in human service agencies. Given the lack of congruence between staff and organizational goals, several mechanisms are suggested as a way of integrating the individual into the organization: recruitment and selection; training; reward and role structures. Psychological methods of control are contrasted with impersonal control mechanisms which are considered more objective and ethical. The power of lower-level employees needs to be understood by professionals as an important influence on their practice.

APPLICATION OF CONCEPTS ON AUTHORITY, CONTROL, AND POWER TO CASE "DISCIPLINARY ACTION"

In the case situation "Disciplinary Action," *ambivalence in the use of authority, control, and power* is evident in the administrator's relations with the supervisor. It emerges in her inability to inform him of his inadequate performance and poor behavior. She seemed to be more comfortable using interpersonal and psychological methods of control.

Authority is defined as legitimated power, and one can speculate as to whether the subordinate viewed the administrator as having the expert power (e.g., administrative expertise) to legitimate her actions. It may be that it was because of her lack of legitimacy that she had to resort to the use of power in influencing the supervisor.

The *need for authority and control* was evident in that there was apparently a *lack of congruence* between the goals of the supervisor and those of the organization. (This had not always been the case, and, in fact, the supervisor's film-making acitivities exemplify how individual needs and goals can be integrated with organizational goals.) Given the general lack of congruence, the administrator was faced with the need to assert her authority and control in order to attempt to achieve a better integration of the supervisor and agency goals. However, she preferred not to confront the differences in her effort to *minimize conflict.* Had she viewed conflict in a more constructive manner she would not have delayed in confronting the supervisor. When conflict finally became unavoidable, the organization was able to constructively resolve it through an adjudication procedure (i.e., disciplinary hearing).

The contrast between the supervisor's lack of performance and his outstanding performance in a previous position suggests that his move to his current position may have involved faulty *procedures for selection* as well as inadequate *methods for training.*

The problem of poor selection and training procedures was perhaps in part attributable to a lack of clear-cut job description and performance standards—that is, an inadequate *role structure.* Not having a clear idea of what expectations are associated with a particular position makes it difficult to design criteria for selecting and screening staff for that position. Similarly, the lack of a specific job description makes it difficult to design an appropriate program for socialization and training.

The inability of the superior to fulfill a *training function* may have also stemmed from the fact that it *conflicted with her administrative and control functions.* That is, the conflict engendered by her administrative role, which including monitoring the performance of the supervisor, and potential use of rewards and sanctions may have constrained her in carrying out the educational function. An alternative she could have pursued is that of in-service educational programs. Training outside of the administrative line of authority is not constrained by the role conflict present within the hierarchical structure.

Rewards and sanctions are another means for *facilitating the integration* of the individual into the organization. In this case, utilitarian sanctions (job suspension) were used to obtain compliance. Apparently the use of symbolic rewards—support and acceptance—had not been effective, perhaps because of the lack of a clear-cut *role structure* with which to link the rewards. That is, lack of clarity as to job responsibility made it impossible to have an objective means for applying rewards or sanctions.

The *use of psychology as a method of control* was also evident in this case situation. The administrator used casework techniques in attempting to get the supervisor to comply with organizational demands. The difficulities attending the use of this strategy emerged quite clearly. The strategy not only failed to obtain compliance but also might have aggravated the situation of an employee who was emotionally upset. The Employee Relations Officer in charge of the disciplinary hearing also used psychology as a means for control, recommending that the supervisor receive psychiatric treatment. Although this solution may have helped the supervisor, it may also have deflected attention from structural factors as a significant cause of the difficulty. The use of *impersonal methods of control* would have been desirable but was not possible given the lack of clear-cut role expectations and standards. Had there been more objective standards for job performance, then such impersonal procedures as performance records could have been used to inform the supervisor that he was not meeting standards. This objective and impersonal approach to control obviates the interpersonal tension created when the supervisor confronts the subordinate directly with poor performance.

This case also illustrates the potential for *conflict between professionals and administrators* over the issue of control and autonomy. The supervisor in this case may have viewed himself as a professional with the prerogative for independent and autonomous action. The administrator, although also professionally trained, had the responsibility of insuring that the production was being maintained. The supervisor may have focused more on the clients served by his unit and therefore been unable to understand the administrator's stress on such matters as dictation on cases.

This conflict between professional and administrator could have been moderated through skilled *leadership* on the part of the administrator. Leadership can bridge the gap, recognizing professionals' need for autonomy by creating a participative structure and giving professionals freedom to decide on the *means* required to do their work while holding them accountable for *results.*

LEADERSHIP

OUTLINE

I. Issues
    A. Should the Leader Be Blamed?
    B. Can Leadership Exist on All Organizational Levels?
    C. How Important Is Personality for Leadership?
    D. Can Leaders Change Agencies?
    E. Is Leadership Necessary?

II. Definition

III. Levels of Leadership
    A. *Executive Leadership*
        1. Critical Decision
        2. Stages of Organizational Development
    B. *Lower-Level Leadership*
        1. Supportive Leadership
        2. Directive Leadership

IV. Leadership Skills
    A. *Upper-Level Leadership*
        1. External System Perspective
        2. Internal System Perspective
        3. Major System Change and External Pressure
        4. Charismatic Leadership
    B. *Middle-Level Leadership*
        1. Subsystem Perspective–Two-way Orientation
        2. Integration of Primary and Secondary Relations–Human-Relations Skill
    C. *Lower-Level Leadership*
        1. Technical Knowledge
        2. Concern for Equity

V. Situational Influences On Leadership

VI. Summary

VII. Application to Case "Mental Health Rules and Regulations"

ISSUES

As funding authorities, accrediting bodies, and consumer advocate groups subject human service programs to closer scrutiny, the spotlight is directed at the administrators of the agencies, who are held responsible for any inadequacies. As funds become more scarce, administrators are called upon to demonstrate in concrete terms the efficiency and effectiveness of their programs. These pressures have led to an increased number of firings, voluntary resignations, and lateral transfers of administrators (see Chapter 7, "Occupational Burnout").

This movement of administrators from one job to another raises several issues regarding leadership in human service agencies and its role in resolving (and creating) problems. The issues focus on the following five questions: (a) Should the leader be blamed? (b) Can leadership exist on all organizational levels? (c) How important is personality for leadership? (d) Can leaders change agencies? (e) Is leadership necessary?

Should the Leader Be Blamed?

The theory that poor organizational performance can be remedied by changing the organization's head assumes that the problem lies in inadequate direction and influence from the top. In this view, the leader is held responsible for lack of performance of lower-level staff, as well as for insufficiencies in organizational resources obtained from funding sources. Holding the leader responsible for poor staff performance could be justified on the grounds that there may be inadequate policies for selection, training, and control, policies for which the leader is responsible. However, given the fact that most top-level administrators come to their positions with lower-level staff in place, holding them responsible for the deficiencies of all those below them seems unjustified.

The view that a lack of resources can be attributed to deficient leadership could be argued for on the grounds that it is the job of the top person to obtain external support. Here too, this position may be unjustified, inasmuch as factors that are outside the administrator's control (e.g., the state of the economy) may be the more critical ones. The issue can be phrased in terms of a question discussed previously in other areas: To what extent can organizational problems be attributed to individual deficiencies, to what extent to situational factors? The definition of leadership to be used in this chapter will incorporate an awareness of both individual and situational factors.

Can Leadership Exist on All Organizational Levels?

The view discussed in the preceding section that the top-level administrators have primary responsibility for agency deficiencies, as well as the power to "make things work," ignores the importance of lower-level influence and leadership. Middle management, for example, can critically constrain the ability of top-level executives to formulate new policies or implement those established. If leadership is defined as *influence,* then it can exist on all levels of the organization. Therefore, all staff of human service agencies, including staff at the practitioner level, have the potential for enabling or restraining change. The recognition of the power of lower-level staff to affect human service programs is essential for effective human service leadership. This recognition leads to delegation of authority and responsibility to lower-level employees, with the expectation that they will assume leadership roles on their levels. The leadership model included in this chapter provides for leadership roles and functions in top, middle, and lower levels of human service agencies.

How Important Is Personality for Leadership?

The notion that personality is critical for leadership pervades American culture. The way Americans cast their vote seems to have less to do with political platform or party affiliation than with the ability of candidates to project "an image." Edward Kennedy's inability to overcome the stain on his character following the accident at Chappaquiddick, the emphasis in political campaigns on personality, and the role of public relations firms in promoting the personalities of politicians—all attest to the importance we place on the "character" and "strength of personality" of our leaders.

The question of whether "brains" or "personality" is more important for leadership will be discussed in this chapter in terms of two kinds of leadership skills: cognitive and affective. In the human service field, as elsewhere, there is a tendency to overemphasize the role of personality in effective leadership and underemphasize the role of knowledge. Both characteristics are essential, given the complexity of organizational life and the need for a wide range of cognitive and affective skills in the analysis and solution of organizational problems.

Can Leaders Change Agencies?

Given that problems in human service agencies require solutions of system change, the question can be raised as to whether leaders can be expected to be the initiators of change. (Organizational change itself will be discussed in more detail in Chapter 11.) To what extent can we expect leadership to be instrumental in accomplishing change in human service agencies? Is change primarily a function of individual skill and ability, or are factors beyond the control of the individual leaders more important? The model presented in what follows, by combining individual and situational factors, takes into account not only the leadership skills required to accomplish organizational change, but also how these skills are related to situational factors.

Is Leadership Necessary?

The question arises of why organizations cannot be designed and structured in such a way as to insure that people will know exactly what they have to do and therefore will not need to be directed by others. Why not establish clear-cut rules, regulations, and job expectations and allow the organization to run itself with a minimum of direction? As has been pointed out (Katz and Kahn 1978:530–535) there are several reasons why organizations cannot be expected to function without leadership:

1. It is not possible to anticipate all situations and to develop the structure that will take into account all problems. This is because there is a disparity between the formal structure and the informal system. Especially in human service organizations where large number of professionals are employed, there is a constant strain between the professionals' need for autonomy and the organization's need for control. This tension requires the influence of leaders to motivate individuals to conform to the organization's rules and regulations.
2. Changes in environmental conditions result in varying demands on the organization which also cannot be predicted in advance. In the human service field the constantly changing environmental pressures are on the increase, and it would be very difficult to design a system to take into account these changes in external demands.
3. The internal dynamics of organizations involve growth and change, in ways that also cannot be anticipated. New functions arise, leading to new internal conflicts, and the need for leadership to adjudicate these conflicts is ever present. In the human service field, major internal changes such as the introduction of new technology or new structures (e.g., decentralization) require the influence of leaders so that these changes may be integrated into the organization.
4. In all organizations the membership are not completely identified with the organization because of divided loyalties. In human service agencies the professional goals of many individuals may not correspond completely with the organization's goals. Leadership is required to exert influence to attempt to achieve as much congruency as possible between the individual's goals and the organization's goals.

In view of the fact that organizations are subject to various kinds of external influences, one might take the position that what happens in a human service organization really cannot be controlled by the members. The extreme sociological view of organizations would say that situational factors surrounding the organization are the most critical ones and, as the leaders have very little influence on the environmental factors, they cannot affect in any significant way what will happen in organizations. This argument could derive support from the contrast between the 1960s and 1970s. In the 1960s, when resources were plentiful, human service organizations were able to grow. They were seen as successful, and their administrators were considered very adequate and effective. However, in the 1970s, when resources became tight, these organizations were criticized for a lack of effectiveness and their administrators blamed. Therefore, a proponent of the situational perspective would argue, the environment is the critical factor and leadership is secondary.

A similar position can be taken with respect to the ability of an individual to influence the internal factors in an organization. There are those who suggest that an organization's goals and structures are the result of power struggles that are ongoing in the system (Gummer 1978). This political view of organizations seems to give little hope that leadership can exert much influence. This view of the powerlessness of leadership is captured in President Eisenhower's statement that "I give an order and watch nothing happen."

Eisenhower's statement notwithstanding, the U.S. presidential form of government underscores the importance leadership is accorded in this country. In contrast, a parliamentary form of government, as in Great Britain, deemphasizes the importance of the individual leader. But, although the U.S. form of government assumes that electing new leaders will result in change, one can question whether this assumption is warranted. That is, it may be that the opportunities and constraints of the times act as the critical influence on the ability of American leaders to institute changes. Moreover, as we saw in Chapter 4, this focus on the individual may divert attention away from basic problems in the system. Electing a new president or firing the boss will not necessarily solve problems related to defective policies and programs. One can infer from this that one of the purposes of leadership is to have someone to hold responsible for decisions, someone who can be blamed or praised for outcomes.

DEFINITION

Leadership is defined as the ability to influence another person to perform *voluntarily* on a level beyond that required for the position that the individual occupies. This "influencial increment" (Katz and Kahn 1978:528) assumes that most people will fulfill their responsibilities at least on the level of the minimum standards prescribed for them by the organization. The leader motivates greater performance through voluntary compliance, in contrast with the use of power based on *involuntary* compliance. This definition of leadership takes into account situational requirements (Follett 1940:277). As different circumstances (e.g., organizational levels) have different types of performance expectations, then the specific leadership skills required will also differ.

Leadership, rather than being an attribute of an organizational position or a characteristic associated with the person, is a category of behavior. This behavior is related to two kinds of power: referent and expert. Thus, to understand the definition of leadership we must first consider the following five-category classification of power:

1. *Legitimate power* is power associated with position in the organization. Legitimate power is equivalent to authority or position power.
2. *Reward power* involves the ability to influence based on the use of incentives, whether symbolic or economic.
3. *Punishment power* is the ability to influence based on the use of sanctions. Both reward and punishment power are usually associated with position in the organization, but this is not necessarily the case. There is evidence that persons on the lower level of organizations can exert considerable power to reward or punish people in the system (see Chapter 8).
4. *Referent power* is the influence that a person exerts because of his or her personality. More specifically, it is influence that is related to a person's ability to get others to identify with him or her because of their admiration of and liking for his or her personality. Charisma is one example of referent power.
5. *Expert power* is the influence a person exerts on others because of their respect for his or her knowledge and expertise. This power is based on ability of the individual to use conceptual and analytical skills.

Thus leadership comprises referent and expert powers which correspond to affective and cognitive skills.

Of the five bases of power in organizations, expert and referent power are the two that *cannot* be conferred by the organization. Therefore, they represent additions to the organization's ability to influence behavior. Referent and expert power are also important in that their use is free of the negative consequence of alienating people in the system, a consequence that often accompanies the use of position, punishment, or even reward power.

Various studies have investigated the perceptions that subordinates and superiors have of the relative importance of these five types of power. In a study focusing on non-Master of Social Work (MSW) social work supervisees

PUNISHMENT POWER!

d.w.a.

(Peabody 1964), position and expert power were perceived as more relevant than referent power in determining the extent to which supervisors influenced behavior. A study of MSW supervisors and supervisees (Kadushin 1974b) found that expert power was viewed as the most relevant type of power. Although supervisees also saw position power as an important source of influence, referent power was not seen as significant. Similar results were found in a study of 31 rehabilitation agencies (Olmstead and Christensen 1973). In all of these studies reward and punishment power were seen as least influential. Thus it appears that the combination of expert and position power can produce the greatest influence. The fact that referent power is less influential is interesting to note given that in the human service field so much emphasis is placed on interpersonal skills. Perhaps in the work situation expert and position power are found to be more practicial in accomplishing the day-to-day service delivery tasks. If so, this would seem inconsistent with findings that there is little difference in professional expertise between supervisors and supervisees in social work (Kadushin 1976:103). This apparent inconsistency can be explained by distinguishing between two sources of expertise: professional and organizational. The expertise that supervisees may find particularly helpful could be that which helps them navigate the system. Supervisors, because of their position and experience, can have more knowledge of how to work within the agency context. This organizational skill may not have been measured in the studies, which focused on practice tasks (Brieland 1959; Brown 1970).

One further point needs to be clarified. Studies of the relationship of personality to leadership reveal that personality traits are unrelated to the ability to influence (Hall 1977:240). As mentioned, referent power does not refer to any particular personality traits or characteristics; it is associated with the ability of the follower to *identify* with the leader as a *person*. The ability of particular personality traits to influence will vary with situational factors.

In summary, leadership is defined as the ability to exert influence on members of the organization that will motivate them to work beyond the minimum prescribed by their particular job. As it is ability that is associated with knowledge and affective skills, it can be exerted by anyone in the organization and is not confined to people on the upper level. However, leadership can have even greater impact if combined with position power. For example, Dr. Jerome Miller was able to achieve major system change in the area of juvenile corrections in Massachusetts, but was unable to accomplish similar objectives in Pennsylvania and Illinois, where he had been given less formal authority (Richan 1980:77–78).

LEVELS OF LEADERSHIP

The situational influences on leadership are evident when leadership is viewed across organizational levels. Here we will examine separately leadership on the top and lower levels of the organization.

Executive Leadership

Executive leadership is particularly concerned with policy formulation related to organizational survival, growth, and effectiveness. Top-level leadership requires the accomplishments of two major tasks: (*a*) directing and coordinating internal operations and (*b*) establishing linkages with the environment (Hasenfeld and English 1974:153).

Critical Decisions

The two major tasks of top-level executives require that *critical* decisions (Selznick 1957) be made in five basic areas:

1. *Formulating the organization's basic mission.* This decision requires the understanding of the task environment, which will determine the kinds of missions that the organization can undertake.

2. *Establishing the legitimation of the organization by negotiating and mediating with external interests groups.* This type of decision making includes obtaining the necessary resources to insure the survival of the organization. It involves interpretating and representating the organization to the community in order to achieve social support and legitimation.

3. *Selecting service technologies to carry out the mission.* This involves deciding which kinds of service technologies are appropriate in light of the particular goals of the organization.

4. *Developing and maintaining internal structure.* This area of decision making involves designing the organization in such a way as to facilitate implementation of basic tasks.

5. *Initiating and implementing change.* This critical area of decision making requires the constant evaluation of programs and the introduction of change in response to changing environmental demands and new opportunities for innovation.

Stages of Organizational Development

The five areas for critical decision making assume different degrees of importance, depending on the stage of an organization's development (Hasenfeld and English 1974:154–155). This relationship is another illustration of how situational factors require different kinds of leadership skills and actions. The stages and associated areas for decision making are as follows:

1. *Founding stage.* Initially an organization needs the kind of leadership that can make decisions related to defining the mission and legitimating the organization. Also critical at this stage is the recruitment of personnel who are committed to the mission and the ideologies of the organization. The kinds of leadership skills required at this stage would necessarily involve the ability to represent the organization to the community in order to obtain support and legitimation.

2. *Production stage.* In contrast to the first stage, the production stage is concerned particularly with the development of the technical aspects

of the organization's functioning and with establishing standardized and formalized procedures and activities. This stage requires leadership that can understand the technical system and the kinds of division of labor needed to achieve an effective service delivery in the organization.

3. *Expansion and differentiation.* In this stage of development the various subunits in the organization evolve and become more complex. Hence leadership must have the skills to coordinate the subunits and resolve any conflicts that emerge among them.

4. *Stability and predictability.* In order to insure the organization's continued growth and stability, the executive must make decisions that protect the organization from negative external pressures. The board of directors assists in buffering against such pressures.

5. *Innovation.* This last stage of organizational development involves changing the structure in response to external demands. The kinds of leadership decision making required at this stage necessitate a systemic perspective, discussed in what follows.

Together, these critical areas of decision making associated with executive leadership can be said to constitute "institutional leadership" (Selznick 1957). Institutional leadership has been described as the type of leadership that emphasizes conceptual and analytical skills more than affective skills.

> Institutional leaders are concerned with policies as well as with persons; they are concerned with content as well as with process. They are concerned with dynamic adaptation of the total organization to its own internal striving and to its external pressures. There may be only a few decisions each year which demand this perspective, but they are crucial and that quality is quite independent of the human relations skills of the manager and of the psychological glamour which he may possess [Katz and Kahn 1978:543].

As indicated earlier, executive leadership requires expert power, which involves the ability to analyze and conceptualize organizational needs and opportunities for change.

Lower-Level Leadership

Studies of leadership have in general dealt more with the supervisory level than with the executive level. These studies have focused on two primary purposes of lower-level leadership, namely, support and direction (Fleishman and Peters 1962:127–143).

Supportive leadership crucially involves *consideration.* Consideration is defined as the "extent to which an individual is likely to have job relationships characterized by mutual trust, respect for subordinates' ideas, consideration for their feelings [Fleishman and Peters 1962]." A supervisor who has this characteristic of consideration is able to develop a nurturing work environment by means such as the following: "(a) creating a feeling of approval, (b) developing personal relations, (c) providing fair treatment, and (d) enforcing rules equitably [M. Austin 1981:299]." Associated with consideration is the role the supervisor takes to encourage *participation* by subordinates. Participation includes "not supervising too closely, promoting worker autonomy and promoting job enrichment [M. Austin 1981:301]."

Directive leadership crucially involves *initiation of structure,* which has been defined as the "extent to which an individual is likely to define and structure his role and that of subordinates towards goal attainment [Fleishman and Peters 1962]." Thus, the supervisor who is a directive leader emphasizes task accomplishment and structures subordinates' roles accordingly. Initiating structure is similar to the *facilitative* function of the supervisor. Facilitation provides technical support, in contrast to consideration, which gives social support.

A study of social work supervisors found that they scored relatively high on consideration but low on initiation of structure (Olyan 1972:178). This general orientation to people rather than tasks was also found in other studies (Cohen and Rhodes 1977; Granvold 1978). Another study found public welfare administrators low on *both* consideration and initiation of structure (Granvold 1977).

This binary classification of supervisory leadership is similar to the distinction between instrumental and social-emotional leadership (Etzioni 1964:61–67). It has been found that the two types of leadership roles are needed in organizations but that it is difficult for one individual to perform both. The performance of the taskmaster role often conflicts with the supportive role. As a consequence, these two roles are usually performed by different persons in the organization.

If we contrast upper- and lower-level leadership, it is evident that top leadership is more concerned with policy, whereas lower-level leadership is more involved with influencing and motivating people. In human service organizations, however, this distinction is somewhat blurred, perhaps because top-level administrators have often moved up from the technical levels and have not shifted from people- to policy-oriented skills. The distinction between policy- and people-oriented skills may relate to the distinction between proactive and reactive leadership (Hasenfeld and English 1974:155). Proactive leadership attempts to actively influence the inside and the outside of the system; it is change oriented. Reactive leadership responds to pressure and, in general, is concerned with maintaining the status quo. It is suggested here that people-oriented leadership skills tend more toward maintaining status quo than do policy-oriented skills.

This discussion of levels of leadership referred to various kinds of skills required of a leader. The next section will elaborate on the kinds of leadership skills appropriate to different organizational levels and purposes.

LEADERSHIP SKILLS

Leadership has been broadly dichotomized into cognitive and affective areas. The following leadership model, drawn from Katz and Kahn (1978:525–576), integrates these leadership areas with organizational level and extent of organizational change to be achieved by the particular type of leadership.

This model is similar to that proposed by several authors. Wilson (1980:112–113) uses Parsons' three functional levels in organizations (institutional, managerial, and technical) in juxtaposition with three skill areas (conceptual, technical, and interpersonal). A further attempt to clarify the relationship between organizational level and administrative skill is contained in a skill matrix with analytic and interactional (cognitive and affective) on one axis and administrative, human relations, and technical skills (top, middle, lower levels) on the other (B. Neugeboren 1980:67). Another contingency model, combining administrative level and three knowledge and skill areas, proposes that the upper level requires policy development skill, the middle level management technologies, and the lower level social service technologies (Gummer 1979c:392).

Upper-Level Leadership

As discussed earlier, executive leadership has to be concerned with both the internal and external aspects of organizational life in order to make the critical decisions required for major change. That is, executive leadership requires the cognitive skill of a *systemic perspective,* which incorporates internal and external perspectives.

External System Perspective

An external system perspective requires skill in the assessment of environmental opportunities and demands. This perspective helps the organization adapt to changes in the environment by planning the innovations needed to respond to these changes. Thus, this perspective ideally looks at the long term as well as the short term.

The relevance of the short- versus long-term perspectives has been noted in relation to the decline of American industry. American industry has tended toward a focus on the short term reinforced by the stress on quantitative measurement in management advocated by schools of business administration (Lohr 1981:45).

In the human service field the external system perspective requires that the executive become involved in long-term as well as short-term planning. This perspective requires an analysis of current trends and potential changes in areas such as funding. For example, in the child welfare field the stress on permanency planning has pressured agencies to return children to their natural parents or have them placed for adoption. This has created a fiscal problem for these agencies, as they are funded to provide foster care. As a result, they have had to diversify their programs in order to obtain other sources of funding. This has led to program development for the mentally retarded people who, with the new policies on deinstitutionalization, are being placed in the community. In fact, deinstitutionalization has provided the opportunity for a range of public welfare agencies to develop protective service programs for disabled adults. For example, agencies that have traditionally served the severely physically handicapped (e.g., Easter Seals) have now developed programs for the mentally handicapped as well.

The external system perspective's concern with long-term planning could be operationalized by instituting 5-year plans as a standard procedure in the human service agency. As knowledge has increased in the area of futurology (Cornish 1970), human service administrators are able to obtain more information to help them anticipate future trends and changes in the field. It is possible that a major change that will occur within the next 5 years is the development of a national health insurance system in the United States. An executive with an external system perspective will explore what opportunities this new national health policy would provide to enable his agency to obtain additional funding for existing programs or to develop new programs.

Internal System Perspective

The internal system perspective helps the executive integrate and coordinate the different subsystems in an organization, each of which has its own goals and values (see Chapter 5). By incorporating the understanding that these differences in values can lead to unresolvable ideological struggles among subsystems, the internal system perspective encourages the executive to direct attention to those areas of disagreement that *are* negotiable.

In the human service field the problem of internal coordination and integration of programs is a substantial one. Given the lack of determinate technologies, agencies operate from ideological beliefs. The potential for ideological conflict is, therefore, particularly great, and it becomes crucial that leadership have an internal system perspective. One strategy for avoiding conflict is to design the division of labor in such a way that professionals with similar ideologies work together. In addition, ideological conflict can be diverted by attending to practical—and negotiable—differences, such as allocation of resources among the various groups. In general, the frank recognition by leadership of human service organizations that there is a lack of validated knowledge should permit experimentation with new and different approaches, as long as consumer benefit remains the outcome criterion. Thus, diversity can be encouraged, with the leadership facilitating the tolerance of different points of view.

Major System Change and External Pressure

As suggested earlier, one purpose of executive leadership is to manage major organizational change (see also Chapter 11). Since major change is not very likely without external pressure the system perspective of top-level leadership needs to take this into account. The external system perspective helps leaders use the impact of external pressure to facilitate their efforts to change the system. The skillful executive can maximize the use of external pressure by making it visible to the agency members. Representatives from external pressure groups can be allowed to present their points of view to agency staff. This kind of pressure can be used by the leader to move the organization in the direction that seems desirable. An example, mentioned earlier, of how top-level leadership can use external pressure to promote change lies in the success that Jerome Miller experienced in achieving reforms in the Massachusetts juvenile corrections system. His efforts were greatly facilitated by a favorable political climate and by support from the press (Ohlin, Coates, and Miller 1974).

Charismatic Leadership

Thus far our discussion of top-level leadership has focused on the cognitive skills aspect. *Affective* skills, associated with *charisma* in leaders, are important as well. For example, major change can also be facilitated by charismatic leadership. In a crisis situation, if a leader is charismatic, subordinates will be willing to place their confidence in the leader and allow him or her to take action. In the human service field, there have been individuals who were able to capture the imagination of the people in the field and to consequently introduce major change. Here we can return to Jerome Miller, whose changes in the Massachusetts juvenile corrections system were in no small measure facilitated by his charisma (Bakal 1973). Wilbur Cohen, who was instrumental in the enactment of Medicare on the national level, is another example of a charismatic leader. Although potentially important, charisma has its limitations. Thus it is probably time limited and very much a function of the stress created by a crisis situation.

Middle-Level Leadership

The purpose of middle-level leadership is to change the system by sup-plementing or bending existing policies, an incremental type of change (see Chapter 11 on organizational change). Location in the middle of the organizational structure requires that leadership perform an integrative function both vertically and horizontally. Middle-level leadership requires two kinds of skills: (a) subsystem perspective—two-way orientation, and (b) integration of primary and secondary relations—human relations skills.

Subsystem Perspective—Two-way Orientation

The cognitive skill of internal subsystem perspective requires an under-standing of how the tasks performed by the different subsystems are inter-related. The middle-level leader assumes the role of a link between different departments and acts as a facilitator in the coordination and integration of these different subunits in the organization. This horizontal linking is com-plemented by the linking on a vertical level. The subsystem perspective re-quires an understanding of the rationale for top-level decision making, in-cluding the impact of external pressures. Possessing such an understanding, the middle-level person has the responsibility of conveying it to the lower levels. The middle-level person must also be a communication channel from the lower-level employees to the upper levels, representing their interests and needs.

In human service organizations this vertical "linking pin" (Likert 1961) function is critical. Human service organizations have a large proportion of professionals, who, as professionals, feel a need to know what is going on in the system, as well as to contribute to the system. If they believe that their ideas are not being considered by upper-level administrators, the result can be a high degree of alienation and feeling of divorce from the policymakers. For these reasons, the "representative" function performed by middle-level managers is crucial, as confirmed by research (e.g., Pelz 1951:49–55) in-dicating that the presence of this representational function in an organization correlates positively with subordinate morale.

The importance of the middle-level communication link in facilitating downward communication stems from similar factors. As we saw earlier, people tend to define problems in terms of where they themselves are located in the system. Thus the lower-level technical personnel must be made aware of the kinds of pressures and demands placed on upper-level administrators by such forces as the funding authorities or boards of directors. This com-munication link from the top to the bottom helps broaden the perspective of lower-level staff and aids in integrating them into the system and reducing their feelings of alienation.

Integration on a horizontal level is also very much needed in human service organizations. Here the objective is to facilitate coordination of different subunits. For example, a middle-level leader might be involved in aiding a management information system unit to obtain information from a service delivery unit so that the information system established will be relevant to and useful for the service delivery unit. The specific kinds of coordination required depend on the field. For example, in the child welfare field there is a need to coordinate foster care functions with adoption functions. In the correctional field the need is to coordinate custodial functions with rehabilitative functions. In hospitals it is necessary to coordinate discharge planning with admission activities. In mental hospitals, in-service treatment programs must be coordinated with after-care programs. Regardless of the specific circumstances, the skill in coordinating and integrating different subunits requires an understanding of the goals of the different subunits and of how these are shared or are in conflict.

Integration of Primary and Secondary Relations—Human Relations Skills

Whereas the subsystem perspective involves primarily cognitive skills, the integration of primary and secondary relations requires affective skills. This middle-level function involves integrating the individual's personal needs and expectations with the organization's goals. The requirements of the individual's organizational role need to be integrated with his or her skills, abilities, aspirations, and interests.

Stress on these human relations skills has been traditional in the human service field, largely because of the transfer of the clinical ethic to administrative situations. However, it should be noted that administrative human relations skills are different from interpersonal skills derived from clinical training. Human relations skills are not used to change problematic attitudes or behaviors. Rather, the assumptions are made that personal problems cannot be appropriately dealt with in the work situation and that individual satisfaction will come primarily from successful job performance. Given these assumptions, the task of the middle-level administrator is to enhance job performance by helping to integrate it with the needs of the particular individual. For example, as the need for support from peer groups is basic to organizational life, the middle-level supervisor will facilitate the development of cohesive work groups. In human service agencies the need of professionals for autonomous practice is also integrated with the official role requirements.

Lower-Level Leadership

The purpose of lower-level leadership is to effectively implement existing policies by the creative use of existing structure. This implementing of policy is termed administration and when done efficiently can be an important factor in maximizing the benefits to the recipients of service. The two skills important to lower-level leadership are (a) technical knowledge and (b) concern for equity.

Technical Knowledge

The line supervisor's technical knowledge can facilitate the efficient and effective use of personnel and resources. Because of his or her knowledge of the tasks that need to be done, the supervisor can provide the structure that the direct service worker needs to perform these tasks (Austin 1981:100–124). This technical knowledge is also crucial to the supervisor in performing the three major functions of supervision—administrative, educational, and supportive (Kadushin 1976). Knowledge of the tasks enables the supervisor to help the subordinate organize work and coordinate efforts with others in the work group. This knowledge of the tasks is necessary to the initiation of structure by the superviser which was discussed earlier.

Concern for Equity

Fairness in the distribution of rewards and sanctions in human service organizations is essential. As indicated in the discussion of organizational change (see Chapter 11), the fairness of an agency's reward structure is a key to good or poor morale. In many human service organizations rewards are not distributed objectively (Steiner 1977). This may be attributable, in part, to unclear job expectations and standards, which stem from the indeterminate nature of the tasks that are performed. The responsibility of line supervisors to insure equity (Austin 1981:188) is critical if lower-level staff are to develop strong motivation and identification with the organization. The "bottom line" for staff who may not agree with policies from above or who work under very stressful conditions is the judgment that the system is *fair*. If promotions and rewards are based on such criteria as flattering the superior or not threatening the boss by asking embarrassing questions, then staff will tend to work at the minimum level required.

SITUATIONAL INFLUENCES ON LEADERSHIP

The discussion of leadership skills emphasized individual abilities but, in showing how different skills are relevant to different organizational levels, pointed also to the situational aspects of leadership. In this section we will consider more directly the ways in which the situation (tasks) influences the effectiveness of leadership skills.

Studies of leadership have found it difficult to obtain consistent relationships between leadership styles and subordinate performance (Hall

1977:244). In some situations effective leaders were supportive whereas in others they were authoritarian. Worker satisfaction was also difficult to relate to leadership styles. As researchers began to take the work situation into account, however, findings became more clear-cut and consistent. In general, it was found that supportive leadership led to greater worker satisfaction and productivity under the following conditions: the work situation was not routine; information could not be standardized; decisions did not have to be made rapidly and, therefore, employee participation in decision making was possible; subordinates felt a need for independence and regarded their participation as legitimate; and subordinates did not need close supervision (Hall 1977:244). When the opposite conditions prevailed in the work situation, autocratic leadership was more effective. In other words, supportive leadership was *not* effective where work situations were structured and stable and where time pressures were significant.

The theory of leadership that takes into account the situational tasks has been referred to as the *contingency theory of leadership*. This theory has implications for the kinds of supervision that may be required in certain types of human service organizations. In the public sector of social welfare (e.g., public assistance and child welfare agencies and mental hospitals), where job pressures are great and there is lack of time for deliberate decision making or staff participation, there may be a need for autocratic supervision. A dilemma arises, however, as decisions in these job situations are usually not routinized, nor is information standardized. The high rate of turnover and burnout in these jobs and the common complaint that supervisor support is not available may thus be understood in light of this contingency theory perspective. A possible solution may lie in redefining the service delivery task. That is, if it is the case that these agencies serve primarily a people-processing rather than people-changing function (see Chapter 14, "Technologies"), then the task may need to be redefined in a more routinized fashion.

Hersey and Blanchard's (1977) model for situational leadership takes into account three factors: task, relationship behavior of the leader, and maturity level of followers. The maturity level is associated with high achievement motivation, willingness and ability to take responsibility, experience and training. The combination of these three factors determines four types of leadership styles which are on a continuum ranging from low to high maturity: telling, selling, participating and delegating. Thus low maturity of the follower requires "telling" which consists of high task and low relationship behavior of the leader.

The discussion of the situational influence on leadership reaffirms the basic thesis here—that leadership cannot be viewed only in terms of individual abilities and skills. The effectiveness of leadership is influenced by the situation, and this fact must be taken into account in organizational design.

SUMMARY

Leadership has been presented as a function not only of individual ability and skill but also of the kind of work conditions that prevail. The different kinds of leadership skills vary in their effectiveness depending on the work situation, on the organizational stage, level, and task. Although the importance of skilled leadership cannot be overemphasized, it must be kept in mind that a change in leadership will not in itself solve systemic or structural problems. Skilled executive leadership can accomplish system change provided there are facilitating situational factors.

APPLICATION OF CONCEPTS ON LEADERSHIP TO CASE "MENTAL HEALTH RULES AND REGULATIONS"

The question of whether the *leader should be blamed* for organizational problems can be explored in the case "Mental Health Rules and Regulations," which involves a change in emphasis of state mental health policy from rehabilitation to social care. The director of the state department of mental health not only was responsible for the provision of service in state mental hospitals but also allocated funds to such autonomous community programs as mental health centers. Thus the fact that the chronically mentally ill were being neglected by these community-based programs could be blamed on this top-level administrator. However, as these community agencies were not directly under his authority and control, one might question whether he should be held responsible. However, the director could be held responsible for the state hospitals which were under his authority.

This question of who should be held responsible for organizational problems is related to another issue—should *leadership exist on other levels* besides just at the top? The mental health service delivery system contains programs administered by a variety of autonomous agencies. Directors of community mental health centers, general hospital psychiatric services, outpatient psychiatric clinics, day hospitals, etc., could also be held responsible for the lack of adequate programs for the chronically mentally ill. The case situation notes that within the state department itself there was an inadequate emphasis on community care for the chronically mentally ill. Leadership could also have been provided within the state hospitals to establish more community based programs.

Yet another related issue is that of the extent to which *leaders can be expected to change agencies.* The director's expectation that he could accomplish a major shift in the goals of mental health programs might be viewed as overly ambitious. How realistic was it to expect that such a change was feasible, given the power alignments in this field? Although the director was able to institute new rules and regulations, how realistic was it to expect that they would be implemented, given the multiplicity and diversity in the organizational auspices of these services?

The issue of whether *leadership is necessary* also can be considered in conjunction with this case. One might speculate that the pressure of the release of the chronics into the community might in itself have forced the creation of new programs for their care. It is also possible that opponents exaggerated the importance of leadership and by focusing their criticism on the director diverted attention from the need to modify basic legislative policies for allocation of funds for community mental health programs.

Leadership has been *defined* as influence. Leadership motivates voluntary effort beyond minimum requirements by using expert and referent power. In this case situation, the extensive resistance to the new rules and regulations suggests that voluntary compliance was not forthcoming. It is possible that part of the difficulty the director had in obtaining voluntary compliance is that he was not perceived as having *expert power* by the professionals in the mental health system. His philosophy of social care was contrary to their ideology of rehabilitation as the most appropriate goal for mental health programs. Also, it may have been difficult for him to exert *referent power,* given his lack of proximity to the local administrators in the various communities. That is, affective leadership skill is probably most feasible in those situations where there is ample opportunity for social interaction between a leader and the people he or she hopes to influence.

Executive leadership roles and functions are relevant to this case situation. The director made *critical decisions* with regard to the *formulation of the basic mission* for his agency. Given the state's responsibility for the chronically mentally ill, he established social care as the primary mission for mental health programs. His *initiation and implementation of change* through the new rules and regulations was another critical decision made, as was the *selection of appropriate service technologies* (i.e., the shift from treatment to social care technologies). The director also attempted *legitimation of the organization through negotiation and mediation with external interests groups,* an attempt that was more successful with the governor's office and the state legislature than with the mental health professional groups. The final critical decision of *developing and maintaining the internal structure* of the state department was also made. This required the recruitment of staff to monitor and evaluate compliance with the performance standards of the new rules and regulations.

The *four stages of organizational development* can also be illustrated by means of this case. Although the state department was not a new organization, its move toward the new goal of social care in a sense put it in the *founding stage* of organizational development. The task of obtaining legitimation and community support is essential in this founding stage. As should be clear, the director was encountering difficulties in achieving this task, because of resistance from psychiatrists, psychologists, and social workers.

The next stage, *production,* involves the development of the technical aspects of the organization, including standardized procedures. This agency developed the necessary technical core to implement the new regulations. The process of operationalizing these new standards required their modification on the basis of experiences with the mental health service providers. *Expansion and differentiation* of the agency occurs as experience indicates a need for new roles and functions. It is possible that if the traditional mental health providers continue to have difficulty implementing service to the chronically mentally ill, the state will have to turn to alternative service providers, who share the state's goals of social care.

The next stage of achieving organizational *stability* involves protecting the organization from negative external pressures. The department was now attempting to establish advisory committees made up of representatives of the service providers. These committees could later be a mechanism for buffering the agency from external pressures. The final stage of *innovation* might involve this agency in reallocating resources for service to the chronically mentally ill to such social care providers as public welfare and physical rehabilitation agencies.

In order to accomplish a major system change, such as this change in the mental health system, two types of upper-level leadership skills are required: *systemic perspective and charisma. External systemic perspective* requires the skill to assess environmental opportunities and demands. In this case it is unclear to what extent the administrator was able to anticipate and plan for the establishment of community care programs for the chronically mentally ill. Deinstitutionalization had been going on for several years prior to the inauguration of the rules and regulations. An external system perspective would have anticipated the need to formulate plans for a new kind of mental health care system that was community based. As indicated earlier, this could have included human service providers whose goals were more congruent with the objectives of social care.

The *internal system perspective* involves the integration and coordination of different subsystems: here the avoidance of ideological conflict is basic. It is evident that in this case ideological conflict was *not* avoided. Some of the state department's major differences with the traditional mental health programs were based on differences in belief systems as to the proper and appropriate way to provide mental health service. It might have been possible to avoid ideological conflict by directing attention to the more practical problem of resource allocation. This latter problem was probably the more basic issue from the point of view of the mental health agencies and could have been negotiated more readily than the ideological differences.

Top-level leadership also requires the affective ability of *charisma*. There was evidence that this executive did in fact have certain charismatic qualities. However, charisma is in part a function of situational uncertainty and turbulence; hence here the lack of environmental instability may have minimized the effect of the director's charismatic personality.

The environment is also a factor in that major system change can be facilitated by strong *external pressure*. In this case, then, the executive's efforts to introduce a shift in mental health policy may have been constrained by the lack of strong external pressure on the mental health department. The active support of the federal government, for example, could have facilitated the change process. Pressure for this change could also have come from those agencies that provide aid for the chronically mentally ill (e.g., public welfare). Finally, the support of the general public, including the business community, could have been sought, as the public is very sensitive to the difficulties the chronically mentally ill pose when they are unsupervised in the community.

The preceding discussion of the effects that external pressure can have on the introduction and implementation of major change also illustrates how *situational* factors can influence leadership. The problem of lack of adequate service to the chronically mentally ill is not a new one. It simply became more visible as the situation was changed, with the release of the chronically mentally ill from the hospital to the community. This changed situation provided the opportunity for the director to assume leadership in changing the goal of mental health programs to that of social care.

ADMINISTRATIVE
DECISION MAKING

dus.

10

OUTLINE

I. Issues
   A. How Rational Can Decisions Be?
   B. Individual versus Situational Influence on Rational Decision Making

II. Definition

III. Decision-Making Model
   A. Introduction
   B. Immediate Pressures
   C. Problem Definition
   D. Problems versus Dilemmas
   E. Organizational Context
   F. Search For Solutions
   G. Evaluation of Anticipated Consequences of Alternative Solutions
   H. Bounded Rationality—Cognitive Limits

IV. Summary

V. Application to Case "From Psychological Work to Social Work"

ISSUES

Decision making is one of the most important organizational activities engaged in by leaders (Hall 1977:257). Critical decisions made at the executive level will impact on the kinds of goals to be established, legitimation obtained from the environment, selection of service technologies, maintainence of internal harmony, and initiation of organizational change (Hasenfeld and English 1974:153). At other levels of the organization decisions are required in areas such as personnel selection and training, labor relations, fiscal management, service delivery, and program evaluation, all of which require judgment involving the evaluation of alternative courses of action. Therefore, decision making is closely linked with the area of leadership discussed in Chapter 9.

The issue of the limits posed by situational factors, which was evident in the discussion of leadership, arises also in the area of decision making. Although the term "decision making" tends to emphasize the individualistic aspect, the organizational context has an ever-present impact on the "rational" decision-making procedure. The first issue, therefore, is that of how rational organizational decision making can be. A related issue is what are the influences of the individual versus the situation on rational decision making.

How Rational Can Decisions Be?

Economists, philosophers, and other scholars have pondered the problem of how humans make decisions and solve problems. From the writings of John Dewey (1910) to the current widespread use of computers, the emphasis has been on rationality in analyzing problems and predicting solutions. If decision making is viewed as an information processing activity, then the potential of such mechanical devices as computers should be great. Computer programs have been developed to do such complex activities as launch space vehicles and perform medical diagnoses. If one can determine all the variables and their relative importance, then a device such as an electronic computer can very readily process this information and arrive at a "rational" decision.

Problems in the human service field, however, are not such that we can know all the variables. It is not possible to weigh all alternative solutions and their consequences (Gruber 1981:13). Although we would like to achieve optimal answers (Sutherland 1977:viii), we usually have to settle for "satisfactory" solutions (March and Simon 1958:169). Such *nonrational* factors as lack of knowledge place limits on our attempts to be rational.

A *rational* approach to decision making includes problem definition, search for solutions, and evaluation of alternatives, leading to the selection of the alternative having the most favorable cost–benefit ratio. However, this effort to be rational is influenced by a variety of *nonrational* factors—not only the limits on knowledge, but also factors relating to the organizational context, including the nature of the goals, structures, and values prevailing in the organization. Therefore, a realistic approach to decision making in organizations takes into account both the cognitive rational processes and the influence of structurally determined nonrational factors. The decision maker aspires to be as rational as possible, but circumstances limit or enhance this rational effort.

Individual versus Situational Influences on Rational Decision Making

In order to understand the role of individual versus situational influences on decision making, it is necessary to distinguish between the terms *non-rational* and *irrational*. Irrationality refers to an individual deficiency, asso-ciated with faulty logic or incompetence in analytical skills and abilities. An individual decision maker can be evaluated in an objective manner as to whether he or she uses logical reasoning in assessing evidence and drawing conclusions. Potential distorters of rationality can be identified; these include subjective psychological processess as overidentification with reference groups, projection, global and undifferentiated thinking, dichotomized think-ing, cognitive nearsightedness, and oversimplification of causation (Katz and Kahn 1978:503–508). *Nonrationality* is associated with situational factors that impinge on the decision-making process, for example, time pressures, lack of information or organizational influences. As these factors are *external* to the decision maker they are termed *nonrational* rather than *irrational*.

The issue of the relative importance of individual and situational factors in decision making can now be viewed in terms of the general problem of the extent to which the individual should be held responsible for good or poor decisions when situational factors are also relevant. Any model used for decision making needs to incorporate in some way both the rational and nonrational elements present. Concentrating solely on the *rational* aspects and ignoring the nonrational factors may achieve intellectual satisfaction but only at the expense of ignoring the importance of the "decision environment."

DEFINITION

Decision making can be classified into two major categories, based on how extensive the impact of a decision will be for members of the organization. The first category of decision making, called policy formulation, involves those decisions that have a major impact on organizational sturcture and policy (see Chapter 11 "Organizational Change"). The second category of decision making is concerned with implementation of existing policy and, therefore, has relatively less impact on this system. This type of decision making includes decisions involving routine day-to-day actions. These decisions require little judgment as they draw heavily upon precedent. An example of a routinized decision is the application of eligibility criteria for client service. In general, most of the decision-making activity in organizations is routinized (Inbar 1979) or "programmed" (March and Simon 1958:177). However, as we have noted, although rules may prescribe decisions to be made under different circumstances, they cannot cover all contingencies, leaving the door open for use of discretion and judgment.

The remainder of this chapter presents a decision-making model, which is applicable to both policy formulation and policy implementation. Before proceeding to discuss the model, however, it must be made clear that making *no decision* is itself a form of action. Administrators will often defer a decision with the expectation that the problem will solve itself. The pressures in the day-to-day work in human sevice organizations generate numerous problems, of which some are addressed and others ignored. As with physical symptoms, many of these organizational problems are self-limiting. Therefore, the decision as to what problems are to be given priority is a basic one; weighing the significance of the various cross-pressures (e.g., when client benefit conflicts with staff benefit) involves decision-making skills.

DECISION-MAKING MODEL

Introduction

The decision-making model presented here, including both rational and nonrational factors, is drawn from Katz and Kahn (1978). The *rational* model includes four sequential stages: (a) immediate pressures, (b) problem definitions, (c) search for solutions, and (d) evaluation of alternatives, leading to choice. The *nonrational* factors include (a) problem versus dilemma, (b) organizational context, and (c) cognitive limitations.

Although the rational model assumes a sequential order, in reality the decision maker may forgo this sequence. For example, in response to external pressures the decision maker may simply adopt the problem definition and solutions advocated by the pressure groups, without attempting a more complete problem analysis, search for solutions, or objective evaluation of all alternatives.

Immediate Pressures

The force behind all decisions is some pressure or felt difficulty. The nature of organizational life is such that opportunities for action are not sought unless there is a conviction that action is needed to solve a problem. This felt difficulty may come from outside the decision maker or from his or her own concerns and convictions. The former sort of pressure may originate outside the organization altogether. As resources have grown scarce, there has evolved a much greater recognition of the fact that human service agencies are interdependent. This realization has led to external pressures for interagency cooperation and coordination. Pressures external to the decision maker may, of course, also originate from inside the organization. This type of pressure probably has more immediate impact on the administrator, because of its proximity and because ignoring it may have serious consequences for day-too-day functioning of the agency. The latter sort of pressure, which *should* be operating, stems from the executive's awareness of problems that are impeding organizational effectiveness. In human service agencies a professional commitment to client benefits should also lead to a felt need to act.

Problem Definition

Basic to any effort to solve problems is the rationale used to analyze the problem. A rational approach to problem definition requires an understanding of both the causes and consequences of the problem. The assumptions made as to the cause of the problem have implications for the kinds of solutions considered. Thus, as we have seen, the cause of organizational problems can be sought in persons and/or policies. If a problem of excessive staff turnover is understood as caused by an incompetent supervisor, then the remedy has to be directed at changing the supervisor. If, however, the problem is perceived as originating in a lack of adequate role definition for the supervisor, then the remedy must involve changing the job specifications for this *position*.

This discussion has assumed that a problem entails a deviation from some standard of performance (Kepner and Tregoe 1965:39–54). A fundamental question is how to determine the criteria.

In defining something as a problem in the first place, we need to keep in mind the fact that the primary purpose of the human sevice organization is to achieve client benefit. Thus staff dissatisfaction and turnover may or may not be an organizational problem depending on its relationship to the standard of client benefit. It is conceivable that turnover may be expected and functional in job situations where extreme stress requires that staff have short tenure because of the high psychological costs. Working with terminally ill patients in a hospice may require a certain amount of turnover in order to insure that staff will continue to function.

As indicated, problems may be defined differently depending on the perspective taken. It therefore behooves the rational decision maker to obtain as comprehensive a problem definition as possible by consulting with a variety of people who would be expected to have different perspectives. People in the lower levels of the organization will view problems differently than will those in the middle levels. It may be important to obtain problem definitions from experts—outside consultants or specialists inside the agency such as program evaluation staff from the adaptive subsystem (see chapter 5). The decision maker, however, must keep in mind that no person is free of bias.

As problem definition is intrinsically related to individual perception and frame of reference, it will be influenced by professional ideologies (see Chapter 13). If one has a belief system that generally attributes problems to individuals, then one will be inclined to view all situations in these terms. Decision makers must therefore be aware of the influence that ideologies, their own as well as others', can have on problem definition. The factual basis for judgments must be sought in order to minimize the influence that subjective professional beliefs will have on problem definition and on the subsequent stages of the decision-making process.

Problems versus Dilemmas

Organizations usually solve problems by use of precedents. Parsimony requires that problems be dealt with today as they were yesterday. These programmed solutions assume that most problems can be solved within the framework of existing policy. Therefore, we can define a *problem* as a difficulty that *can* be solved by using existing procedures and policy. When existing policy *cannot* adequately solve the problem we are confronted with a *dilemma*. A dilemma requires a *reformulation* of existing policy. For example, if high staff turnover was caused by inappropriate agency goals, then in order to solve this difficulty, the organization would have to change its basic purposes. More specifically, if a child welfare agency has as its official goal the treatment of child abuse cases and the more appropriate goal is social care, then the solution to the difficulty of excessive staff turnover would be to modify the goal and associated staff practices. Continued efforts to accomplish people-changing goals when environmental-changing objectives are required will simply result in further staff frustration and turnover.

Organizations are generally very reluctant to acknowledge dilemmas, because to do so would then entail making major changes in policy. Refusal to confront a dilemma, however, results in repeated unsuccessful efforts to solve the difficulty by applying existing policies. This continued failure to achieve a solution is seldom recognized as being related to the fallacy of treating dilemmas as if they were problems. As a result, the difficulty persists because the frame of reference used to analyze it (precedent) is not adequate.

The other side of this coin is the tendency that some staff members have of trying to turn problems into dilemmas. For such individuals, solving a problem by using precedent is not challenging enough, and therefore, their response to all problems is innovation and change. In some cases, this tendency simply stems from an inadequate understanding of existing policy. For example, students who are new at a university may pressure for new policies because they are not aware of existing policies which are suitable for solving their problems.

Organizational Context

As mentioned earlier, an important associated nonrational factor in decision making is the influence of the organizational context—the goals, structures, ideologies, and technologies present in the organization. These relatively fixed aspects of organizational life (e.g. "walls of the maze" see Chapter 4) narrow the focus of the decision maker, in that problems are viewed in terms of the assumptions underlying existing policies on goals, structures, ideologies, and technologies. For example, if an organization has a hierarchical structure, then this may preclude the recognition of the possibility that the problem of turnover stems from a lack of participation by professional staff in organizational decision making. If the organization is a mental health center with psychological treatment as its primary purpose and ideology, then there will be a tendency to view staff turnover as a psychological problem requiring treatment (see Chapter 7, "Occupational Burnout").

Search for Solutions

The third stage in this rational model for decision making, following problem definition, is the search for solutions to the problem identified. In general, the amount of effort expended at this stage is limited, because of pressure for quick solutions. As already implied, the search will start by examining precedent. Every effort will be made to solve the problem by using existing policy. If satisfactory solutions are found, then search efforts will stop. That is, optimal solutions will not be attempted if minimal and painless solutions are possible (see section on bounded rationality). If, however, the difficulty cannot be solved using existing policy, then we are confronted with a dilemma, which requires a more experimental search process, in order to find an innovative solution.

Evaluation of Anticipated Consequences of Alternative Solutions

The last stage of the rational decision-making process is an attempt to assess the costs and benefits of alternative solutions. The evaluation of consequences varies with organizational level; in general, executives tend to *underestimate* the feasibility problems, whereas lower-level staff tend to overestimate them. The line operational staff are concerned with whether the solution will *work*—that is, whether it can be implemented without undue cost to the agency operations. This short-range view can defeat a long-range planning perspective. They also overestimate the practical problems of implementation of "radical" changes. Ultimately, from their vantage point, proposals for innovations may be "pie in the sky" when compared to the day-to-day problems of service management and delivery.

This resistance of line personnel to change can be illustrated by the efforts of a public child welfare agency to introduce permanency planning. In such an agency, the day-to-day operations are directed at responding to crisis and emergency situations of child abuse and neglect. Pressures on line staff are numerous and are compounded by requests coming from corrections, mental health, education, and public welfare agencies. In light of these pressures, the proposal to do "permanency planning," which requires a long-range perspective, may appear somewhat unrealistic, even through rationally it can be demonstrated that the solution to this crisis-dominated service is the provision of more permanent and stable home situations for the children. In this situation, administration will often use a demonstration units that is outside of regular operations. If this demonstration unit can show that the innovation can "work" then operational units might be convinced to try it. However, the tension between operational staff and upper-level personnel who advocate change is basic to organizational life and needs to be recognized and resolved. In order to avoid both bias in the evaluation of alternative solutions and resistance to the solution selected, it is advisable to involve lower levels of the organization in this stage of the decision-making process.

Bounded Rationality—Cognitive Limits

In evaluating alternative solutions, the decision maker is, as we noted earlier, constrained by a lack of information on these alternatives and by an inability to predict fully, the consequences of selecting a particular one. These cognitive limitations may result in a trial-and-error method of decision making, which has been termed the "simplification process" (March and Simon 1958). This process has the following characteristics:

1. Optimizing is replaced by satisficing—that is, the attempt is not to seek the best solutions but merely satisfactory answers that are acceptable to persons in the system.
2. The search process is one of trial and error, instead of systematic evaluation of the relative advantages and disadvantages of several alternatives.
3. Programmed solutions are used—that is, the established ways of doing things are followed.
4. The organization sets the boundaries for problem definition and solution—decisions have to fit into existing organizational context.

We can observe a possible instance of the simplification possess by looking at the case situation "Mental Health Rules and Regulations" in which a state planning agency attempts to provide services for the chronically mentally ill at community mental health centers. A rational analysis could have revealed that human service agencies with a rehabilitive goal (the CMHCs) were not the appropriate means for providing social care services to the chronically mentally ill. Therefore, the *best* solution might have been to have shifted funds to agencies that had social care as their primary function, for example, physical rehabilitation services or public welfare agencies. However, because shifting financial support away from community mental health centers would have created conflict (and, in particular, would have been unacceptable to that powerful system), a *satisfactory* solution was selected—to attempt to influence the CMHCs to modify their programs and goals. This solution confined itself to the existing system and organizational context.

SUMMARY

This chapter emphasized that administrative decision making has both rational and nonrational elements. Placing stress on the rational aspect can result in assigning too much responsibility for outcome to the decision maker, as nonrational situational factors may have been equally important. Although we need to be more rational and logical in making decisions, we also need to be aware of how the "decision environment" impinges on the process.

The decision-making model presented in this chapter incorporated both the rational and nonrational aspects and suggested how both administrators and practitioners can maximize professional accomplishment by taking into account the interplay between the two in organizational decision making. Only if these two emphases are balanced can decisions be made that will enhance client benefit.

APPLICATION OF CONCEPTS ON DECISION MAKING TO CASE "FROM PSYCHOLOGICAL WORK TO SOCIAL WORK"

The problems confronting the new director in the case "From Psychological Work to Social Work" can serve to illustrate the concepts of the decision-making model. We shall first look at the *rational* decision-making model and then consider the influence of *nonrational* factors.

The *immediate pressures* on this administrator at the outset came from upper-level authorities, the staff, and the community, as well as from his own professional concerns and standards. The central office upper-level managers were concerned with inadequacies in service delivery, including clients not being served and poor systems for accountability. The pressure from the staff was reflected in low morale, discontent over high workloads, and high turnover. The pressures from the community came from various sources, including the courts, the schools, and welfare and mental health agencies. The administrator himself was concerned with what he perceived as the inappropriateness of the service delivery model in use. This service delivery model stressed rehabilitation rather than a social care goal, which the administrator thought would be more beneficial to clients.

Each of these sources of pressure focused on specific problems and advocated specific solutions. The upper levels wanted the cases served and a new accountability system implemented. The staff felt overwhelmed and wanted caseloads reduced. The other community agencies wanted the agency to respond more rapidly to their demands for service in various urgent case situations.

In order to know what action to take, this administrator needed to understand better the causes and consequences of the problems confronting the agency. This *problem definition* indicated the following five problem areas:

1. *Inadequate accountability system.* There was a lack of systematic procedures for service delivery, including job specifications and clear-cut goals and objectives.
2. *Inappropriate organizational goals.* Given the social nature of clients' needs, the rehabilitation goal, which focused on changing clients, was inappropriate. (Here, however, staff disagreed with the administrator, because of basic ideological differences.)
3. *Dysfunctional power structure.* The agency's problems were exacerbated by the inordinate amount of power and control exerted by the hiring officer and the manager of administrative support.
4. *Inadequate procedures for staff selection.* Related to (2) and (3) was the fact that staff selection and promotional procedures actually worked against the kinds of personnel who would be most appropriate for the new goal of social care service delivery. Inadequate procedures for staff selection had also resulted in the understaffing of the clerical department.
5. *Work overload.* The excessive caseloads stemmed in large part from two of the problems already mentioned—the lack of systematic service delivery procedures and the excessive control exerted by the hiring officer and the manager of administrative support.

The following diagram illustrates how these various factors were interrelated:

PROBLEM DEFINITION

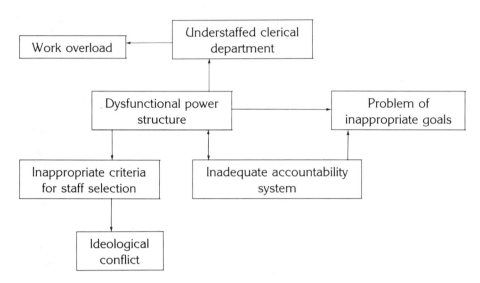

By diagramming the multiple causes of the problem the administrators developed comprehensive analysis which helped specify which factors were the critical ones, requiring priority attention. That is, by defining the basic problem as one of inappropriate agency goals, he was able to examine the various factors as they related to this problem. Throughout the decision-making process—in defining the problem and in evaluating *alternative solutions*—the administrator used as the basic standard the effects on client benefit.

Examination of the diagram reveals that a key factor influencing other difficulties was the *dysfunctional power structure*, which gave the hiring officer and manager of administrative support excessive influence. This situation was made particularly problematic by the fact that both individuals opposed the administrator's plans for change. The administrator therefore decided to concentrate on this power structure problem. To deal with the two individuals, the administrator could select from among various *alternative solutions*, including the following: (a) persuade them to voluntarily relinquish their power and conform to his wishes for changing the agency's goals and procedures; (b) use organizational structure to constrain their activities, thereby reducing their influence and power, and (c) attempt to replace them by bringing disciplinary action against them.

The *rational* approach to decision making would have the administrator evaluate the consequences of each alternative solution and, after carefully weighing the costs and benefits, make a decision as to which solution is the best. Use of the persuasion alternative would involve the *cost* of acknowledging the power of these staff members and perhaps diminishing the administrator's authority. A *benefit* would be that this consensus strategy would generate a minimum of conflict. The second alternative—using organization structure to constrain their activities and power—has the potential *cost* of creating conflict, as these individuals were unaccustomed to being limited in their roles. A *benefit* would be that the specification of job performance standards in accordance with the civil service rules was a legitimate responsibility of the administrator; that is, he had the *legal authority* to do this. The last alternative—namely, replacing these staff members—would have the *cost* of generating substantial conflict, particularly as other staff members might mobilize in support of these two individuals. The *benefit* would be that removing these individuals would quickly change the power structure and permit the administration to move ahead with other changes.

The actual decision made was to use the structure to constrain the power of these two staff members. With the establishment of specific job expectations, they faced the possibility of unsatisfactory performance ratings which could lead to dismissal. Under this kind of pressure both staff members decided to leave the agency.

The dysfunctional power structure can be viewed as a problem, rather than as a *dilemma*. By definition a problem is solved by use of existing policy and structure. Thus, the administrator was able to solve this problem of the overconcentration of power by applying existing rules. He did not have to introduce an official policy change.

In actuality the series of acts he became involved in, including the establishment of specific job performance criteria geared to social care objectives, eventually led to a shift in the goals of the agency. Therefore the aggregation of the many "uses of structure" resulted in a major policy change.

As already mentioned, the administrator identified the basic problem in this agency as that of inappropriate goals. This posed a *dilemma* which could *not* be solved by a continuation of existing procedures. The reason the administrator was confronted with so much resistance was that he was endeavoring a major policy change. This means, by definition, that the activities of staff needed to change (see Chapter 11).

The *organizational context*, which includes the goals, ideologies, structure, and technologies of the system, can constrain or facilitate decision making. In this agency, underlying all these aspects of organizational context was a strong clinical emphasis. The administrator's attempt to establish a more structured operation ran counter to this clinical philosophy, which relied heavily on interpersonal relationships. Therefore, the organizational *context* was a major *constraint* on the administrator's efforts. However, the *official* structure of this state agency was that of a bureaucracy. This aspect of structure provided a *context that facilitated* the administrator's efforts to establish clear job performance standards and an objective system for accountability.

Understanding both the opportunities and constraints allowed him to skillfully direct his efforts to change the system.

Another nonrational factor is the *cognitive limits* on rationality: It is impossible to know the full range of factors relevant to a decision or to foresee all potential consequences. Perhaps because of such limits, the administrator, in making a decision regarding the two staff members, followed basically a trial-and-error procedure—the *simplification process* in decision making. He first tried the least painful solution—convincing the two staff members to cooperate. Only after this failed did he proceed with the more difficult alternative of using structure to control them. Throughout the case there are examples of the unanticipated consequences of decisions made. Solving one problem creates other problems. The cognitive limits on this administrator precluded anticipation of the series of events that occurred to thwart his efforts—such as the supervisory civil service lists.

ORGANIZATIONAL CHANGE

OUTLINE

I. Issues
   A. Will Changing Individuals Change Organizations?
   B. Source of Resistance to Change
   C. Persuasion or Power—Which Is More Effective?

II. Definition

III. Resistance To Change
   A. Ideological Factors
   B. Self-Interest
   C. Technological Factors
   D. Lack of Knowledge

IV. Opportunities For Change
   A. External Pressures
   B. Natural Change Processes

V. Types of Change
   A. Goal Change
   B. Procedural Change
      1. Internal Change
         a. Structural Change
         b. Organizational Assessment
      2. Changes in External Relations
         a. Closed System Strategies
         b. Open System Strategies
   C. Degree of Change
      1. Major Structural Change
      2. Bending Structure
      3. Using Structure
   D. Organizational Growth
   E. Benefits of Change

VI. Individual versus Organizational Change
   A. Individual Change Strategies
      1. Behavior Change Strategies
         a. Attitude Change
         b. Behavior Change
      2. Replacement Strategy

ISSUES

The need to change human service organizations becomes more urgent as evidence accumulates of their lack of efficiency and effectiveness. Administrators and practitioners are being pressured by external forces to initiate and implement change. Funding authorities, client advocates, and professional peers look to organizational innovation as a solution to dysfunctioning human service programs. Numerous changes have been suggested, including decentralization of internal structure in mental hospitals and use of case management systems in probation departments. Although proposals for change are readily developed, successful implementation is more difficult. In this chapter we discuss several issues associated with change in human service agencies: (a) Will changing individuals change organizations? (b) What is the source of resistance to change? (c) Which is the more effective change strategy: persuasion or power?

Will Changing Individuals Change Organizations?

If organizations are collectivities of individuals, then logic seems to suggest that a people-changing strategy is appropriate to achieve organizational change. The proponents of the human relations model (see Chapter 3) advocate this strategy for organizational innovation. The individual change strategy delegates the task of organizational change to the staff and emphasizes such means as information giving, training, counseling, selection, and removal.

Criticism of the individual approach to organizational innovation has centered on what has been termed the "psychological fallacy" (Katz and Kahn 1978:658). That is, the approach makes a fundamental oversimplification in assuming that the behavior of organizational members is separate from such situational and structural factors as organizational role and function. It fails to distinguish clearly between behavior determined by structural factors and behavior determined by personality needs and values. Changing the attitudes, motivations, and perceptions of individuals does not change patterns of behavior that are related to role, power, reward, communication, and interorganizational structures (Holloway and Brager 1977:355).

The individual approach to organizational change has also included group strategies, such as the use of sensitivity-training groups. The idea is that group interaction can be used to achieve change of individuals. Also associated with the human relations school is the strategy of encouraging staff participation in order to achieve greater consensus and commitment and hence change the organizational climate. Such changes are all directed at the informal system, and their value is limited by the fact that they have little effect on the formal structure.

As most organizational change can be expected to generate resistance, it can also be postulated that the greater the participation of staff in the change process, the *more* likely that they will have an opportunity to coalesce and organize against the change. This is especially true when major system change is at stake. In such cases, use of power and authority may be required to effectively initiate the change.

Source of Resistance to Change

The questions that arose in the preceding section, of whether staff members' cooperation is required in initiating change and of how such cooperation can be obtained, can only be answered by considering the source of the opposition to change. Resistance may be based on threat to self-interest, ideology, a simple lack of knowledge, or to technological factors. If it is based on lack of knowledge, then communication and discussion can be expected to elicit cooperation. If it is based on threat to self-interest, then some bargaining and compromise strategy is probably required. Threats to values or ideologies are usually not resolvable through either education or compromise. Resistance associated with the introduction of new service delivery technologies may be based on a combination of threats to self-interest, ideology as well as lack of knowledge. Thus, change from people to situation changing technologies can be resisted by staff because of their concern that their lack of the new skill may threaten their jobs. They also may oppose the change on the grounds that they do not believe this approach is appropriate for the clients. Finally, their lack of understanding of the particular technology may result in unwarranted anxieties and concerns based on lack of knowledge of what may be involved.

These three sources of resistance to change need to be differentiated so that the appropriate strategies can be selected. For various reasons, it is often difficult to make this differentiation. For example, what appears to be ideological opposition may be primarily a screen for self-interest. This dynamic is evident in the controversy to deinstitutionalize the chronically mentally ill and the reluctance of community mental health centers to provide them service. The rehabilitation-oriented clinicians in the mental health centers justify not serving the chronics on the ground that they are not "treatable." Although it is probably correct that rehabilitation approaches are not appropriate for this group, the underlying source of resistance may be the fear that if the mental health center accepted these patients, the staff's lack of appropriate technology would become apparent, with the result that more appropriate staff might be hired or government funding shifted to other programs.

It is commonly assumed that most resistance to change can be overcome by open communication (Hasenfeld 1980:509). Underlying this belief is the premise that misunderstandings and misperceptions are often the basis for resistance to change. However, even in situations where this is the case, ideological and political factors might also be at work. Unless these "hidden agendas" are recognized, it will be difficult to overcome the resistance by "open" communication, as staff members may not admit to all of the sources for their opposition.

The assumption that cooperation can be achieved and resistance overcome by open communication is evident in the emphasis on "teamwork" in the human service field. What this emphasis overlooks is that interdisciplinary teams are made up of professionals with different philosophies and different degrees of power which can be a serious barrier to cooperation and group decision making. Both sources of difficulty are evident in the mental health teams in outpatient or inpatient programs: The differences in ideologies between psychiatry (medical model), psychology (psychological model), and social work (social model) can provide a basic source of disagreement. The fact that the doctor has more power and status and can unilaterally make final decisions because he has ultimate medical responsibility can further reduce the ability of the group to have "open" and "free" communication.

Persuasion or Power—Which Is More Effective?

Persuasion and power are the two basic strategies for achieving change, and their relative effectiveness depends on the source of resistance. If the source of resistance is self-interest, then persuasion may be successful. In such a case, both parties can objectively evaluate the costs and benefits of the changes proposed, and negotiations based on persuasion can lead to mutually acceptable agreements. This scenario assumes that the parties involved have relatively *equal* amounts of power (Slavin 1978:534). If, however, the party that perceives the change as contrary to its self-interest is *less* powerful, then the other party will resort to a power strategy to accomplish the change. The use of raw power is not unusual in hierarchically based systems. Upper-level managers frequently use power to institute changes (Hasenfeld 1980:244–245), particularly if the changes are major.

As already indicated, if the source of resistance to change is a lack of knowledge, then persuasion by communication of information can be effective. However, this assumes that the change does not threaten self-interest or ideology (Slavin 1978:534).

Ideologically based resistance is the most difficult to overcome (see Chapter 13). Because ideological convictions have a very strong emotional base, they are not readily compromised. Hence a persuasion strategy generally cannot be effective, and it may be necessary to resort to the use of power, with the understanding that alienation will probably result.

DEFINITION

Organizational change is defined in behavioral terms. An organization is changed if the activities of the staff—its day-to-day tasks, roles, and functions—have been modified. Major system change can mean change in organizational goals and/or in the basic strategies for achieving these goals. Change in organizational goals is a change in the direction in which the organization is moving. For example, an organization can change its goals from social care to social control or from social control to rehabilitation. Measures of goal change will involve the examination of the activities of the staff in relationship to these purposes. In contrast, change in the major strategies for achieving organizational goals involves modifying the internal structural arrangements that allow the organization to accomplish its goals. Changes in strategies also include changes in the manner in which the organization copes with the external environment.

RESISTANCE TO CHANGE

The behavioral definition of change used here has implications for the extent that change will be resisted by members of the organization. A basic assumption is that in most instances people will be reluctant to modify the way they have been doing things unless they are very dissatisfied with the existing arrangement. The nature of organizational life is such that most members establish a pattern of activity (structure) that provides them with some stability and security. In the human service field these activities, and the associated technologies and skills, are often the result of extensive education, on-the-job training, and experience, and hence are believed to be valid and effective. In short, unless special circumstances prevail, resistance to change is likely to be strong. As already mentioned, the particular source of resistance varies from case to case and may involve ideological factors, technological factors, self-interest, or lack of knowledge.

Ideological Factors

The lack of validated knowledge on the cause–effect relations of human service technologies (see Chapter 14) requires that organizational members rely on belief systems to guide and justify their actions. Change efforts that question these ideological and value bases for action will be viewed as threats (Brager and Holloway 1978:3–7). Challenges to ideology can provoke very strong emotional responses, as they are in a sense similar to questioning a religion.

Ideological resistance to change is often manifested in situations where program goals are modified. Organizational goals are by definition based on value preferences (Simon 1957:45–60), as they are outcomes that are deemed intrinsically desirable.

Thus, social care, social control, and rehabilitation as goals of human service programs are equivalent to different values or ideologies. These goals are based on the conviction—unsupported by empirical evidence—that they are desirable ends toward which human service agencies should strive. When attempts are made to modify these goals, resistance can be expected to be ideologically based. For example, a proposed merger of two agencies that have different goals will encounter resistance because the staff of each will believe that its agency's goal is preferable to that of the other. Ideologically based resistance to change is also exemplified in the case situations "From Psychological Work to Social Work" and "Mental Health Rules and Regulations," both of which involve an attempt to change from a rehabilitation to a social care goal.

Because the two are closely related ideological differences may sometimes be screened behind differences in technological approaches to service. Different service modalities, such as individual versus family-centered therapies, have different underlying philosophies. Thus, in the merger of a psychiatrically oriented child guidance agency and a family oriented family service organization, resistance centered around differences in service philosophies.

Ideological opposition is also evident in resistance to efforts to introduce outcome-oriented services. "Process"-oriented professionals have perceived stress on accountability and outcome as "unprofessional" and as ignoring the essential interpersonal dynamics between client and helper. Resistance to use of statistics and management information systems has also been based on ideological grounds, as exemplified by the criticism that use of quantitative data is "dehumanizing."

Strategies for dealing with ideologically based resistance must start with the recognition that strong, emotional convictions are involved. Direct confrontation would be likely to engender greater resistance to the change. A strategy that accepts the ideology as a given and respects it as *one* legitimate way of viewing the world would tend to mitigate the potential for an open ideological conflict. The stage is then set for diverting attention to issues that are debatable and negotiable, such as issues based on self-interest.

Self-interest

Change that requires a modification of staff behavior might be resisted if it threatens a person's power and status (Brager and Holloway 1978:82-83). Resistance based on self-interest can also be related to the individual's need to have control over his or her job. Most people want a secure job situation, where there is a minimum of uncertainty. Change can threaten this job security.

Self-interest is a factor not only at the individual level, but also at the level of organizational subunits. Thus change can be seen as a threat to a department's autonomy, power, and status. The movement towards decentralization in mental hospitals, for example, has been seen as a threat to the power of the various specialized disciplines (e.g., psychiatry, psychology, social work, and nursing).

Self-interest is a fundamental basis for resistance to organizational change, given the essentially political nature of human service organizations (Gummer 1978; Hasenfeld 1980). Previous discussion of subsystems (Chapter 5), management models (Chapter 3), and organizational structure (Chapter 4) have all referred to the importance of individual and collective self-interest as a dynamic in organizational life. An organizational change that poses a threat to self-interest can provoke strong staff resistance. Self-interest can be pursued in an economic sense (e.g., salary increases) or in a political sense (the enhancement of power and control over one's own activities or over other people). Regardless of the form it takes, the importance of self-interest as a dynamic is evident.

Given its importance, self-interest must be taken into account in planning and implementing organizational change. It is necessary to be aware that even when other reasons are given for resistance to change, self-interest may be the real cause. It is more socially acceptable to oppose a change on grounds that it violates certain cherished values (e.g., the welfare of clients) than on the grounds that it threatens one's power and position.

Technological Factors

People have an investment in the skills and practices they learned in school or on the job. Technology is therefore another area in which there is strong resistance to change, especially if the change is major. For example, a worker who uses a direct service casework methodology, with its various techniques of support, clarification, and insight, will find it difficult to switch to behavior modification technologies, which require different techniques of reenforcement, desensitization, and conditioning (see Chapter 14).

The increase in specialization of human service modalities has resulted in the rapid introduction of new approaches and techniques. Staff members who were educated in the older methods are understandably threatened by the newer methods. Although some retraining is possible it is difficult to expect a person who has invested years of training and experience in a specific modality to adopt a different and alien approach to serving clients. Whether the changes are from people-changing to environmental-changing technologies, from process- to goal-oriented services, or from rehabilitation to care, the difficulties of adopting new ways of doing the job are a considerable inconvenience for workers, if not a threat to their self-esteem and self-worth.

Lack of Knowledge

The body of knowledge on which we can draw is rapidly growing. Research on organizational functions, structures, and process in industry has been conducted for some time. Much of this research is applicable to human service organizations. More recently, information pertaining directly to the human service field, discussing the kinds of structures and techniques needed for more effective design and administration of programs, has been appearing in journals such as *Administration in Social Work* and in a variety of books (e.g., Abels and Murphy 1981; M. Austin 1981; Gates 1980; Hasenfeld 1983; Hasenfeld and English 1974; Lewis and Lewis 1983; Meringoff 1980; Patti 1983; Perlmutter and Slavin 1980; Slavin 1978; Sarri and Hasenfeld 1978; Weiner 1982). However, as most practitioners and administrators in human service agencies are unfamiliar with this literature, they would probably resist organizational change that attempted to apply the new findings. Therefore, it is crucial that mechanisms be developed to communicate research results and hence overcome resistance based merely on lack of knowledge. In fact, methods for communication and dissemination of information are developing rapidly; for example, the research literature on social change has been codified and translated into practice principles and techniques to facilitate communication (Rothman, 1974, 1976, 1978a, 1978b, 1980a, 1980b).

OPPORTUNITIES FOR CHANGE

Just as certain factors are sources of resistance to change, other factors facilitate change. These facilitating factors include external pressures and the natural change processes that exist in most human service agencies.

External Pressures

The pressures exerted by forces outside of the organization (funding authorities, competing organizations, etc.) can have considerable influence on the potential for change (Hasenfeld 1983:245–246). This influence may be either constraining or facilitating in nature (Hasenfeld 1980:513). The internal resistance to major change can be counteracted if there is considerable external pressure (Katz and Kahn 1978:536).

Accreditation procedures, formal external reviews, and citizen review boards, although they increase pressure for accountability, enable the administrator to introduce changes that would otherwise not be possible. For example, in the case "From Psychological Work to Social Work," the director of the child welfare agency used the requirements established by an external review board to develop and enforce a management information system, despite staff resistance.

Natural Change Processes

Emphasis has been placed on the constraints on organizational change. However, if one observes organizational life one sees continuous movement and change. This movement and change is possible because of the opportunities for discretion in the interpretation of rules. Although the constraints on major change may be substantial, there are occasions when minor or incremental changes are possible. The opportunity for better *use of structure* is present if one has sufficient knowledge of the system. By understanding the existing structure, one becomes aware of which natural change processes provide the greatest potential for movement within the particular organization.

TYPES OF CHANGE

As indicated earlier, changes in staff activities can be translated into innovation in organizational purposes and/or the strategies for achieving these purposes.

Goal Change

Changes in organizational goals may take many forms, including the following: (a) goal clarification, (b) shift in priorities of goals, (c) addition of new goals, and (d) shift in the mission (Katz and Kahn 1978:479–480).

The *shift in the mission* of human service organizations can be illustrated by means of the National Foundation For Infantile Paralysis: Once the foundation had accomplished its original goal of preventing polio, it developed and implemented the alternative goal of providing service to people with birth defects. The *shift in the priorities* given to goals is illustrated by the change in the emphasis of service to the mentally disabled from social control in institutions to social care services in the community. The *addition of new goals* is illustrated in the area of services for the chronically ill, with the introduction and implementation of the new goal of support systems in the community.

Goal clarification is the process of assessing the relationship between the means and ends of human service programs leading to change. This process makes it possible to determine the extent to which the goal of client benefit may have been displaced by any of the means being used. For example, in the child welfare field the ultimate goal is the normal development of children, and foster home care has been a major strategy for achieving this goal. There is increasing evidence, however, that foster placement has become an end in itself, to the detriment of the children (Rapp and Poertner 1978). Foster homes are temporary, and the children are exposed to unstable, unpredictable life circumstances, which may adversely affect their development. A child welfare agency that clarifies its goals would make explicit this kind of goal displacement and establish more appropriate means for achieving the goal of child welfare, such as providing assistance to the natural families or developing adoption services.

Of the four types of goal changes discussed, goal clarification is the most common. Shifts in the organization's mission are relatively rare.

Procedural Change

Changes in the strategies for achieving goals have been referred to as substantive procedural change (Katz and Kahn 1978:515). Policy formulation that involves substantive procedural change is thus concerned with general, overall strategies for achieving the organization's goals. Procedural change can affect the internal structural arrangements or the relationship the organization has with the external environment.

Internal Change

Innovations in the internal arrangements are concerned with (a) structural change (see Chapter 4, "Organizational Structure") and (b) methods for organizational assessment.

Structural Change. Change from centralized to decentralized structure generally involves modifications in the distribution of authority and power within the organization. This type of change has become common in the human service field, with the move to decentralize program implementation (Perrow 1976). Although policymaking remains centralized, implementation is delegated to community levels, in keeping with the rationale that service delivery must be related to the needs of the individual community. In New Jersey, for example, state-level agencies in the fields of child welfare, mental retardation, and mental health are regionalizing service delivery, with the central offices maintaining budgetary control. This type of change, then, provides increased responsibility and authority to the service delivery level.

Other internal changes in substantive procedures may affect the role structures of service delivery staff. The emphasis in Title XX programs on concrete services could help precipitate a major shift in human service agencies that have traditionally stressed client-changing technology (B. Neugeboren 1979:181). Introduction of new service delivery technologies, as occurs in the shift from people changing to people processing, requires changes in the role structure.

It should be noted that the notion of internal change used here differs from that used in the political economy perspective. According to that approach, significant change is necessarily linked to shifts in power and resource allocation (Hasenfeld 1980:511). In the approach taken here, although power and resource allocation are seen as factors (major changes in staff activities may require power realignments and resistance to change often stems from threats to group interests), it is held that large-scale change is possible without power shifts. For example, there are times when external pressures can mitigate the power of internal groups (e.g., pressure from funding authorities can lead to agency mergers despite internal resistance). Also, organizations may be in such turmoil as to preclude the formation of strong power groups. This situation often is found in public human service agencies with high turnover rates. In short, the change emphasized in the power politic model is categorized here as a change in organizational authority or power structure. However, we also acknowledge the possibility of change in the role, reward, communication, and interorganizational structures, which may or may not affect the power structure. Thus, a change in the reward structure to performance appraisals based on results of employee efforts may be perceived as legitimate by staff and not as a threat to their power and authority. This change could nonetheless have significant repercussions, ultimately affecting staff members' day-to-day methods of doing their work.

Organizational Assessment. The second area of internal organizational change involves the strategies used by the organization to assess its progress.

In general, organizations can use either of two major strategies for assessing progress: (a) objective assessment and (b) self-fulfilling prophecy (Katz and Kahn 1978:518).

Objective assessment involves the use of systematic procedures to determine whether or not the organization is achieving its purpose and if not, why not. In human service organizations this means determining whether the goal of client benefit is being met and evaluating how particular organizational structures help or hinder achievement of this goal. Objective criteria for assessment must be established. In the nursing home field, for example, the longevity of patients could be used as a criterion for effective care. In the field of service to the chronically mentally ill, community adjustment as measured by performance in a job is a possible criterion. Measures of consumer satisfaction through opinion survey is another approach for assessment of results of service.

Use of objective appraisal as a strategy for assessing organizational progress requires ongoing feedback of the results of program efforts to administrators and service delivery staff, so that problem areas encountered can be dealt with. For example, the comparative information obtained on the relative effectiveness of various inputs could be used to modify programs. Administrators should be prepared to introduce program change—including substantive policy change—when the feedback indicates this is required. It would also require significant changes in the activities of service delivery staff who would be evaluated in terms of case outcome. The nature of reporting data would have to be modified to provide the needed information required for objective assessment. It can readily be appreciated that this type of substantive policy change would be a major shift from the usual practice of justifying efforts on such input criteria as number of hours worked or number of clients served. The increased emphasis on accountability in the human service field has promoted more objective assessment strategies.

Self-fulling prophecy is the assessment strategy that assumes that an organization is effective if it survives and has sufficient demands for its service. This strategy assesses effectiveness on the basis of the size of the waiting lists and the numbers of clients served rather than on the basis of results of service. Although this has been the predominant strategy in the human service field, it has come under increasing attack. The new emphasis on accountability has made it difficult to defend the use of the self-fulfilling prophecy as a strategy for assessing progress.

As indicated, process-oriented technologies emphasize the details of client–worker interactions. Hence, where such technologies are used, service is generally measured on the basis of these interactions, and the effect is to reinforce the self-fulfilling prophecy strategy. This occurs even if there are systematic criteria for the deciding on an adequate process; the outcome in terms of client benefits is usually displaced.

Change in External Relations

Organizational strategies for coping with the external environment fall into two general categories: closed and open system strategies. In recent years the movement has been toward open system strategies.

Closed System Strategies. Closed system strategies assume that human service organizations can function independently of other organizations and do not need to develop interorganizational relations. Human service organizations that are very highly specialized (e.g., general hospitals) can justify their isolationism on grounds that they have all the services required by their clients and therefore do not need to seek aid from other organizations. Traditional correctional institutions and mental hospitals have been described as "total institutions" (Goffman 1959) because they provide for all of the inmate's or patient's needs.

Human service agencies that define consumer needs within a narrow and circumscribed framework do not recognize the need for an open system strategy in interorganizational relations. A child welfare organization that views child abuse as caused by deficiency in the parents can develop counseling programs to correct this problem. As child abuse is narrowly defined the solution does not require the help of other agencies or resources. The same is true of a mental hospital that views the appropriate solution of chronic mental illness as custodial care. Yet evidence accumulates that social problems are multidimensional, closed system strategies become difficult to defend. The pressure of external groups such as the public advocate and citizens review boards also makes it difficult for human service agencies to remain isolated.

Open System Strategies. Open system strategies assume that human service organizations cannot fulfill their purposes without the help of other organizations. Such strategies have become increasingly important in the human service field, as recognition of the interdependencies among organizations has led to greater coordination and integration. The shift from closed to open system strategies has been accentuated by the policy of deinstitutionalization. As mental hospitals, facilities for the mentally retarded, and prisons become more concerned with community, rather than institutional, functioning as outcome, they have had to develop linkages with other organizations, for example, through affiliation agreements.

A change to open system strategies requires the development of procedures to facilitate interagency communication and cooperation. It also requires a major shift in staff attitudes—from an attitude of being isolated from or in competition with other agencies to one of cooperation and coordination. Ultimately, the shift hinges on an understanding of the dynamics of interorganizational dependency as based on shared goals and resource exchange (see Chapter 12).

Degree of Change

The behavioral definition of organizational innovation links change with modification in activities of personnel.

An important dimension of organizational change is that of the degree or extent of the change. The behavioral definition of change that we adopted can help us understand the differences between minor and major change, allowing us to more accurately estimate feasibility. In the human service field, the term "social change" has been applied to changes that varied greatly in the extent to which policies and programs were modified. For example, demonstration programs which have had minimal impact on systems, have been described as major systems change (Rein and Miller 1966).

Rothman's guidelines for promoting change in organizations and communities also stress the demonstration or "incremental" strategy (Rothman, Erlich, and Teresa 1976:23). Incremental changes are, however, different from major system change. The degree of change is therefore an important variable which has not been fully recognized in the change literature. In part this lack of recognition may stem from the assumption that the main barrier to change is deficiency in information, an assumption that underlies the diffusion of innovation literature (Rogers 1962). This emphasis on diffusion of information and hence change fails to take into account major structure change which requires significant shifts in staff activities and power arrangements.

If we consider the factor of degree of organizational change, we see that changes fall into several distinct categories: (a) major structural change— policy formulation, (b) change that bends structure, and (c) change that uses structure (Katz and Kahn 1978:536).

Major Structural Change

Major structural change, or policy formulation, is defined as a substantial change in the activities of the personnel of an organization. This change may be directed at goals and/or procedures. Major structural change occurs, for example, when an agency shifts from serving a nonchronic population to serving a chronically disabled group (e.g., a geriatric population): This shift would require a major change in goals and technologies, as well as the development of more extensive interorganizational relationships. As indicated earlier, major structural change is relatively rare; it probably occurs only in the face of extreme pressure from the external environment. Such pressure is often evident in organizational mergers, which are another example of major change. In mergers, not only are changes extensive, but large-scale disruptions occur on all levels (e.g., board, execution, line) of the agencies that are involved.

Bending Structure

The bending of structure refers to a *moderate* degree of change. It is associated with a process in organizations whereby minor changes are introduced without being officially recognized. The creative interpretation of rules and use of discretion leads to changes in areas such as staff roles and the types of people served. Gradually these changes become cumulative, so that at some point in time there is a significant change in the activity pattern, affecting the goals and/or strategies for achieving goals. An example of this type of incremental change is evident in the evolving pattern of community care for seriously disabled children and adults. As the funds for serving this population in institutions are withdrawn and community agencies assume the responsibility, ad hoc arrangements have arisen, stressing networks for community support (Garbarino, Holly, et al. 1980). As these changes in service delivery patterns occur, the goals of community service programs change also. These changes now are being officially recognized and formal policies are being promulgated. Thus, dramatic shifts in goals and strategies are occurring as the result of an incremental and cumulative change process (Donnison & Chapman 1965). Therefore, although the bending of structure generally results in moderate change, it can in some instances lead to major structural change if the changes cumulate over a period of time. The formal recognition of these major changes by policy makers has been referred to as "retrospective policy formulation."

The gradual or incremental change phenomenon is also evident in the case "From Psychological Work to Social Work." Over a period of several years the administrator moved his agency from a rehabilitative to social care goal through use of discretionary authority. He was able to replace key staff, introduce more effective systems for control, redesign the roles and functions of supervisory and line staff, and develop relationships with other community organizations. His new "caseload management" approach to child welfare services was subsequently legitimized by the top-level administrators in the state capital and was used as a model for the other district offices. Thus, persistent bending of the system eventually resulted in a major shift in goals and strategies.

Using Structure

Effective and creative implementation of existing policies can itself be an organizational change process (Pruger 1973). By capitalizing on opportunities for discretionary action, members of human service agencies can be innovative in carrying out daily tasks. A line worker can provide more effective service by moving beyond the "rule book" to work cooperatively with staff in other agencies. When resources needed to help clients appear to be lacking, a staff member can actively seek out "hidden" resources (B. Neugeboren 1979:180). A supervisor can creatively carry out his or her role by initiating structure that will help subordinates perform their jobs. Use of structure by definition requires that changes be within the framework of existing policies. Although this requirement may make it impossible to achieve the optimal outcome, use of structure nevertheless can produce significant movement toward a desirable goal.

Organizational Growth

Organizational change is possible during periods of growth. It is more feasible to add on new programs than to reallocate existing resources from one program to another. During the 1960s, when resources were available, the human service field changed greatly through the expansion of existing programs and the addition of new ones. In general, four kinds of organizational growth are possible: increase in unit size; increase in the number of parallel units; increase in differentiation and specialization; and merger (Katz and Kahn 1978:78–81). These forms of organizational growth have different repercussions for organizational change.

Increases in unit size or in the number of parallel units are possible without any basic modification or restructuring of the organizaiton. For example, unit size is increased by adding clerks or direct service staff without changing the functions and roles performed. Similarly, the establishment of a branch office need require no structural change.

Organizational growth through an increase in differentiation and specialization involves more basic change, because it requires the performance of new functions and tasks, as well as the use of new technologies. Not only does the division of labor change, but the administrative structure must also change, in order to coordinate and integrate the new specialties. Thus such specializations as caseload management require changes in both staff roles and coordination mechanisms (R. Neugeboren 1976). Given the recent rise and evolution of numerous areas of specialization in the human services, this source of growth and change will be an important one.

The fourth type of organizational growth—mergers—also requires structural change. The joining of two organizations necessitates creation of new authority and role structures. Whereas in the 1960s the human service field expanded by adding new programs, the resource scarcity of the 1970s and 1980s has led to the merger of agencies in order to conserve resources. The inflationary squeeze has prompted the United Way of America to recommend that any agency with an annual budget of less than $100,000 be considered for merger (Long 1975:6–7) Although economic pressures may be the primary stimulus for mergers, the underlying agenda "involved job tenure, working relations, leadership program development and a host of other personal and organizational issues [Blumberg and Wiener 1971:89]."

The assumption that the merger of two organizations into a larger unit will result in greater cost efficiency and/or effectiveness remains to be proven. Economics of scale have been the basis for centralization of organizational units. Furthermore, as has been noted, there is currently a movement to increase client access to human services, for example, through regionalization and the establishment of locally based operations. Consolidations, however, may result in reduced client access; the evidence thus far is unclear. In general, the research findings have been mixed. Findings indicate only minimal savings through reductions in personnel costs, considerable expenditure of time on planning and implementation, and an adverse impact on staff morale (Rambeck 1976:37). However, it has also been found that the increased size, scope, and power of agencies created from mergers enabled them to compete more successfully for resources (Sieverts 1972:51). The expansion in the variety of services available may result in a more effective service delivery. Thus, the merger of an institutional program with a community-based child welfare service permitted more flexibility and expedited coordination in moving children back and forth between the community and the source of institutional care.

A final possible negative consequence of mergers relates to reduction in competition. In the human services, as in industry, the market mechanism (A. Kahn 1979:145-146), which makes possible consumer choice, may be undercut by mergers. The impetus for some mergers is avoidance of duplication of services. However, this duplication and overlapping of services does provide consumers with some choice, assuming that the services offered are not identical. That is, clients have an opportunity to compare and evaluate service and select those which they feel are most relevant for their particular needs. In short, comprehensive human service could provide a "supermarket" of products, representing an expansion of choices or a consolidation of service with a reduction in options (see Chapter 12).

Benefits of Change

Throughout this discussion of organizational change it has been suggested that change in activities does not in itself necessarily yield positive outcomes for the consumers of human service programs. This is in contrast to the belief, which was particularly evident during the 1960s, that change always has beneficial effects and hence is inherently desirable. The consequences of change must be constantly scrutinized to be certain that the change has beneficial effects for clients (Resnick and Patti 1980:6). Some of the changes that have been instituted have been found to have harmful consequences (e.g., deinstitutionalization). Mergers may result in cost–benefit ratios that ultimately have not worked for client welfare.

INDIVIDUAL VERSUS ORGANIZATIONAL CHANGE

As discussed in Chapter 4 on organizational structure, the relationship between individual change and organizational change is basic, but not fully understood. Must people be changed in order to change policies? If policy is changed will this cause people to change?

In the literature on organizational change there has been considerable emphasis on changing people as a strategy for changing systems. The argument for this individual change strategy is that since organizations are made up of people we can change an organization by changing its members. As indicated earlier, this argument has been challenged on the grounds that it is based on a "psychological fallacy" which "ignores the situational factors that shape behavior." This failure to take situational factors into account is illustrated by human relations training programs that emphasize openness and trust as a strategy for gaining cooperation and support for change. When a person who is involved in such a training program returns to the organizational situation where competition and conflict prevail, he or she finds it difficult to function in this "jungle" by using the newly acquired human relations skills. Thus, the person may have been changed but the situation has not.

This lack of transferability of the training to the job situation has been addressed by structuring training in "family groups." That is, training involves the entire organizational unit (e.g., a supervisory unit may constitute a sensitivity training group). However, such efforts have the same problem as efforts directed at the individual: the organizational unit that has had the training has to cope with the larger system which has not. This dilemma is dramatically illustrated in the case "From Psychological Work to Social Work" where the change in a county child welfare office (e.g., recruitment of social care staff) was undermined by the larger state civil service structure whose examinations stressed rehabilitation.

Individual Change Strategies

Behavior Change Strategies

The first kind of individual change strategy, behavior change, may in fact be pursued in two ways—either by trying to change attitudes that affect behavior or by trying to change the behavior itself.

Attitude Change. Attitude change strategies involve information giving, training, and counseling. These strategies are concerned with *persuading* individuals that the desired change will be beneficial to them, to the organ-

ization, and ultimately to the client. Information giving is a strategy that assumes that the resistance to change is based on a lack of knowledge as to
the purpose of the change—and not, for example, on perceived threat to
beliefs or self-interest.

Training as a basic strategy for achieving organizational change has received much attention. Human relations experts have advocated the use of
T groups and of other forms of peer group interaction as an effective strategy
for achieving organizational change through change of staff attitudes and
perceptions. Staff development and training departments have been established and claim expertise in "organizational development" and change. Despite the attention and claims, the use of a training strategy to achieve change
may run into a number of difficulties. In a public welfare agency, for example,
efforts to train staff in a task-centered approach to casework had a negative
outcome; the staff simply resisted the training, even though the approach
was highly relevant to the work they were doing (Reid and Beard 1980:81).
The limitations of the training strategy relate, in part, to where in the organization this function is being performed. If training is performed in the maintenance subsystem (see Chapter 5), then the general thrust of this subsystem
toward stability will counter organizational change purposes.

The use of psychological techniques such as counseling and psychotherapy is limited in that, although this fact is not always recognized, personality
change requires extensive investment of time and resources. A more basic
limitation, alluded to earlier, is that such techniques do not affect the situation
to which the individual must return. The gains achieved through a therapeutic
relationship are not easily transferred to the organizational situation.

Behavior Change. An alternative strategy to modifying behavior by first
changing attitudes is to change behavior directly. This behavior change strategy is based on the assumption that changing a person's situation will modify
that person's attitudes. Use of this strategy requires that the leadership have
the power to mandate a change in staff activities. Thus, staff of mental health
centers who served only neurotics could be required to serve chronic schizophrenics. When confronted with day-to-day problems of serving this new
population, the staff will, in order to adapt, change their attitudes and develop
the appropriate techniques and skills. A behavior change strategy was successfully used in a poverty program: In order to adapt to changed job requirements, clinically oriented social workers had to change their practices
and attitudes to those of social care (B. Neugeboren 1970b).

Replacement Strategy

The second kind of individual change strategy is the replacement strategy.
This strategy assumes that changing individual attitudes and behavior is very
difficult and that the only real option, therefore, is to replace the individual

who will resist changes with one who—for ideological reasons, as well as from self-interest—will support them. The axiom that "a new broom sweeps clean" suggests that in order for new leadership to be able to implement changes, it must replace the "old guard" with new personnel who can be expected to be loyal and supportive of the change efforts.

A potential limitation of the replacement strategy involves selection of new personnel. Personnel selection as a routinized procedure may have a very conservative thrust (see Chapter 5, "Subsystems"): The usual procedure is to bring in personnel who will support the existing system. Therefore, it is critical that those responsible for changing the system gain control over this "gatekeeper" function (see case "From Psychological Work to Social Work").

Another problem with the strategy is, of course, that it is difficult to terminate employees. Although there are alternatives to direct dismissal, such as lateral transfers (Peter and Hull 1969) or demotions, the constraints on unilateral job changes are considerable. For example, civil service regulations and union contracts both limit the power of administrators to reassign or dismiss employees. However, the high turnover rates in many human service agencies (e.g., public welfare agencies) provide opportunity for replacement (see case "From Psycholgical to Social Work".) Although the official power to replace individuals may be limited, the unofficial power to pressure individuals to "move on" is substantial. Superiors can make the work life of individuals very stressful by strictly monitoring their work and increasing the job expectations. Even with protections offered by employee grievance machinery, the subordinate is still basically powerless to counteract this type of pressure. This successful use of pressure is illustrated in the case "From Psychological Work to Social Work," where the manager of administrative support operations decided to retire early, after being pressured by the administrator to fulfill the requirements of his position.

As indicated, the replacement strategy of dismissal of employees is constrained by civil service systems, union contracts, and personnel policies. However, most human service agencies do provide for dismissal on the basis of unsatisfactory performance. In general, such provisions are not made use of, because of the time and skill required to use them effectively. In most disciplinary actions the superior has to follow strict due process procedures to insure that the employee is not the victim of arbitrary and discriminatory action. Basic preconditions for disciplinary action include the clear specification of what is expected of the employee and the provision of adequate resources to enable the job to be done. Once performance expectations are clearly specified, then it is the responsibility of the supervisor to monitor and *document* whether these standards are being met. Many human service supervisors find this documenting task very time consuming and also somewhat alien to their definition of their role. However, because the replacement strategy is potentially very important for overcoming resistance to organizational innovation, it is crucial that supervisors and administrators master the skills that are involved in utilizing provisions for the dismissal of employees (M. Austin 1981:186–190).

Organizational Change Strategies

Definition

The target of organizational change strategies is the *actual* organizational structure (see Chapter 4). This may include the role structure (functions and tasks performed by staff), reward structure (system for rewards and sanctions), communication structure (information access), authority structure (distribution of power), and interorganizational relationship structure (cooperation versus conflict).

Studies of Organizational Change

Studies of organizational change have focused on the effects of modifying three structural variables: authority structure, reward structure, and role structure (Katz and Kahn 1978:682–710). When moves from centralized to decentralized systems changed authority structure by increasing the participation of lower-level employees, the result was consistently a positive change in staff productivity and satisfaction. When the reward structure was changed, generally by increasing economic rewards, the result was again greater staff productivity and satisfaction. Changes of role structure, which involved job enlargement and enrichment, also produced positive results. Although these findings were for industrial organizations, they are probably applicable to human service agencies as well.

A survey of the relative impact of individual and organizational change strategies suggests that the "direct manipulation of organizational [structural] variables is a more powerful approach to producing enduring systemic change [Katz and Kahn 1978:711]." The importance of organizational change strategies is clearly evidenced in the cases presented here. The case "From Psychological Work to Social Work" involved changes in the role, reward, authority, and interorganizational relationship structures. In contrast the case "Mental Health Rules and Regulations" the state agency was unable to influence directly the organizational structures of community mental health centers, as these centers were not under its direct supervision.

CONDITIONS CONDUCIVE TO ORGANIZATIONAL CHANGE

Seven organizational characteristics have been found to be associated with organizational innovation: Complexity, decentralization, formalization, stratification, production, efficiency, and job satisfaction (Hage and Aiken 1970:30–55).

Complexity

Degree of complexity is measured by the number of different occupations or specialties in an organization, as well as by the extensiveness of training and the intricacy of the tasks performed. In general, it has been found that more complex organizations have a greater potential for innovation than less complex organizations (Hage and Aiken 1970:32–38).

This association of diversity in staff skills and background and potential for organizational change is understandable in terms of the stimulation that different points of view can offer. Human service agencies that consist of a single discipline may provide an environment where similar ideologies reinforce and justify continuing the existing ways of doing things. Interdisciplinary arrangements within agencies such as teamwork, may be needed to avoid the provincialism of organizations dominated by one discipline (Zaltman, Dunca, and Holbech 1973:135). Human service agencies that utilize a variety of specialties may be firm ground for innovation. It has been suggested, however, that although the presence of different points of view make *initiation* of change easier, it may make *implementation* of change more difficult (Zaltman *et al.* 1973:135). Therefore, mechanisms for integration and negotiation of differences between specialties are probably required in the implementation phase of organizational change.

Decentralization

Decentralization is defined as a delegation of power downward and a high degree of staff participation in decision making. The evidence suggests that the greater the delegation of power and authority to lower levels, the greater the rate of program change (Hage and Aiken 1970:38). One explanation for this lies in the fact that as most change will impact on the organization's power structure, a centralized organization will tend to block innovation in order to maintain its authority and control. Furthermore, a decentralized organization facilitates expression of different points of view from low levels, which encourages diffusion of ideas and results in change. Centralized hierarchical structures, in contrast, restrict communications and consequently hinder feedback and ideas for change (Zaltman *et al.* 1973:143). Decentralized structures permit greater participation in decision making, which has itself been found to correlate positively with innovation.

As with complexity, the situation changes somewhat when we consider the implementation, as opposed to initiation, phase of change. Although centralization may be dysfunctional for initiation of change, it may be functional for implementation (Zaltman *et al.* 1973:145). The reason for this is that implementation requires coordination and control to reduce conflict and disagreement among staff.

Formalization

Formalization is the extent to which written rules and regulations prescribe what is required by personnel. It has been found that greater formalization results in lower rates of program change. The reason is that highly structured jobs discourage initiative because they emphasize uniformity. Less specific rules provide greater opportunity for individuals to exercise discretion. Again, the effect of formalization may vary depending on the stage of the change process. Although *low* formalization may facilitate initiation of change, *high* formalization may be necessary at the *implementation* stages when specific rules and regulations are required to avoid role conflict and role ambiguity (Zaltman *et al.* 1973:140).

Stratification

Stratification refers to the extent to which rewards—both utilitarian (money) and symbolic (prestige)—are equitably distributed. The greater the stratification, the greater the disparity in allocation of rewards between upper and lower levels and the greater the difficulty in upward mobility.

A high degree of stratification has also been found to correlate with low rates of program change (Hage and Aiken 1970:45). The reason for this is that systems that are based on privilege will thwart change efforts, in order to preserve the status quo which favors those in power. A lack of fairness in reward systems is probably one of the most dysfunctional aspects of organizational life. If rewards are based on criteria other than merit, then a motivational basis for effectiveness is destroyed. It is not difficult to understand why this kind of environment constrains innovation and change.

Production

This variable refers to the emphasis on quantity rather than quality of work. It has been found that the higher the volume of production, the lower the rate of change (Hage and Aiken 1970:49). The explanation for this is that as innovation requires temporary interruption of work, it does not fit with an emphasis on quantitative productivity. A qualitative emphasis, in contrast, tends to be associated more with critical evaluative criteria, which can be an impetus for change.

Efficiency

Efficiency is defined as stress on cost reduction and conservation of resources. The greater degree of efficiency, the lower the rate of change (Hage and Aiken 1970:51). Because innovation is costly, it may not be encouraged in an organization that is concerned primarily with efficiency. This finding has particular relevance to the human service field, in view of the current emphasis on cost containment and the use of experts in fiscal management. Administrators should keep in mind the potentially dysfunctional consequences of the emphasis on short-term fiscal concerns.

Job Satisfaction

It has been found that the higher the level of job satisfaction and morale, the greater the program change (Hage and Aiken 1970:53). People who are satisfied with their jobs are more committed to the organization and therefore more receptive to improving the program. Here again, the effect of this factor may be different for the initiation and implementation phases of change. Satisfied employees are the more receptive to new ideas, but the change that is implemented may cause disruption and strain, leading to lower job satisfaction.

Summary

The discussion of organizational conditions that are conducive to change suggests that different strategies may be needed for the initiation versus implementation phases of change. Initiation of change may require lower levels of centralization, formalization, stratification, efficiency, and production and higher levels of complexity and job satisfaction. The fact that implementation of change requires many of the opposite characteristics poses an apparent dilemma. The answer may lie in the development of ad hoc structures (e.g., task forces) that are free to formulate new ideas and proposals, which are then fed into the more structured system. To some extent, the dilemma remains, however, as the nature of the existing structure will still have an influence on innovation.

The discussion of organizational conditions conducive to innovation was based almost entirely on research that examined agencies in the human service field. All of the variables discussed pose potentially important considerations for human service administrators in their efforts to introduce organizational innovation and change.

CONSENSUS VERSUS POWER TACTICS FOR ORGANIZATIONAL CHANGE

Implicit throughout the preceding discussion was the question of when achieving consensus is possible and desirable and when power and authority are needed to insure that change will occur. It was evident that staff participation and consensus were functional during the initiation stages, whereas control and structure were useful in the implementation stage. In this section we will look directly at power and consensus—the two tactics for accomplishing organizational change (Walton 1969).

Power Tactics

Power is defined here as the ability to obtain the nonvoluntary compliance of organizational members. Power tactics are based on the assumption that change necessarily involves conflict, which is resolvable only through domination and submission. Conditions in which one group is dependent on another for resources, legitimacy, etc., allow the use of power tactics.

The use of a power strategy is often associated with *rapid* organizational change. The ability to quickly institute a change by edict from the top avoids the problem of the opposition mobilizing and coalescing against the change. This "fait accompli" tactic is common in hierarchical systems where decisions are made at the upper levels. This unilateral use of authority may be perceived as legitimate or illegitimate, depending on the willingness of subordinates to accept the right of the upper levels to make decisions. The power strategy is advocated by those who favor the structuralist model of management, as it conforms with their belief that conflict is inevitable.

Consensus Tactics

Consensus tactics are based on the assumption that it is possible and necessary to convince participants that the change proposed is worthwhile. Consensus tactics allow for compromise, if necessary, and in general stress the development of trust and the acceptance of mutual dependence. Intrinsic to this tactic is the use of communication to facilitate understanding of shared beliefs, goals, and interests. Openness and honesty are valued as facilitating communication and development of rapport. The human relations school of management has emphasized the value of consensus tactics on the grounds that conflict can be avoided through frank discussion and differences resolved through compromise. A fact that proponents of this tactic overlook is that in order to compromise there has to be equality between the parties involved. If the power of the people or groups involved is not equal, then the more powerful side can dominate the less powerful.

Combination of Power and Consensus Tactics

As indicated earlier, power and consensus tactics may be appropriate at different stages of the organizational change process. Participatory tactics are more appropriate at the initiation stage and power tactics at the implementation stage. The dilemma here is, of course, that these two sets of tactics are incompatible. Use of coercion alienates (Etzioni 1964:60) and will tend to discourage openness and trust. One way of dealing with this dilemma is to have two different leaders use these tactics. The combination of instrumental and expressive leadership styles has been found to be functional, and usually the styles are associated with different people within the organization (see Chapter 9). In small group processes (Bales 1958) change processes fluctuate from one emphasis to the other depending on whether the need of the group is for support or task accomplishment. This fluctuation probably occurs in organizations as well.

SUMMARY

This chapter on organizational change discussed the alternative strategies of changing the individual versus the organization, as well as the basic opportunities and constraints on organizational innovation. The various organizational conditions conducive to change and tactics associated with change were also reviewed. Organizational change was viewed as being possible on all levels of the organization, as long as there existed an understanding of the potential areas of movement within a particular system. In short, change is an ongoing phenomenon in all organizations and it is the responsibility of the human service professional to capitalize on this potential in order to maximize client benefits.

APPLICATION OF CONCEPTS ON ORGANIZATIONAL CHANGE TO CASE "MENTAL HEALTH RULES AND REGULATIONS"

In the case "Mental Health Rules and Regulations," the State Mental Health Department established a set of new rules and regulations, with the aim of influencing community mental health agencies to give more service to the chronically mentally ill. The regulations attempted to shift the goals of these local services from rehabilitation to social care, which was assumed to be more appropriate for the chronic population. As indicated in the case, the resistance to this policy change was very great. The *source of this resistance* lay in a combination of ideological, political, technological, and cognitive factors.

The *ideological basis of the resistance* was evident in the defense of the medical model as the preferred treatment for the mentally disturbed. The rules and regulations had come out quite directly in favor of a social deviancy model, which the mental health agencies viewed as completely contrary to the medical or disease models. The regulations' stress on normalization and levels of functioning, rather than on diagnosis of pathology, added further fuel to the ideological fire.

The *political basis of the resistance* to the new policy was related to the fear that the economic viability of community programs would be jeopardized by the inclusion of the chronics. Perceived *self-interest* held that this new selective approach, with priority given to the severely mentally ill, would threaten service to the less ill, who came from the middle-class population and who could help pay for the service received. Therefore, the basic legitimacy of the community programs was threatened by the policy change.

Resistance based on threat to *self-interest* was also evident in the fear that the rules and regulations would reduce local control over the programs. The detailed specifications of the qualifications required of service providers and the types of service deemed appropriate was viewed by these community mental health agencies as a direct threat to their autonomy. In addition, there was concern that the new standards would entail further administrative costs for the local programs.

The *technological basis of the resistance* to the new rules and regulations was related to the fact that existing treatment technologies were inappropriate for service to the chronically mentally ill. The new goal required, not traditional therapeutic modalities such as individual and group psychotherapy or drug treatment, but rather, educational-based approaches such as teaching the patients the skills of daily living (shopping, budgeting, self-care, using public transportation, etc.). The psychiatrists, psychologists, and social workers at the community agencies had invested much time and energy in developing their therapeutic skills and would find it extremely difficult to replace them with techniques that they were not familiar with or did not consider legitimate.

Another basis for the resistance to the new rules and regulations was probably the *lack of knowledge* on the part of workers at the community mental health agencies. Such sociological principles as normalization and social deviancy would probably be unfamiliar and alien to psychiatrists, psychologists, and social workers. These medically oriented personnel might also have difficulty with the concept of a "unified mental health system" and the stress on community support systems.

In examining this effort at major system change, we need to determine what *opportunities* were available *to facilitate this change*. One essential precondition for major change is *external pressure*. In this case situation pressure favoring change existed but was limited. The mandate for this change came from a higher administrative authority (the governor), and deinstitutionalization may have led to some pressure from the community for more adequate care for ex-patients. However, the groups favoring the change were insignificant in number compared to the many agencies and professional groups that opposed it. Although legislative support was initially present, it was uncertain whether it would hold in the long run, given the strong political base of the opposition.

In addition to external pressure, there are opportunities for change associated with *natural change* processes. There were probably some community-based programs that were in the process of developing programs for the chronically mentally ill. Programs for the severely physically handicapped and for the mentally retarded which have been involved in skill training and community support services, have been expanding to include the mentally ill. Any of these programs could be used to demonstrate the feasibility of this new approach to service to the chronically ill.

In an analysis of policy change, it is useful to determine what *type of change* is involved. Is it a *goal and/or procedural change?*

It is evident that this new policy was directed at a *change in goals* for community mental health programs, which were to *add the new goals* of social care. In the state hospitals there was a *shift in priorities* from social control to social care, perhaps as a result of *goal clarification.* The traditional state hospital programs assume that hospitalization is the desirable means for achieving the goal of successful community adjustment. Goal clarification might have led to the conclusion that goal displacement had occurred, that is, that hospitalization had become the end, displacing the intended goal of return to the community. Successful goal clarification here might also determine a more appropriate means for achieving the desired goal of successful community adjustment.

A change in the *strategies for achieving organizational goals* is termed *procedural change.* Procedural change can involve modification in strategies for external relations, internal organizational arrangements, and methods for assessing organizational progress.

The goal of normalization in community living for the chronically mentally ill requires a change in the *external relations* of the hospitals and community programs, so that an *open system* strategy can be implemented. That is, because these clients require a multiplicity of community support services, the hospitals and community programs serving them must have close working relationships with other community agencies. This necessitates a philosophy that views interagency collaboration and cooperation as desirable and legitimate. (In contrast, the traditional state hospital and community clinical services can operate with *closed system* strategies, as they assume that they can provide all of the necessary services.)

The rules and regulations also had impact on the strategies for *internal* operations of the community mental health programs. As indicated previously, service for the chronically disabled requires technologies that stress environment- rather than people-changing techniques. To adopt these technologies, the centers would need to obtain caseworkers, supervisors, and administrators with the appropriate skills and orientation. New reward systems would have to be developed to insure proper job performance of staff. This change in the community programs from rehabilitation to social care would therefore affect the role, reward, authority, and communication structures.

In addition to change in structure, the rules and regulations also affect the *strategies for assessing organizational progress*, with a shift to more objective procedures. It is noted in the case that the new standards required detailed monitoring of agency performance. Specific criteria defining the target population gave the state department the basis for determining in an objective manner whether the community agencies were fulfilling the requirements. For example, the target population was defined as persons who had previously been hospitalized in a mental institution. This objective strategy for organizational assessment was in sharp contrast with the prior system of evaluation based on the *self-fulfilling prophecy*—that is, whether the organization is busy serving clients.

In addition to understanding the types of change it is important to determine the *degree of organizational change*. A behavioral definition of organizational change would evaluate the extent to which the activities of staff are modified. In the case situation, given the changes that would be required in staff roles vis-à-vis both clients and other human service agents, the *intention* of the regulations is to effect a major change in the daily activities and functions performed by the staff. If this intention were to be realized, the organizational change would be categorized as *policy formulation—major structural change*. To show that this had in fact occurred, one would need empirical data indicating that staff had significantly modified their daily activities (e.g., data showing an increase in the proportion of staff *time* devoted to serving chronics). In the case situation, *demonstration* programs were successful in enabling the chronically mentally ill to adjust to living in the community. However, these programs were a very small proportion of the total activity of the mental health system in the state.

The fact that a change occurs does not tell us whether it was successful in terms of *client benefit*. Patients may be able to stay out of hospitals, but this in itself is not evidence of successful functioning in the community. Therefore, the consequences of the change need to be evaluated in terms of the change's ultimate purpose—consumer benefit.

Strategies to achieve change can focus either on changing people or on changing policies. The rules and regulations were directed at changing written policies and procedures. Specifically, they modified the rules on role expectations in terms of the target population to be served. Therefore, the basic strategy was to directly change the *behavior* of the staff by changing policy. The *implementation* of the change also included efforts to change *attitudes*, through personal persuasion directed at both professional and state legislators.

Various *organizational conditions* have been associated with the successful *initiation* and *implementation* of change. In general, the appropriate conditions for initiating change are those associated with nonbureaucratic structures. Although the case does not contain information on the structures of the mental health agencies, the state hospitals were probably more highly bureaucratized than the community programs, which in general tend to be small in size. If so, other things being equal, *initiation* of change should be more feasible in the community programs than in the hospitals. However, as the opposite organizational conditions are conducive to *implementation* of change, this phase should be more readily achievable in the hospitals. It should be kept in mind that these principles on the organizational conditions conducive to change were derived from studies of innovation within rather than across systems. Thus, the principles might not be fully applicable in case of the community agencies, which were not under the direct authority of the state department, but they should apply in the case of the hospitals, which were under direct control. In fact, we see that in the hospitals, bureaucratic structure may have constrained the *initiation* of change.

The final concepts to be applied to this case concern the kinds of *tactics appropriate to achieving organizational change—consensus versus power.* As already noted, the state department by issuing the rules and regulations used a *power* tactic to initiate the change. Some of the critics complained about the lack of participation of provider groups in the formulation of the new regulations. This use of power may have been necessary, as resistance in this case would inevitably be based on factors that could not be negotiated (ideology) and hence change had to be initiated quickly to avoid mobilization of the opposition. However, the change having been initiated, consensus tactics could then be introduced in the implementation phase.

INTERORGANIZATIONAL RELATIONS

OUTLINE

ISSUES

As resources become increasingly scarce, human service organizations are compelled to confront a long-standing problem—the lack of coordination among agencies (Hasenfeld 1983:50). When resources are abundant, there is little pressure to deal with such problems as duplication, fragmentation, and overlapping programs. Economic scarcity, however, requires agencies to find ways of maximizing resources. One such way is to work more cooperatively to achieve better coordination with other agencies. The question arises as to why coordination has not been successful in the past. What are the barriers to interagency coordination? What might the costs and benefits be?

In the human service field the difficulties in achieving interagency collaboration are not only long-standing, but also pervasive and problematic. In public welfare, for example, there has been a lack of coordination between child welfare and public assistance. In the criminal justice system, serious problems have resulted from the inability to coordinate probation, institutional corrections, and parole. The mentally ill have suffered because of a lack of coordination between community mental health centers and the state mental hospitals. Why haven't these agencies been able to work out cooperative arrangements to maximize service to the various consumer groups?

Policymakers have begun to address this problem and are advocating various comprehensive models for service coordination and integration. Evaluation of actual efforts to achieve coordination point to continued difficulties (D. Austin 1978:20–28). Turf protectiveness, ideological differences, and funding sources that facilitate specialized rather than integrated programs are some of the reasons given for the inability of agencies to work together (Morris and Lescohier 1978:21–50).

The recent focus on interorganizational cooperation has pointed up several issues. These issues will be discussed here in conjunction with the following questions: (*a*) Is interorganizational coordination desirable? (*b*) Can interorganization coordination be forced?

Is Interorganizational Coordination Desirable?

If overlapping and duplication of human service programs can be avoided by more coordination among agencies, then it would seem inherently desirable to work toward more coordination. Before accepting this conclusion, however, we must look more closely at two assumptions made, which may not be valid, namely, the assumptions that programs that are identical result in duplication and that competition among agencies is undesirable.

The first assumption fails to take into account the fact that two similar human service programs may have very different goals. A child welfare agency may have a rehabilitation goal and a public assistance agency a social care goal. Coordination of these two agencies may result in one or the other goal being displaced. Similarly, one community mental health service may stress treatment of neurotics while another may focus on care of the chronically ill. Attempting to coordinate these different types of agencies may make it difficult for them to accomplish their different purposes. Only if their goals are similar will coordination be functional. The exchange model presented in what follows assumes that coordination between agencies is *feasible* only if their goals are shared.

The assumption that competition among human service agencies is undesirable can be argued against on the grounds that consumer choice is desirable. If the market mechanism is valid in the human service sector, then it is desirable that human service agencies compete for consumers. This competition would give consumers more equality in their relations with agencies, and such equality is considered beneficial for service outcome (Hasenfeld and English 1974:469). The charge that agency competition and resulting service duplication is inefficient runs counter to the philosophy that a free market will produce the most economical result.

Interagency coordination *can* result in more efficient and effective programs if the coordinating agencies provide complementary services, so that resource exchange is feasible. The model of interorganizational coordination presented in what follows assumes that cooperation requires an interdependence based on shared goals and the exchange of mutually needed resources.

Can Interorganizational Coordination Be Forced?

The issue of whether interorganizational coordination can be forced has come to the forefront as pressures for service integration have increased. Funding authorities, in particular, are pushing for more "comprehensive" and integrated service delivery models.

Poor coordination is evident not only among human service agencies but also intraorganizationally. Administrators are frequently unable to achieve interdepartmental cooperation and integration, even when they ostensibly have the power and authority to do so. Often the problem is that certain subunits in the organization have developed so much power that they have become somewhat autonomous. Consequently, competition and conflict are at least as common within organizations as between autonomous agencies. The exchange model presented here assumes that defensiveness over organizational territoriality can be moderated by the inducements of resources not otherwise available. It assumes, therefore, that *voluntary participation* is a prerequisite for successful interorganizational cooperation and coordination. With self-interest as the motivating force, an agency will relinquish some of its autonomy in order to obtain the resources needed to achieve its goals.

A MODEL FOR INTERORGANIZATIONAL COORDINATION

Interorganizational Coordination—Definition

Interorganizational coordination is defined as the *voluntary* exchange between two or more *autonomous* agencies of *complementary resources* needed to achieve *shared goals* (Reid 1965:359).

Although coordination as defined here has been relatively infrequent; there is ample evidence of regularized patterns of interaction among human service organizations. Thus an organization has an "organizational set": the network of organizations with which it interacts (Lauffer *et al.* 1977:47–54). Coordination as used here is a more specific type of collaboration, requiring the four conditions specified by Reid (1965) in the definition, namely, (*a*) voluntary participation, (*b*) agency autonomy, (*c*) shared goals, and (*d*) complementary resources.

Voluntary Participation

Voluntary participation, the first condition for interagency coordination, requires that human service organizations have the option of *not* engaging in a cooperative arrangement. Coordination that is mandated, for example, under a single administrative authority, would not meet this criterion of voluntary participation. It should be noted that application of this criterion is not always straightforward. For example, if funding authorities require interagency coordination, does compliance with this requirement constitute voluntary participation? As organizations have options in applying for grants, it is assumed that even though there is some economic pressure, the agency is participating on a voluntary basis. (Although, as noted earlier, the problems of internal coordination are in many ways similar to those of interorganizational coordination, internal coordination does not meet this criterion of voluntary participation.)

Agency Autonomy

The second condition for interorganizational coordination is that of *agency autonomy*. Autonomous agencies are separate from and independent of the agencies with which they wish to coordinate. They are legally accountable to an authority that is different and distinct from the other organizations. Voluntary agencies (e.g., YWCA) under the authority of a board of directors are incorporated as autonomous organizations. Human service agencies in the various levels of government (e.g., county and state) are considered autonomous because they are under independent, legally recognized authorities. Even though a state-level agency may provide a substantial amount of funds for a county-level agency, the agencies are still under different legal authorities and, therefore, autonomous. Some of the difficulties in coordination between state- and county-level agencies may stem from a failure on the part of the state agency to recognize the autonomous nature of the county agency.

Shared Goals

Shared goals, the third condition for interagency collaboration, refers specifically to *perceived* goals, which may or may not be the official or operative goals. If members of two agencies *believe* that their agencies' goals are different, then interagency collaboration will be difficult, even if the goals are in fact similar. In general, if an organization has disparate official and operative goals (see Chapter 2), it will be unable to establish lasting interagency agreements. For example, if a child welfare agency's official goal is care and its operative goal is rehabilitation, then the agency will find it difficult to implement an agreement with a public welfare agency whose operative goal is care. Presumably, the situation would not even arise if the agencies shared operative goals but differed in official goals. As official goals are the basis for agency legitimation and support, they are also the basis for the *initiation* of cooperative efforts among human service organizations. It is the actual *implementation* that depends on the extent to which operative goals are shared.

Sharing of goals implies not only goal similarity but also goal interdependence—the situation in which each agency, in accomplishing its own goals, facilitates goal accomplishment of the other agency. The Work Incentive Program can be used to illustrate simultaneously goal interdependence and lack of goal interdependence. In New Jersey the Work Incentive Program (WIN) involved the collaboration of the United States Department of Labor, the state child welfare agency, and the county welfare board. The overall purpose of WIN was to enable low-income women with children to obtain job training and subsequent employment. In order to complete their training, the women needed both day care aid and financial assistance, which were provided by state child welfare and county welfare respectively. The Department of Labor's goal of increasing employment complemented the goal of the public assistance agency, which was to help low-income persons to become economically self-sufficient. The third collaborator, however, did not have such a complementary goal.

Traditionally, the goal of the child welfare agency has been to enhance the normal development of children, usually by providing a "normal" home environment, which includes good parental care. Hence, the day care that was needed to allow the mother to obtain training and employment might have been perceived by child welfare staff as conflicting with the need of children for a normal home environment. Therefore, the goals of the child welfare agency may be not only not shared but acutally in conflict with the goals of the other two agencies. It is of interest to note that recent developments in New Jersey have recognized the lack of shared goals between child welfare and public assistance with shifting of the auspices of the WIN program from child welfare to the public assistance agencies.

In general, child welfare and public assistance agencies exemplify the consequences of a lack of shared goals. Traditionally, child welfare has focused on people-changing or rehabilitative goals, whereas public welfare has stressed concrete services or social care. The inability of these two types of organizations to develop cooperative programs even though they serve the same clientele is attributable at least in part to the difference in their goals.

The lack of coordination between mental hospitals and mental health centers is another case in point. Mental hospitals have had goals that are a combination of social care and social control. Mental health centers have been primarily involved in rehabilitation. With deinstitutionalization, community mental health centers are being pressured to serve the chronically mentally ill. Hospitals and community centers have had difficulty developing the collaborative working relations needed to serve this population, because their goals are so distinctly different (see case "Mental Health Rules and Regulations").

Resource Exchange

The fourth condition for interagency coordination, the *exchange of complementary resources*, underscores the fact that coordination is based on a system of *exchange*. Resource exchange can involve such resources as personnel, information, funds, legitimation, equipment, office quarters, etc. The need for resources possessed by some other organization is a key element of interdependence necessary for interorganizational coordination. It is probably the most critical factor in influencing a human service agency to consider cooperating with another organization.

The tendency to view clients' problems in more comprehensive terms has increased awareness of the need for resource exchange. In the past, when the problems of clients were segmented, each agency could supply its particular service, independent of those offered by other human service organizations. The understanding of social problems as a *syndrome* of interrelated needs (health, housing, education, economic, legal, etc.) compels the human service organization to recognize that coordinated efforts are required.

The movement of deinstitutionalization has also served to increase the importance of resource exchange. Such groups as the mentally ill, mentally retarded, ex-offenders, physically handicapped, and elderly all require a variety of services in order to function in the community. The schizophrenic discharged from a mental hospital requires housing, health care, training in skills needed for daily living, mental health service, and social support services. Community support networks, both formal and informal, are being advocated for these chronically disabled populations (Stein 1979). Case management programs are evolving, with one agency assuming responsibility for coordinating the large variety of services needed by clients. However, the effectiveness of this coordination often depends on the ability of an individual's case manager to elicit cooperation. This *ad hoc case coordination* (see discussion in what follows) has been the traditional method used by practitioners.

As indicated, exchange of resources depends on the perceived need for resources possessed by other agencies. The more specialized a human service organization is, the less it needs resources from other agencies. Mental health centers specializing in psychotherapy will not need resources other than its treatment staff. At the other extreme, self-sufficiency is possible in large multifunctional agencies, which have a wide range of services under one roof (e.g., general hospitals). In between these two extremes, however, agencies are generally not self-sufficient and hence can potentially benefit from resource exchange and coordination.

Impetus for greater coordination comes also from the new economic pressures, which have motivated human service agencies to seek resources elsewhere in the community. Despite the widespread belief that community resources are being fully utilized, there is evidence of untapped resources and programs (B. Neugeboren 1979:180). Agencies have found that locating resources is in itself a time-consuming task, requiring specialized skill. As a result, such functions as resource coordination are being developed and centralized data banks are being established to coordinate and disseminate information on what resources are available and how to obtain them (R. Neugeboren 1976).

LEVELS OF COORDINATION

As the preceding discussion implied, agencies may be coordinated to greater or lesser extents. There are three main levels of coordination: ad hoc case coordination, systematic case coordination, and program coordination

(Reid 1965:358). The three levels of coordination are characterized in terms of the extensiveness of the exchange, which also has implications for the amount of resources involved and the extent of the impact on daily operations. As has been noted repeatedly, one of the reasons that interagency coordination is difficult to achieve is that it is perceived as threatening agency autonomy (turf). Coordination can also require changes in activities of staff and diminish *their* autonomous functioning. Therefore, one of the important differences among the three levels of coordination is that they have different degrees of impact on both agency and staff autonomy.

Ad Hoc Case Coordination

As mentioned earlier, ad hoc case coordination refers to the traditional way in which individual practitioners from different agencies share information when their cases overlap (Mathiesen 1971). This type of coordination depends on the direct service staff member's interest in coordination, as well as on the contacts he or she has with other agencies. As this is an individually determined activity, staff members tend to keep their information on community resources private and use it only for their own clients.

The development of community resource data banks in agencies was motivated by the inequities and inefficiencies associated with ad hoc case coordination. This formalized approach to assessing the availability of community resources provides a more comprehensive, uniform, and equitable basis for service. Different staff members are assigned particular resource areas (e.g., housing, health, mental health, legal) and develop a comprehensive information system on the services available in that area and, even more important, on how one can obtain these services for the consumer. Although the resource data bank makes obvious the inefficiencies of ad hoc case coordination, it does not deal with the need for interagency coordination and systematic case coordination.

Systematic Case Coordination

The next level, systematic case coordination, consists of a more systematic effort to coordinate services on a case basis. Two or more human service agencies agree on specific rules and procedures for division of labor between the organizations in handling different types of cases. These agreements may include referral procedures, information exchange, and routine case conferences.

This level of coordination is becoming increasingly important as efforts are made to "track" clients who have been deinstitutionalized. Funding authorities often require this type of coordination through interagency affiliation agreements. Interagency agreements serve a number of functions. For example, agreements between state hospitals and community mental health centers requiring case conferences on patients prior to hospital admission provide for routine screening to insure that referrals are appropriate. This kind of activity has increased as mental hospital admission policies have become more restrictive. Child welfare agencies and juvenile courts have also developed case coordination agreements to facilitate proper referrals.

As effective case coordination is dependent on accurate knowledge of agency purposes and programs, systematic efforts are sometimes made to familiarize staff with other community agencies through "cross-training." Cross-training occurs when each of two agencies includes staff from the other agency in its routine staff development and training programs. This "inside look" gives staff a more valid picture of programs of other agencies than they can get from just using the community service directories put out by planning and coordinating agencies. However, it does require agencies to risk giving "outsiders" access to "organizational secrets" (Gouldner 1963). The willingness of human service organizations to open their doors to out-siders, whether agency professionals or client advocates, requires an open system philosophy (see Chapter 11). This philosophy is most evident in the third level of coordination—program coordination.

Program Coordination

Program coordination provides for the integration of two or more *programs*. Agencies performing different but related specialized functions may agree to program coordination. The Work Incentive Program discussed earlier is one example of program coordination. The possibilities for program co-ordination are numerous. In the child welfare field, for example, a community-based foster care and protective service agency may develop a joint program with an institutional-based child service program.

Program coordination by definition requires agreements on the policy level of the coordinating agencies. As it requires major modifications in staff activities, it is the most difficult type of coordination to accomplish. Human service organizations generally will not engage in program coordination unless external pressure is exerted by some superordinate body that has control of funding resources.

BARRIERS TO COORDINATION AND STRATEGIES FOR OVERCOMING THEM

The preceding discussion on interorganizational coordination made nu-merous references to barriers to coordination. In this section we review these barriers and suggest strategies for overcoming them. The barriers are related to the costs that coordination efforts have for human service organizations. There are three kinds of costs: political, economic, and psychological costs.

Political Factors

A basic political cost incurred in interagency collaboration is the relinquishment of a certain amount of autonomy (the amount varies with level of coordination). Organizational autonomy is associated with institutional identity (Gouldner 1959: 241–270). Hence, a possible consequence of interdependence is a loss of identity, which may also lead to greater vulnerability to competition from agencies having similar goals. To some extent, however, the concern for loss of autonomy is simply based on fear of the unknown: Any organizational change will usually be viewed as a possible threat to autonomy. Thus, it may be possible to partially mitigate the problem by delineating in advance the areas of staff activity that will be affected. As real autonomy becomes less possible, given increasing accountability to government and other regulatory agencies, its importance as an issue in interorganizational coordination can be expected to diminish. The fact that agencies and their staff will become accustomed to coordination, as it becomes a more common phenomenon, will in itself make autonomy less of an issue.

Political barriers to coordination generally require political solutions. If interagency collaboration is perceived as a threat to the self-interest of the parties involved, then a political solution could be the negotiation of agreements that make explicit the costs and benefits of cooperation. A common problem is a lack of awareness of the potential benefits to be gained from collaboration. Therefore, a strategy for overcoming resistance to collaboration is to *induce* awareness of interdependence. As suggested earlier, funding authorities can sometimes use coercion to force cooperation between agencies. Federal- and state-level human service umbrella agencies have been committed to service coordination and integration. The administrator can utilize this external pressure from funding authorities to facilitate coordination on the community level (see Chapter 9).

Economic Factors

Despite the economic pressures for greater interorganizational coordination in the human service field, an administrator must be cautious in calculating potential economic benefits. Coordination has certain economic costs: Control procedures are needed to insure that the coordination is going according to plan, and these controls take time and money. The economic costs increase with level of coordination, as greater coordination requires more sophisticated monitoring mechanisms. Costs also depend on whether the activities being coordinated are routinized or complex. Coordination of the provision of concrete services will be less costly than that of people-changing services, which require much staff conference time. Another factor that adds to costs is the need to integrate control mechanisms into the structure of the agency, a need that may require considerable time from administrative personnel.

Given these various costs, the use of a strictly economic rationale for interorganizational coordination may not be justified in particular cases. If it is not, then the argument for coordination must be made in terms of consumer benefit. A strategy for overcoming these economic barriers would therefore be to make explicit the trade-off with more effective services.

Psychological Factors

Psychological costs are associated with staff concerns that interagency collaboration will threaten their independence and indentity. Therefore, a barrier to interorganizational coordination is both the lack of awareness of organizational interdependence and potential benefits of interagency collaboration. Often, possibilities for coordination among human service agencies exists in terms of shared goals and complementary resources but administrator and staff are not aware of it. An obvious strategy for overcoming this psychological barrier, then, is to facilitate this awareness. For example, community planners might formally investigate the potential for interorganizational coordination and communicate their findings to the relevant parties. Administrators can take an active role in increasing staff awareness.

COORDINATION VERSUS INTEGRATION OF HUMAN SERVICES

Service integration differs from service coordination in terms of the structural arrangements established. Service integration assumes a single administrative authority which has the power to mandate cooperation and integration. This situation has been termed simple structure, as opposed to a federated structure, in which units are autonomous (Rein and Morris 1962). Coordination applies to the latter.

Although service integration has been successful in Europe, this success has not been matched in the United States. Evaluations of attempts to establish integrated programs in the United States reveal several basic constraining factors (D. Austin, 1978). Most important, funding tends to be categorical, as the political base for programs continues to rest with specialized constituencies (elderly, mental health, child welfare, etc.) (Morris and Lescohier 1978). Ultimately, therefore, limits to service integration in the United States relate to the basic tendency against centralization of authority in government.

Another factor hindering service integration is the lack of shared goals between the different programs. As indicated earlier, different programs may emphasize care, control, and rehabilitation to varying degrees. A program that strives for service integration may not be possible given the inevitable differences among the goals of the individual services.

The studies of service integration attempts to question not only their feasibility in the American context, but also their efficiency and effectiveness (D. Austin 1978; Weiner 1982:149). Integrating programs showed little cost saving. Some have questioned the need for integrating on the local level as with chronic multiproblem families where integrating services has been relatively unsuccessful. Integrated services appear most effective in the area of dispensing information (Perlman 1975).

Moreover, it has been argued that the U.S. "pin-ball" model for service delivery (Cummings 1967: 132), in which clients "bounce" from one agency to another, while in certain respects inefficient, allows for greater consumer choice. A comprehensive and rational service delivery system could eliminate the existence of competing agencies and hence of consumer choice. Thus even if it were feasible, service integration might not be fully desirable.

Service integration, as it has been discussed here, refers to attempts to integrate a variety of services under one umbrella. Integration on a more limited basis is the merger of agencies. Agency mergers have increased with the pressure for more efficient services. Here again the question arises as to whether such integration in fact achieves economic gains. A more basic question is whether it enhances consumer benefit.

SUMMARY

This chapter has discussed a model for interagency coordination based on the condition of shared goals and resource exchange. Three levels of coordination are discussed: ad hoc case coordination, systematic case coordination, and program coordination which involves varying degrees of exchange and threat to agency autonomy. Political, economic and psychological barriers to coordination were analyzed along with the strategies for overcoming them.

Interagency coordination can be a means for solving some of the economic problems in human service organizations. More important, it can contribute greatly to consumer benefit. In fact, given the multiplicity and interrelatedness of human needs, service coordination has become essential. Although service integration may, from an ideal point of view, be the best solution for dealing with the problems of fragmentary and duplicated services, in the United States it does not appear to be very feasible.

APPLICATION OF CONCEPTS IN INTERORGANIZATIONAL RELATIONS TO CASE "MENTAL HEALTH RULES AND REGULATIONS"

In the case "Mental Health Rules and Regulations," the state mental health department mandated that state mental hospitals and community mental health programs collaborate to give priority to the severely mentally ill who had previously been hospitalized. Elaborate and detailed regulations were promulgated, requiring that particular kinds of services be provided with the general purpose of making community-based social care available to the chronically mentally ill.

One issue in this area of interorganizational relations is that of *whether cooperation between agencies is desirable.* Two assumptions underlie this issue — the assumptions that *similarity between programs results in duplication of services* and that *competition is undesirable.*

In this case, the department's aim was to get the community mental health centers, which traditionally gave priority to the lesser disturbed, to cooperate with the state hospitals, the primary agency serving the chronics. Therefore, the problem here was not that services were duplicated but that the community programs were discriminating against the chronically mentally ill. What was advocated was not that the hospitals and community centers cooperate to better serve a similar clientele, but that the community mental health centers assume responsibility for the persons being discharged from the hospitals. The second assumption, of whether competition is desirable, also fails to apply in this case, for similar reasons. Although these assumptions are not relevant here, they do implicitly raise the question of whether it is desirable from the point of view of service provision for the chronically mentally ill to attempt to promote cooperation between agencies that have such disparate goals.

Another issue in this area of interorganizational relations is *whether cooperation can be forced.* The state department did mandate that the hospitals and mental health centers comply with the new regulations. Although the department had direct line authority over the hospitals, it was related to the community programs only in that it was a source of funding. Hence, with respect to these programs the regulations were forced on them. The tremendous amount of resistance encountered may have resulted from the involuntary basis for initiating the change.

The model for interorganizational relations proposed here assumes that coordination is feasible under the following conditions: (a) the agencies are autonomous; (b) relations are on a voluntary basis; (c) goals are shared; and (d) the agencies need each other's resources.

The first condition that cooperating agencies be *autonomous* was met by the community mental health centers. These programs were not under state auspices, but were sponsored by such authorities as voluntary general hospitals, united funds, and county govenment. The state hospitals, however, were *not* autonomous, as they were under the direct authority of the department.

As already noted, the mental health department's regulations were mandated. Therefore, the requirement that participation be on a *voluntary* basis was *not* met.

The third condition, that agencies have *shared goals,* was also absent. The hospitals' primary goal was social control, whereas the community mental health centers' was rehabilitation. (Neither of these, moreover, coincided with the social care goal expressed by the new regulations.) Not only were the goals not shared, but they may have been perceived as being in conflict. The dichotomizing of the social deviancy and the medical models suggests that their advocates (mental health departments and mental health centers respectively) saw the goals of care and treatment as mutually *contradictory.*

The last condition, perceived need for *resource exchange,* did not obtain: As the two kinds of organizations had different purposes, they, not suprisingly, viewed each other's resources as not being of use. This analysis reveals, then, that none of the four conditions for coordination were met.

In analyzing the difficulties encountered in interagency cooperation, one also needs to examine the level on which coordination is occurring. The higher the level of coordination, the greater the threat it poses to agency autonomy. As the rules and regulations promulgated new policies, they fostered *program coordination.* This requires extensive collaboration of staffs on all levels and therefore can pose a significant threat to the autonomy (turf) of the agencies involved. As indicated in the case description, the department instituted elaborate reporting requirements and controls. The community agencies complained that these procedures were very costly and also violated their autonomy.

One can speculate that whereas program coordination was difficult because of the extensive changes required, case coordination might have been more feasible. In this type of coordination, cases are referred and the practitioners involved attempt to work out a collaborative relationship. Thus, the feasibility of case coordination would have depended on the interests and skills of the lower-level service employees.

The barriers to coordination may be analyzed in terms of three kinds of perceived costs: political, economic, and psychological. All three were evident in the case situation.

The *political* costs of collaboration were extensive from the point of view of the community mental health agencies. These agencies were afraid they would lose their identity as service providers to the middle-class patient. This might in turn lead to loss of legitimation and community support. In addition, the extensive controls imposed by the state threatened their autonomy, by curtailing their ability to manage their own operations.

Economic costs have already been mentioned. A major complaint was the large amount of staff time required to implement the new regulations.

Psychological costs involve the staff's awareness that interagency coordination would not jeopardize their independence. Awareness of interdependence also involved the fact that the department, by imposing greater demands on the community programs, made explicit the programs' dependence on the state for funds. The increased awareness on the part of local program staff, however, may ultimately result in some collaboration and cooperation.

The problems confronted by the state department in implementing the new regulations may be related to its *failure to differentiate between program coordination and integration.* The distinction between coordination and integration relates to whether programs are legally autonomous or under a single authority. The state department may have incorrectly assumed that as it supplied funds to the local programs it had the authority to direct and control these programs. In reality, local mental health programs have been able to exert considerable political power, for example, at the level of the state legislature. Those who advocate integration assume much more centralization of authority than actually exists in American society.

In this case situation, therefore, a combination of elements — lack of centralized authority, lack of shared goals, and absence of facilitating conditions—made service integration for the chronically mentally ill a very difficult objective to achieve.

PROFESSIONAL IDEOLOGIES

13

OUTLINE

I. Issues
   A. Ideological Basis for Lack of Consensus
   B. Conflict Based on Professional Ideology versus Self-Interest
   C. Are Prfoessional Ideologies Useful?

II. Definition

III. Management Ideologies

IV. Service Delivery Ideologies
   A. Definition
   B. Economic
   C. Political Ideology
   D. Social Ideology
   E. Psychological Ideology
   F. Ecological Ideology
   G. Somatic Ideology
   H. Cultural Ideology
   I. Legal Ideology
   J. Implication of Professional Ideologies for Human Service Practitioners

V. Relationship of Ideology to Organizational Areas
   A. Program Goals—Care, Control, and Rehabilitation
   B. Decision Making
   C. Leadership

VI. Summary

VII. Application to Case "From Psychological Work to Social Work"

ISSUES

Interprofessional disagreements, which are fairly widespread in the human service field, may often be traced to differences in beliefs and values. Such differences are common in situations where there is a lack of validated knowledge to guide action. In the human service field, where technologies are indeterminate (see Chapter 14) and cause–effect relationships are not clear, practitioners and administrators use ideologies to justify their actions. Decisions on program design, allocation of resources, and service delivery roles need to be made even if "facts" on which to base them are lacking. These "value" decisions (Simon 1957) are therefore based on the individuals' convictions that their rationales are the correct ones. As professional belief systems play such a significant function in the human service field, it is important to understand their consequences not only for administration decision making but also for professional–client relations and staff member interactions.

The discussion on the role of professional ideologies in human service organizations will focus on the following three topics: (a) lack of consensus caused by ideological differences; (b) conflict based on professional ideology versus conflict based on self-interest; (c) the usefulness of professional ideologies.

Ideological Basis for Lack of Consensus

It is evident that lack of consensus in dealing with organizational problems can stem from ideological differences (Brager and Holloway 1978:3–7). The persistence of disagreements as to the kind of decisions that need to be made in case or administrative situations suggests that these disagreements have underlying ideological components. Indeed, there are few decisions that do not. The decision as to whether to dismiss an employee because of inadequate performance will be influenced by the decision maker's ideological conviction as to whether, in general, difficulties are attributable to people or system problems. The decision as to whether to use a consensus or power strategy in introducing and implementing an organizational change will relate to the decision maker's management ideology (Weiner 1982:16; see Chapter 3, "Management Models"). Thus, an appreciation of the widespread influence that ideology has on the behavior of human service professionals is essential (Wolfensberger 1972:7). An understanding of the fact that decisions often have an ideological component makes it possible both to accept various viewpoints as legitimate and to focus on areas in which this component is minimal, as conflicts are more resolvable if not based on ideology.

Conflict Based on Professional Ideology versus Self-Interest

Conflict in human service agencies may be based on differences in self-interest rather than ideology. Whereas ideologically based conflict is extremely difficult to resolve through compromise, disagreements based on self-interest *are* resolvable in this way, as differences can be negotiated. Understanding whether conflict is ideological or political can aid the human service administrator or practitioner in selecting the appropriate strategy for resolution. As ideological differences cannot readily be debated or "reasoned," a strategy to "agree to disagree" would be appropriate. For example, assume that an administrator and his subordinate, who is a line supervisor, have conflicting managerial philosophies, based on the classical versus human relations model. This underlying difference could be reflected in the kinds of supervision advocated, as the classical model stresses control, whereas the human relations model favors staff participation and freedom. Recognition of this as a value difference could enable the superior and subordinate to move on to the more critical question of the results of supervision—for example, the productivity of the line workers. Differences on productivity measures could be negotiated and an agreement reached without any discussion of the ideological dispute.

Understanding the difference between ideology and self-interest makes it possible to discover the use of ideology as a screen for self-interest. This use of ideology is not uncommon in human service organizations. For example, an individual might argue for a certain program on the grounds that it would be best for the clients, when in reality he is motivated primarily by self-interest (e.g., the program might entail a promotion for him). Another example of how ideology may mask self-interest lies in the tendency of lower-level staff to advocate a participatory management model and of upper-level management to support the classical model. This apparently ideological conflict can be related to the different interests of lower- and upper-level staff: It is in the interests of lower-level employees to advocate participation in decision making, as this would enchance their power; upper-level management would prefer to not include staff in decision making, as this would be time consuming and would diffuse power. The use of ideology to manipulate situations for political objectives needs to be understood to achieve more successful conflict management.

Advocates of a more objective or "scientific" approach to professional practice might question whether professional ideologies are necessary for the operation of human services agencies. This issue will be discussed next.

Are Professional Ideologies Useful?

If professional ideologies are unproven philosophies, then one can question whether they have a legitimate place in professional practice. Shouldn't human service administrators and workers strive for objectivity in decision making? Doesn't the use of approaches that have not been empirically val-idated negate the very essence of a profession (Fischer 1981:199–207)? The use of ideology as a basis for decision making is problematic; however, there may be no alternative. Administrators and practitioners have to take action. Decisions have to be made on what the goals of human service program should be, on how to select staff, allocate resources, and deliver services to clients. Practitioners need to confront the day-to-day problems of delivery of human services (Hasenfeld 1983:120). Without a framework within which to act, they would have to treat every situation as unique—an approach that would be extremely inefficient. Because of the indeterminancy of the work performed in the human service field, practitioners need a philosophy or ideology on which to base decisions. The lack of a philosophy to guide action would probably result in paralysis.

DEFINITION

Professional ideology may be defined as a set of ideas on cause–effect relationships that are logical and internally consistent but have yet to be proven empirically (Rapoport 1960:269; Strauss 1964:8). It is a belief system that helps explain social phenomena and thereby facilitates professional action and decision making. As can be seen from this definition, an ideology is in many respects similar to a religion.

The need for ideologies in the human service field is related to the in-determinate nature of the problems dealt with. Empirical studies on the ef-fectiveness of clinical interventions have yet to demonstrate cause–effect re-lations (Fischer 1973). Despite this lack of validated knowledge, human service practitioners must respond to the demands for help by consumers or to pressures to solve administrative and organizational problems. They require a frame of reference, which will be viewed as rational and legitimate, to justify their actions (Hasenfeld 1983:119). These frames of reference are professional ideologies.

Ideologies have been defined here as a single set of ideas which the individual holds. For example, classical management is an ideology which includes among many other ideas the notion that insufficient staff productivity reflects the lack of a strong control and accountability system. However, some would argue that it is not possible to hold this notion as well as the human relations management ideology which assumes that staff are motivated by recognition and appreciation. Others would argue that people do not nec-essarily operate from a single ideology—that it is possible to be an eclectic, a believer in several ideologies. This eclectic approach to social work practice is often advocated (e.g., Siporin 1975:153–155). The question of whether it is possible to be a multiple believer is, however, an empirical one. A study of social workers values found that social and clinical orientation were in-dependent of each other (Tabor and Vattano 1970). Studies of professional ideologies in the field of mental health (Strauss 1964) confirm this tendency for practitioners to adhere to a single ideology. It therefore appears that belief in more than one ideology is difficult because of basic differences in underlying assumptions.

Another possible philosophical stance is that of the nonbeliever: the individual who will believe only what has been proven. In the human service field it used to be assumed that researchers fell into this category. However, some have questioned whether research is in fact "value free" (Kuhn 1962). In actuality, an individual who saw all sides to problems would have great difficulty in taking action; such an individual would suffer from what has been termed "analysis paralysis" (Livingston 1971).

We have seen, then, that the availability of professional ideologies facilitates action. What effect do ideologies have on the benefit received by the consumer? How do various belief systems affect client outcome? Studies of the effectiveness of various psychological therapies have, in general, revealed them to be all equally effective (Eysenck 1965). It may be that—in the area of psychological treatment, at least—outcome is influenced not so much by the content of the ideology as by the professional's conviction that the ideology is correct.

A study of treatment environments in two mental hospitals illustrates how professional belief may influence outcome. This study compared a traditional treatment philosophy, which stressed control and system maintenance, with a social system approach, in which patients were given more autonomy and responsibility. In the initial phase of the study each hospital had equally favorable environments and approximately equal discharge rates. However, when the traditional program moved toward a more progressive philosophy the result was a decrease in discharge rates and decline in staff morale and program effectiveness (Moos 1974:110). The explanation may be that the attempt to introduce a new philosophy weakened the initial traditional belief system, making it less effective. If so, this underscores the importance of ideologies in the human service field.

The influence that staff ideologies can have is evident in the relative effectiveness of two different kinds of people-changing strategies: changing attitudes versus changing situations (Kennedy 1980:219). When attitudes are based on ideological beliefs, the possibility of changing them directly is generally remote. In such cases, changing people's situation may readily produce a change in their beliefs. Thus, experiments in integrated housing have demonstrated that situational changes can decrease racial prejudice (Deutch and Collins 1951).

The relationship between work behavior and ideologies was shown by a study in the mental health field (Strauss 1964). This study utilized a mental health ideology scale, which distinguished three belief systems concerning the causes of and treatment for mental illness: psychological, social, and physical. The *psychological* ideology locates the cause in the personality and therefore assumes that psychotherapeutic treatments are indicated. The *social* ideology views mental illness as having an environmental cause and therefore proposes that the appropriate solution lies in changing the social conditions. The *physical* or somatic ideology locates the cause of mental illness in the body and requires physical treatments such as drugs, shock, or surgery. This mental health ideology scale demonstrated both reliability and validity. It was validated by being administered to three professional associations of psychiatrists, each known for its adherence to one of the ideologies.

Data that was then obtained in a mental hospital revealed that different ideologies prevailed in different parts of the hospital. On the chronic ward the professionals had an organic or physical ideology. On the acute ward, however, the social ideology predominated, as did the psychological ideology in outpatient service. This pattern of variation suggests that the work situation can shape a person's belief system. An alternative explanation is that professionals seek to work in situations that are compatible with their beliefs.

In this same study, mental health ideologies were also found to differ among professions in predictable directions. Psychiatrists favored the somatic ideology, psychologists the psychological ideology, and social workers the social ideology. Nurses favored all three ideologies, a finding that may also be explained in terms of work situation. In mental hospitals nurses generally are involved with a variety of treatments and therefore may come to view them all as equally valid.

Another illustration of the relationship between education and job experience and on professional values was found in a study of social workers (Varley 1966). Community organization and administration practitioners were found to be more socially oriented than caseworkers and group workers. The opposite pattern emerged when psychological orientation was considered.

The preceding discussion has implications for personnel selection. Programs with a social care goal should recruit social workers educated in community organization and administration, whereas programs with a rehabilitation goal should recruit those with casework and group work training. An apparent problem arises, however, when human service agencies have *both* social care and rehabilitation goals. In the field of social work there has been a stress on the integration of social and psychological approaches; "psychosocial" casework practice attempts to both change the person *and* the situation. Yet it is unclear that the two emphases coexist in actuality. If, as stated earlier, people tend to favor a particular ideology, then practitioners would probably emphasize one approach over the other. Given the time pressures in practice, direct service personnel are forced to establish priorities, and these priorities are ideologically determined (see cases "From Psychological Work to Social Work" and "Mental Health Rules and Regulations").

The movement toward generic practice in social work has been based on the assumption that different intervention methods can be integrated (Siporin 1975; Pincus and Minahan 1973). Evaluation of these generic models, however, reveals that they tend to be primarily people changing, in their focus (E. Schwartz 1977). This would support the contention that the ideological base for practice, including practice theories, emphasizes single belief systems.

MANAGEMENT IDEOLOGIES

In Chapter 3 on management models three different approaches to understanding organizations were discussed: classical, human relations, and structuralist. (A fourth approach, the systems model, was an integration of the three others.) These three philosophies of management were seen as making different assumptions regarding both the basic factors that motivated staff in organizations and the extent to which individual and organizational goals were congruent. In addressing the question of influences on staff behavior, the classical model emphasized economic motivation, the human relations model interpersonal factors, and the structuralist model self-interest. Both the classical and human relations models assumed that individual and organizational interests could be congruent, whereas the structuralist model held that conflict was inevitable because the individual and organization had competing interests. These three philosophies of management are ideologies, because they are logical and internally consistent but have not been validated as practice theories.

In keeping with our discussion of the nature of professional ideologies, we may say that most managers probably tend to favor one philosophy or another. Different types of management education will also be likely to stress one or another philosophy. Business administration schools, which have been heavily influenced by the field of economics, will probably stress the classical model. The human relations model has been more closely linked to the field of industrial psychology, whereas the structuralist model is closer to organizational sociology. The literature in social work administration has tended to favor the human relations model, as this people emphasis is more akin to this field (see Abels and Murphy 1981).

If we assume that administrators will favor one management philosophy over another, then we must ask what consequences this will have for the goals of human service programs. It is conjectured here that human service administrators are most inclined toward the human relations model, because of their education and the expectations of staff. If so, then this emphasis might have several consequences. For example, it has been found that therapeutic agencies lack formal structure (Rosengren 1967). It has also been found that voluntary human service agencies have low productivity (B. Neugeboren 1970a), in part because much time is devoted to staff participation in meetings. In this way, use of the human relations model, with its emphasis on staff satisfaction, may result in less efficiency and hence have adverse consequences for the consumer. Unfortunately, we lack systematic studies of the effectiveness of human service organizations, and it is therefore difficult to assess the consequences of the various models.

As indicated, the systems model was proposed as an approach to integrate the other three management philosophies. It was suggested that as an ideal approach it would use different ideologies under different circumstances (subsystems). However, the problem would remain of how to overcome the tendency of professionals to favor one or another ideology. The systems model might also provide a solution for this problem: Organizational structure—that is, the subsystems—can be used to segregate the different philosophies. This "birds of a feather" approach or homophyly (Blau and Scott 1962:137) would facilitate communication and cooperation within these subunits or work groups. However, the problem of ideological conflict among subunits would remain.

If the "ideological imperative" is present, then it would seem useful to recognize this fact and, as suggested earlier, create an atmosphere to "agree to disagree." Again, open recognition of the legitimacy of these different management ideologies can help focus conflict on practical areas which are more easily negotiated.

SERVICE DELIVERY IDEOLOGIES

Ideological issues occur in the service delivery area of human service programs as well as in the management area. In this section we will discuss eight different ideological perspectives on the causes of and solutions for various social problems. These different belief systems have different implications for the design of service delivery programs.

Definition

Service delivery ideologies are defined as causal models that explain the source of social problems and suggest remedies for solving them. Although these belief systems serve as guides for activity for direct service personnel, they also have implications for administrative functions: policy formulation, program design, staffing, controlling, etc.

The influence of ideology on service delivery in the human services is evident in the following description of "human management models":

> Human management models affect and often dictate the location, design, and operation of human management facilities .... For instance, much has been

said and written about the medical model which generally implies the perception of the consumer of a human service as a "sick" "patient" who, after "diagnosis", is given "treatment" or "therapy" for his "disease" in a "clinic" or "hospital" by "doctors" who carry primary administrative and human management responsibility assisted by a hierarchy of "paramedical" personnel and "therapists", all this hopefully leading to a "cure". Not only daily management practices, but also the social organization of service systems and manpower structures are usually consistent with and related to the prevailing human management concepts and models [Wolfensberger 1972:8].

This medical (somatic) model is one of the eight service delivery ideologies that will be discussed. These service delivery ideologies are: *(a)* economic, *(b)* political, *(c)* social, *(d)* psychological, *(e)* ecological, *(f)* somatic, *(g)* cultural, and *(h)* legal.

Economic Ideology

The *economic* service delivery ideology assumes that social problems are primarily caused by the system of distribution of wealth in the society. Drawing on evidence that social problems such as child abuse (Pelton 1981) and mental illness (Hollingshead and Redlich 1958) are class related, and that there is a correlation between rate of unemployment and state mental hospital admissions (Brenner 1973), this model suggests that a possible solution lies in the provision of a guaranteed income. Attempts have been made (e.g., Froland and Bell 1979) to systematically evaluate the effects on behavior (e.g., family stability and work) of the provision of different levels of income. Although the results of these income maintenance experiments are incomplete, there is a conviction among some (especially economists) that the distribution of material resources is the key factor influencing social problems. Whether the point of view is radical (Galper 1975) or conservative (Stoner 1983) the basic position is that social problems should be dealt with more directly through more adequate income policies.

Thus, the economic service delivery model suggests that programs that serve lower-income clients could best help these clients by providing cash or other material benefits directly (or indirectly, by facilitating access to public assistance). Implications for service delivery are that either the agencies would need to move funds for these purposes (e.g., rent, food, clothing, etc.) or practitioners would be required to have the skill to link clients with these resources in the community (Keefe 1978).

Political Ideology

The *political* service delivery ideology stresses distribution of power as the key factor causing social problems. The "power to the poor" advocates in the 1960s took the position that poverty was caused by the lack of power in the lower classes. Their solution was to organize low-income groups to press for their rights and entitlements (Brager and Specht 1965). The field of community organization in social work has stressed organization of consumers so that as a group they can influence the power structure (Kramer and Specht 1969). Citizen participation in human service programs initially was through lay boards of directors. This has broadened to the point that government now mandates that clients be involved in policymaking boards. The Title XX, community mental health, and health planning programs require citizen input into decision-making processes. Although it is not clear that this trend represents a sharing of power rather than simply "citizen manipulation" (Grosser 1973: 201), the involvement of clients and citizens in policymaking and monitoring functions is on the increase. Further examples of such redistribution of power strategy are the use of citizen review boards to monitor foster care placement and the client advocacy movement, which includes a public advocate financed with government funds.

The suggestion that more equality is needed in the area of organization–client relations (e.g., Hasenfeld and English 1974:469) is based on this political ideology. The various strategies for achieving equality between clients and organizations (e.g., giving clients more choice as well as allowing them to organize collectively in relating to the agency) assume that redistribution of power will improve service delivery outcomes. Whether this in fact occurs has not been conclusively demonstrated. In any event, the democratic ethic in the United States supports the inclusion of citizen groups in the administration of human service programs. Administrators and practitioners are becoming painfully aware of the increased power of the consumer, especially through legal suits (see section on legal ideology). Malpractice insurance for human service professions is needed not only for the private practitioner but also for those working in public agencies. Professionals are no longer in an omnipotent position, and the human service practitioner, whether in administration or direct service, must keep this fact constantly in mind.

Social Ideology

The *social* service delivery ideology assumes that social conditions are the key factor determining human problems. These conditions include the variety of social-environmental factors that influence our lives, beginning with the way in which society is stratified into social classes and social mobility constrained or facilitated (Hasenfeld 1983:42). A social solution, therefore, would be directed at the practitioner rectifying the inequalities in the social system. While the political ideology advocates having the deprived mobilize power to change the system, the social ideology places the responsibility for change on the human service practitioner. An example is the stress given in the poverty programs of the 1960s to opening up the opportunity structure through job training and employment programs (B. Neugeboren 1970b).

This stress finds ample support in sociological theory. For example, Cloward and Ohlin (1960) explained the socially deviant behavior of juvenile delinquents in terms of their using illegitimate means for achieving goals for which all citizens strive, because of lack of access to legitimate means (e.g., jobs).

Sociological theories of deviancy such as labeling theory (Scheff 1975) are based on a social causal model. These theories suggest that not only does behavior deviate from societal norms for social reasons, but that once this deviancy is officially recognized, the individual is labeled and compelled to continue in the deviant role (e.g., mental patient, criminal). The view of mental illness as a "contingency" rather than a sickness (Goffman 1959:135) is based on the fact that only a small proportion of mentally ill persons are officially diagnosed as such and that the factors associated with their being identified are not psychological but social (Scheff 1968:510). Social deviancy theory has been used to explain a variety of social problems, including mental illness, crime, addiction, poverty, ill health, marital conflict, and discrimination (Clinard 1963). The main thrust of deviancy theory is that social factors help precipitate, complicate and reinforce human problems. The implications for human service agencies is that, as in the example of the poverty programs, interventions must address these social factors.

The goal of social care in human service programs, discussed earlier, is based on the social ideology. Creating positive social environments, whether in institutions or in the community, involves changing situations to facilitate human functioning. The development of community support systems for the deinstitutionalized population is a *social* strategy, based on the assumption that environments must be changed (see Chapter 14, "Technologies").

In the child abuse area the social ideology has become increasingly important. Thus, the myth that child abuse is classless is being exposed (Pelton 1981a). For example, a national study has revealed that child abuse is in fact associated with lower-class status (Gil 1970). Proposals for community support systems for victims of child abuse (Garbarino and Stocking 1980) and the program emphasis on concrete services such as housing, health care, and employment are also based on the social ideology.

There are major implications of this social ideology. Since many human service programs have as their official goal change in the social environment, it is important that this emphasis be recognized and reflected in agency recruitment and selection of personnel with a social ideology. In Chapter 8 we discussed the difficulties of recruiting personnel with a social ideology, given that most human service educational programs emphasize people changing. We also suggested that persons from the lower classes should be recruited since they may be more inclined to have this ideology, as they are the "victims" of social inequality. Recruitment from such specific fields as sociology or *macro* specialization in social work may also help in selection of socially oriented personnel. Situational tests with a situation-changing emphasis may facilitate selection of personnel with a social ideology (see "From Psychological Work to Social Work").

Psychological Ideology

The *psychological* service delivery ideology is based on the assumption that human problems can be explained by defects in the individual's personality. Therefore, the appropriate solutions lie in various psychological treatments, such as psychotherapy, psychoanalysis, behavior modification, casework, group therapy, counseling, and other people-changing technologies.

The American inclination toward psychological "determinism" is reflected by terms such as the "cult of personality" or the "psychiatric state" (Szasz 1963). The period of 1930–1970, with the "New Deal," "Fair Deal," and "New Society," moved toward society's responsibility for human problems. In the 1970s and 1980s there has been a shift back to the "me" society, which emphasizes individualism, self-expression and introspection. The rapid development of different types of psychological treatments, including sensitivity groups, scream therapy, group encounters, etc., is evidence of the increased stress on psychology as the basis for understanding human and social problems. The mushrooming demand for psychological services by the middle classes has had a great impact on the human services field. With insurance companies now including psychological treatment in their major medical coverage, the human service clinical agencies and private practitioners are receiving increased funds and legitimacy.

Although the psychological ideology has important implications for human service administration, practitioners must avoid the tendency to view all problems in terms of personality. This applies to organization problems as well as to the problems of clients. The assumption that organizational problems or even individual employee performance problems are personality-based leads to solutions (treatment) that are not achievable in the organizational setting. Counseling employees takes away time from clients and, more important, may result in a failure to recognize the organization's basic structural problems. But, because the impact of the psychological ideology in human service programs has been great (Gummer 1979a:214; Rosenberg 1978:91; Field 1980; Weich 1981) administrators must be cautious in attempting innovations that conflict with this ideology, as the resistance may be substantial (see case "Mental Health Rules and Regulations").

Ecological Ideology

The *ecological* ideology assumes that human problems are caused by physical-environmental problems. The influence of the physical environment on human behavior has been the concern of physical planners and architects. Studies of crowding (Calhoun 1963) have demonstrated the negative consequences that lack of physical space can have on animals and people. Climate can affect behavior; the urban riots in the summer of 1965 were perhaps exacerbated by the discomforts of hot weather (Moos 1974:22). The effects of physical factors should be an important consideration in design. For example, the fact that different colors have different effects on human behavior has been taken into account in painting buildings that house mentally disturbed patients. The architectural design (long corridors) of public mental hospitals has been found to increase the visual distortion of images by mental patients. The design of rooms and buildings can influence the social interactions of persons living or working there in ways that help or hinder their functioning and performance (Wolfensberger 1972:56–77).

The "ecology movement" has received much support from environmentalists, who have made clear the negative consequences of such physical-environmental factors as air and water pollution. Air pollution is believed to be an important cause of cancer. "Acid rain" has damaged lakes and affected fish. Water supplies are endangered by the disposal of toxic waste.

If physical-environmental factors exert an important influence on human problems, then human service agencies should be aware of this fact and work closely with the physical planners (Morris and Frieden 1968). If crime rates in large public housing sites are high because design factors limit visibility (Jacobs 1961), then human service planners should work to remedy such factors. The administrators of service delivery agencies (hospitals, welfare boards, etc.) also have a stake in environmental planning. The fact that physical environment influences human problems needs to be more fully recognized by practitioners in human service organizations.

Somatic Ideology

The organic or *somatic* ideology assumes that the causes of human difficulties are in the body and that the appropriate solutions involve some form of physical intervention. Our society has turned more and more to somatic intervention to solve human problems. In the health field, drugs have been used extensively and often inappropriately. The indiscriminate use of tranquilizers, barbiturates, and pain killers has resulted in various addictions. Although the iatrogenic side effects of drugs have received increasing publicity, many factors function to encourage the use of drugs as a solution to problems. Television commercials inform the viewer that whether the problem is constipation, tension, insomnia, overweight, wrinkles, or something else, there is a drug that will take care of it. The use of mind altering drugs has gained popularity even in middle-class professional groups.

Human service programs providing service to substance abusers have increased as a result of the wide availability and use of drugs. Also, a wide range of human service agencies uses drugs as a regular part of their programs. Thus, drugs are used to sedate hyperactive children in schools, as well as mental patients in hospitals or in the community. The inappropriate use of drugs is evident with the elderly: a lack of coordinated health care in the community can result in an elderly person going to several specialists who prescribe different drugs that may produce overall negative effects (Glassman 1980).

As with any form of treatment, the rational use of drug therapy requires specialized knowledge. Most physicians do not have detailed knowledge in the area of pharmacology. Human service agencies would therefore need access to experts in this area, in order to implement drug therapy programs and to be able to help consumers who lack the knowledge to coordinate their own use of drugs.

Cultural Ideology

The *cultural* ideology assumes that the cause of human problems lies in discrepancies in values between client groups and the dominant society. The existence and effects of differences in cultural values have been much studied. Anthropologists have identified different value orientations for different American ethnic groups, such as Irish, Italians, and Jews (Spiegel 1964). The effects of different ethnic cultures on lifestyle were analyzed in relation to blacks, Puerto Ricans, Jews, Italians, and Irish in New York City (Glazer and Moynihan 1963). Some dispute the relevance of culture, however, claiming that class is the more critical factor. Attributing human problems to "caste" when they are due to "class" is viewed as another form of "blaming the victim" (Ryan 1971). Others have explained value differences between the lower and middle classes as a "value-stretch," in that members of the lower class identify with society's basic value system but modify it to meet their current needs (Rodman 1965).

Various studies of psychological problems in particular groups support the cultural ideology. For example, psychological problems have been shown to differ among ethnic groups (Roberts and Myers 1954). Mental problems in women have been seen as related to the role women play in American society (Chesler 1972). The high incidence of mental illness among newly arrived immigrants is another source of evidence for a relationship between culture and human problems (Grob 1973).

Recognition of the relevance of culture in the delivery of human services has increased as different ethnic groups have pressured for separate programs which would take the cultural factors into account. Historically, the various religious-sponsored social agency programs have attempted to preserve and foster particular culture values (Marty 1980). This has been evident in the Jewish community center field and in the Catholic social service agencies. Today ethnic groups such as Italians, Puerto Ricans, Chicanos, and Chinese are establishing separate human service programs. The creation of programs for women also reflects the emphasis on social and cultural factors.

The realization that human problems are related to value conflicts could have a significant impact in human service delivery programs (Jenkins 1981; Devore and Schlesinger 1981). In the field of child abuse, it could lead to an appreciation of value differences regarding the use of physical punishment. Middle-class social workers, who generally have a permissive child-rearing philosophy, often find it difficult to understand the more traditional, "spare the rod and spoil the child" philosophy of lower-class clients (R. Neugeboren 1981).

Counseling in such areas as mental conflict, parent–child relations, adjustment problems of adolescents from different ethnic groups, etc., must separate value issues from the psychological focus. Given that people are reluctant to change their values, value conflict problems are difficult to resolve. Perhaps this may explain the inadequate results obtained from psychological therapies (Fischer 1973). The basic principle suggested earlier in relation to ideological organizational conflicts can apply to direct service as well: It is often best to recognize differences in values and to agree to respect these differences.

The staffing patterns of human service organizations would also be affected by the recognition of the importance of cultural and value differences in human problems. Staff members would need to be recruited from the various ethnic groups being served, in order to insure understanding of the value systems of those groups.

Legal Ideology

The *legal* ideology is an orientation that places emphasis on individual *rights*. Advocates of this belief system stress the value of fair and equitable treatment with respect to both clients and staff members. For example, they argue that the wide discretion available to human service personnel can result in actions that discriminate against the consumer (Handler 1973, 1979). The legal approach essentially sees the provision of social service in a "political framework with clients trying to secure needed resources from recalcitrant and paternalistic welfare bureaucracies [Gummer 1979a]."

The legal ideology has received impetus from the increased involvement of lawyers and law in the administration and delivery of human services. This involvement is exemplified by court cases aimed at protecting the rights of hospital patients, mental patients, servicemen, teachers, students, women, suspects, poor, reporters, gay people, and prisoners. Handbooks have been written to assist these groups in being aware of their particular rights (Dorsen and Neier). It is also shown by the development of the new areas of law, including welfare, housing, health, poverty and mental health law (Dickson, 1976), and by client advocates such as public advocates, ombudsmen, legal services for the poor, and agencies established as "watchdogs" over human service programs.

As indicated earlier, the use of legal procedures to insure individual rights has become widespread within the human service field itself. Personnel policies, civil service regulations, and union contracts have established grievance procedures to protect staff from "arbitrary and capricious" decisions affecting their welfare. Administrators find it more and more difficult to dismiss, demote, or sanction employees. In order to do so they have to provide "documentation" based on "facts." Similarly in the area of direct service, human service workers, whose training has emphasized "feelings," also have difficulty adjusting to the increasing use of legal procedures. They find to their dismay that when asked to testify in court they cannot readily verify the factual basis of their actions (R. Neugeboren 1981). With the growing number of court decisions and statutes regulating the human service field, however, it has become imperative that administrators and practitioners develop expertise in this area or employ persons with legal backgrounds (Dickson 1977).

Implications of Professional Ideologies for Human Service Practitioners

Having discussed eight different service delivery ideologies, we can now ask how this knowledge might be used by administrators and practitioners in human service organizations.

Administrators will need to determine what ideologies are especially relevant to the goals of their organization. Service directed at ethnic groups would have to take into account the cultural ideology. Programs for the lower social classes probably would need to include the social ideology. As, by definition, all ideologies have some validity, it would be difficult to arbitrarily exclude anyone. The "eclectic" approach would be to use the different ideologies for the purposes to which they are appropriate.

For the practitioner, awareness of the wide range of ideologies available can lead to a broadened perspective. Acceptance of the legitimacy of other ideologies—the "agreement to disagree" with colleagues who have different ideologies—can help minimize interprofessional conflict.

The ideologies discussed vary in their assumptions as to whether human problems are primarily caused by the individual or the situation. If the causes of problems lie outside the individual but the responsibility for solving them is placed on the individual, then we have a situation in which the victim is being blamed (Ryan 1971). Blaming the victim can occur when problems are defined as psychological, cultural, or somatic if, in fact, the cause is outside the person, for example, in the environment. Victim blaming can also be associated with the political ideology. The "power to the poor" strategy, which emphasized community organization and self-development, had for some of its advocates, an underlying assumption that the lower classes had to group together to enhance their self-image if they were to unite as a power group. This has been described as "community sociotherapy" (Rein 1970); that is, social action is a tool to transform the individual personality.

RELATIONSHIP OF IDEOLOGY TO ORGANIZATIONAL AREAS

Program Goals—Care, Control, and Rehabilitation

As organizational goals are by definition value positions (Simon 1957), the goals of human service programs may be equated with ideologies. These goals are justified on the basis that they are intrinsically good and worthwhile to accomplish.

As discussed earlier, human service programs may be seen as having three primary goals: social care, social control, and rehabilitation. It is self-evident that social care is related to the social ideology and rehabilitation to person-changing—psychological and somatic—ideologies. The goal of social control also may be viewed as having an ideological base. In the field of corrections, the use of punishment to deter crime is based on the belief that the criminal is a rational person, who engages in deviant behavior not because he is disturbed but because he has calculated that he can get away with it. This assumption of a rational basis for human action is also found in the economic ideology, which holds that the consumers are rational and if given choice will exercise good judgment in maximizing their self-interest. This assumption that deviants can be controlled by sanctions is also made in the justice and deterrent models in the correction field which are gaining much support today (Conrad 1973). The "fixed sentence" which insures equality of punishment is believed by some to be more effective and fair.

Decision Making

The problem definition stage of decision making (see Chapter 10) will be influenced by the ideological positions of those formulating the problem. This occurs because problem formulation is an analytic process in which the causes and consequences of a particular problem are made explicit and ideology is a causal model. Thus, if one holds a political ideology, one will tend to emphasize power as the cause of problems. Applying this to a morale problem in an organization one might see the cause of the problem as lack of staff power to influence decision making. The solution could be a change in organization's power structure. Alternatively, if operating from the psychological ideology, one attributes poor morale to a lack of sensitivity to employees' needs, then the solution might be seen as lying in the establishment of human relations program. Thus, other stages of decision making can also be influenced by ideological predilections. The kinds of solutions considered and the way they are evaluated tend to depend on values.

The nonrational factor of organizational context in the decision-making process is linked to ideologies. The basic service ideologies in the human service organization will provide the opportunities and constraints for decision making. They focus the attention of the decision maker on those areas that they define.

Leadership

In Chapter 9, we discussed the leadership skill of top-level administrators as requiring a systemic perspective. This perspective includes the understanding that the potential for ideological conflict in human service organizations is very great given the indeterminate nature of the tasks. Leadership skill also involves the ability to divert conflict into areas that are nonideological in order to improve the changes for resolution. Understanding the ideological basis of conflicts in the service delivery will help the leader to support the validity of all ideological positions and provide the opportunity for all approaches to demonstrate their effectiveness. Placing the emphasis on the results in terms of consumer benefit will minimize the polarization of staff. Although this competition among ideologies may foster tension, it will provide an objective basis for determining which approaches are valid in the particular agency.

SUMMARY

Professional ideologies have been presented as an important factor influencing the delivery of human service. The indeterminate nature of the field requires practitioners to develop belief systems to justify and legitimize their decision and actions. These beliefs reinforce existing patterns of professional activity and can be a major constraint to change. Although there are strategies for influencing individuals' beliefs, in general, ideologically based convictions are very difficult to change. Recognition of the existence of different professional value systems can facilitate cooperative effort if it leads to acceptance of differences rather than ideological warfare. Understanding the importance of professional ideologies can facilitate practice by administrators and direct service personnel in human service organizations. This chapter has presented a range of professional ideologies related to human service management and service delivery. The service delivery ideologies discussed included: economic, political, social, psychological, ecological, somatic, cultural and legal.

APPLICATION OF CONCEPTS ON PROFESSIONAL IDEOLOGIES TO CASE "FROM PSYCHOLOGICAL WORK TO SOCIAL WORK"

In the case situation "From Psychological Work to Social Work," the *lack of consensus* between the child welfare agency administration and staff was in part attributable to *ideological differences.* The administrator's *social* ideology for delivery of services to clients was in direct contradiction to the *psychological* ideology held by most of the staff. The conflict that occurred was not resolvable, as both belief systems were strongly held, ruling out any possibility for negotiation and compromise.

The issue of whether the conflict is *based on ideology and/or self-interest* was also relevant here. The hiring officer was apparently using ideology as a means of protecting his power and control. A power struggle ensued between the administrator and the hiring officer over who would control the operations of the agency. Although this type of conflict is suitable for negotiation, it was not possible in this situation; this may indicate that genuine ideological differences were involved.

The *utility of ideologies* in facilitating decision making and action was also evident in this case. Prior to the new administrator's introduction of the change to a socially oriented service delivery model, the staff had apparently performed their jobs at a level that was at least minimally satisfactory. After the new philosophy was introduced, the staff found it so difficult to function that they felt compelled to ask for transfers to other offices in the agency. In other words, when they were not permitted to use their professional belief system they became unable to act.

The *relationship between changing attitudes and behavior* was also evident in this case situation. Certain staff members were able to change their behavior and move toward a socially oriented program. Under the pressure from administration, they did implement the caseload management model utilizing community resources, even though this was contrary to their ideological convictions. Therefore, the strategy of this administrator to change the work situation rather than the staff's attitudes was effective. A direct attempt to change their attitudes probably would have been less effective.

The presence of different *management ideologies* was also evident. The administrator in his use of structure and control could be identified as favoring the *classical model* of management. His constructive use of conflict and sensitivity to environmental pressures would align him with the *structuralist model* as well. In contrast the staff favored the *human relations model.* They complained because, compared to the previous administration, there was less opportunity for staff participation in decision making. Their objections to the emphasis on structure and their fear that structure would constrain their freedom were also in keeping with the human relations model. The human relations model emphasizes the importance of the *informal system.* As noted in the case description, there was an extensive informal communication network, which operated to enhance the power of the hiring officer. The administrator's appreciation of this led him to restrict this informal contact by establishing specific role definitions for staff.

Different *service delivery ideologies* were present as well. The basic change introduced involved movement from a *psychological* to a *social* ideological approach to service delivery. The administrator favored the *social* approach; that is, he emphasized the provision of concrete services to the clients, who came from the lower social classes. The caseload management service delivery model stressed *environmental modification* on the assumption that social class was the key factor that created problems for these clients. In order to obtain staff with this orientation the administrator devised situational tests which successfully screened for a macro emphasis in service delivery.

As indicated, the prevailing service delivery ideology in this agency had been *psychological.* This was evident not only in the service delivery area, but also in the use of psychological techniques in staff supervision. The education of the professional staff in social casework reinforced this ideological stance.

Certain problems that arose in this case could be explained by means of the *cultural ideology.* Staff were recruited from ethnic groups similar to that of the clients to facilitate understanding of clients' needs. The conflicts between the newly recruited minority staff who came from a lower social economic class and the middle-class workers were probably in part related to differences in culturally derived values. This conflict could have revealed itself in different points of view regarding the use of physical punishment in child rearing. The inability of these new staff members to understand the value of psychiatric supervision was probably also related to differences in cultural orientation.

The stress placed by the new service delivery model on client and worker *rights* suggests the operation of a *legal* ideology. The caseload management model tried to reduce areas of discretion of the staff to insure greater protection of the rights of clients. The use of grievance procedures, including due process procedures, also exemplifies the operation of legal philosophy in this agency.

As *organizational goals* are based on value premises, they are by definition ideologically bound. This agency's goals included social care, social control, and rehabilitation. Although the staff was reluctant to recognize their social control functions in the child abuse area, they were required to investigate and assist in the prosecution of parents who violated the child abuse law.

Administrative decision making can also be influenced by professional ideology. This administrator's attempt to change his agency was very much constrained by the organizational context of the psychological belief system that prevailed among the staff. In general, the administrator's managerial philosophy seemed to be influenced by a *political* ideology. He saw as a key problem the way *power* was distributed in the agency, and one of his first actions was to change this power structure (see case application in Chapter 10, "Decision Making").

Effective *leadership* skills require the understanding that *ideological conflicts* should be avoided as they are generally unresolvable. This administrator did attempt to avoid such conflicts, by focusing on structural issues. His official position was that the staff would be judged on the *outcome* of their efforts in terms of client benefit, regardless of the philosophy they used to achieve this outcome. This willingness to allow diverse approaches probably helped minimize the ideological conflict.

HUMAN SERVICE
TECHNOLOGIES

14

OUTLINE

I. Issues
   A. People versus Situation-Changing Technologies
   B. Quality versus Quantity in Human Services
   C. Human Service Technologies for the Poor

II. Definition
   A. People-Changing versus People-Processing Technologies
   B. Determinate versus Indeterminate Human Service Technologies
      1. Knowledge of Cause—effect Relationships
      2. Objective Feedback System of Evaluation
      3. Reliability and Validity of Human Service Technology
      4. Training Potential of Technology

III. Staffing Arrangements
   A. Specialization
   B. Teamwork

IV. Organizational Auspice and Service Delivery Pattern

V. Goals of Social Care, Social Control, and Rehabilitation and Human Service Technologies
   A. Social Care Technologies
      1. Social Ecology
      2. Social Provision
      3. Resource Systems
      4. Community Support
      5. Least Restrictive Environment
      6. Normalization
      7. Habilitation
      8. Opening Opportunity Structures
      9. People Processing
      10. Situational Analysis

ISSUES

The service delivery technologies used in the human service field have, over the last ten years, expanded to include a variety of roles and techniques. Whereas previously the direct service practitioner's role was confined to psychological support and counseling, now the practitioner acts as a broker, advocate, mediator, resource coordinator, caseload manager, expediter, and even "procurer" (*Rules and Regulations* 1980:47). As the literature on human service technologies grows rapidly, with numerous descriptions of new roles and approaches (Hasenfeld 1983:389; Siporin 1975:136–156), the human service administrator must have some way to determine what kinds of technologies are appropriate for achieving the purposes of his or her organization. Practitioners also can benefit from being aware of the new technologies and can choose to master those that might prove relevant.

In our earlier discussion of practitioner ideologies (Chapter 13) we suggested that as cause–effect relationships were often not known in the delivery of human service, ideologies were necessary to justify and legitimate action. Although ideologies are useful, this indeterminate situation creates tension and uncertainty for both administrators and practitioners. How can an administrator be sure that allocation of resources to one technology or another will result in effective and efficient service? How—apart from ideology—can direct service practitioners, when confronted with clients' demands, have assurance that the procedures and techniques used are the appropriate ones?

These questions concerning technologies in the human service field will be analyzed around three issues: *(a)* people- versus situation-changing technologies, *(b)* quality versus quantity of services, and *(c)* technologies for the poor.

People- versus Situation-Changing Technologies

Some believe that the people- versus situation-changing dichotomy is a false one and that an integrated technology is more often found (e.g., W. Schwartz 1969:22, 22–43). The position presented here is that conceptually and operationally, a distinction can be made between these two roles. Moreover, such a distinction is desirable from the point of view of both administrator and practitioner, in that it facilitates clear-cut performance standards and accountability. As suggested earlier, the two activities are appropriate for different kinds of human service objectives—social care versus rehabilitation.

Making the distinction does not resolve the problem of when it is appropriate to use one or the other technology. Are the skills and techniques needed to change situations basically different from those needed to change people? This issue was previously discussed in terms of the differences between changing people versus policies (see Chapter 5) and in terms of the relationships that exist between these two intervention targets (see Chapter 1). For example, in acting as a broker for a client to enable him to obtain health services, should the human service practitioner motivate the client to demand his right to health services (people change)? Should the practitioner attempt, instead, to "convince" the health service intake staff member to provide service to the client (person *and* situation change)? Alternatively, should the focus of the human service practitioner be on the policies of the health agency and the use of the structure to insure that the client is receiving the services to which he is entitled (situation change)?

This illustration indicates the complexity of distinguishing between people- and situation-changing technologies. However, it is important to attempt to make the differences clear in view of the tendency in the human service field to assume that people change is the *same* as situation change and that interpersonal skills are the primary techniques for task accomplishment.

The distinction between people and situation change is illustrated by a research demonstration project in public welfare (E. Schwartz 1967). In this project supervisors had overall responsibility for the study, diagnosis, classification, and formulation of case plan, with workers assigned specific, time-limited tasks. Workers, therefore, did not have caseloads, but rather, workloads. After completion of a task with one client they would terminate their contact and be assigned tasks with a different client. The worker could work in specialized areas (housing, health, employment, etc.) and could be described as a technician rather than a counselor. A key assumption underlying this project was that a one-to-one relationship between worker and client was *not* essential. In contrast, in most people-changing technologies, a client–worker relationship is considered a basic requirement.

Another way to understand the distinction between people and situation change is to examine the difference between process and product. In people-changing technologies the *process* of interaction between client and practitioner is given much importance. This area of practice usually requires detailed process recording of the interactions between worker and client. Some have even suggested that for this area the maxim would be that "process is our best product." The stress on product or outcome, in contrast, would leave open the choice of means (process) to achieving a particular goal, assuming that there may be many "roads to Rome."

It is suggested that it is important to distinguish between people- and situation-changing technologies because these are in fact quite different in the techniques and skills required. Only by clarifying the difference can administrators be clear as to alternatives for action. To better understand the issues involved, one can examine the differences between "hard" and "soft" services in the human service field, which have been identified as requiring "determinate" and "indeterminate" technologies, respectively (Hasenfeld and English 1974:280). The distinction between determinate and indeterminate technologies is important for human service administrators because the two kinds of technologies differ greatly in the extent to which they may be monitored and their success evaluated. A determinate technology assumes that the cause–effect relationships between inputs and outcomes are known. For example, the provision of social security benefits is a determinate service because the required input and outcome has been operationalized. The same may be said of other "social provision" areas such as health care, homemaker service, employment, etc. Determinate technologies are characterized by the following attributes: *(a)* cause–effect relationship is known; *(b)* evaluation by feedback of results is possible; *(c)* the technology is reliable and valid; and *(d)* persons can be readily trained in the technology (Perrow 1961:856–860). In contrast, the indeterminate technologies, which are used in people-changing human service agencies, lack many of these attributes.

One would think that given their advantages from a practitioner and administrative point of view, the determinate technologies would be preferred over the indeterminate ones. It has been suggested that a Gresham's Law of human services results in hard services driving out soft services (Gummer 1979c:389). The opposite seems to be the case, however. The explanation is that the influence of psychology on the human service field has led to an emphasis on people change as the most appropriate form of intervention (Johnson and Rubin 1983:52). This phenomena of a profession using a single technology from a specific type of training has been termed "the law of the instrument". This law is illustrated in the analogy that states: "give a small boy a hammer and he will find that everything he encounters needs hammering" (Kaplan 1964:28). This is also evident in the health field where people-changing activities have more prestige than situational modification (Coulton 1981:32). The concrete service strategy tends to be dismissed as "unprofessional" and "simplistic," and the provision of concrete services is delegated to the untrained or paraprofessional staff.

The fallacy in these assumptions can be illustrated by examining what might be involved in the provision of a concrete service, such as helping a client obtain adequate housing. Imagine a welfare client who is living in a very inadequate slum apartment, which lacks space (one bedroom for family of five) and such essential services as heat. The worker contacts the public housing agency and discovers that they prefer not to accept welfare clients. The worker must be aware of the official policies of this housing agency to determine if exclusion of his client is justified. Assuming it is not, the worker then advises the client to go to the legal services program for help. At the same time this worker speaks to the housing specialist in his agency and discovers that there exists an affiliation agreement between the housing agency and his organization, specifying mutual roles and expectations. This affiliation agreement was mandated by a state agency that supplies funds to both agencies. The administrator of this worker's agency is then informed of the apparent violation of the affiliation agreement. At the same time, the client's lawyer is preparing to sue the housing agency on the basis of discriminatory action.

As one can see from this example, the kinds of knowledge and skills required in resource provision can be extensive. These include an understanding of official policies, of community resources, and of the dynamics of interorganizational cooperation, power, and conflict (Johnson and Rubin 1983:53). The practitioner must be able to work "with institutional networks and organizational structures ... with their policies, regulations, procedures, and forms; with organizational bureaucracies; with the ways maximal use can be made of their benefits and services [Siporin 1975, p:140]." Thus, the assumption that the skills required in this type of technology are "not professional" reflects a lack of understanding of what is involved. Ultimately, the activities of personnel engaged in resource provision require an understanding of how to establish "systematic links with external recipient units ... that are part of larger organizational networks [Hasenfeld 1974:62]." This knowledge of the community as a "system" is quite different from the knowledge emphasized in the people-changing technologies.

Quality versus Quantity in Human Services

Given the lack of evidence on the effectiveness of human service programs the assumption has been made that *quality* of service is associated with *intensity* while quantity is linked with less frequent intervention of client contacts (e.g., B. Neugeboren 1970a:41). The idea that "more is better" is based on the premise that if existing technologies are valid and the input is increased, outcome will, of necessity, be improved. This assumption of linearity is in part derived from the field of psychoanalysis, in which greater depth of the therapy is achieved by frequent sessions and is assumed to result in more effective outcomes.

This assumption that intensity correlates with effectiveness was questioned by studies of brief and extended casework, which found the former to be more effective than the latter (Reid and Shyne 1969). Similarly, although staff often translate the assumption that "more is better" into a demand for smaller caseloads (Weissman 1973), studies in the field of probation have found little relationship between caseload size and outcome: "The conclusion was that the concept of a caseload is meaningless without some kind of classification and matching of offender type, service to be offered, and staff [*Corrections* 1973:319]."

The question of whether "more is better" oversimplifies the issue, as it assumes the intervention and its target are fairly uniform. Although this may be true in psychoanalytic therapy, it certainly is not the case in human service programs, where the types of problems brought by consumers are so varied. Although psychiatric nomenclature recognizes the wide range of diagnoses that are possible, treatment modalities are somewhat more limited. Consequently, in the psychiatric treatment field the situation is one of different diagnoses but *undifferentiated* treatments.

The issue of quality (more intensive) versus quantity (less intensive) is important for administrators, as it is very much related to the efficient use of resources. If *less* intervention is sometimes more effective, then a policy using brief contacts can save funds and permit more services to more consumers.

Human Service Technologies for the Poor

The findings from a variety of studies of human service programs indicate that social class is a key variable associated with social problems. Epidemiological surveys revealed that the incidence and prevalence of schizophrenia are correlated with lower economic class (Mechanic 1980:49). Child abuse (Gil 1970), death rates, mental retardation, cerebral palsy, epilepsy, behavior disorders, reading disability (Romanyshyn 1971:181), disability of the elderly (Nelson 1982), and crime (*President's Commission on Law Enforcement and Administration of Justice* 1968) are also class related.

The poverty programs of the 1960s were concerned with the development of human service technologies specifically suited to meet the needs of the lower classes. This concern was stimulated by evidence that most of the human service technologies in existence were more suitable to the values and expectations of the middle class (Richan and Mendelsohn 1973:103–104). Making a distinction between middle and lower classes in terms of values risks the criticism of "blaming the victim" (Ryan 1971); (see also Chapter 13). Some have suggested that since the individualized treatment model is based on middle class values it is invalid in the criminal justice field (American Friends Service Committee 1971). Therefore, there was ample evidence supporting the need for a different service modality. For example, it was found that lower-class patients expected psychological therapists to assume a more active medical role and that when this did not occur they tended to become dissatisfied and stop their treatment (Overall and Aronson 1963:421–430). Characteristics that have been attributed to members of low-income groups include toughness, smartness, excitement, fate, autonomy, stress on family and kinship, neighboring, anti-intellectuality, authoritarianism, intolerance, pessimism, nonverbalness, traditionalism, action, belief in luck, and nonjoining (Reisman, Cohen, and Pearl 1964:114). New approaches in assessment of problems were advocated not only because of such value differences, but also because the usual methods of intake and diagnosis were found to be biased (Reisman, Cohen, and Pearl 1964:241–274). New service approaches were also advocated and included brief contacts, treatment in the home, role playing, and game and other "active" and nonverbal approaches.

In addition to new technologies, different organizational arrangements were introduced to facilitate greater utilization of human service programs by low-income clients. Decentralization of service involved moving offices into the low-income neighborhoods, with outreach workers actively seeking residents who needed aid (B. Neugeboren 1970b). Neighborhood centers were established similar to the British citizen advice bureaus (Kahn et al. 1966; Perlman and Jones 1967). Access to human services was emphasized and advocacy techniques were used to insure that lower-class clients would be helped to navigate through hostile bureaucratic systems (Kahn 1970:95–102). Social service offices were established in such systems as local public schools, housing projects, and employment centers (B. Neugeboren 1970b). "Radical casework" was proposed as a means for changing policies within dysfunctional bureaucratic systems (Rein 1970:23–25).

The staffing patterns also underwent modifications. Indigenous non-professionals were hired on the assumption that their personal understanding of the problems of poverty could be used as a bridge between middle-class professionals and lower-income clients. Indigenous nonprofessionals are better able than professionals to deal with external client groups (Katan 1974:558–567) and are more oriented to service provision (Lowenberg 1968). Professionals can have a trained incapacity to work with the poor; that is, they may overlook material deprivations as cause of malfunctioning in their stress on personality inadequacy. They react to the helplessness of clients as "dependency" and therefore are constrained from "doing" for the client (Geismar and Krisberg 1967:294–304).

Although indigenous nonprofessional staff were able to perform important roles in linking the agency with lower-class consumers, they tended to lose their unique skills as they became integrated into the professionally dominated agency culture. One mechanism used for dealing with this problem was the "compartmentalization" of the nonprofessionals where they had a separate supervisory structure and where peer reinforcement was facilitated (Hardcastle 1968:56–64).

DEFINITION

Technology has been defined as a "set of institutionalized procedures aimed at changing the physical, psychological, social or cultural attributes of people in order to transfer them from a given status to new prescribed status [Hasenfeld 1983:111]." Technologies may be directed at people or situation change. The distinction between these two types of change can be clarified through a discussion of people change and people processing technologies.

People-Changing versus People-Processing Technologies

People-changing technologies are directed at altering the behavior of clients indirectly or directly through change of attitudes. Attitude changes are achieved through such approaches as counseling, psychotherapy, group therapy, symbolic interaction, existentialism, and problem solving. Direct behavior change is achieved through behavior modification (Thomas 1967). People-changing organizations have as their major purpose socialization and social control. They use interpersonal methods by structuring staff–client relations (Vinter 1963).

People-processing technologies are directed at changing the public status of the person without altering the person's behavior. They are directed at changing societal reactions to the client by influencing the range of social opportunities available (Hasenfeld 1974:61). Although the literature on people-processing functions stresses the classification and disposition of clients through diagnostic or screening activities, a more important function relates to change of public status. It is here that people processing differs markedly from people changing. The basic assumption is that the person's functioning is not the critical factor, but rather that the environment is the problem and that the task is therefore to relocate the consumer into a more functional situation.

People processing was demonstrated in a program to enable chronic psychotics to work and function in the community, a project called the "Lodge" (Fairweather 1969). The assumption underlying this program was that mental illness involves two problems: *(a)* the need to control the deviant behavior of the mentally ill, and *(b)* the judgment society makes of their capacity to assume rights and duties. The former problem influences the latter; that is, the need to control deviancy leads to unrealistically low expectations of the capacity of the mentally ill to assume responsibilities. Thus the mentally ill are accorded an inferior social status. This results from the following sequence of events:

1. Official diagnosis forces individuals from an acute to a chronic patienthood status through cultural labeling.
2. Inside the total institution of the mental hospital this chronic status is reinforced.
3. In the discharge process, the individuals become involved with various institutions such as after-care clinics, halfway houses, and sheltered workshops, all of which emphasize their patient status.

Thus, they are locked into a permanent system of dependency and an inferior social status.

In the Lodge program discharged male schizophrenic patients lived together and worked together in a house-cleaning business. The goal of the program was to transfer all the functions of running this business to the residents, so that they would be placed in nondeviant roles. The controls that were established were from the peer group, so that the community social control agents (e.g., police and social workers) would be kept at a distance. In general, the effort was to reduce public visibility of these chronic psychotics. A new social status was created with various situational supports. The results were that although these *chronic* schizophrenics continued to have such symptoms as delusions and hallucinations, they were *able to function* in the performance of the tasks in this house maintenance business. Thus they adequately performed house cleaning tasks and were perceived as "normal" by the customers once they learned to conceal their symptoms. This project thus demonstrated how it is possible to counter society's perpetuation of the sick, subordinate, inferior status role of the mentally ill—a status that is derived from an evaluation of people that is based on their *psychological adjustment* and that disregards their behavioral competence. The project also indicated that professionals tend to *underestimate* the capabilities of the chronically ill. In this regard it is of interest to note that when these men worked in the homes of the staff from the hospital their functioning deteriorated. This is related to the more general tendency in society to classify people as *either* sick *or* well. A chronic condition, therefore, becomes identified as "sick," even though the individual may be able to function (e.g., person with a chronic heart condition). This tendency is reinforced by the stress on the goal of *cure*.

This description of the Lodge experiment, then, should serve to illustrate the nature of people-processing technologies and, in particular, their emphasis on changing the *public status* of the person rather than changing his or her behavior.

Determinate versus Indeterminate Human Service Technologies

An ideal technology is one that provides clear-cut criteria for its successful implementation. Such a technology is termed a determinate technology, and it displays a number of specific characteristics (Perrow 1965). Indeterminate technology, in contrast, lack these characteristics.

Knowledge of Cause–Effect Relationships

The first characteristic of determinate technologies is that they make it possible to understand what effects or consequences for the solution of human problems specific procedures and actions will have. Knowing in advance which means will lead to which results is important for achieving efficient and effective human service programs. If we are clear as to the amount and nature of the input required for particular outcomes, we can develop monitoring and control mechanisms to insure that such input is implemented. The difficulty in operationalizing this criteria in the human service field rests with lack of systematic data on the relationship of input to outcome.

However, recent reports indicate some positive results of treatment with behavioral therapy which is somewhat more effective than family therapy which is more effective than individual therapy (Thomlinson, 1984).

Knowledge of cause–effect relationships in the delivery of human service does vary depending on the nature of the program. Program operationalization and determinancy is more feasible in the delivery of *hard* services, for example, in employment, day care, family planning, and health care programs. It has even been suggested that Gresham's Law of planning mandates that routinized programs will replace nonprogrammed activity (March and Simon 1958:125). Although routinization is useful from the point of view of reducing uncertainty, it tends to go counter to the human service professional's need for freedom and autonomy. There is strong belief that routinized activities, which do not require judgment and discretion, are by their very nature "unprofessional" and therefore less valid in serving consumers. This bias against routinized technologies is further reinforced when the ideological basis of the technology is questioned. This is evident in the use of drug therapy in the mental health field. Drugs are probably one of the least expensive and more routinized of the human service technologies. The introduction of methadone maintenance in the area of heroin addiction was and still is viewed as not very legitimate by professionals in the field of drug addiction. A similar situation arises with the use of tranquilizers in the treatment of mental disturbance.

The desirability of knowing cause–effect relations in the use of human service technologies is self-evident. However, what are administrators to do in their day-to-day decision making when this knowledge doesn't exist? An alternative is to base decisions on the results obtained. Take, for example, a child welfare office where a variety of technologies are used, including both hard and soft services. The administration may encourage these different approaches on the grounds that they have to demonstrate their validity in terms of case outcome (see case "From Psychological Work to Social Work"). A comparison could then be made of the relative effectiveness of hard versus soft services (B. Neugeboren 1979:186) in terms of such outcome criteria as "permanency planning" or the normal development of the child. This "competition" among various technologies could thus eventually demonstrate the superiority of one over the others, leading to a policy of allocating more program resources to that approach to service delivery.

Objective Feedback System of Evaluation

The second attribute of an ideal technology is a feedback system on the consequences of action. The importance of a system of feedback on the consequences of various human service technologies relates to the need for a mechanism to guide administrator and practitioner decisions. Feedback could include data on input such as the number of contacts and/or results of intervention (e.g., client functioning). A difficulty here is that one can never be certain that the consequences are the direct result of the particular intervention technique. Nevertheless, assessment is possible on a relative basis using aggregate data. Thus, staff productivity would be evaluated in terms of an average for the group. Such data might include the number of interviews conducted in a given time period by staff. This quantitative data is often dismissed by professionals, who argue that "quality" is much more important. Thus the administrator may be placed in the very difficult situation of trying to convince staff that quantitative measures are legitimate. Often the administrator will resort to arguing that funding sources pay on the basis of quantity or that monitoring is necessary because "those people in Washington" require it.

Measures of the content of technological input are more complicated than measures of the *quantity* of this input. Evaluative studies in social work have been criticized on the grounds that the measures of input were too gross and did not take into account such factors as the level of training of the social workers (Fischer 1973:13; Wood 1978:438). Measurement of the *content* of input is probably less difficult in the delivery of such concrete services such as day care, homemaker services, or health services. It seems more feasible to define in specific terms what actions are appropriate to help a client find a job or an apartment than to define what is needed to help a client develop more self-confidence or esteem. Therefore, in the soft service area the evaluation of the nature of a technological input becomes more complicated and an objective feedback system more difficult to achieve.

Reliability and Validity of Human Service Technology

The *reliability* of a human service technology refers to the ability to repeat the performance of the method so that each execution is similar to the others. Given their indeterminate nature, most human service technologies are difficult to standardize. For example, the reliability of psychiatric diagnosis has been found to be quite low (Schmidt and Fonds 1956; Beck 1962; Mechanic 1980:93). Here again, there is a wide range of variation. Administration of drug dosage is a very reliable technology, as the exact amount can be measured. Unless technological input is standardized to a greater degree it will be very difficult to determine why certain technologies are more effective than others. An exception is in the behavioral approaches: The reliability of the technologies in the behavior modification area can be tested because of the focus on specifically defined actions (Thomas 1967).

The *validity* of human service technologies refers to its effectiveness. As has been stressed throughout this book, the effectiveness of human service programs is tied to client benefit. Therefore, a valid technology would be one that demonstrated improvement in the client's situation. As indicated earlier, the emphasis on cure and the dichotomizing that occurs in the health field (sick versus well) may be too stringent an expectation for most human service technologies. It should also be noted that the degree of success of human service technologies will vary depending on the problem being served. The rate of success in treatment of schizophrenia will be quite different from that of an adjustment problem of adolescence. Therefore, in determining the validity of a particular technology the nature of the problem has to be kept constant.

The decision as to what rate of success justifies use or discontinuance of a technology has to be based on a cost–benefit calculation. That is, given the limitation of resources, the administrator and practitioner have to decide on the *relative* value of different technologies in terms of the goal of the human service agency. Assume that a mental health agency has the goal of enabling schizophrenics to live in the community. Assume, further, that with community support technologies this goal can be achieved with a 50% success rate at an annual cost of $5,000 per patient. The judgment as to whether 50% is adequate will depend whether alternative technologies are available that can achieve a better cost–benefit ratio. If no other technologies have a better ratio, then this agency has no choice but to accept this level of success. The authorities that fund this agency will also have to judge what rate of success is acceptable, and they can do so by comparing various mental health organizations.

The outcome of client benefit is ideally measured in behavioral terms— the extent to which the client's situation has improved. As this type of measurement can be difficult to obtain, it may be necessary to substitute a measurement of client satisfaction. But, although such measurements are readily acceptable in the marketplace, in the human service field they are doubted. For example, the evaluation of university teaching by student opinions has been criticized as invalid even though there is considerable evidence to support it (*Academe* 1979). Similar doubts are raised at the validity of clients' opinions of the benefits they derived from a service.

Training Potential of Technology

The last attribute of an ideal human service technology is the extent to which it can be communicated and ease with which personnel can be trained in its use. The training potential of technologies will vary with their complexity and determinancy. If the cause–effect relations are unknown and the technology is not sufficiently operationalized to allow for a determination of its reliability or validity then it probably will be difficult to communicate in such a way that others can master it.

Given that human service technologies are being introduced at an ever more rapid rate, the ability to train personnel in new technologies becomes extremely important. There are limitations, however, in educational programs offering human service practitioners practical training. Traditionally professionals have received their basic training in the university, which has stressed conceptual rather than technical skills. As a result, lawyers need to take courses in how to make wills or draw up mortgages after they graduate from law school. The skill aspect of professional education is often left to the practicum component, which may not be under the direct control of the university. Some professional training schools either do not require practicums (e.g., law) or have very limited ones (e.g., health administration). Public and business administration programs training students for careers in human service administration usually do not even require field experience. Another alternative to the teaching of technical skills has been classroom simulation of practice (Rothman and Jones 1971). However, regardless of the method used, there will probably always be some difficulty in bridging the gap between university training and the technologies required in the world of practice.

Given this gap, it becomes the responsibility of agency-sponsored staff development programs to train personnel in human service technologies. A basic constraint here, which was discussed in Chapter 11, is the tendency for in-service training to be oriented to perpetuating existing technologies.

In recent years, the function of upgrading technological skills in the human service field is increasingly being filled by postgraduate continuing education programs (B. Neugeboren 1981). The extent to which these programs will be oriented toward specific technical skills is yet to be determined. These postgraduate noncredit progrms can provide the opportunity for professional schools to add technical education to its base by bringing in experienced practitioners as instructors.

Given the many difficulties involved in training, the ability to train personnel efficiently and effectively in a particular human service technology is highly advantageous. In agencies plagued by turnover, technologies that have a high training potential are particularly important, as they can help minimize the instability.

STAFFING ARRANGEMENTS

Specialization

The increase in the number of technologies used in human service organizations has been accompanied by a corresponding increase in specialization, that is, in the different kinds of personnel employed. Human service organizations employ personnel from a wide range of professions, for example, doctors, psychologists, nurses, teachers, social workers, and lawyers. In addition to these professional specialties, we find different levels within each profession. For example, in social work there are people trained on the bachelors, masters, and doctoral levels. Nursing and psychology are also characterized by several levels of education. Within each profession there is also a variety of subspecialties. And, as discussed earlier, human service organizations also employ indigenous nonprofessionals. The human service administrator is thus confronted with the problem of deciding which professional specialties or subspecialties are needed to deliver the services of his or her organization.

This kind of decision might be fairly straightforward if one could assume that these different specialty areas were mutually exclusive. In fact, however, much of the education of these human service professionals is quite similar. For example, the stress on counseling and human relations training has become dominant in the fields of psychiatry, psychology, social work, and nursing. The mental health team, which was once justified on the grounds that each discipline contributed a unique expertise, is now fairly uniform as team members all emphasize therapeutic skills. Similarly, although one approach to the division of labor would be to assign more complex tasks to persons with higher levels of education, studies of the relative effectiveness of persons with different levels of education have found few differences in performance (Barker and Briggs 1968; B. Neugeboren 1970b:51). However, it was previously noted that less educated indigenous personnel had unique skills based on their special life experiences that could be a *complement* to the professionals. The distinction here is that it may be more functional to have specialization by *person* rather than by *task* (V. Thompson 1961:Chapter 3).

Teamwork

The use of teamwork in the human service field has also been increasing (Weissman 1973:Chapter 1). The assumptions behind the team concept are that each team member has unique expertise and that there is equality among members leading to open communication and effective problem solving. These assumptions may in fact be incorrect. In all group situations, status hierarchies naturally occur (Blau and Scott 1962:121–123) even if there are no apparent status differences. In human service teams there *are* obvious status differences, for example, among psychiatrists, psychologists, social workers, and nurses. Therefore, the effectiveness of teamwork, insofar as it relies on democracy and open communication, might be diminished.

The appropriateness of teamwork will also depend on the task to be performed. Experiments with small group problem solving differentiate between two tasks: the creative problem solving involved in discovering new and innovative solutions and the problem solving required to arrive at a single correct solution. The distinction is evident if we compare the task of *constructing a crossword puzzle* and that of finding the *one correct answer in completing a crossword puzzle*. These two types of tasks require two different kinds of structures. In finding the *one* correct answer, a group structure is useful. Furthermore in order to facilitate the error-correction mechanism of the group process, free and open communication is needed. Therefore, in this type of group problem-solving situation it is imperative that open communication be facilitated and hierarchical barriers minimized. Skilled leadership may be able to perform this function of facilitating open communication.

In contrast, creative problem solving may be more effectively accomplished by individual effort. We are all familiar with the frustrations that occur when a committee attempts to do such creative work as writing a report. The main problem here is that of achieving effective *coordination*. Although hierarchies can facilitate coordination of members of a group, the group process of open communications itself may work against effective coordination (Blau and Scott 1962:119).

The implications of the preceding discussion for efficiency and effectiveness of human service programs should be self-evident. The efficiency or cost of programs will be heavily influenced by use of teamwork, as the expense in terms of manpower can be considerable. Before allocating resources to teamwork technology, the administrator should be clear that it is appropriate for the task and that an individual decision-making model is not in fact preferable. As much of the decision making in human service programs involves creative solutions, it may in general be more appropriate to utilize an individual problem-solving model.

The continued popularity of the teamwork technology in the human service field is probably related to the strong belief in the value of participatory management (see Chapter 3, "Management Models"). Another factor encouraging teamwork is the strain and tension present in the day-to-day activities of the staff of human service organizations (see Chapter 7, "Occupational Burnout"). As groups function to provide social support to their members (Blau and Scott 1962:119), their value in alleviating stress may explain their widespread use. Thus, from an administrative and organizational point of view, the issue can become one of deciding where the priorities lie—in meeting staff needs or in providing the most efficient and effective service to the consumer. The advocates of teamwork should be able to justify this expensive technology not only on the grounds that it fulfills staff needs for participation and support, but also on the grounds that it effectively accomplishes the task at hand.

The assumption that team members have unique expertise has been questioned earlier in this chapter. Although a diversity of knowledge can be useful, the human service administrator should not take for granted that it will exist among personnel with different credentials. However, teams made up of persons with complementary skills can be highly effective as was demonstrated in a poverty program, where the teams consisted of professionals and indigenous nonprofessionals. It was found that cases serviced by both professionals and nonprofessionals achieved better outcomes than those serviced by only a professional or nonprofessional. The professionals were more successful in helping residents obtain employment whereas nonprofessionals were more effective in helping clients receive financial assistance and housing (B. Neugeboren 1970b:51). It was evident here that the skill diversity between the professional and nonprofesssional facilitates teamwork.

ORGANIZATIONAL AUSPICE AND SERVICE DELIVERY PATTERNS

This section will present information on the relationships of organizational auspice and service delivery patterns in community psychiatric clinics. How the organizational situation can affect the methods used in the delivery of services will be illustrated here. The data in this section was obtained from a study of 245 psychiatric outpatient clinics in the state of New York (B. Neugeboren 1970a).

Organizational auspice is defined as consisting of these separate organizational characteristics: *(a)* public versus voluntary sponsorship, *(b)* hospital versus community setting, and *(c)* specialized versus unspecialized service.

Sponsorship relates to whether the organization is under the authority of a governmental or nongovernmental agency. A county-government-sponsored clinic would be classified as under *public* sponsorship. A private-sponsored child guidance center under a community board is an agency under *voluntary* sponsorship. *Setting* is classified in terms of hospital or community. A *hospital* setting is characteristic of programs affiliated with a medical institution such as a general hospital. A nonhospital, *community* setting is characteristic of programs not associated with a medical institution. A *specialized service* is devoted to a particular target group or problem; examples include programs for the retarded, alcoholics, drug addicts, criminal offenders, children, etc. Unspecialized services provide help to all groups in the population.

The major finding of the study of psychiatric outpatient clinics was that organizational auspice was significantly associated with two service delivery patterns: intensive and extensive. These two service delivery patterns characterize the way service resources are allocated among pathological and socially deviant patients. An *intensive* service delivery pattern is one in which few patients are served but those that are seen receive a relatively large number of contacts. The patients receiving intensive service were typically the less socially deviant and pathological. An *extensive* service pattern is one in which more patients receive service but each person has relatively few contacts. The patients receiving this type of service tended to be among the more deviant and pathological.

Public sponsorship and hospital setting were both associated with an extensive service pattern, voluntary sponsorship and community setting with an intensive service pattern. Specialized programs were found to have *both* intensive and extensive service patterns.

The aspect of organizational auspice that most influenced service delivery patterns was public–voluntary sponsorship: "Wholesale" (extensive) psychiatric services were provided by publicly sponsored agencies, "retail" (intensive) services by nongovernment agencies. Thus, like other institutions in our society, human service agencies are socially stratified. The poor tend to be served in the extensive, publicly sponsored agencies; a criticism that has often been made of voluntary agencies is that they neglect the poor (Cloward and Epstein 1967; Sarri 1982:27). The problem is exacerbated by differences in funding: Hospitals under public and voluntary sponsorship differ significantly in the amount of financial support they receive (Elling and Halebsky 1961). Also private auspice was found to *constrain* innovation (Tucker 1980:43).

The differences between agencies under public versus voluntary sponsorship have major implications for the required technologies. Publicly sponsored agencies will require service approaches appropriate to the groups they serve: lower-class clients (Kupers 1981:22–24; Jansson 1979) and more pathological and deviant psychiatric patients. In general public social service agencies typically are involved in such activities as "outreach, brokerage, mobilization, care giving, behavior changing and information processing," whereas private treatment agencies might engage in such rehabilitative approaches as reality therapy, activity therapy, psychodrama, crisis intervention and milieu treatment [M. Austin 1981:9]."

The work environment characteristic of public human service agencies, in which external pressures are quite extreme, also requires different abilities and skills at both the practitioner and administrator levels. The lack of these skills is probably responsible for high turnover of staff and burnout (see Chapter 7).

Part of the reason staff in public agencies lack needed skills relates to their prior training. Much of the field training in the human services occurs in agencies under voluntary sponsorship. In the study of psychiatric clinics it was found that clinics under voluntary sponsorship that received no public funds did more training than those that were grant supported and that publicly sponsored clinics did the least amount of training of all. This pattern held regardless of area—it characterized the training of psychiatrists, psychologists, and social workers (B. Neugeboren 1970a:160–162). The inability of publicly sponsored clinics to provide training is probably due to the lack of time because of excessive demands for service. As a result, the cycle is perpetuated whereby the training institutions promote the "trained incapacity" of the human service professional to perform in public programs. The consequences can be dramatic. For example, it was found that in a public child welfare agency the turnover rate of casework educated staff was twice that of staff educated in social work administration (B. Neugeboren 1978). This difference can be explained by the inability of clinically educated professionals to use their skills in a public agency, where work demands prevent them from giving "intensive" services. Direct service workers in public agencies need skills in case and resource management as much as, if not more than, they need therapeutic skills (Gummer 1979b:14).

The problem that public agencies have in providing field training was confirmed in a study of the training experiences of students in social work administration. Outcome data on students' satisfaction and performance indicated that learning experiences were less adequate in agencies under public sponsorship than in agencies under voluntary sponsorship (B. Neugeboren 1977:20).

In conclusion, organizational auspice is a significant factor influencing the technologies used in human service programs. The implications for administrators of human service organizations relate to policies on hiring and in-service training. Policies need to take into account the potential for professional incapacity in cases where individuals were educated under one auspice and are practicing under the other. Given that most training occurs under voluntary sponsorship, "remedial" in-service training efforts will be especially crucial in public agencies. However, given that the staff working in training

units in public agencies themselves came out of an educational system influenced by the voluntary context, there are also limits to their ability to provide
the skills needed for public agency practice. The cycle can be broken only
if institutions of higher education develop specialized programs for training
for the public human service sector.

GOALS OF SOCIAL CARE, SOCIAL CONTROL, AND REHABILITATION AND HUMAN SERVICE TECHNOLOGIES

As technologies are means, it is important to understand for which goals
they are or are not suitable. In this section we will explore the relation of
human service technologies to the three major goals of human service programs: social care, social control, and rehabilitation. Clarification of means–
ends relationships can facilitate more apropriate service on the practice level
and better accountability and control on the administrative level.

In order for such clarification to be useful, however, it must be remem-
bered that service evaluation must be tied to client benefit. Historically, the
human service field has tended to shift from one service approach to another
before validated knowledge was available on the costs and benefits. The current movement for deinstitutionalization, its achievements notwithstanding,
has shown again that simplistic solutions can create new problems. As
Wing (1978) suggests, "A good hospital is better than a poor hostel or
a poor family environment. A good hostel is better than a poor hospital or
a poor family environment [p. 254]."

The following discussion of the technologies associated with each of the
three primary goals of human service programs is intended to foster greater
understanding of the consequences of different service alternatives for program design and implementation. In this discussion of social care, social
control, and rehabilitation technologies, somewhat more attention will be given
to social care as this is an area that is currently being emphasized in human
service programs.

Social Care Technologies

In Chapter 1 *social care* was characterized as emphasizing the provision
of an environment that could enhance positive human functioning. The goal
of social care is to facilitate the individual's use of existing potentials, however
minimal these may be. Although social care is considered particularly appropriate for chronically disabled groups such as the mentally ill, mentally
retarded, elderly, and physically handicapped (R. Morris 1977:353–359), it
can apply to any human problem that can be alleviated by environmental
modification. Environmental change is functional not only for a person who

is confined to a wheelchair and hence could benefit from the provision of a barrier-free environment, but also for a young person who needs to move from his parents' home in order to establish his independence.

Here we will address the question of what kinds of human service technologies are most appropriate for achieving environmental change. Social care technologies will be discussed in terms of the following principles and concepts: *(a)* social ecology, *(b)* social provision, *(c)* resource systems, *(d)* community support systems, *(e)* least restrictive environment, *(f)* normalization, *(g)* habilitation, *(h)* opening opportunity structure, *(i)* people processing, *(j)* discharge planning and case management and *(k)* situational analysis.

Social Ecology

Social ecology is concerned with the impact on human beings of physical and social environments. Moos (1974) has characterized its emphasis as being on the "short term evolutionary adaptive consequences of these environments [p. 20]," and has described six major categories that relate various aspects of environments to human functioning [pp. 22–29]: *(a)* geographic–meteorological–architectural, *(b)* behavior settings, *(c)* organizational structure, *(d)* characteristics of inhabitants, *(e)* psychosocial characteristics and organizational climates, and *(f)* reinforcement analysis of environments. Together, these six categories provide a fairly broad framework for the assessment of physical and social environments.

Geographic–Meteorological–Architectural. The physical environment has been shown to exert an important influence on personality and behavior. Extremes of heat and cold can affect "general health, intellectual performance, admission to mental hospital and organizational participation [Moos 1974:23]." As pointed out earlier, urban riots tend to be associated with hot summers. The priority given to summer youth employment programs may in part be related to the realization of the effect of temperature on antisocial activity ("Sparing of Social Programs" 1981). Color, size, and shape of rooms and hallways can all affect social interaction. For example, a two-hundred-bed, two-story nursing home with one or two persons per room will have many more rooms and longer corridors than a three-story home with two or three persons per room. The former will constrain social interaction and groupings and have more of an institutionalized effect than the latter because of the long corridors and relatively greater isolation of the patients (Gitterman and Germain 1981:47).

These physical factors can be taken into account where relevant in human service delivery programs. Building plans can take into account the effect of architecture on human mood and behavior. Excessive heat and cold can be remedied by allocation of resources for electric heaters and air conditioners. Manipulation of the physical environment can be at the center of program goals, as in summer camp programs and "fresh air" funds for slum residents.

Behavior Settings. The term "behavior settings" refers to the various environmental factors that produce different kinds of behavior expectations. That behavior expectations in turn have consequences for behavior was pointed out in our earlier discussion of the functional consequences that setting high expectations can have for the emotionally disturbed. Many environmental factors have been found to relate to behavior expectations. For example, in schools with smaller numbers of students the expectations are higher than in larger schools.

The Lodge experiment discussed earlier was a behavior setting that provided high levels of performance expectations. The human service practitioner needs to be aware of how different settings are associated with different performance expectations and levels. For example, it has been found that discharged mental patients perform differently depending on whether they return to parents or conjugal families. Parents tend to have much lower expectations than spouses. Consequently, mental patients returning to parental family will perform at a much lower level and continue to remain in the community because their situation tolerates their deviancy. Conjugal families require a higher level of performance, and consequently a greater number of patients discharged to these families return to the hospital (Freeman and Simmons 1963:6). This kind of knowledge could be used by the human service practitioner to provide service that is congruent with the expectations in different kinds of behavior settings.

Another way of characterizing family behavior settings was suggested by Wing (1978:253). He classified the negative social environments for schizophrenics as potentially *over-* and *under*stimulating. Overstimulating situations were found in homes where relatives placed too many pressures on the individual, understimulating situations were characteristic of old-fashioned mental hospitals, where low expectations resulted in "institutionalism." This kind of differentiation, which anticipates negative outcomes, can be a useful guide in formulating service policies and plans.

Organizational Structure. The effect that organizational structure can have on patients has been revealed in various studies of mental hospitals. In hospitals that had informal structures characterized by a high level of staff member disagreement, there was often manic excitement among patients (Stanton and Schwartz 1954:364). Another study found that a suicide epidemic in a hospital was related to changes in the financial and social structure of that organization (Stotland and Kobler 1965).

Organizational size has been found to be an important variable affecting the performance of human service practitioners. Social workers in small branches of a state welfare organization had more of a service orientation and performed better than workers in large branches (Thomas 1959:30–37).

An extensive study of institutional and community treatment environments found that smaller program size and/or higher staffing leads to an emphasis on relationships with patients and a deemphasis of staff control. Increased size and/or decreased staffing creates pressures for more rigid structure and control (Moos 1974:331). Another structural factor, then, is staffing pattern. In a study of treatment environments in community programs it was found that programs with professional staff stressed treatment dimensions, whereas those with nonprofessionals stressed system maintenance dimensions (Moos 1974:332).

The negative consequences of "total institutions" on patients have been extensively documented (Goffman 1959). This information has been utilized by planners and designers of mental institutions to make them more humanistic (Vail 1966).

There are various ways in which human service practitioners can make the organization more responsive to people. For example, administrators can restructure their organizations into smaller work units to capitalize on the value of smaller size. Direct service practitioners can help compensate for the negative effect of dysfunctional structure on their clients, for example, by attempting to modify scheduling procedures that require clients to wait for long periods of time (Coulton 1981:33). Even if constrained by a lack of power and authority, direct service practitioners can exert influence on those in positions of power to make organizational structure more responsive to consumers' needs.

Individual Characteristics. To a great extent, the social and cultural environment depends on people. Therefore, such characteristics as age, ethnicity, religion, socioeconomic class, educational attainment, and mental status all exert an important influence on the environment.

In institutional settings it would seem that homogeneity or diversity could be a significant factor affecting programs. These factors establish standards for behavior expectations which can affect social interaction. Grant (1970) found that age-homogeneous housing contributes to high morale and life satisfaction for the aged. However, patients admitted to an age integrated psychiatric ward had a stimulating effect on social interaction (Kahana and Kahana 1967). The fact that religious and membership organizations (e.g., unions) have sponsored such programs as housing projects, nursing homes, hospitals, etc., may reflect the desire of people to associate with those who have values and experiences similar to their own. In the nursing home field it appears that institutions under religious auspice may provide a more effective service than nonsectarian institutions.

Institutions often tend to separate patients on the basis of personal or behavioral characteristics. Mental hospitals may have different wards for chronic and acute patients. Geriatric patients are sometimes separated from younger residents. In nursing homes the more severely mentally handicapped may be segregated from those who are less handicapped. This emphasis on homogeneity may be questioned, however. My own observations of a nursing home that did *not* segregate patients indicated that diversity had a positive influence. The lower-functioning patients were pressured by other patients to "behave normally," and this high expectation atmosphere seemed to have beneficial effects. The higher-functioning patients also benefited in that they were able to see themselves in a more favorable light. The staff would use this implicit comparison to urge the higher-level patients to strive to improve their performance (e.g., through physical therapy), by suggesting that if they did not they might become like the lower-level patients. It is interesting to note that the patients had a relatively high tolerance for one another, in contrast to the visiting relatives, who perceived the mixing of patients as detrimental to the better-functioning individuals.

Integration versus separation of more deviant individuals has been an issue also in the field of education. "Mainstreaming" of groups such as the mentally retarded, emotionally disturbed, and socially deprived is intended to "normalize" the environment of the handicapped without detrimental effects on others.

The implications of this discussion for human service administration and planning relates to the issue of efficiency and effectiveness. Will integration require more staff effort at maintaining order or less? The need of the organization to maintain order and control must be balanced against the consequence of client benefit. Public relations factors also come into play, as the different publics may or may not approve of integration or separation. Whereas relatives may favor separation, the funding authorities may not.

For the direct service practitioner, the environmental effects of client characteristics need to be taken into account in helping clients and their families to plan for appropriate placement.

Psychosocial Characteristics and Organizational Climates. The specific norms and values present in an organization can help shape its climate. They are in a sense the organization's "cultural heritage" (Katz and Kahn 1980:50). Three dimensions that distinguish different kinds of organizational climates are: *(a)* the relationship dimension, *(b)* the personal development dimension, and *(c)* the system maintenance and system change dimension (Moos 1974:27–28).

The *relationship dimension* refers to the extent to which individuals in the organization's environment support and help one another. The *personal development dimension* refers to the ways in which personal growth and development occur in a particular environment. These include *autonomy* (extent to which people are encouraged to be self-sufficient), *practical orientation* (extent to which program works toward practical goals such as training for future jobs), *personal problem orientation* (the stress on understanding of feelings and problems), and such other emphases as competition, cooperation, intellectuality, and religious orientation. The *system maintenance and system change dimension* is concerned with order and organization, clarity of expectation, and control as opposed to independence, autonomy and open expression of feelings.

Moos studied the organizational climates of hospital- and community-based treatment programs and found all three dimensions to be related to patient morale, indices of coping behavior, and treatment outcome. For example, patients treated in a hospital that allowed some autonomy had better post-hospital work adjustment than patients treated in a hospital that stressed order and control. However, better symptom improvement occurred in the more controlled program.

An understanding of the effects that organizational climates have on service outcome can be useful to the administrator, both in planning new programs and in changing existing ones. Decisions on staffing and in-service training could be influenced by the knowledge of what results are associated with different kinds of environments. The program design plans could take into account the staff roles conducive to more or less autonomy, system maintenance or system change, etc.

The availability of standardized instruments to measure organizational environments provides the human service administrator with the tool to analyze the organization and change it by feeding back to staff the results of this assessment. In a university hospital program, for example, positive change was achieved through feedback of discrepancies between real and ideal treatment climates (Moos 1974:329).

The direct service practitioner must be aware of organizational environments in order to make client referral decisions. The problem here is how to obtain accurate data, as program descriptions, which have a public relations purpose, tend to emphasize positive aspects. A systematic comparison of descriptions and programs revealed significant discrepancies (Moos 1974:272).

Reinforcement Analysis of Environments. The *social learning* perspective stresses that environments are influenced by systems of sanctions and rewards. This emphasis is reflected in the reinforcement approach used in such behavior modification programs as token economies. In the field of education, climates that reinforce the achievement motivation and the kinds of work habits considered desirable can be created through use of specific rewards and sanctions (Moos 1974:28).

The use of this approach in the establishment of different kinds of service environments has received less attention. Given the operational nature of behavior modification, it may have significant potential as an administrative tool for creating and changing organizational environments.

This discussion of social ecology has presented a comprehensive framework for viewing social environments. As social care is concerned with environmental change, this framework can provide guidance as to how and where change should occur. From this somewhat broad view, we shall now turn to more specific principles and concepts associated with the area of social care.

Social Provision

Social provision refers to the use of nonmarket mechanisms to substitute for, supplement, or replace such resources as income, medical care, and housing (Coulton 1981:32). The process is intended "to assure all individuals, as a citizen right, equitable access to those provisions essential for some defined level of well-being [Romanyshin 1971:51]." It thus represents a "quest for social security and social justice [Romanyshin 1971:201]."

Assuming that society provides these benefits the human service delivery system needs to assist the consumer in obtaining them, that is, in overcoming the various institutional barriers to "access to and use of social utilities [Siporin 1975:140]." In order to accomplish this, the human service practitioner must be able to focus on the

> macroenvironmental aspects of the case or service system . . . with an understanding of people in terms of their institutional memberships . . . required to have a . . . skill in working with institutional networks and organizational structures; for example, with a social security, public welfare, or a public school system; with their policies, regulations, procedures and forms; with organizational bureaucracies; with the ways maximal use can be made of their benefits and services [Siporin 1975:140].

Resource Systems

Resource systems have been classified into three categories: informal, formal, and societal (Pincus and Minahan 1973:4). Informal resource systems are natural systems (Delgado and Delgado 1982) such as "family, friends, neighbors, co-workers, bartenders, and other helpers. The aid given by such informal relationships includes emotional support and affection, advice and information, and concrete services or resources such as baby-sitting or loan of money [Pincus and Minahan 1973:4]." *Formal resource systems* are membership associations, such as labor unions, that promote the interests of the members by providing resources which help them negotiate in different systems. *Societal resource systems* are the official government and voluntary agencies that are mandated by the community to fulfill various social provision functions.

The human service practitioner who is attempting to influence and change the situation for the consumer needs to view the environment in terms of these three resource systems (Jenkins and Cook 1981). This is particularly important as changes in the informal resource systems, such as the displacement of the extended family with the nuclear family and the rise of the single-parent family, have required that the formal and societal resource systems assume certain functions previously performed by the informal systems. This "institutional" view of human service functions stresses that "mutual support" of the needy has become necessary as such institutions as family and religions are unable to deal with rapid social and technological change (Gilbert and Specht 1974:9; Froland 1980).

Appreciation of the relevance of societal resource systems has increased under the pressures of deinstitutionalization of chronically ill and dependent persons. Evidence suggests that the mentally ill have been institutionalized for extended periods of time not because they were a threat or required treatment but for social care purposes. The need for institutional care stemmed from the unwillingness or inability of the family or other informal care systems to provide for the needs of the mentally ill in the community (Mechanic 1975:313). With deinstitutionalization the need for care in the community has led to establishment of *community support* systems (Turner 1976; Stein 1979).

Community Support Systems

A community support system differs from traditional bureaucratically organized, single-agency human service programs in the nature of the task to be accomplished. Traditional human service agencies, such as mental health centers, child welfare departments, and probation offices, identify specific areas for service and through time-limited interventions attempt to solve particular problems. In contrast, community support systems are concerned with the entire life situation of the person and attempt to insure that all needs such as housing, health, employment, recreation, and income are met. As no single agency is capable of meeting all these needs, the social care provider must have the skills to coordinate the activities and functions of a variety of human service agencies (Froland *et al.* 1979). "Professions in this context become brokers who must negotiate among varying interests and agencies (Mechanic 1975:316)."

A new approach to develop a comprehensive community support system for the elderly is being done in the "Long Term Care Channeling" project. Channeling refers to comprehensive needs assessment and case management, which in turn involves planning and arranging for care services and then providing monitoring and ongoing assessment (Baxter, et al., 1983). This program attempts to remedy in part the inability of the medical care system to adequately plan for patients who need long-term care, as its technologies are more suited for treatment of acute and episodic disease. Developing patterns of care over extended periods is a considerably more complex task than short-term treatment. It involves "forms of organization outside the medical institution and types of coordination and integration of programs and agencies that require particularly skillful administration [Mechanic 1979:53]."

This assumption of responsibility for the total life space of the individual served potentially has the same negative consequences as "total institutions" (Goffman 1959). This leads us to the principles of *normalization* and *least restrictive environment.*

Least Restrictive Environment

The principle of *least restrictive environment* is related to the legal principle of "least restrictive alternative," which has been stated as follows: "[When] government has a legitimate communal interest to serve by regulating human conduct it should use methods that curtail individual freedom to no greater extent than is essential for securing that interest [Chambers 1975:25]." When applied to services for the mentally ill, this principle entails that "alternatives to commitment ... be assessed in terms of whether they provide needed protection or habilitation, not in terms of their effectiveness in serving the improper function ... of simply screening from sight those who make others in society feel uncomfortable [Chambers 1975:29]."

The difficulties in implementing this principle are shown by the continued lack of adequate protection for the mentally ill who live in the community. Many deinstitutionalized mental patients live in unsupervised boarding homes. The consequences have been numerous and serious. In New Jersey, for example, a series of fires in some of these homes resulted in death of 74 persons within a 6-month period ("Psychiatric Ghettos" 1981). Reports of neglect and even starvation of unsupervised chronically ill in the "back wards" of the community (*Back Wards to Back Streets* 1978) highlight the need for a comprehensive community care program (Comptroller General's Report 1977). The evidence indicates that mentally ill persons *can* live in the community and function—provided they have continuing support and assistance (Test 1975). A basic problem that arises when continuous aid and assistance is given is the risk of creating a low expectation environment that accentuates the chronicity. The principle of *normalization* addresses this problem.

Normalization

Normalization as a principle in the delivery of human services was introduced in the field of mental retardation in the Scandinavian countries. It has been defined by Wolfsenberger as "utilization of means which are culturally normative as possible, in order to establish and/or maintain personal behaviors and characteristics which are culturally normative as possible [Wolfsenberger 1972:28]."

Because normalization attempts to achieve "normative" behavior it is relevant to the phenomenon of *social deviancy,* where deviancy is behavior that "departs from, or conflicts with, standards which are socially or culturally accepted within a social group or system [Himmelweit 1964:196]." Persons who are perceived by the community as "different" will have this deviant status reenforced by the expectation that they will continue to behave in a manner that is unusual. Community attitudes toward such groups as the mentally retarded, the physically handicapped, the cosmetically disfigured, the aged, epileptics, legal offenders, etc., suggest that members are perceived as socially deviant. Until 1920 a range of individuals including "the idiotic, imbecilic, and feeble-minded, deaf, dumb, blind, epileptic, insane, delinquent and offenders" were simply grouped into one class called "defectives" (Wolfsenberger 1972:15). Moreover, even those differences that are not usually seen as disabilities can render the individual "deviant" (e.g., the characteristic of being tall, short, or the member of a racial minority). Negative attitudes toward behavior that is "different" may stem from the idea that "goodness, truth and beauty are related to each other, and that any deviations from norms ... must be related to evil and ugliness [Wolfsenberger 1972:14]."

As deviant status carries with it certain role expectations, the behavior of persons who are so labeled will be very much influenced by the attitudes of others (see Chapter 13). In essence, they will be compelled to conform to these role expectations, and the result is a self-fulfilling prophecy. Characterizations accorded to deviant persons include those of "subhuman organism, menaces, object of dread, object of pity, holy innocent, diseased organism, object of ridicule and eternal child [Wolfsenberger 1972:16–24]."

Normalization involves human service technologies aimed at "undoing the stigma" (Goffman 1963: Lowenberg 1981). For example, an individual might be trained to "behave like others" in his dress, walking, talking, etc. This goal may be difficult to accomplish with individuals who have severe physical and mental defects. For example, a retarded adult living independently may overeat and become obese. However, if this person lived in a supervised apartment situation his diet could be regulated. Thus, the structuring of the environment can be a crucial strategy in the normalization process.

In the Lodge experiment discussed earlier (Fairweather 1969) schizophrenics who continued to hallucinate could function in the community because they lived in a motel where their deviant behavior was screened. On the job, they learned to do their work "without talking" and consequently were not identified as deviant.

The normalization concept stresses the importance of high expectations for normal behavior performance. Support for this position comes from studies of mental breakdown under combat conditions in World War II: Mentally disturbed soldiers who remained on the front lines recovered much more rapidly than those who were sent to hospitals and placed in a "sick" role (Mechanic 1980:104). Thus, in the Lodge experiment, the tendency of human service professionals to "underestimate" the abilities of the mentally ill was taken into account. The project was designed so that the patients were gradually given total responsibility for the operation of the janitorial service. It was found that the expectations the patients set for each other were also high. Interestingly, it was when patients were assigned to clean the houses of hospital staff members who knew their identity that lowest levels of performance resulted. The potential dysfunctional consequence of the professional tendency to foster dependency in clients has been stressed by Mechanic: "We must remain vigilant to the fact that care that encourages dependency rather than incentives to cope can be exceedingly detrimental. Focussing on life difficulties and symptoms may reinforce an illness behavior pattern which reduces coping effectiveness. Mental health professionals must never forget that chronicity of illness is one of the few widely recognized reasons for failing to meet social responsibilities [1978b:317]."

The impotance of high expectation attitudes on the part of human service practitioners is also evident in the field of physical rehabilitation. The rehabilitation of a paraplegic or a stroke victim requires an ability to maintain a persistent effort despite a slow rate of progress. Human service professionals who have been trained to help "normal" persons may lack this kind of ability.

As previously stated, social care emphasizes the creation of benevolent environments. This often requires the restructuring of social systems that impact on the individual—whether school systems or job situations. However, attempts at public education in the mental health field have not been very successful. A study of mental health education in Canada revealed that it had the opposite effect from that which was intended—it created stigma (Cummings and Cummings 1957). Similar results can occur if the human service practitioner intervention facilitates the labeling process (Ginerich, Kleczewski, and Kirk 1982).

Achieving a balance between the need for a protective and high expectation environment is a difficult and complex task. Normalization through community integration requires that the chronically disabled have as much interaction with "normals" as possible in an environment that is sufficiently protective to facilitate functioning. Therefore, it is preferable that living arrangements be made in small rather than large residences, because the community can integrate only a limited number of people (Wolfsenberger

1972:36). Application of these principles to the sick elderly who require specialized, around-the-clock nursing care would suggest the establishment of neighborhood-based nursing homes, which would give these people the kinds of services they need and yet allow them to remain in the community and maintain their social contacts.

Habilitation

Habilitation shares with normalization the assumption that high expectations will result in higher levels of performance. The goal of habilitation is to enable the individual to approach or achieve a level of performance held in the recent past. In contrast to rehabilitation it does not seek to enhance potentials not previously realized. Whereas rehabilitation strives to solve problems whose origins are in the past, habilitation makes no assumptions regarding the relationships between past difficulties and present ones. Habilitation assumes that all people desire to perform at their capacity if provided the chance. The basic problem is therefore lack of opportunities rather than lack of motivation. The basic task is to provide *social opportunities* by supplying concrete resources and/or restructuring the individual's immediate environment. Suppose, for example, that an elderly person who has been depressed since the loss of her spouse becomes withdrawn, refuses to leave her bed, and suffers a mild stroke. Rehabilitation could either counsel the person to help her understand the cause of her depression or provide antidepressants and tranquilizers. Habilitation would change her environment, for example, by moving her to a facility where the structure would compel her to get out of bed and give her the opportunity of interacting with others. In an actual situation of this kind, the person responded with anger to being forced out of bed, and this expression of anger helped her overcome her depression. The environment also enabled habilitation of another sort: through the structure it provided and through physical therapy, this individual was able to recover partly from her stroke.

Although habilitation has been applied primarily to service to severely disabled persons, it also is relevant for service to persons with long-standing social deficits, for example, the "hard-core" poor. This segment of the lower classes is characterized by chronic unemployment, health difficulties, lack of vocational skills, family instability, and other life stresses associated with poverty (Miller 1964:139–154). The expectation that this poverty group will be able to oversome social and personal deficits within a short period of time is probably unrealistic. Although there is a risk of underestimating their potential, the more serious problem that the human service practitioner faces here, as with the severely disabled, is that unrealistic expectations will lead to perceived failure and hence withdrawal on the part of both the client and the service provider. A more realistic strategy, then, is a habilitative one, where progress is measured in small incremental changes and the emphasis is on long-term, episodic (not necessarily intensive) service provision.

Open Opportunity Structures

The role of human service practitioners in opening opportunity structures was emphasized in the poverty programs of the 1960s. This focus was derived from sociological theory which suggested that there was "disjunction between cultural goals and socially structured opportunity [Cloward 1959]." When a society reaches a balance between culturally prescribed goals and the institutionalized means for achieving these goals, then integration, social stability, and conformity result. When, however, there is a gap between the goals and the capacity of individuals to achieve them, then deviancy occurs. That is, when legitimate means for goal achievement are unavailable, individuals will turn to illegitimate means. The availability of legitimate means differs among social classes. Members of the lower class generally have fewer of the "connections" that are so necessary for opportunities in education and employment. Socially structured barriers thus limit the opportunities available to lower-class persons, preventing them from achieving the material "success" that our society so esteems. An illustration of how society differentially allocates opportunities is provided by studies comparing educational achievement and income of white and nonwhite groups in the United States. These studies suggest that because of the basic problem of discrimination in employment, education has less pay-off for nonwhites (*Social and Economic Conditions of Negroes in the United States* 1967:21; Center for Study of Social Policy 1983).

Given its impotance, the human service practitioner who wants to influence the environment to enhance individuals' performance must intervene into this opportunity structure. One such poverty program with this major emphasis has been termed "opportunity-centered social services" (B. Neugeboren 1970b). This program had as its primary purpose the facilitation of upward economic mobility for lower-class clients. It sought to achieve this goal by enabling clients to use three focal opportunity systems: employment, housing, and education. Hence social service offices were established within these opportunity systems to allow for direct intervention. The underlying assumption was that lower-class persons, because of the various social concomitants of poverty, were not able to take advantage of those social opportunities that existed. For example, poor physical health, resulting from inadequate nutrition and health care, might be a barrier to utilizing an opportunity for employment. Thus in this kind of situation the human service practitioner would intervene to facilitate the provision of health care and at the same time explain to the employer why the individual could not meet his job obligations. Similarly, adequate housing was assumed to be a prerequisite for adequate social performance. The social service office in a public housing project would be automatically notified by the housing authority if any clients were not paying rent and in danger of eviction. Intervention into this type of situation usually revealed that the client did not have income because of loss of employment. The worker would then intervene with the public welfare agency to insure that the individual received the assistance he required and, if possible, would also help with employment or job training.

As the preceding examples indicate, this program also assumed that the poor, not unlike middle-class people, require assistance in dealing with complex bureaucratic systems. Such assistance is especially crucial because lower-class persons are much more dependent on bureaucratic organizations for their survival. And, whereas middle-class individuals can obtain "broker" types of services through such expeditors as lawyers, accountants, physicians, or personal connections, lower-class individuals cannot. Thus social workers, as in this program, take on an expeditor role, which is in some respects similar to that of the settlement house worker and political ward leader in the early 1900s (Perlman and Jones 1967:8–9).

People Processing

The intervention into the opportunity structure to aid lower-class individuals to achieve economic mobility is an example of the task of facilitating status change for people. The goal of status changing is also a primary purpose of "people-processing" technologies.

The function of the people-processing human service technologies is to change the public status of the individual. Such technologies are concerned not with behavior change, but rather with identifying and defining "the person's attributes, social situation, and public identity, which ... typically results in both societal and self-reaction. It is through these anticipated reactions of significant others that the organization tries to change its clients' social position and future behavior [Hasenfeld 1974:61]."

The basis of people-processing technologies lies in the classification and disposition of clients. This process requires that the social worker undertake the role of mediator in placing clients in various external units. Therefore, people-processing technologies hinge on the understanding and use of interorganizational exchange relations. Human service organizations that perform primarily people-processing functions include diagnostic clinics, university admissions offices, employment offices, and juvenile courts. However, any human service agency engages in people processing if in its decision-making processes it—intentionally or not—confers a different status on persons served. Admission to a mental hospital, prison, or public assistance program confers on the individual a status different from that of an ordinary citizen.

The concept of a patient "career" (Goffman 1959:125–169), in which the mental patient moves from pre-patient to inpatient to ex-patient status, captures the way in which human service agencies can affect the public status of persons served. The literature on people processing and social labeling has emphasized the dysfunctional aspects of people processing. The term itself has the implication that people are dealt with like inanimate objects and given cursory attention (Prottas 1979:1–12).

The rationale for the inclusion here of people processing as a social care technology is to emphasize the *functional* purposes of changing the status of the human service consumer. In line with social deviancy theory, the objective of people processing can be to change the public status of clients to *facilitate social opportunities.* This objective involves destigmatization by *delabeling.* As indicated earlier, however, human service agencies unintentionally place persons into deviant roles and statuses by classifying them as eligible for their services. Thus, admission to a hospital places an individual into a "sick" role. Often human service professionals assume that decisions that place persons in various classificiations or diagnostic categories are neutral in their consequences for those being served (Scheff 1968:289). The possibility that such classifications will have iatrogenic consequences tends to be overlooked. The problem is compounded because in situations of uncertainty the practitioner, in order to minimize risk, may err on the side of classifying individuals as sick (Scheff 1975:105).

It is therefore crucial that human service practitioners who utilize people-processing technologies understand both the positive and the negative consequences of classifying clients. This process of client categorization must be seen as having consequences for how society will react to the client and hence as influencing the client's opportunities for performing normally, whether on the job, in a classroom, or in some other situation.

As indicated, people-processing technologies require the practitioner to perform mediator or boundary roles. Intrinsic to these boundary roles is an understanding of the interdependent relationships among organizations (Hasenfeld 1974:63). Such relationships are based on the need for resources that can be supplied by other organizations. The factors influencing interorganizational interdependence (e.g., shared goals and complementary resources) must be understood (see Chapter 12). Thus, the amount of discretion available to external organizations in controlling their intake will influence the ability of a people-processing organization to dispose of its clients to such organizations. This discretion will be affected by the kinds of formal and informal agreements existing between the two organizations. For example, the acceptance of persons on parole for employment placement will depend on the kinds of resources that can be exchanged in this situation. The employment placement agency—the external organization—may benefit from the enhanced public image achieved through the service it performs for the community by helping rehabilitate ex-offenders. The technology of people processing, therefore, includes an analysis of the opportunities and constraints on interorganizational cooperation and coordination.

Discharge Planning and Case Management

The previous discussion of social care technologies directed attention to various environmental areas for intervention by human service agencies. This section on case management and discharge planning focuses on two specific human service technological areas which influence the environmental area of inter-organizational practice (see Chapter 12). Case management and discharge planning are related also to other social care areas such as people processing, social provision, resource systems, community support systems and opening opportunity structures which were previously discussed. All these areas are concerned with environmental manipulations—linking clients with services in the community. Stein indicates that case management has become increasingly popular because of "less concern for client pathology and more concern with the social environment and how it contributes to clients' problems" (Stein 1981:75).

Although these two technological areas have been viewed as separate and distinct interventions they are interrelated through the continuum of services. Thus, planning for client discharge from institutional care precedes the coordination of post-discharge case management services. The reverse also occurs in that case management services may be used to prevent institutionalization. Traditionally both these intervention areas have focused on people changing goals. They are included here under the social care rubric because of the specialized environmental skills used when coordinating with other agencies.

Case management and discharge planning functions have received increased attention along with pressure for deinstitutionalizing the mentally ill, the developmentally disabled, and the elderly. The interconnectedness of the two functions have been highlighted by the discharging of chronics without adequate planning for services in the community (Lindenberg & Coulton 1980:49). Large numbers of the chronically mentally ill have been discharged placing the burden of coordinating patient resources on the community.

The increasing importance of case management and discharge planning is highlighted by the current struggle between the social work and nursing professions over which group could legitimately claim ownership of this area (Davidson 1978:51, Miller & Rehr 1983:94). Historically social workers have downgraded the task of discharge planning and case management as not requiring professional training (Kane 1980:2, Johnson & Rubin 1983:50, Davidson 1978:45–48). Also, social workers have in the past given up the discharge planning function to nurses (Meyer 1983:419). In this interprofessional competition the validity of each profession claims may hinge on their competence in the direct service role and in the interorganizational practice area (Steinberg & Carter 1983:41).

Case management has been defined as "a mechanism for linking and coordinating segments of a service delivery system ... to insure the most comprehensive program for meeting an individual client's need for care." It has been noted that it refers to "management of a system of services, not to management of a person" (Sancier 1983:3). The principle functions in long term care are: (1) "screening and determining eligibility (2) assessing the need for services and related needs (3) case planning (4) requisitioning services (5) implementing the service plan, coordinating service delivery, and follow-up, and (6) reassessing, monitoring, and evaluating services periodically" (Austin 1983:16).

Discharge planning had been defined by the American Hospital Association as primarily an administrative responsibility (vacating beds) (Davidson 1978:50). Social work has viewed discharge as a service that helps patients to cope with their illness and its effects so they can move through the hospital system and return to the community with the necessary support (Rossen 1977).

The following discussion of discharge planning and case management will focus on the source of authority for the service coordiantor (see Chapter 8). The importance of linking power and authority with community resources has received little attention (Austin 1983:17). The absence of this consideration may in part be associated with the tendency for case managers and discharge planners to give prime emphasis to client-worker interaction (Austin 1983:21, Case Management Research Project 1980:33, Kane 1980:2). However, it would seem self evident that the task of influencing autonomous agents to provide the needed services assumes a level of legitimacy and authority that is beyond what is available to most direct service staff. Two approaches to this problem have been suggested: (1) inter-organizational cooperation based on resource dependency (2) a purchase of service mechanism.

Interorganizational exchange theory suggests that resource dependence between agencies can be a powerful motivational source for cooperation and coordination (Austin 1983:17). A situation where two agencies are dependent on each other for resources can provide the basis for interagency service agreements which sanction the case manager and discharge planner linkage role.

The purchase of service mechanism can also aid in sanctioning and legitimizing the case manager role (Steinberg and Carter 1983:77). For example, the financial control model which was used in the channeling project authorizes the case manager to allocate funds to purchase services for elderly clients. This program gives the case manager the "authority to limit, alter, or terminate services in response to change in client needs or of a failure of a provider to deliver services of adequate quality" (Baxter et al. 1983:27).

As case management is extended to services for child protection, mental health and the elderly, discharge planning becomes critical. In order to facilitate deinstitutionalization it seems essential that everyone involved temper their expectations of case managers and discharge planners considering the difficulty in coordinating such a complex array of services from autonomous agencies. Knowledge and skill in this interorganizational arena of practice needs to be explicated to make it possible for case managers and discharge planners to successfully perform their given tasks.

Situational Analysis

The operationalization of the various principles and concepts associated with social care technologies requires a methodology for environmental assessment. *Situational analysis* is the procedure used to assess how environmental factors affect the individual. Thus, the human service practitioner analyzes the client's situation and, with the agreement of the client, proceeds to modify it. This "structural approach" of adjusting the environment to the needs of the individual follows from the underlying assumption of social care technologies that the situation can be a basic constraining or facilitating force. It is based on the position that "inadequate social arrangements are predominantly responsible for many of the situations that are frequently defined as products of those who suffer from them [Middleman and Goldberg 1974:26]."

The persistent tendency to blame individuals for the situations they are in makes situational analysis difficult. This shift of focus from the situation to the individual may occur through an emphasis on the *interaction* between individuals and their environments ("Working Statement on the Purpose of Social Work" 1981:6). Thus, emphasizing the importance of the individual's perceptions of his situation as a key to its modification shifts attention away from the situation to the individual. Yet such an emphasis is not uncommon. One author, in describing strategies of situational intervention, states that "the way one sees through a situation changes the situation [Laing 1969]." Another indicates that "the redefinition of the client's life situation needs to be based on an assessment that emphasizes alternative and more positive perceptions of it [Siporin 1975:238]." Therefore, the human service practitioner who provides social care services must be constantly aware of the pressures to blame the victim, through stress on intrapsychic factors. It has been suggested that such an emphasis will become especially prevalent in periods of political conservatism (Levine and Levine 1970:8).

The complexity of the task of situational analysis can be appreciated from the earlier discussion of the variety of social-environmental factors that may be involved. Perhaps the simplest and most straightforward procedure is to use "common-sense" judgment in responding to the consumer's definition of need and to direct efforts at overcoming situational barriers to meeting this need. Common-sense judgment enters in in several ways. To begin with, an understanding of the needs of people with certain general problems can aid in efficient and effective situational analysis. For example, an understanding of the social isolation of the older person who has outlived family and friends will guide the human service practitioner in linking such a person with substitute social networks. Similarly, an understanding of the fact that the mentally ill person who has been deinstitutionalized needs skills for daily living will lead the human service administrator to plan for programs to teach such skills. In short, the situational analysis undertaken for an individual client will not be completely idiosyncratic and unique. Moreover, professionals' definitions of human *needs* will often be much more complex than consumers' definitions of their *wants* (Goodenough 1963:49–60). Persons who are the victims of social problems identify their wants in terms of basic survival needs. For example, in the surveys in the urban areas that had riots in the 1960s, the residents pinpointed such wants as employment and housing (*Report of the National Advisory Committee on Civil Disorders* 1968). If assessment of client needs is difficult, assessment of the environmental barriers to the fulfillment of these needs is even more so, because it requires an understanding of how complex bureaucratic systems operate. Thus defining a problem may be less difficult than developing an understanding of how to resolve it. Crucial to the situational analysis required in social care technology, therefore, are the skills of intra- and interorganizational analysis. In contrast, professionals define what the clients want in this situation as being the need for internal, psychological, and personal change (Richan 1969).

Rehabilitation Technologies

Rehabilitation technologies are people changing in that their goal is to assist individuals to regain a prior level of functioning or achieve a higher one. In contrast with "habilitation," discussed earlier, rehabilitation strives to remedy maladaptive functioning. It focuses on treating persons to provide them with the social competence for effective functioning. Although rehabilitation and social control overlap to some extent and are sometimes treated in conjunction in the literature (e.g., Romanyshin 1971:153; Vinter 1963:33), here they will be dealt with separately. The distinction between rehabilitation and social control technologies is that the primary purpose of the former is to help the person achieve a better level of functioning whereas that of the latter is to meet the community's need to control deviant behavior. Although rehabilitation often enables the person to function in a manner more acceptable to community norms and standards, this is not its main purpose. Moreover, although social control sometimes involves changing behavior by changing attitudes, it may also involve physical control and containment via institutionalization. Therefore, in social control but *not* rehabilitation technologies the *client* served is *primarily* the community.

Rehabilitation is conducted by treatment organizations. Treatment organizations can be differentiated from socialization agencies, such as schools, in that they are concerned with problematic behavior whereas socialization agencies deal mainly with normal behavior (Vinter 1963:35).

Rehabilitation, or people-changing technologies, vary from education to treatment to coercion.

Treatment

The technologies used in therapeutic settings stress modification of feelings and cognition through interpersonal change. Clients' participation is voluntary, and only those who are "motivated" are served. Because each client is perceived as unique, individualized assessment and treatment are required. *Treatments* include such approaches as psychoanalysis, interactional, existential, and problem-solving (Siporin 1975:141–149). Treatment technologies need not be psychological; they may also be physical or social.

Physical treatments include use of vitamins and drugs, surgery, and electrical shock. Use of physical treatments has increased as psychological therapies have failed to demonstrate their effectiveness. For example, the practice of using tranquilizers to influence problematic behavior has been adopted by numerous in-patient and out-patient human service agencies. As discussed earlier, the somewhat indiscriminate prescription of tranquilizers by physicians has had negative repercussions. Although it is commonly believed that use of psychosurgery has stopped, evidence suggests that in fact such surgery continues to be performed (President's Commission on Mental Health 1978). The recent popularity of diet therapy has led to the use of vitamins as a form of treatment for emotional problems, particularly schizophrenia. In short, physical treatments are diverse and pervasive.

Social treatments such as miliem therapy have been popular since World War II. The "therapeutic community" (Jones 1968) and variety of group therapy approaches are derived from social treatment modalities.

In assessing the utility of these various treatment technologies one could theoretically use as a measuring rod their efficiency and/or their effectiveness. Although there is new evidence indicating some modest success for treatment, conclusive proof of its effectiveness has not been demonstrated (Thomlinson 1984). As their effectiveness has not yet been demonstrated, then the assessment could be made in terms of efficiency.

In considering treatment technologies one needs to consider the implications of applying the "medical model" to the delivery of human services (Weick 1983). This model implicitly assumes that perfect health and hap-

piness—"cures"—are possible (Dubos 1959). This model assumes further
that effective treatment is based on accurate understanding of the etiology
of the problem and the diagnosis of the signs and symptoms. In many human
service programs, however, these assumptions cannot be justified, so that
the diagnostic process becomes purely ritualistic (Mechanic 1974:180–181).
Moreover, treatment has potential negative, or iatrogenic, consequences,
which need to be taken into account in planning and administering human
service programs (Illich 1976). For example, in the mental health field chronic
patients may become dependent on the professionals who treat them (Mechanic 1980:175; Gaylin 1978:29–30).

Education

The human service technologies directed at skill development are classified here as educational technologies. There is evidence that individual
malfunctioning may be related to lack of coping abilities (Mechanic 1977).
Although the psychological approaches often assume that successful coping
and adaptation require the ability to understand "reality," it may also be that
"too much self-awareness or introspection retards successful coping efforts
[Mechanic 1974:171]."

The usefulness of such technologies will depend on how important the
specific skills and information that are being taught are for effective adaptation.
The skills of daily living—dressing oneself, budgeting money, shopping, using
public transportation, and basic social skills—are essential for community
adjustment.

Educational technologies have been seen as particularly appropriate for
service to chronic schizophrenics—patients who lack the information, skills,
and abilities needed for community adaptation. Mechanic (1980) suggests
that these persons need to learn: "(1) The way persons anticipate situations;
(2) The way they seek information about them; (3) The extent to which they
plan, prepare, and rehearse them in a psychological and social sense; (4)
The way they test problem solutions; (5) The way they consider and prepare
alternative courses of action should the situation require it; and (6) The way
they allocate time and effort [pp. 173–174]."

Educational technologies have an advantage over treatment technologies
in that maladaptive behavior is seen in meaningful social contexts, rather
than in a clinical setting. This has been accomplished in European industrial
rehabilitation programs for the mentally ill where service outcomes are within
the work context (Furman 1965; Wing 1967). Another advantage of educational technologies is that they minimize stigma (Mechanic 1980:177). This
is particularly evident in programs for the mentally retarded, which in many
states are under the jurisdiction of the education rather than mental health
department.

The educational approach is also important because information that people need in order to understand and accept disabilities may not be readily available. Doctors often fail to give information to patients, perhaps because of time constraints. The success of various self-help groups may stem from the fact that they provide an opportunity for persons with similar problems to share factual information. Similarly, the great popularity of Spock's book on child development and care is probably attributable to the fact that its specific information on stages of child development reassured parents that their children's problems are normal and developmental.

The behavior modification approach can be classified as an educational technology. This approach is based on learning theory which suggests that maladaptive behavior is the result of inadequate reinforcement systems (Thomas 1967). It uses operant conditioning to help individuals unlearn maladaptive behavior patterns. As suggested earlier, the very specific nature of this approach facilitates its operationalization, trainability, and monitoring for administrative purposes.

Coercion

Coercive technologies stress the use of negative sanctions (Vinter 1963:37). Traditionally they have been used in prisons and other correctional facilities, where sanctions may take the form of physical punishment or deprivation of freedom. Coercive technologies are also used in mental hospitals, where electric shock or physical isolation may punish deviant behavior.

American society has long used coercive methods for controlling deviant behavior. During the colonial period, the mentally ill, the poor, and others considered deviant were often punished by whipping, stoning, burning, and hanging (*Action for Mental Health* 1961:26). Although punishment as a form of treatment has generally fallen into disfavor, it has gained renewed support in the criminal justice field, where capital punishment and the "fixed sentence" are being advocated as a means of deterrence. As mentioned earlier, the use of punishment to deter assumes that deviant behavior is rationally determined and that the criminal will rationally calculate whether it is to his advantage to commit the deviant act (Sutherland and Gressy 1978). Thus coercive technologies share with certain educational technologies the assumption that deviant behavior is learned and can be controlled through rewards and punishments.

Although many may disapprove of coercive technologies, the use of various forms of punishment continues in the human service field. And, after all, it cannot be denied that human beings are influenced by sanctions and rewards. Our driving on a highway, for example, is very obviously influenced by the presence of a highway patrol car. Therefore, the effectiveness of punishment as a human service technology is very much related to the assumptions concerning the "rationality" underlying deviant behavior. If we assume deviant behavior is the result of "sickness" and is beyond the control of the individual, then coercive techniques would be difficult to justify as a people-changing technology.

Social Control Technologies

Social control refers ultimately to the fact that in all social interaction the individual is limited by the norms and standards of the community. Social control has thus been defined as "the arrangements by which society influences the behavior of the members to achieve conformity with its norms [Gilbert and Specht 1974:5]." By this definition, all efforts to socialize persons to accept community value and standards have a social control purpose. Provision of in-kind services (Gilbert and Specht 1974:83) and treatment as a people-changing technology (Vinter 1963:33) are therefore both seen as having social control as a major function. The social worker is viewed as an agent of social control, as the "moral agent" for the community (Siporin 1975:39).

In contrast, as defined here, social control is limited to efforts of the human service organization to control an individual *because of the pressure being exerted by the community*. In order to appreciate the difference in scope of these definitions, it is necessary to understand that most deviant behavior does not gain official and public recognition (Scheff 1968). As discussed earlier, official recognition of deviance is often related to social characteristics of the individual, such as culture and class (Mechanic 1980:95).

Human service administrators and practitioners are often under significant pressure to base service delivery policies and decisions primarily on community concern and only secondarily on client needs and interests (Kupers 1981: 26–28; Rosenberg 1978:91). For example, the decision of a mental health center to send an adolescent to a treatment institution rather than serve him on an out-patient basis may be due to community pressure. Many people who have been institutionalized in mental hospitals did not require in-patient treatment but were put there because of community discomfort with their behavior. Thus, the hidden agenda in many human service programs is the performance of a social control function. Although the technologies utilized may be those of social care or rehabilitation, the primary purpose is to serve the community rather than the client. This situation is exemplified in the corrections field by the stress on "diversion," by which deviant young people are diverted from correctional agencies to institutional treatment agencies. Although they are kept out of corrections institutions, they may spend much more time incarcerated in a treatment institution—and hence away from the community (Lerman 1975).

In the design, delivery, and monitoring of human service programs, it would seem essential that administrators and practitioners be aware of the social control goals and technologies of their organizations. Recognizing the differences between client and community objectives can lead to a clearer understanding of when it is in the client's best interest to remain in or be removed from the community. Awareness that community pressure to control deviant clients has to be dealt with can lead to community-based programs that are more appropriate for these types of clients. The mass movement of deinstitutionalized people into the community has exacerbated pressures for social control. An appropriate response to these pressures is essential if community backlash is to be avoided. As Mechanic (1978a) has noted:

> One of the major difficulties in organizing community environments for the care of the mentally ill is the lack of predictability of the social and political climate. . . . We have not yet learned how to balance, or even measure, the social costs for the community against the advantages and ideologies of community care. No legal theory or social ideology . . . can substitute for the willingness of the community to provide the resources for adequate care [pp. 317–319].

Program effectiveness requires that human service agencies examine the implications of social control objectives. Assuming that social control is a legitimate function for the human agency does not preclude the careful weighing of how this function can be performed without compromising client benefit.

Since community rejection of the deviant client is the basis for social control activity, the human service worker needs to develop social control technology. When developing this technology the worker needs to influence key persons in the community who are pressuring for removal of the deviant person. This would require reaching key persons who are in a position to counteract the pressure for control and removal. One strategy would be for a human service worker to contact a high status board member who may have the needed connections with those in the community power structure. These contacts could aid in alleviating pressure to remove the client. This type of intervention skill, which is common among community organization practitioners, needs to be developed by direct service personnel.

SUMMARY

This analysis of the goals and techniques associated with human service technologies has provided a broad survey of the variety of approaches available in the delivery of human services and has highlighted a number of issues. The emphasis on the *social* technologies is intended to provide information in an area that has not received adequate attention in the human service literature (Gitterman and Germain 1981:45). Moreover, social technologies may prove most relevant for the remediation of *social* problems. Human service administrators and practitioners may find it difficult to resist society's move toward the "cult of personality" and the "therapeutic state" (Szasz 1963:216–218). However, if client benefit is the primary criterion for the design and delivery of human services, then it behooves the administrator and practitioner to be aware of the relevance of social technologies for human service programs.

APPLICATION OF CONCEPTS ON HUMAN SERVICE TECHNOLOGIES TO THE CASE "MENTAL HEALTH RULES AND REGULATIONS"

It will be recalled in the case "Mental Health Rules and Regulations" the State Department of Mental Health established policies giving priority to services for the chronically mentally ill. Community mental health programs were mandated to stress such approaches as "normalization" and "levels of functioning," rather than the pathology-oriented therapeutic models they traditionally followed.

The *issues of whether people- or situation-changing technologies* are relevant for helping the chronically mentally ill is brought out by this case situation. Do the severely mentally ill require counseling to help them understand the cause of their internal stress, or should efforts be directed at enabling them to obtain jobs, housing, and the basic skills of daily living? Will changing their environment alone suffice to enable them to function in the community? The policy of the state department, which was based on social deviancy theories, assumed that many of the problems confronting the severely mentally ill stemmed from the lack of adequate environmental supports in the community. The professionals operating the mental health centers took the position that psychosis was a disease that had to be treated directly.

Related to the question of the relative value of people- versus situation-changing technologies in the chronically mentally ill is the issue of whether the effectiveness of technology is associated with its intensity—*quality versus quantity of services.* In other words, is more better. Many psychotherapeutic models assume that the greater the intensity or amount of service given to the individual patient, the greater the effectiveness. In contrast, social deviancy based approaches hold that less public attention may be more beneficial in the case of those who are chronically ill. In this view, treatment, by definition, places the mentally ill in a deviant status and encourages the society to treat them with lower expectations. "Normalization" thus attempts to provide as normal an environment as possible for the chronically ill.

Another issue that arises in conjunction with models for service to the mentally ill is that of whether *different technologies are required for persons from the lower social classes.* Studies have found that the incidence and prevalence of mental illness are greater in the lower socioeconomic classes. As persons from the lower classes have different orientations to treatment, technologies need to be used that take these differences into account. Also, as material deprivation is by definition associated with lower social class, then service for the chronically mentally ill should, when relevant, meet these resource needs. The mental health department's new rules and regulations attempted to take these class-related factors into account.

The use of *people-changing versus people-processing* technologies was also a consideration in this case. People-changing technologies are directed at altering behavior, people-processing technologies at changing public status. The department's new policy, which emphasized normalization rather than treatment, was directed at changing the deviant patient status of the ex-hospitalized patients.

The question of the extent to which human service *technologies are determinate or indeterminate* also emerged in the case. The concrete nature of the services advocated in the new mental health policies contrasted with the indeterminancy of the more traditional psychotherapeutic treatments. For example, the objective of instructing the mentally ill in such skills of daily living as shopping, housekeeping, using public transportation, self-care, etc., can be clearly operationalized. Given the determinate nature of such service, the department had an objective basis for monitoring and evaluating compliance with the regulations. In contrast, the indeterminate nature of the psychotherapeutic modalities would make it much more difficult to monitor and control.

These differences between the technologies advocated in the new mental health policies and the therapy practiced in the community programs raise questions as to appropriate *staffing arrangements.* Are the specializations of psychiatry, psychology, social work, and nursing all appropriate for the kinds of technologies proposed in the new rules? Which specialties are best equipped to carry out the new policy's *environmental* approach to service? Although historically social workers have been identified with this approach, today their training emphasizes counseling and therapy. Given the lack of any particular professional group that sees environmental manipulation as its specialization, it may be appropriate to recruit nonprofessionals, who may have a more practical approach to responding to human needs. Another possibility is to select ex-patients who are aware of the value of resource provision in helping mental patients to adjust in the community. Professionals who have an understanding of community resource systems (e.g., community organizers) could collaborate with ex-patients in teams to help the chronically mentally ill find the necessary resources.

Organizational auspice is another factor that needs to be taken into account in human service programs for the severely mentally ill. *Public agency sponsorship* often characterizes service to more deviant and pathological patient groups. In the case situation the community mental health programs were generally under *voluntary agency sponsorship.* Voluntary sponshorship tends to constrain service to deviant groups, and the state department would need to take this fact into account in allocating funds. That is, it might have to give priority to public agencies such as welfare boards and county psychiatric centers.

In this case situation, as elsewhere, choice of technologies related to the issue of goals. The new policies advocated technologies related to *social care* as the most appropriate for the chronically mentally ill. The basic task was the creation of positive social environments to allow the severely mentally ill to adjust in the community. The various social care technologies available would need to be assessed in terms of their relevance for this group. Technologies that might be particularly appropriate include social provision, resource systems, community support systems, least restrictive environment, normalization, habilitation, and people processing. The principles and concepts associated with these technologies could be used to develop a comprehensive service delivery model for the chronically mentally ill group. The *educational rehabilitation* technologies would also be relevant for service to the chronically mentally ill, particularly with regard to the task of training in the skills of daily living. *Social control* has traditionally been a major goal of programs for the chronically mentally ill, who have generally been confined in hospitals away from the community. Implementation of new regulations would have to take into account the pressures present in the community to control psychotic individuals by separating them from the mainstream of community life. State monitoring systems would be needed to insure that social control does not become the primary objective, with social care and/ or rehabilitation serving merely as means to achieve this end.

EPILOGUE

Throughout this book three major themes have been emphasized: (a) the need for practitioners in the human services to develop bureaucratic expertise; (b) the importance of integrating three primary goals—social care, social control, and rehabilitation—with practice; and (c) the need to understand the causes and solutions of organizational problems in human service agencies in terms of systemic and political factors (Gummer 1978). This concluding chapter will discuss these three themes and their implications for education and practice in the human service field.

BUREAUCRATIC EXPERTISE

Practitioners in the human services, whether in direct service or in supervisory and administrative positions, need in addition to technical skills the knowledge of how the organizational context influences practice. This understanding of the organizational opportunities and constraints on their practice enables them to develop the "bureaucratic expertise" needed to survive within the bureaucratic work environment. This kind of expertise is needed because the bureaucratic lines along which human service agencies are structured result in various strains and stresses for workers, particularly for professionals who value autonomy in their practice. To be effective these practitioners must appreciate the limits imposed by the structure as well as the opportunities available for discretion in decision making and action. The "good bureaucrat" is the practitioner who uses the knowledge of organizational structure and process to help withstand the strains of working in bureaucratic systems. That is, knowledge of the systemic sources of organizational pressures allows the "good bureaucrat" to persist in his or her efforts fully understanding that change takes time (i.e., to have staying power). Organizational opportunities are seized with the understanding that rules imposed by the organizational structure are of necessity stated in general terms and therefore leave room for interpretation. Structure becomes the servant rather than the master. Bureaucratic rules and regulations are therefore seen less as constraints than as challenges and as problems to be solved. They are viewed as a means to achieve the ends of human service programs rather than as ends in themselves.

INTEGRATION GOALS OF SOCIAL CARE, SOCIAL CONTROL OR REHABILITATION WITH PRACTICE IN THE HUMAN SERVICES

At the outset of this book, the distinction was made between the organizational mission of client benefit and the goals of social care, social control, and rehabilitation in human service programs. That is, it was emphasized that these goals are themselves merely means for achieving the mission of client benefit and that their validity must be assessed accordingly. A distinction was also made among care, control, and rehabilitation, as these goals are relevant to different types of client problems and needs. Moreover, although rehabilitation has generally been considered the primary goal in human service programming, social control is often present as a hidden and latent purpose, and its presence needs to be made explicit. The existence of a social control goal has become particularly evident in recent years, as deinstitutionalization policies have led to the discharge of such socially deviant client groups as the mentally ill and retarded. As institutionalization of these clients had a social control basis, their discharge has made overt the societal pressures for control. Human service practitioners need to be aware of such pressures. Social control as a goal for human service progams has also been evident in such areas as child abuse, drug and alcohol addiction, crime, and delinquency. Human service practitioners in these areas have to reconcile this goal with their own goals of rehabilitation and care. To insure accomplishment of client benefit, the potential means–ends relationships between social control and care and rehabilitation need to be clarified and linked to service outcome.

The explication of the three major goals for the human services is also necessary to aid in the design of the structures and technologies relevant for these different purposes. Here again, there is a need for means–ends clarification so that the organizational arrangements established are efficient and effective in achieving organizational goal and mission. The need for such clarification has been evident in the development of programs for the chronically disabled client groups. The inappropriate establishment of rehabilitation as a goal for such groups as the mentally ill, mentally retarded, elderly, and chronically poor highlights the importance of defining appropriate means–ends relationships between program goal and client benefit.

The discussion of social care as an important goal and technology for human service programs pointed to the need for greater attention to intervention directed at environmental manipulation. Although this type of intervention has in fact had a long tradition in social welfare and the human services, its theoretical and empirical bases were developed relatively recently (Moos 1974). A failure to clearly differentiate social care from rehabilitation has obscured the special and unique characteristics of the social care goal and technology. Thus, special efforts are needed to develop and evaluate the kinds of technologies and organizational structures appropriate for this social care goal. Two of the cases used in this book ("From Psychological Work to Social Work" and "Mental Health Rules and Regulations") exemplify attempts to move toward social care and to develop relevant technologies. The requirement for greater interagency coordination is an illustration of the special kinds of organizational arrangements needed to achieve this goal.

Although human service agencies have been developing social care programs in response to deinstitutionalization policies, there has not been a concomitant development of professional education in this area. For example, social work education continues to focus on rehabilitation intervention strategies (Thomas 1983:415). Hence it is important that educational programs in the human services develop curriculum content in the social care area, including both relevant theoretical knowledge and skill training. A basic understanding of *chronicity* needs to be developed, given the current almost exclusive emphases on intervention for acute problems. Field practicum experiences need to be developed in agencies that are particularly concerned with chronic social problems, for example, public child welfare agencies, mental hospitals, nursing homes, and programs for mentally retarded and for the elderly. This emphasis on social care as a goal for the human services should lead to reintroduction of the "social" into the field of social work (Miller 1981; Stewart 1981).

PRACTICE WITH A SYSTEMIC PERSPECTIVE

A systemic perspective views practice in structural and political context. Problems on the administrative and practitioner levels are seen as related to dysfunctional policies as well as the interplay with political and organizational factors. Intrinsic to a systemic perspective for practice in human service organizations is an understanding of the difference between viewing problems in individual versus organizational terms. Given the individual orientation prevalent in the general culture of the United States and more specifically in the human service field, it is essential that the practitioner be able to ascertain whether problems that arise in daily practice have an individual or structural cause.

The distinction between individual and systemic views of practice was initially discussed in relation to the concept of organizational structure (Chapter 4). Organizational structure was defined *behaviorally* in terms of the patterns of staff activities linked to five structural areas: role, communication, authority, reward, and interorganizational structure. This behavioral definition of structure was equated with the operative policies of the organization. Therefore, such problems as lack of role prescriptions, inequitable promotional policies, inadequate channels for communication, poor fit between authority and responsibility, and inadequate relations with other agencies were seen as requiring solutions involving changes in agency policies. To attribute such problems to individual dysfunction would be inappropriate, as changing individual attitudes and/or behavior—or even replacing the individual—would not in itself achieve policy changes and concomitant changes in the patterns of staff activities. For example, changing the director, supervisor, or direct service staff member who is not performing adequately cannot solve a problem that is rooted in an inadequate role definition for the positions. Thus, it is essential to distinguish between structural and individual dysfunction in order to avoid attributing problems to "people" when their source in fact lies within the "policies."

This theme of individual versus systemic cause and solution of problems in human service organizations underlies the distinction made between the concepts of bureaupathology and bureausis (Chapter 6). Bureaupathology was defined as referring to the dysfunctional organization, bureausis as referring to the incompetent individual. Human service practitioners at all levels need to understand this difference, as their actions in solving problems will be guided by whether they perceive the causes as located in the individual or the system. The consequencies of failing to make the distinction may be serious. For example, if problems that are the result of inadequately defined job expectations are attributed to individual personality difficulties, then the steps taken to "resolve" the problem may further accentuate frustration and burnout.

This distinction between individual and systemic is crucial not only in problem definition, but also in other organizational areas, including decision making; authority, control, and power; organizational subsystems; management models; leadership; organizational change; and service ideologies and technologies. In each of these areas, systemic factors are involved and need to be recognized as such.

Decision making (Chapter 10) is influenced by the *decision environment,* which includes the organization's goals, structures, ideologies, and technologies. Decision makers "satisfice" (i.e., take action that will create the fewest problems) because political influences prevent them from following the optional course of action.

Authority, control, and power (Chapter 8) also relate to political and system influences. If human service organizations are viewed as political systems, with various interest groups (e.g., line staff, supervisors, administrators, different departments and programs) in competition for power and influence, then the individual participants are less important than the interests they represent. Systems of control are needed precisely because there is a lack of congruence between staff and organizational goals. This lack of congruence is a basic source of conflict which needs to be negotiated and mediated. The structuralist and subsystems management models (see Chapter 3) are based on this political definition of organizational life. Similarly, professional ideologies (Chapter 13) which are an important source of conflict in human service agencies may mask self-interest and politically based goals (Hasenfeld 1983:146).

Leadership (Chapter 9) is another area influenced by the organizational context. Effective leadership skills vary with the organizational level. This contravenes the assumption often made that lower-level leadership abilities can be readily transferred to the upper levels. The "Peter Principle" (Peter and Hull 1969), which states that the individual will be promoted to his or her highest level of incompetence, recognizes that leadership competence on one level may not be transferable to the other levels. Therefore, leadership depends on not only individual characteristics, but also on organizational level as well as the nature of tasks performed and the influences from the external environment.

In the area of organizational change (Chapter 11) the human service practitioner needs to appreciate the distinction between changing people and changing policies. Changing attitudes and behavior of some individuals will not necessarily result in change of programs and policies. Furthermore, the process of changing individual behavior is often complex. The stress on human relations training as a strategy for organizational change does not take into account the fact that self-interest is frequently a basic source of staff resistance to change. This political perspective is basic to the systemic view of organizational change (Kennedy 1980).

Human service delivery technologies (Chapter 14) also require systemic perspective. As indicated earlier in this chapter, in the discussion of social care as a goal of the human services, there is a need to develop service intervention policies and procedures directed at influencing situations. Such a development will require a systemic perspective, as will the development of interagency cooperation to achieve more effective comprehensive services. This latter also requires a political understanding of power and turf issues that must be negotiated among agencies. Social care technologies require, in addition, an understanding of how situational and environmental forces— including the bureaucratic environment of the agencies themselves—impact on clients. Attributing clients' problems to individual personality deficiencies can be another form of blaming the victim.

The human service field has emphasized an individual orientation to practice, and this emphasis has been reflected in educational programs for people entering the field. It is proposed here that this emphasis be broadened to include a systemic and political perspective. Educational programs in psychology, social work, nursing, medicine, and teaching need to incorporate content on the systemic perspective to practice in the human services. It is important that training cover the organizational context for practice on which we have focused here.

In conclusion, it is proposed that the human service practitioner requires an organizational perspective—an awareness of the structural and political influences on practice. The specific technical skills required for any given position need to be supplemented with systemic and political knowledge, so that opportunities may be maximized and constraints on practice minimized. This bureaucratic expertise is not in itself sufficient to achieve effective practice, however. To insure that client benefit is accomplished the human service practitioner need to be clear as to the appropriate mission and goals of human services. Clarity regarding the difference between social care, social control, and rehabilitation, and their potential use as means or ends, will also maximize client benefit. Finally, this bureaucratic skill and clarity regarding goals must both be related to a systemic and political orientation to practice. Again, this systemic and political knowledge and skill needs to be viewed as a means to achieving client benefit, in order to avoid displacement of efforts away from the basic mission of human service organizations.

APPENDIX: CASES

DISCIPLINARY ACTION

The Outburst

The employee relations officer of a large state child welfare agency received a call for advice from a frantic administrator who related the following incident: During a briefing by that administrator to bring staff up-to-date on the activities of the agency, a supervisor stood up and began to shout and clench his fists. Moving toward her, he yelled, "I'm going to get you. This is a conspiracy. The workers and the clients are the ones who suffer!" He proceeded to shout out confidential information which had been discussed with him in private. Although he was asked politely to return to his seat, the employee continued his tantrum. Finally he was asked to leave the room. When he did so, he began a confrontation with another worker, whom he subsequently threatened to come after with a baseball bat. It was at this point that the administrator hurried to call the employee relations office for advice.

The supervisor had been with the agency for nine years and had consistently received satisfactory or better evaluations until a short time before this incident. His employment record revealed that his functioning on the job had always been at least adequate. There was evidence that his previous work at a residential center, which involved less direct contact with clients, was outstanding, whereas his current functioning at a district office, which entailed more direct client contact, was not as good. Protective service work in the district office subjected him and his workers to extreme pressures from community agencies concerning their clients.

When he was transferred out of a residential center and into a district office, his behavior changed markedly. His attendance record became irregular, with unexcused absences and excessive tardiness. He had recently called in sick and, with hardly any documentation to substantiate this claim, proceeded to go to Florida in order to recuperate.

His director had had occasion to consider requesting disciplinary action before. She had become concerned about the fact that the workers under his supervision were not performing adequately. They had not dictated on cases for numerous months and were farther behind than the norm for the office. When confronted, the supervisor had complained that the administration was only concerned with production and not the needs of clients and staff. On a certain occasion, the supervisor had been told to leave the courtroom while representing the agency. He had also had an explosive incident with another supervisor. Yet the director had not filed a disciplinary action, because she felt she should give him another chance. The present outburst, however, was the last straw.

After listening to the director, reviewing the man's work history, and much deliberation, the employee relations officer recommended a 15-day suspension from work and a referral to a psychiatrist. In this way, the supervisor would be kept out of contact with clients and other employees until some conclusions could be reached as to his mental status and his ability to continue working.

The Hearing

When the employee received the appropriate government forms recommending the disciplinary action he requested an appeal. He also requested, and was granted, union representation at an appeal hearing.

As initiator of the action, management had to substantiate its case. During the appeal, nine witnesses were called to testify about the appellant's actions at the office. Management presented evidence concerning the outburst and numerous incidents of odd behavior. However, management could not prove that the employee had been made aware that such behavior was unacceptable.

The major point in the appellant's case was that the administrator had misperceived his actions. He admitted that he felt as if he was burning himself out, that he had been taking on too much, and that he was more than willing to go for psychiatric assistance even if the state did not pay for it. However, he claimed that his behavior had not been very different from his usual way of expressing himself and that he had never been told that it was inappropriate. According to him, the person he had threatened was a good friend and he had not expected her to take him seriously. Never in the course of his nine years at the agency had he received any formal description of how his performance was to be evaluated or any written standards for workers' performances. Verbal communication from his supervisor had never included any direction as to how he could improve his work performance. He had never received any indication that his work was unsatisfactory. The director was generally very supportive of him and in times of stress had provided him counseling. He felt that his present endeavor was a credit to the agency. He was developing, writing, and producing a new film for the agency, with funding from a grant that he had initiated himself.

The hearing outcome was a compromise. The employee was given an unsatisfactory rating along with a 3-day suspension. It was stated that this disciplinary measure was to be corrective rather than punitive tool. In addition, he was moved out of the district office into a programmatic area where he had fewer direct service responsibilities interfering with his work on the film. Psychiatric care is being provided free of charge. Evidence of burnout syndrome is diminishing, and his work has been quite satisfactory.

FROM PSYCHOLOGICAL WORK TO SOCIAL WORK

A state child welfare agency was mandated to provide protective services to children. The families served were for the most part from low-income and minority groups.

In the provision of protective services to children the agency operated a variety of programs. These included supervision of child care for children in their natural home, day-care and homemaker services, transportation, tutoring, psychological evaluations and treatment, foster care, residential placement, and numerous other services for the protection of children and the enhancement of family life. The agency was staffed primarily by social workers with a BA degree; about 12% of the staff had graduate education. The agency's higher supervisory levels were filled by social workers with MSWs. At the time that a new director arrived, the agency, part of a larger state child welfare system, was subjected to a variety of pressures.

Agency Under Attack

Pressures included discontented direct service staff, whose ineffectiveness was justified by the high number of cases in their caseload. Service discontinuity resulted from direct service staff turnover of 47% in a year. Most of the cases under supervision had been active in the agency for many years with no clear objectives established. Uncovered caseloads resulted in cases remaining under supervision and receiving little or no services. Also, lack of documentation about service provision provoked frequent reviews, criticisms, and sanctions from the agency's higher administrative structure. The agency on a statewide basis had undergone a study conducted by a governor's task force, which reported severe pitfalls in service delivery and fiscal accountability. The new director found no formalized record-keeping procedures nor any kind of tracking system to monitor social workers' activities and the quantity and type of services being provided to clients. More importantly, there was little information on the effectiveness of the services in terms of the welfare of the children under supervision.

This new director also found that his agency was operating in an extremely hostile community environment. There was close scrutiny of agency operations by advocacy groups and the judicial system, much antagonism from the other service agencies in the county, and strong criticism from the public at large. Following the dissemination of studies on the negative effects of long-term foster care placement of children, a legislative act was passed, requiring external review of all cases of children in placement. The agency was being openly challenged for the way it handled its protective service program and for its placement of children outside the home for indefinite periods.

The new director immediately identified the need to design systems to document service provision for fiscal accountability purposes. He recognized the need to account for workers' activities, type and quantity of services being provided, and case outcome resulting from the social work intervention. However, when workers and supervisors were required to plan activities and maintain records of services provided, they looked upon these new assignments as "irrelevant" extra burdens. They felt that the director, in his desire for statistics, was underestimating their efforts to keep up with their caseload service demand. The overall feeling in the agency was that accountability measures were a constraining element placed upon the professional's efforts to deliver quality services to clients.

Staff versus Client Goals

The most important area of controversy, however, was that the director found that the type of services the staff deemed appropriate were in fact incongruent with client needs. The great majority of this client population came from poverty-stricken homes; their families had experienced social breakdown and lacked knowledge about community support systems. The service delivery modality advocated and provided by this agency, however, was highly clinical. There was a need for staff with an orientation toward intersystemic intervention, yet the majority of workers possessed knowledge primarily of intrapsychic intervention. The workers saw this new role of obtaining concrete resources for clients as being in conflict with therapeutic intervention.

The child abuse law under which the agency operated required that the staff investigate complaints of parental abuse of children. Workers were expected to investigate these violations of the law and to present evidence in court proceedings. This legal role was to be performed within the context of the protection of client rights. The clinically oriented staff had difficulties in carrying out these activities, again because they viewed them as being contradictory with the goals of rehabilitation.

Leadership Structure

The new director, forseeing the battle that would ensue from his effort to change the service modalities, analyzed the agency leadership structure that supported the existing clinical approach. After some investigation he learned that the hiring function was the responsibility of a staff member who gave preference to workers with a clinical approach. The responsibility for the selection of personnel gave this staff member ample power to shape the goals of the agency.

There also existed a leader for the clerical staff—the manager of the administrative support operations. In hiring, he had a distinct preference for "middle-class housewives who know how to type." This preference had created a great problem for him, because of the changing demography of the city. As middle-class housewives moved to the suburbs, the size of the clerical staff decreased. Over the last ten years the manager had only filled one-third of the positions open for clerical staff. He routinely refused assignments on the basis of the staff shortage. This created an ever-growing amount of clerical work for the professional staff who eventually became overworked and overwhelmed. Without a clearly established policy on job expectations and with the inordinate amount of paperwork imposed upon them, many professional workers suffered from the burnout syndrome. Their discontent was reflected in the 47% turnover rate and in frequent group grievances threatening job actions.

Community Linkage

As his awareness of different aspects of the situation increased, the director's mission took shape. He wanted to establish a social work intervention modality that would insure protection of the child while assisting the parents to improve the family living situation. In order to "change the situation" for these families, however, he had to have a staff oriented toward *social* needs rather than psychological problems. Thus the director operationalized the basic mission into a series of goals. One such goal was to establish a caseload management service delivery system for maximization of client services with resources available. An integral part of the caseload management system was to "link" community agencies' services on behalf of natural parents. These linkages would enable staff to navigate their clients through the maze of community systems and would be a force in changing the situation. Implementation of accountability devices would serve to measure achievement of agency and client goals.

In an effort to develop linkages with other community agencies—the community mental health center, board of education, juvenile court, and public welfare agencies—the administrator actively negotiated affiliation agreements establishing the basis for resource exchanges. For example, the

CMHC was to provide diagnostic and treatment services in exchange for transportation and child care services. Similar agreements were established with the board of education and juvenile court. Competition with the public welfare agency precluded the establishment of coordination agreements.

Another strategy for achieving close coordination and cooperation with other community organizations was the use of "cross-training." This is a procedure whereby agencies permit each other's staff members to participate in their regular in-service training programs. As staff become more familiar with the purposes and programs of the other agencies, closer linking of services is facilitated. Interagency coordination was also aided by the creation of the staff role of "resource coordinator." This staff member had the full-time responsibility of maintaining data on the programs available in other agencies and maintaining contacts with these agencies to determine the extent to which they had shared goals and could benefit from the exchange of needed resources.

As a result of this development of community linkages, the agency's public image improved. Public acceptance was also enhanced with the establishment of a speakers' bureau, through which staff members were made available to talk to community groups about child abuse and neglect. Further legitimation was achieved through staff participation on various statewide committees.

In planning, the director was aware that there would be barriers to achievement of his plans. The staff perceived the "new" orientation as a threat to their professional expertise. Measurement of case outcome instead of process was considered inappropriate as the "process" of therapeutic intervention was considered the essence of the real work to be done. Moreover, with such an orientation, staff had never developed the ability to establish working relationships with other systems in the community and now felt uncomfortable with the stress placed on interagency activities. Another discouraging factor was the dearth of technologies for systems coordination.

Changing Attitudes versus Structure

The director first attempted to persuade the staff to change their attitudes and behavior. After this failed he reversed the ideological orientation, by removing the hiring power from the leader of the professional staff. He established criteria for hiring staff with a macro-orientation and went so far as to develop instruments in order to measure this characteristic in applicants. He soon found that most of the persons whose scores indicated a high degree of macro-orientation had had personal experience in dealing with community service systems. Generally, they seemed to be from minority groups. The director also redefined the hiring officer's functional responsibilities with strict adherence to the civil service job description. He was able to achieve more specific job expectations for all staff by implementing a system establishing standards for role performance according to specific positions. This was a statewide job performance expectation system, which had never been operationalized in the agency.

The new system revealed that the hiring officer had become a consultant to workers with personal problems and as a result had gained great power within the organization. By redefining his responsibilities, the director had placed a limit on his communications and, therefore, on his power as well. The hiring officer was informed that his frequent meetings with other members of the staff were considered dysfunctional and could be the basis for an unsatisfactory evaluation. He was required to use the structure of the organization in intervening in personal problems and was required to communicate any such problems to the director. Workers had grown accustomed to having their personal problems attended to during work hours as part of their training to handle clients' emotional responses to the social work intervention. Most of them, especially supervisors, had lost the ability to differentiate between being supportive on a professional versus personal level. When this "personal counseling" was eliminated by the director in favor of more efficiency in services to clients, strong objections were voiced. The director was accused by both supervisors and line workers of being unconcerned about his staff. He remained firm, nonetheless. He continued to hold the hiring officer accountable for this time in the office and limited his ability to interact with and influence other staff. The director was able to document subversive activities on the part of the hiring officer. Under the potential threat of disciplinary action the hiring officer decided to resign.

The director utilized the opposite strategy in dealing with the manager of support operations. Instead of removing certain functions from his purview, he informed him that it was his responsibility as a manager to see that *all* of the clerical work to be done in the agency was completed regardless of how many clerical positions he had filled. This expectation was also included as a criterion for evaluating his job performance. After an unsatisfactory evaluation, this seat of power was eliminated when the manager suddenly decided on an early retirement.

Process versus Outcome

Having changed the leadership structure, the director's next step was to impact upon the workers themselves. Workers were informed that their performance would be measured by task and case outcome, not by process. Their interventions were to be viewed as means and not as ends. Training programs were implemented which stressed clients' and workers' rights, utilization of community support systems, and cooperation with other people and agencies in the community. The new performance standards for supervisors and the move away from clinical intervention created an exodus of supervisors from the agency. With this increase in turnover at the supervisory level came a corresponding overall decrease in turnover at the line worker level. The new director used the opportunity presented by the turnover to hire staff who possessed a macro-orientation to social work practice. He also established new selection and promotional procedures, including the tests mentioned earlier which measured this macro-orientation.

With the recruitment of more minority staff another problem arose. Many of these new employees had only limited work experience in bureaucratic structures. Because of their bureaucratic imcompetence and their inability to engage in a psychiatric supervision process, these workers were isolated from the rest of the staff and became easy targets for disciplinary action from their supervisors. The result was a staff that was markedly divided in terms of their approach to social work intervention. Time-consuming personnel conflicts arose constantly, preventing the director from fully implementing his caseload management service delivery system.

The director believed that the major reason for "burnout" was the disproportionate expectations in a crisis-oriented social service agency. He saw no solution for morale problems, other than to make the job expectations more realistic. In particular, he felt that the psychological model that had been followed contributed to burnout because it was inappropriate for the problems being served. He felt that the caseload management service delivery system would be more relevant for the clients and hence partially alleviate burnout. However, the changes in staffing were not occurring fast enough to facilitate the implementation of the caseload management system. Staff opposition was too strong.

Accountability System

Unable to change the service delivery modality by directly dealing with staff resistance, the director used the requirements established by a newly created external review board to develop and enforce a management information system. The implementation of the management information system required quality control procedures from direct service supervisors and casework supervisors. Data about case outcome had to be submitted to the director on a monthly basis, reporting type and quantity of services provided to client in accordance with clearly established criteria for social work intervention. However, only the staff assigned to generic caseloads—who, incidentally, were overburdened by large numbers of cases—were under the pressure to adhere to the service delivery criteria measured by the quality control procedures.

Staff opposition to the conversion of a caseload management service delivery system was also associated with structural factors. These factors were the geographic work structure and the specializations.

The work of the agency had previously been structured around geographical areas for generic units. It was firmly believed that assigning workers to geographical areas would be beneficial for clients because the workers would gain familiarity with a particular community. However, this work structure did not permit the balancing of caseload levels for individual workers, as it is not possible to control intake in a public agency or to control from which areas clients will come. Frequent redistribution of geographical boundaries, and the high turnover that was probably encouraged by high caseload, seemed to prevent workers from becoming familiar with their community, defeating the purpose of the geographic work structure. Nonetheless staff were violently opposed to the director's suggestion that caseload be lowered by eliminating geographical areas for generic units.

The specializations system was also supported by staff strong belief in its effectiveness. The staff sustained a conviction long accepted in the social work profession—that expertise in an area of practice contributes to positive case outcome. In addition, the specialists were assigned to low workload and jealously guarded their status in the agency. The generic workers, meanwhile, saw those specialties as career goals for themselves. As a result of such factors, the staff decided to strike if the director eliminated the specialties.

Divide and Conquer

In the middle of staff unrest the director came up with a strategy to conquer the problem of burnout and ineffective services to clients. The strategy involved diverting attention to another problem within the agency. A severe shortage of space had existed in the office for some time, as the agency had remained in the quarters that had been rented when the staff was less than one-third its present size. As there were no available places for expansion, the director submitted a proposal to divide the county into three offices. Such a division required dismantling the geographical areas and restructuring the agency in newly created offices. Redistribution of staff among three offices did not permit assignment of staff to a specialty because of the necessary reduction of staffing levels for each office. In that manner, by using the problem of office space, the director managed equalization of caseloads and dissolution of geographical assignments. These changes were intended not only to prevent worker burnout, but also to facilitate the implementation of a caseload management system.

The director, through the new record-keeping systems, developed data to prove that changes have indeed occurred despite the resistance. He has found that workers have been closing a larger number of cases than in the past, and that they have been focusing more on providing concrete services. By reading staff writings and through discussions, he also has become aware that workers have developed a better understanding of permanency planning for children and the need for accountability. He presented this data to staff as evidence that the changes achieved positive results. The data gathered also included service delivery achievements obtained through joint intervention with other community agencies. The staff received recognition from the judiciary, school, and mental health systems for effective social work intervention. Regardless of their differences of opinion, workers are bringing their actual behavior into line with the director's objectives. Moreover, hiring social workers with socioeconomic backgrounds similar to those of the clients, the director hopes to reverse the present system of "blaming the victim" and to preserve the rights of clients to due process and social services.

The Results

A year-and-a-half after the change to caseload management system, the staff turnover rate had been reduced to 10%, and the affirmative action report indicated a 15% level of minority staff, including five individuals promoted to supervisory positions. Nor were there any grievances during this 18-month period; in fact, agency morale was higher than it had ever been in their whole history. The director was asked by higher administrative levels to present his service delivery model to the directors of similar county offices around the state.

Civil Service List

The smooth functioning of this agency was abruptly disrupted, however, when the civil service list for line supervisors was announced. Whereas most of the staff recruited and promoted by the administration had a "social" rather than clinical orientation, the civil service tests stressed a clinical approach. As a result, the staff who had been recruited and promoted, and who were performing efficiently and effectively on the job, achieved low grades on the civil service exam. In contrast, the older, clinically oriented staff, who had resisted the director's efforts to change the agency, achieved high grades on the test. The director was thus confronted with another problem—how to keep qualified and effective supervisors from being displaced by those who had a philosophy contrary to the new thrust of this agency.

The civil service list for the line supervisors position involved *130* staff members. The list included not only personnel from inside this district office, but also others throughout the state. Undaunted, the administrator spoke to all of the relevant staff members by phone, indicating that they would be displacing a person who was already in the position, providing a brief description of the duties involved with emphasis on the caseload management aspects, and asking for permission to obtain references from their supervisors. Following these telephone conversations about 10 persons decided not to seek the promotional opportunity. Their decisions may have been related to the fact that their supervisor would be asked for specific data on the activity in their caseloads, including number of contacts with clients and involvement in community-oriented activities. Although this type of data was routinely collected in this office, it was not done in other offices.

The Test

The director also planned to include a situational test as part of the interview procedures. This test had been used previously in the selection of casework supervisors and was found to be valid. Although a grievance had been filed against the use of this written test on the grounds that it duplicated the test given by the civil service and that it discriminated against minorities, the director had been successful in defeating the grievance on both grounds. In fact, the persons who did best on this test were minority staff members.

A similar grievance was now filed against the use of this situational test for the group of staff on civil service supervisory list. Because of time constraints, the director decided that rather than use the written test he would incorporate the test into the interview procedure. His plan was to have each person read a case situation just prior to his or her interview and then respond to questions verbally in the interview situation. Following this, the director would discuss the answers with the applicant. The primary purpose of this procedure was to make clear to the applicant the social approach used in service delivery in this office. The director anticipated that most applicants would have a psychological approach and that the discrepancy between their orientation and that of the office might persuade them to withdraw. However, the interviews with the persons on the list were abruptly interrupted as a result of a major retrenchment that followed large cuts on the federal level. Many staff persons, including the director, received notices that they could be "bumped" out of their positions. At first it appeared that this "bumping" would completely disrupt this office. However, it turned out that the outside staff members who were considering coming to this office had decided not to seek positions in this socially oriented agency. And as a consequence of the retrenchment it was decided to make the new supervisory list inactive. Therefore, the staff remained in place and are currently working toward a social approach to child protective services.

MENTAL HEALTH RULES AND REGULATIONS

The Sickness in the System

Having been given the mandate to "reform the system," the Department of Mental Health uncovered what appeared to be a most glaring inequity—discriminatory practices toward the seriously and chronically mentally ill.

Those patients most in need of services were receiving the least, both in quantity and in quality.

The roots of this serious problem lay in various practices and perspectives of the mental health system as a whole. One such perspective was the stress placed on the disease model in diagnosing patients. Practitioners attributed maladaptive behavior to some sort of pathology *within* the patient, which was hopefully "curable" through "treatment." The Department of Mental Health took the position that, providers of care, by adopting this disease model, were disregarding important situational factors as reasons for maladaptive behavior. If primarily a response to situational stress, this behavior could be alleviated more easily by providing patients with opportunities, concrete services, and training which would "change the situation" for them. And through such services, chronic patients could be brought up to a certain level of functioning in the community, so that institutionalization would be unnecessary.

A further problem was that community-based clinics and private hospitals, with the most advanced technologies and a large number of highly trained practitioners, were "creaming" the more "desirable" patients (i.e., less severely mentally ill, middle-class patients who could afford to pay a fee for treatment) and excluding the patients with the least resources and the greatest need. This selection process was pervasive, even though the stated purpose of the agencies was to serve the entire community. Hence, state hospitals, known for their poor conditions, had become "receptacles" for this socially undesirable population. The state hospitals emphasized provision of custodial care, with corresponding deemphasis on return of the patient to the community.

One possible strategy was to improve conditions in the state hospitals for these needy patients. However, the Department of Mental Health set as its mission a more far-reaching task—to reform the *total* system by getting at the roots of the discriminatory practices.

Planning the Attack

Once basic malfunctions had been identified and the overall mission of reform enunciated, it became necessary to establish goals. The goals established were as follows: *(a)* to shift priorities to service for the chronically mentally ill in funding community mental health programs; *(b)* to promote the unified mental health system by coordinating services and funding in counties and regions; and *(c)* to shift emphasis away from the disease model to a conceptual framework that emphasized "normalization" and "levels of functioning," so that services, supports, and opportunities would be provided for the patients to live up to their highest level of functioning.

To prove that many people who were in hospitals did not have to be there, the Department of Mental Health first funded a few demonstration projects. The patients in these projects had been institutionalized an average of 15 years. It was successfully demonstrated that with community supports and advocacy they were able to live in the community.

Care or Cure?

The department started by making changes in the state hospitals, including revision of their admissions policies, in an attempt to increase community involvement and strengthen the voice of workers and patients.

In order to create a more unified system, the department scheduled regional meetings and began more frequent and closer monitoring and evaluation of community mental health centers. The department threatened the funding of those who did not cooperate in these ventures, and as a result, received increasing compliance.

The department also required service contracts for each patient upon admission to a state hospital. The service contracts were to include the plan for the patient while in the institution and for the patient's support and supervision by the community mental health facilities and other agencies upon discharge. These contracts emphasized normalization and levels of functioning, rather than diagnosis based on individual pathology.

According to Department of Mental Health officials, the results of the contract program have been startling: 3,000 ex-patients appear to be living and adjusting in the community.

Or Control?

The department soon found that the strategies implemented were insufficient, in that discriminatory practices against chronically and seriously mentally ill patients continued. It became obvious that the essence of the problem was that state hospitals were operating as social control mechanisms by eliminating "undesirables" from the community. Allowing chronic patients into the mainstream of society through community support systems was too threatening—hence the continuance of discriminatory practices despite the new strategies. Moreover, community mental health centers and private hospitals were still being selective in whom they accepted for treatment, and needy patients were still getting "dumped" into state hospitals. This meant that the community-based centers had to be dealt with directly, and it was here that the department met its greatest challenge. By attempting to interfere with the operation of these agencies, the administration of the Department of Mental Health was risking its own existence. There was tremendous community resistance and political pressure for the department *not* to interfere with these centers.

The Opposition

The strategy chosen for the confrontation was to rewrite the rules and regulations that dealt with how community mental health programs would receive state aid. These rules and regulations had not been revised for 8 years. They existed as vague, general guidelines and allowed a great deal of leeway. A task force was organized; its members represented a cross-section of interest groups and included two representatives from the department, the president and vice president of the Community Mental Health Association, and other community representatives. By rewriting the rules and regulations into a thick, explicit document, the department created its instrument of reform. These regulations specified in detail rules for agency operations, including the criteria for service priority, the qualifications of staff, the roles and functions to be performed by staff and, the nature of agency community relations. In terms of service priority the lesser disturbed patients had low priority.

But the War Goes On

Soon after the rules and regulations were distributed, the governor was deluged with letters and telegrams expressing opposition. Even the president of the Community Mental Health Association, who had been a member of the task force, publicly rejected the new regulations. Opponents were numerous and included a large number of politically powerful professional organizations such as the Health Department, the Psychiatric Association, the Medical Society, the Hospital Association, the Association of Mental Health Agencies, the Association of Social Workers, and the Association of Mental Health Administrators, in addition to a large number of clinics and centers across the state. The attack was staged on a number of fronts: an appeal was sent to the commissioner to stop the regulations, and pressure was placed on various other professional groups and organizations and local legislators to come out against the regulations. The goal of the attack was to stop implementation, appoint a new task force, and rewrite the regulations once again.

Support did exist, but these groups were much less vocal. They included private advocacy groups, the public advocate, various other legal projects, many county mental health boards, and a number of clinics. However, because most supporters remained silent, it appeared to legislators that the regulations had met with widespread opposition and very little support.

Reasons for opposition were numerous. It was felt that the task force that wrote the document had not been representative of the provider or professional community involved, nor of the consumer population. Opponents also stated that the new regulations would create a lack of balance in the mental health services as the target population was too narrow. The real need, they claimed, was for a gradual expansion of mental health services for various target populations, rather than a shift to one of them. The new regulations would exclude a vast majority of those seeking mental health services in the state: They would cause a reduction of major preventive and early treatment services and would force providers to discriminate against clients who required immediate mental health services but not hospitalization. One opponent claimed that the shift in emphasis would in effect "contribute to a formation of a new generation of chronic, incurable mental patients."

Survival

Economic considerations were also brought to the surface as opponents elaborated upon their criticism of the focus on the chronic population. Opponents predicted that outpatient services in the community would collapse due to lack of financial support. They urged that the statement of the rules and regulations be modified to include provision of general outpatient services and acute inpatient services to a broader spectrum of clients or potential clients.

Critics also claimed that the rules and regulations mandated numerous specific activities and services for which funding was not provided. Some of the expectations, they claimed, were unrealistic given the low level of funding. For example, it was unrealistic to expect general hospitals to alter the composition of their boards of trustees in compliance with the new regulations, simply in order to receive .1% of the budget per institution. On a more general level critics expressed surprise that a state agency that only provides one dollar per capita outpatient allotment to mental health services could propose such explicit regulations. For example, one regulation mandated an individually written medication information fact sheet for each prescription the patient was given. This change would greatly increase the amount of time physicians must spend with each patient. Moreover, the rules and regulations stated that each inpatient unit should be furnished to create a homelike environment, without making any suggestions about how to pay for this decor. Critics also pointed out that a possible consequence of creating a homelike environment in an inpatient unit was that clients would be encouraged to stay in the unit instead of going back to the community. One of the most frequently expressed concerns was that the new rules and regulations would increase administrative costs because of requirements relating to evaluation, information gathering, and record keeping. The fear was that this cost increase would result in a reduction of clinical services for residents of the state.

There were other criticisms as well: Some of the new regulations were potentially dangerous, as certain "crisis prone" individuals might need more emergency services than anticipated or more supervision than could be provided through off-site services. The document and its philosophy implied that hospitalization was *never* indicated, whereas it is, in fact, the treatment of *choice* for certain patients at certain times. Providers were also being asked to engage in a form of pretense that real alternatives already existed in the communities, with "natural support systems." Moreover, by restricting mental health agency services to the most seriously disturbed population, the rules and regulations might increase the stigma attached to these programs and endanger support from the community.

The Autonomy Issue

Autonomy was clearly a central concern. One county mental health association came out strongly against the rules and regulations, stating that they imposed "escalated requirements" which were excessively detailed and had the effect of minimizing local autonomy in favor of centralized control.

For example, the rules and regulations state that funded mental health programs should submit credentials of individuals to be hired as program element director/coordinator or executive director to the Department of Mental Health for approval. Opponents felt that this would undermine the power and authority of the governing boards. Although it was reasonable that the state should establish minimum criteria for professional training and length of experience, it seemed to be an unnecessary assumption of power and authority for the state to have final approval on the selection of particular persons to be hired.

Discontent about intrusion on autonomy did not stop with these administrative concerns. Restrictions on treatment were also considered unjust. This included the requirements that agencies had to submit to the Department of Mental Health for prior approval procedures concerning nonstandard treatment procedures, research-oriented procedures, or education demonstration programs.

Perhaps the most original statement in opposition to the regulations was made by the director of one of the community mental health centers. He stated that the new rules and regulations would have exactly the opposite effect of what was intended. He stated that any community organization effort that would promote the mental health of the community at large could result in strategies excluding the chronically, seriously disabled and others who deviated from the general norms of the community. He ventured to guess that a sampling of community residents would indicate that their mental health would be enhanced if they did not have to deal with "troublesome people who acted in a deviant fashion."

Seeking Support

Despite all the controversy, the director of the Department of Mental Health and his staff, without losing sight of the political power of their opponents, are attempting to gain more visible support for their position. They feel that by doing so, they will win the favor of legislators as well. Their major strategy had been to meet, without hostility, all parties interested in discussing the situation. The director's office had become a place where anyone in need of help can go, and in this way many new supporters have been acquired.

The agency has also sought support from the federal government, but thus far has had little success.

Ideology versus Self-Interest

And what of the department's response to the issues raised by the opposition? Although the opposition's objections appear to be stated with the best interest of the clients in mind, the director of the Department of Mental Health, a psychiatrist, interprets them as expressions of self-interest by the professionals involved and as a reaction to a conceptual model that contradicts their basic ideology.

The new rules and regulations place a greater responsibility on professionals because they point to a target population in need of continuous and comprehensive care. This necessitates that professionals put in longer hours. It could also mean less monetary remuneration, in that community clinics might lose clients who have the ability to pay fees. The stress on normalization and community living is detrimental to those involved with the hospital association, because all efforts would be placed on moving patients out of the hospital and keeping them out. Perhaps one of the most threatening aspects of the new regulations is that they take away from the practitioners some autonomy in decision making. Implementation of new screening procedures for admissions and mandated contracts and plans for discharge constrain autonomous professional judgment.

But beyond these restrictions for professionals lies an even more basic issue: The ideology reflected in the new regulations contradicts the one that these professionals hold. Opponents state that those who prepared the rules and regulations were unwilling to differentiate between mental disorder and social misfortune. They claim that it is convenient for the Department of Mental Health to redefine psychological disorders as social disorders. They further state that the rules and regulations would necessitate conversions of outpatient clinics to social service delivery systems. That is, they feel that the regulations imply that social service supports are sufficient to handle the chronic patient, and the care of mental patients is thus reduced to the satisfaction of their basic human needs. This approach, opponents feel, ignores the complexity of the problem and wastes precious public funds.

In contrast, the philosophy behind the regulations is that the patient and his or her problem should be viewed in the broadest sense possible, a perspective that allows for simplified procedures at all levels of care. By looking at the social situation, and not just at the person, this philosophy deemphasizes the importance of professional judgment and individualized treatment. It stresses social supports over medication and therapy.

REFERENCES

Abels, Paul, and Michael Murphy. 1981. *Administration in the Human Services.* Englewood Cliffs, N. J.: Prentice-Hall.

Academe. 1979. "Evaluating Teachers." 65.

Ad Hoc Committee on Advocacy. 1969. "The Social Worker As Advocate: Champion of Social Victims." In *Social Work* 14: 16–22.

Alexander, Leslie B., and Toba Schwaber Kerson. 1980. "Room At the Top: Women in Social Administration." In *Leadership in Social Administration.* Felice D. Perlmutter and Simon Slavin, eds. Phil.: Temple University Press, pp. 200–211.

American Friends Service Committee. 1971. *Struggle for Justice.* New York: Hill and Wang.

Argyris, Chris. 1970. "Being Human and Being Organized." In *American Bureaucracy,* ed. Warren B. Bennis. Piscataway, N. J.: Transaction Books.

———. 1972. *The Applicability of Organizational Sociology.* New York: Cambridge University Press.

Austin, Carol D. 1983. "Case Management in Long-Term Care: Options and Opportunities." *Health and Social Work* 8(1): 16–30.

Austin, David M. 1978. "Consolidation and Integration." *Public Welfare* 36 (3): 20–28.

Austin, Michael J. 1981. *Supervisory Management for the Human Services.* Englewood Cliffs, N. J.: Prentice-Hall.

Back Wards to Back Streets: A Study of People in Transition from Psychiatric Hospital to Community. 1978. Montclair, N.J.: Mental Health Association of Essex County.

Bakal, Yitzhek. 1973. *Closing Correctional Institutions.* Lexington, Mass.: D. C. Heath.

Bales, R. F. 1958. "Task Roles and Social Roles in Problem Solving Groups." Eleanor Maccoby, T. M. Newcomb, and E. L. Hartly. *Readings in Social Psychology* 3d ed., New York: Holt, Rinehart and Winston.

Barker, Robert, and Thomas Briggs. 1968. *Differential Use of Social Work Manpower.* Silver Spring, Md.: National Association of Social Workers.

Baxter, Raymond, Robert Applebaum, James J. Callahan, Jr., Jon B. Christianson, and Stephen L. Day. 1983. *The Planning And Implementation of Channeling: Early Experiences of the National Long-Term Care Demonstration.* Princeton: Mathematica.

Beck, A. T. 1962. "Reliabilty of Psychiatric Diagnoses, 1: A Critique of Systematic Studies." *American Journal of Psychiatry* 119 (September): 210–216.

Bendix, R. 1960. *Max Weber: An Intellectual Portrait.* Garden City, N.Y.: Doubleday.

Bennis, Warren. 1966. *Beyond Bureaucracy.* New York: McGraw-Hill.

Bernstein, Paul, 1976. *Workplace Democratization: Its Internal Dynamics.* Kent, Ohio: Kent State University Press.

Better Services for the Mentally Ill. 1975. London: Her Majesty's Stationery Office.

Blau, Peter, and Richard Scott. 1962. *Formal Organizations.* New York: Chandler.

Bloom, Alan A. 1978. "Pitfalls of a Managerial Approach to Supervision in a Public Welfare Agency." *Administration in Social Work* 2 (4): 482–487.

Blumberg, Arthur, and William Wiener. 1971. "One from Two: Facilitating as Organizational Merger." *Journal of Applied Behavioral Science.* 7 (1).

Bosk, Charles L. 1979. *Forgive and Remember: Managing Medical Failure.* Chicago: University of Chicago Press.

Brager, George, and Stephen Holloway. 1978. *Changing Human Service Organizations: Politics and Practice.* New York: Free Press.

Brager, George, and Harry Specht. 1965. "Mobilizing the Poor for Social Action." In *Social Welfare Forum.* New York: Columbia University Press.

Bramhall, Martha, and Susan Ezell. 1981. "How Burned Out Are You." *Public Welfare* 39 (1): 23–28.

Brenner, M. Harvey. 1973. *Mental Illness and the Economy.* Mass.: Harvard University Press.

Brieland, Donald. 1959. *An Experimental Study of Adoptive Parents at Intake.* New York: Child Welfare League.

Brown, Edwin G. 1970. *Selection of Adoptive Parents: A Videotape Study.* Ph.D. dissertation. School of Social Service Administration, University of Chicago.

Brown, G. E. (ed.). 1968. *The Multi-Problem Dilemma: A Social Research Demonstration with Multi-Problem Families.* Metuchen, N.J.: Scarecrow Press.

Calhoun, John B. 1963. "Population Density and Social Pathology." In *The Urban Condition,* ed. Leonard Duhl. New York: Basic.

Caplan, Gerald (ed.). 1964. *Principles of Preventive Psychiatry.* New York: Basic.

Center for Study of Social Policy. 1983. *A Dream Referred: The Economic Status of Black Americans.* Washington, D.C.

Chambers, David L. 1975. "Community Based Treatment and the Constitution: The Principle of the Least Restrictive Alternative." In *Alternatives to Mental Hospital Treatment,* ed. Leonard I. Stein and Mary A. Test. New York: Plenum.

Chafetz, Morris, and Harold W. Demone, Jr. 1962. *Alcoholism and Society.* Fairlawn, N.J.: Oxford University Press.

Chernesky, Roslyn. 1979. "A Guide for Women Managers: A Review of Literature." *Administration in Social Work* 13 (1): 91–97.

Cherniss, Gary. 1980. *Staff Burnout: Job Stress in the Human Services,* Beverly Hills, Calif.: Sage.

Chesler, Phyllis. 1972. *Women and Madness.* New York: Avon Books.

Clinard, Marshall B. 1963. *Sociology of Deviant Behavior,* rev. ed. New York: Holt, Rinehart and Winston.

Cloward, Richard A. 1959. "Illegitimate Means, Anomie and Deviant Behavior." *American Sociological Review* 24: 166–176.

Cloward, Richard A., and Irwin Epstein. 1967. "Private Social Welfare Disengagement from the Poor: The Case of the Family Adjustment Agencies." In *Social Welfare Institutions,* ed. M. N. Zeld. New York: Wiley.

Cloward, Richard A., and Lloyd Ohlin. 1960. *Delinquency and Opportunity.* New York: Free Press.

Cohen, Neil, and Gary Rhodes. 1977. "Social Work Supervision: A View toward Leadership Styles and Job Orientation." In "Education and Practice." *Administration in Social Work* 3 (1): 281–291.

Comptroller General's Report of the United States. 1977. *Returning the Mentally Disabled to the Community.* Washington, D.C.: Department of Health, Education and Welfare.

Conrad, John B. 1973. "Corrections and Simple Justice." *Journal of Criminal Law and Criminology* 64: 208–217.

Cooper, Cary L., and Judi Marshall, 1978. "Sources of Managerial and White Collar Stress." In *Stress at Work,* ed. Cary L. Cooper and Roy Payne. New York: Wiley.

Cornish, Edward. 1970. "The Professional Futurist." In *Mankind 2000,* ed. R. Jungk and J. Galtung. London: Allen and Unwin.

Corrections. 1973. National Advisory Commision on Criminal Justice Standards and Goals. Washington, D.C.: U.S. Government Printing Office.

Coser, L. 1956. *The Functions of Social Conflict.* New York: Free Press.

Coulton, Claudia J. 1981. "Person–Environment Fit as the Focus in Health Care." *Social Work,* 26 (1).

Cummings, Elaine. 1967. "Allocation of Care to the Mentally Ill, American Style." In *Organizing for Community Welfare,* ed. M. Zald. New York: Quadrangle.

Cummings, Elaine, and John Cummings. 1957. *Closed Ranks.* Cambridge, Mass.: Harvard University Press

Cupaivolo, Anthony A., and Michael J. Dowling. 1983. "Are Corporate Managers Really Better?" *Public Welfare* 41 (3): 13–17.

Daley, Michael R. 1979. "Burnout: Smouldering Problems in Protective Services." *Social Work* 24 (5): 375–379.

Davidson, Kay W. 1978. "Roles In Health Care: The Case of Discharge Planning." *Social Work In Health Care* 4 (1): 43–54.

Davis, E. W., and M. Barrett. 1981. "Supervision for Management of Worker Stress." *Administration in Social Work* 5 (1): 55–64.

Day, Peter R. 1981. *Social Work and Social Control.* London: Tavistock.

Delgado, Melvin, and Denise Homan. 1982. "Natural Support Systems: Source of Strength in Hispanic Communities." *Social Work* 27 (1): 83–89.

Demone, H., and D. Harshbarger. 1974. *A Handbook of Human Service Organizations.* New York: Behavioral Publications.

Deutsch, M., and M. E. Collins. 1951. *Interracial Housing: A Psychological Evaluation of a Social Experiment.* Minneapolis: University of Minnesota Press.

Devore, Wynetta, and Elfriede Schlesinger. 1981. *Ethnic Sensitive Social Work Practice.* St. Louis, Mo.: C. V. Mosby.

De Weaver, Kevin L. 1983. "Deinstitutionalization of Developmentally Disabled." In *Social Work* 28 (6): 435–439.

Dewey, John, 1910. *How We Think.* New York: D. C. Heath.

Dickson, Donald. 1976. "Legal Skills for Social Workers." In *Social Work Practice,* ed. Bernard Ross and S. Khinduka. Silver Spring, Md.: National Association of Social Workers.

Dickson, Donald. 1977. "Law and Social Work." *Encyclopedia of Social Work.* Silver Spring, Md.: National Association of Social Workers.

Donnison, David, and Valerie Chapman. 1965. *Social Policy and Administration.* London: George Allen Unwin.

Dorsen, Norman, and Aryeh Neier (eds.). 1971, 1973, 1974, and 1983. *American Civil Liberties Union Handbooks.* New York: Avon.

Dressel, P. 1982. "Policy Sources of Worker Dissatisfaction: The Case of Human Services in Aging." *Social Service Review* 56 (3): 406–423.

Dubos, Rene. 1959. *Mirage of Health: Utopias, Progress and Biological Change.* Garden City: N.Y.: Doubleday.

Elling, Ray H., and Sandor Halebsky. 1961. "Organizational Differentiation and Support: A Conceptual Framework." *Administrative Science Quarterly* 6 (2): 183–209.

———. 1965. "Support for Public and Private Services." In *Social Welfare Institutions,* ed. M. Zald. New York: Wiley.

Etzioni, Amitai. 1964. *Modern Organizations.* Englewood Cliffs, N.J.: Prentice-Hall.

Eysenck, H. J. 1965. "The Effects of Psychotherapy." *International Journal of Psychiatry* 1: 99–142.

Ewalt, Patricia L., and Robert M. Honeyfield. 1981. "Needs of Persons and Long Term Care," *Social Work* 26 (3): 221–223.

Fairweather, George. 1969. *Community Life for the Mentally Ill.* Hawthorne, N.Y.: Aldine.

Fiedler, F. E. 1967. *A Theory of Leadership Effectiveness.* New York: McGraw-Hill.

Field, M. H. 1980. "Social Casework Practice During the 'Psychiatric Deluge'." *Social Service Review* 54 (4): 482–507.

Finch, Wilbur A. 1976. "Social Workers vs. Bureaucracy." *Social Work* 21 (5): 370–375.

Fischer, Joel. 1973. "Is Casework Effective?" *Social Work* 18 (1): 5–20.

———. 1981. "The Social Work Revolution." *Social Work* 26 (3): 199–209.

Fleishman, E. A., and D. R. Peters. 1962. "Interpersonal Values, Leadership Attitudes and Managerial Success." *Personnel Psychology* 15: 127–143.

Follett, Mary Parker. 1940. *Dynamic Administration: The Collected Papers of Mary Parker Follett.* ed. Henry Metcalf and L. F. Urwick. New York: Harper & Row.

Freeman, Howard, and Ozzie Simmons. 1963. *The Mental Patient Comes Home.* New York: Wiley.

Friedson, Elliot. 1970. "Dominant Professions, Bureaucracy and Client Services." In *Organizations and Clients: Essays in the Sociology of Service,* ed. William Rosengren and Mark Lefton. Columbus, Ohio: Charles F. Merrill.

Froland, Charles. 1980. "Formal and Informal Care: Discontinuities in a Continuum." *Social Service Review* 54 (4): 572–587.

Froland, Charles, and Joseph Bell. 1979. "Policy Experimentation: Framing the Welfare Debate." *Social Service Review* 53 (3): 441–451.

Froland, Charles, Gerry Brodsky, Madeline Olson, and Linda Stewart. 1979. "Social Support and Social Adjustment." *Community Mental Health Journal* 15 (2): 82–93.

Fuchs, Victor. 1974. *Who Shall Live.* New York: Basic.

Furman, Sylvan, S. 1965. *Community Mental Health Services in Northern Europe.* Public Health Service Publication 1407. Washington, D.C.: U.S. Government Printing Office.

Galm, Sharon. 1972. *Issues in Welfare Administration: Welfare—An Administrative Nightmare.* U.S. Congress, Subcommittee on Fiscal Policy of the Joint Economic Committee. Washington, D.C.: U.S. Government Printing Office.

Galper, Jeffry H. 1975. *The Politics of Social Services.* Englewood Cliffs, N.J.: Prentice-Hall.

Garbarino, James; Holly S. Stocking; Alice H. Collins; Benjamin H. Gotlieb; David L. Olds; Diane L. Pancoast; Deborah Sherman; Anne Marietietjen, and Donald I. Warren. 1980. *Protecting Children from Abuse and Neglect.* San Francisco: Jossey-Bass.

Gardos, George, and Jonathon O. Cole. 1976. "Maintenance Antipsychotic Therapy: Is The Cure Worse Than The Disease?" *American Journal of Psychiatry* 133.

Gates, Bruce L. 1980. *Social Program Administration.* Englewood Cliffs: N.J.: Prentice-Hall.

Gaylin, Willard; Ira Glasser; Steven Marcus, and David Rothman. 1978. *Doing Good.* New York: Pantheon.

Geismar, Ludwig, and Jane Krisberg. 1967. *The Forgotten Neighborhood.* Metuchen, N.J.: Scarecrow Press.

George, Vic, and Paul Wilding. 1976. *Ideology and Social Welfare.* London: Routledge & Kegan Paul.

Gerhart, Ursula, and Alexander Brooks. 1983. "The Social Work Practitioner and Antipsychotic Medications." *Social Work* 28 (6): 454–460.

Germain, Carel B., and Alex Gitterman. 1980. *The Life Model of Social Work Practice.* New York: Columbia University Press.

Gil, David G. 1970. *Violence Against Children.* Cambridge, Mass.: Harvard University Press.

Gilbert, Neil. 1982. "Policy Issues in Primary Prevention." *Social Work* 27 (4): 293–297.

Gilbert, Neil, and Harry Specht. 1974. *Dimensions of Social Welfare Policy.* Englewood Cliffs, N.J.: Prentice-Hall.

Gilbert, Neil, Henry Miller, and Harry Specht. 1980. *An Introduction to Social Work Practice.* Chicago: University of Chicago Press.

Gingeviol, W., M. Kleczewski, and S. Kirk. 1982. "Name Calling in Social Work." *Social Service Review* 56 (3): 366–374.

Gitterman, Alex, and Carel B. Germain. 1981. "Education for Practice: Teaching about Environment." *Journal of Education for Social Workers* 17 (3): 44–51.

Glassman, Marjorie. 1980. "Misdiagnosis of Senile Dementia: Denial of Care to the Elderly." *Social Work* 25 (4): 288–292.

Glazer, Nathan, and Daniel Patrick Moynihan. 1963. *Beyond the Melting Pot.* Cambridge, Mass.: M I T Press.

Glisson, Charles. 1981. "A Contingency Model of Social Welfare Administration." *Administration in Social Work* 5 (1): 15–30.

Goffman, Erving. 1961. *Asylums*. Garden City, N.Y.: Doubleday.

——. 1963. *Stigma: Notes on the Management of Spoiled Identity*. Englewood Cliffs, N.J.: Prentice-Hall.

Goldberg, E. Matilda, and R. William Warburton. 1979. *Ends and Means in Social Work*. London: Allen and Unwin.

Goodenough, W. H. 1963. *Cooperation in Change*. New York: Russell Sage Foundation.

Gould, Julius, and William Kolb (eds.). 1964. *Dictionary of the Social Sciences*. New York: Free Press.

Gouldner, Alvin W. 1954. *Patterns of Industrial Democracy*. New York: Free Press.

——. 1959. "Reciprocity and Autonomy in Functional Theory." In *Symposium in Sociological Theory*, ed. LLewellyn Cross. New York: Harper & Row

——. 1963. "The Secrets of Organizations." *Social Welfare Forum*. New York: Columbia University Press.

Grant, D. P. 1970. "Architect Discovers the Aged." *Gerontologist* 10: 275–281.

Granvold, Donald K. 1977. "Supervisory Style and Educational Preparation of Public Welfare Administrators." *Administration in Social Work* 1 (1): 79–88.

——. 1978. "Training Social Work Supervisors to Meet Organizational and Worker Objectives." *Journal of Education for Social Work* 14 (2): 38–45.

Grob, Gerald N. 1973. *Mental Institutions in America*. New York: Free Press.

Grosser, Charles. 1973. *New Directions in Community Organizations*. New York: Praeger.

Gruber, Murray (ed.). 1981. *Management Systems in the Human Services*. Philadelphia, Penn.: Temple University Press.

Gulick, L., and L. Urwich (eds.). 1937. *Papers on the Science of Administration*. New York: Institute of Public Administrators.

Gummer, Burton. 1978. "Power Politics Approach to Social Welfare Organization." *Social Service Review* 52 (3): 349–361.

——. 1979a. "On Helping and Helplessness: The Structure of Discretion in the American Welfare System." *Social Service Review* 53 (2): 214–228.

——. 1979b. "Is the Social Worker in Public Welfare an Endangered Species?" *Public Welfare* 37 (4): 12–21.

——. 1979c. "A Framework for Curriculum Planning in Social Welfare Adminstration." *Administration in Social Work* 3 (4): 385–396.

——. 1982. "Life Begins at Forty: Alienation, Burnout and the Midlife Crisis." *Administration in Social Work* 6 (4): 85–94.

Gurin, Arnold. 1978. "Conceptual and Technical Issues in the Management of Human Service." In *The Management of Human Services*. Rosemary C. Sarri and Yaheskel Hasenfeld, eds. New York; Columbia Press, pp. 289–308.

Hage, Jerald, and Michael Aiken. 1967. "Relationship of Centralization to Other Structural Properties. *Administration Service Quarterly* 12: 72–91.

——. 1970. *Social Change in Complex Organizations*. New York: Random House.

Hall, Richard. 1977. *Organizations: Structure and Process*, 3d ed. Englewood Cliffs, N.J.: Prentice-Hall.

Handler, Joel F. 1973. *The Coercive Social Worker: British Lessons for American Social Services*. Chicago: Rand McNally.

——. 1979. *Protecting the Social Service Client: Legal and Structural Controls on Official Discretion*. New York: Academic Press.

Hardcastle, David. 1971 "The Indigenous Non-Professional in the Social Service Bureaucracy." *Social Work* 16 (2): 56–64.

Harrison, W. David. 1980. "Role Strain and Burnout in Child Protective Service Workers." *Social Service Review* 54 (1): 31–44.

Hasenfeld, Yaheskel. 1974. "People Processing Organizations: An Exchange Approach." In *Human Service Organizations,* ed. Y. Hasenfeld and R. English. Ann Arbor: University of Michigan Press.

———. 1980. "Implementation of Change in Human Service Organizations: A Political Economy Perspective." *Social Service Review* 54 (4): 508–520.

———. 1983. *Human Service Organizations.* Englewood Cliffs, N.J.: Prentice-Hall.

Hasenfeld, Yaheskel, and Richard A. English (eds.). 1974. *Human Service Organizations.* Ann Arbor: University of Michigan Press.

Hashimi, Joan K. 1981. "Environmental Manipulation: Teaching Coping Skill." *Social Work* 26 (4): 323–326.

Hershey, Paul and Kenneth H. Blanchard. 1977. *Management of Organizational Behavior: Utilizing Human Resources,* 3d. ed. Englewood Cliffs, N.J.: Prentice Hall.

Himmelweit, H. 1964. "Deviant Behavior." In *Dictionary of the Social Sciences,* ed. Julius Gould and William L. Kolb. New York: Free Press.

Hollingshead, August B., and Frederick C. Redlich. 1958. *Social Class and Mental Illness.* New York: Wiley.

Holloway, Stephen, and George Brager, 1977. "Some Considerations in Planning Organizational Change." *Administration in Social Work.* 1.

Human Service Reporter. 1980. "System to Help Disabled Elderly." (New Jersey Division of Human Services) 3 (3): 1,10.

Hummel, Ralph P. 1982. *The Bureaucratic Experience. 2nd Ed.* New York: St. Martin's Press.

Illich, Ivan. 1976. *Medical Nemesis.* New York: Random House.

Inbar, Michael, 1979. *Routine Decision Making.* Beverly Hills, Calif.: Sage.

Indik, Bernard P. 1964. "The Relationship Between Organizational Size and Supervision Ratio." *Administrative Science Quarterly* 9 (3): 301–302.

Indik, B., and F. Berrien. 1968. *People, Groups and Organization.* New York: Teachers College Press.

Jacobs, Jane. 1961. *Death and Life of the American City.* New York: Random House.

Jansson, Bruce. 1979. "Public Monitoring of Contracts with Nonprofit Organizations: Organizational Mission in Two Sectors." *Journal of Sociology and Social Welfare* 6 (3): 362–374.

Jenkins, Lowell, and Alicia S. Cook. 1981. "The Rural Hospice: Integrating Formal and Informal Helping Systems." *Social Work* 26 (5): 414–416.

Jenkins, Shirley. 1981. *The Ethnic Dilemma in Social Servies.* New York: Free Press.

Johnson, Peter J., and Allen Rubin. 1983. "Case Management in Mental Health: A Social Work Domain?" *Social Work* 28 (1): 49–56.

Joint Commission of Mental Illness and Health. 1961. *Action for Mental Health.* New York: Basic.

Jones, Maxwell. 1968. *Social Psychiatry in Practice: The Idea of the Therapeutic Community.* New York: Penguin Books.

Kadushin, Alfred. 1974a. *Child Welfare Services.* New York: Macmillan.

———. 1974b. "Supervisor–Supervision: A Survey." *Social Work* 19: 288–298.

———. 1976. *Supervision in Social Work.* New York: Columbia University Press.

Kahana, E. and B. Kahana. 1967. "The Effects of Age Segregation on Interaction Patterns of Elderly Psychiatric Patients." Paper presented at annual meeting of American Psychological Association, Washington, D.C.

Kahn, Alfred J. 1970. "Perspectives on Access to Social Services." *Social Work* 15 (2): 95–102.

———. 1976. "Service Delivery at the Neighborhood Level: Experience, Theory and Fads." *Social Service Review* 50 (1): 23–56.

———. 1979. *Social Policy and Social Services* 2d ed. New York: Random House.

Kahn, Alfred J., Laurence Grossman, Jean Bandler, Felicia Clark, Florence Galkin and Ken Greenwalt. 1966. *Neighborhood Information Centers.* New York: Columbia University Press.

Kahn, Robert. 1978. "Job Burnout: Prevention and Remedies" *Public Welfare* 36 (2): 60–63.

Kahn, Robert, D. M. Wolfe, R. P. Quin, S. D. Snock, and R. A. Rosenthal. 1964. *Organizational Stress: Studies in Role Conflict and Ambiguity.* New York: Wiley.

Kane, Rosalie A. 1980. "Discharge Planning: An Undischarged Responsibility." *Health and Social Work* 5: 2–3.

Kaplan, Abraham. 1964. *Conduct of Inquiry.* San Francisco: Chandler.

Karger, Howard J. 1981. "Burnout As Alienation." *Social Service Review* 55 (2): 270–283.

Katan, Yosef. 1974. "The Utilization of Indigenous Workers in Human Service Organization." In *Human Service Organizations,* ed. Y. Hasenfeld and R. English. Ann Arbor: University of Michigan Press.

Katz, Daniel, and Robert Kahn. 1978. *Social Psychology of Organizations,* rev. ed. New York: Wiley.

Keefe, Thomas. 1978. "The Economic Context of Empathy." *Social Work* 23 (6): 460–465.

Kennedy, Marilyn. 1980. *Office Politics.* New York: Warner Books.

Kepner, Charles, and B. Tregoe. 1965. *The Rational Manager.* New York: McGraw-Hill.

Kettner, Peter M. 1973. *Some Factors Affecting Use of Professional Knowledge and Skill by the Social Worker in Public Welfare Agencies.* D.S.W. dissertation, School of Social Work, University of California, Berkeley.

Kramer, Ralph, and Harry Specht. 1969. *Readings in Community Organization.* Englewood Cliffs, N.J.: Prentice-Hall.

Kuhn, T. S. 1962. *The Structure of Scientific Revolutions.* Chicago: University of Chicago Press.

Kupers, T. A. 1981. *Public Therapy.* New York: Free Press.

Kurland, Carol H. 1982. "The Medical Day Care Program in New Jersey." *Home Health Care Services Quarterly* 3 (2): 45–61.

Kurzman, Paul A. 1977. "Rules and Regulations in Large-Scale Organizations." *Administration in Social Work* 1 (4): 421–432.

Laing, R. D. 1969. "Interventions in Social Situations." In *The Politics of the Family.* New York: Pantheon.

Lauffer, Armand, Lynn Nybell, Carla Overberger, Beth Reed, and Laurence Zeff. 1977. *Understanding Your Social Agency.* Beverly Hills, Calif.: Sage.

Lee, Laura J. 1983. "The Social Worker in the Political Environment of a School System." *Social Work* 28 (4): 302–307.

Lerman, Paul. 1975. *Community Treatment and Social Control.* Chicago: University of Chicago Press

———. 1982. *Deinstitutionalization and the Welfare State.* New Brunswick, N.J.: Rutgers University Press.

Levine, Murray, and Adeline Levine. 1970. *A Social History of Helping Services.* New York: Appleton-Century Crofts.

Levy, Charles S. 1982. *Guide to Ethical Decisions and Actions for Social Service Administrators.* New York: Haworth Press.

Lewis, Judith, and Michael D. Lewis. 1983. *Management of Human Service Programs.* Monterey, Calif: Brooks Cole.

Likert, R. 1961. *New Patterns of Management.* New York: McGraw-Hill.

Lindenberg, Ruth E. and Claudia Coulton. 1980. Planning for Post-Hospital Care: A Follow-up Study." *Health and Social Work* 5: 45–50.

Lipsky, Michael. 1980. *Street Level Bureaucracy: Dilemma of the Individual in Public Services.* New York: Russell Sage Foundation.

Litwak, Eugene. 1961. "Models of Bureaucracy That Permit Conflict." *American Journal of Sociology* 67: 173–183.

———. 1978. "Organizational Constructs and Mega Bureaucracy." In *The Management of Human Services,* ed. Rosemary Saari and Yaheskel Hasenfeld. New York: Columbia University Press.

Livingston, Sterling. 1971. "Myth of the Well Educated Manager." *Harvard Business Review* 49: 79–89.

Lohr, Steve. 1981. "Overhauling America's Business Management." *New York Times Magazine* (January 4).

Long, David F. 1975. "Mergers of Groupwork Agencies in the Seventies." *Social Agency Management* 1 (5).

Lowenberg, Frank. 1968. "Social Workers and Indigenous Nonprofessionals: Some Structural Dilemmas." *Social Work* 13 (3): 65–71.

———. 1981. "The Destigmatization of Public Dependency. *Social Service Review* 5 (2): 434–452.

Mailich, D, and A. Ashley. 1981. "Politics of Interprofessional Collaboration: Challenge to Advocacy." *Social Casework* 62: 131–137.

March, J. G., and H. A. Simon. 1958. *Organizations*. New York: Wiley.

Marty, Martin E. 1980. "Social Service: Godly and Godless." *Social Service Review* 54 (4): 463–481.

Maslow, Abraham, H. 1970. *Motivation and Personality* 2d ed. New York: Harper & Row.

Mathieson, Thomas. 1971. *Across Organizational Boundaries*. Berkeley, Calif.: Glendessey Press.

Mechanic, David. 1962. "Sources of Power of Lower Participants in Complex Organizations." *Administrative Science Quarterly* 7 (3): 349–364.

———. 1974. *Politics, Medicine, and Social Service*. New York: Wiley.

———. 1975. "Alternative to Mental Hospital Treatment: A Sociological Perspective." In *Alternatives to Mental Hospital Treatment*, ed. Leonard Stein and Mary Test. New York: Plenum.

———. 1976. *The Growth of Bureaucratic Medicine*. New York: Wiley-Interscience.

———. 1977. "Illness Behavior, Social Adaptations, and the Management of Illness: A Comparison of Educational and Medical Models." *Journal of Nervous and Mental Disease* 165 (2): 79–87.

———. *Medical Sociology*, 2d ed. 1978. New York: Free Press.

———. 1979. *Future Issues in Health Care*. New York: Free Press.

———. 1980. *Mental Health and Social Policy*, 2d ed. Englewood Cliffs, N.J.-Prentice-Hall.

Meringoff, Marc L. 1980. *Management in Human Service Organizations*. New York: Macmillan.

Merton, Robert. 1957. *Social Theory and Social Structure*, rev ed. New York: Free Press.

Meyer, Carol H. 1983. "Declassification: Assault On Social Workers and Social Services." *Social Work* 28 (6): 419.

———. 1979. "What Directions for Direct Practice?" *Social Work* 24 (4): 267–273.

Meyer, H. J., E. E. Borgatta, and W. C. Jones. 1965. *Girls at a Vocational High: An Experimental Study in Social Work Intervention*. New York: Russell Sage.

Middleman, Ruth R., and Gale Goldberg. 1974. *Social Service Delivery: A Structural Approach to Social Work Practice*. New York: Columbia University Press.

Miller, Henry. 1981. "Dirty Sheets: A Multivariate Analysis." *Social Work* 26 (4): 268–271.

Miller, Rosalind S., and Helen Rehr. 1983. *Social Work Issues in Health Care*. Englewood Cliffs. N.J.: Prentice-Hall.

Miller, S. M. 1964. "The American Lower Classes: A Typological Approach." In *Mental Health of the Poor,* ed. Frank Reissman, Jerome Cohen, and Arthur Pearl. New York: Free Press.

Monk, Abraham. 1981. "Social Work with the Aged: Principles of Practice." *Social Work* 26 (1): 61–68.

Moos, Rudolf. 1974. *Evaluating Teatment Environments*. New York: Wiley.

Morris, Noval. 1974. *The Future of Imprisonment*. Chicago: University of Chicago Press.

Morris, Robert. 1977. "Caring for vs. Caring about People." *Social Work* 22 (5): 353–359.

Morris, Robert, and Delwin Anderson. 1975. "Personal Care Services: An Indentity for Social Work." *Social Service Review* 49 (2): 157–174.

Morris, Robert, and Bernard Friden. 1968. *Urban Planning and Social Policy*. New York: Basic Books.

Morris, Robert, and Ilana Lescohier. 1978. "Service Integration: Real vs. Illusory Solutions to Welfare Dilemmas." In *The Management of Human Services,* ed. Rosemary C. Sarri and Yeheskel Hasenfeld. New York: Columbia University Press.

Mullen, E. J., R. M. Chazin, and D. H. Feldstein. 1970. *Preventing Chronic Dependency.* New York: Community Service Society.

Murdach, Allison D. 1983. "Skills and Tactics in Hospital Practice." *Social Work* 28 (4): 279–284.

Nelson, Gary. 1982. "Social Class and Public Policy for the Elderly." *Social Service Review* 36 (1): 85–107.

Neugeboren, Bernard. 1970a. *Psychiatric Clinics: A Typology of Service Patterns.* Metuchen, N.J.: Scarecrow Press.

———. 1970b. "Opportunity-Centered Social Services." *Social Work* 15 (2): 47–52.

———. 1971. "Developing Specialized Programs in Social Work Administration in the Masters Degree Program." *Journal of Education for Social Work* 7 (3): 35–47.

———. 1977. "Barriers to Education in Social Work Administration—The More Things Change the More They Remain the Same." Paper presented at Council on Social Work Education Annual Program Meeting.

———. 1977. "Evaluation of Field Education for Social Welfare Administrators." Paper presented at the Western Conference on Curriculum Design for Social Welfare Administration, San Francisco.

———. 1978. "Turnover of MSW's in Public Child Welfare Agency." Unpublished paper, Rutgers University School of Social Work.

———. 1979. "Social Policy and Social Welfare Administration." *Journal of Sociology and Social Welfare* 6 (2): 168–197.

———. 1980. "Field Education for Social Welfare Adminstration: Integration of Social Policy and Administration." *Administration in Social Work* 4 (2): 63–74.

———. 1981. "Post-Masters Program in Human Service Administration—Survey and Proposal." Unpublished paper, Rutgers University Graduate School of Social Work.

Neugeboren, Ramona. 1976. "Caseload Management in Action: A Sociological Model for Service Delivery in Public Agencies." Paper presented at Northeastern Regional Meeting of the American Public Welfare Association, Atlantic Ciy, N.J.

Neugeboren, Ramona, Colleen McGuire, and Bernard Neugeboren. 1981. "The Medical Model in Protective Services." Paper presented at the International Conference on Child Abuse.

Nuehring, Elaine M. 1979. "The Technological Character of Barriers to Primary Preventive Activity in Mental Health: A Framework for Analysis." *Administration in Social Work* 2 (4): 451–468.

Ohlin, L. E., R. B. Coates, and A. D. Miller. 1974. "Radical Correctional Reform: A Case Study of the Massachusetts Youth Correctional System." *Harvard Educational Review* 44: 74–111.

Olmstead, Joseph, and Harold E. Christensen. 1973. *Effects of Agency Work Contexts: An Intensive Field Study.* Research Report No. 2. Washington, D.C.: Department of Health, Education, and Welfare, Social Rehabilitation Service.

Olyan, Sidney. 1972. *An Exploratory Study of Supervision in Jewish Community Centers as Compared to Other Welfare Settings.* Ph.D. dissertation. University of Pittsburgh School of Social Work.

Overall, Betty, and H. Aronson. 1963. "Expectations of Psychotherapy in Patients of Lower Socioeconomic Class." *American Journal of Orthopsychiatry* 33 (3): 421–430.

Palmer, Sally E. 1983. "Authority: An Essential Part of Practice." *Social Work* 28 (2): 120–125.

Panzetta, Anthony F. 1971. *Commmunity Mental Health: Myth and Reality.* Philadelphia: Lea & Febiger.

Parsons, Talcott, 1960. *Structure and Process in Modern Society.* New York: Free Press.

————. 1970. "How Are Clients Integrated in Service Organizations." In *Organizations and Clients*, ed. W. R. Rosengren and M. Lefton. Columbus, Ohio: Charles E. Merrill.

Patti, Rino J. (ed.). 1979. *Educational Innovations in Social Welfare Administration*. Monograph #1. Center for Social Welfare Research. School of Social Work, University of Washington (September).

————. 1983. *Social Welfare Administration: Managing Social Programs in a Developmental Context.* Englewood Cliffs, N.J.: Prentice-Hall.

Patti, Rino J. and Michael J. Austin. 1977. "Socializing the Direct Service Practitioner in the Ways of Supervisory Management." *Administration in Social Work* 1 (3): 267–180.

Patti, Rino J., Elenore Diedreck, Dennis Olson, and Jill Crowill. 1979. "From Direct Services to Administration: A Study of Social Work Transitions from Clinical to Management Roles." *Administration in Social Work* 2 and 3: 131–152; 265–276.

Peabody, Robert L. 1964. *Organization Authority: Superior-Subordinate Relationships in Three Public Service Organizations.* New York: Atherton.

Pearl, Arthur, and Frank Reissman. 1965. *New Careers for the Poor: The Non-Professional in the Human Service.* New York: Free Press.

Pelton, Leroy H. (ed.). 1981a. *The Social Context of Child Abuse and Neglect.* New York: Human Sciences Press.

Pelton, Leroy H. 1981b. "Child Abuse and Neglect: The Myth of Classlessness." In *The Social Context of Child Abuse and Neglect*, ed. Leroy H. Pelton. New York: Human Sciences Press.

Pelz, D. C. 1951. "Leadership Within a Hierarchial Organization." *Journal of Social Issues* 7: 49–55.

Perlman, Robert. 1975. *Consumers and Social Services.* New York: Wiley.

Perlman, Robert, and David Jones. 1967. *Neighborhood Service Centers.* Washington, D.C.: U.S. Department of Health, Education and Welfare.

Perlmutter, Felice, and Simon Slavin (eds.). 1980. *Leadership in Social Administration.* Philadelphia, Penn.: Temple University Press.

Perrow, Charles. 1961. "The Analysis of Goals in Complex Organizations." *American Sociological Review* 26: 856–866.

————. 1965. "Hospitals: Technology, Structure and Goals." In *Handbook of Organization*, ed. J. G. March. Chicago: Rand McNally.

————. 1970. *Organizational Analysis: A Sociological View.* Belmont, Calif.: Wadsworth.

————. 1972. *Complex Organizations.* Glenview, Ill.: Scott, Foresman.

————. 1976. "The Centralized Decentralized Bureaucracy: Forms of Control." Paper presented at 71st Annual Meeting of the American Sociological Association, New York.

————. 1978. "Demystifying Organizations." In *The Management of Human Services*, eds. Rosemary C. Sarri and Yaheskel Hasenfeld. New York: Columbia Univesity Press.

Peter, L. F., and R. Hull. 1969. *The Peter Principle.* New York: Bantam.

Pincus, Allen, and Anne Minahan. 1973. *Social Work Practice: Model and Method.* Itaska, Ill.: F. E. Peacock.

Pines, Ayala, and Ditsa Kafry. 1978. "Organizational Tedium in the Social Services." *Social Work* 23 (6): 499–507.

Piven, Frances Fox, and Cloward, Richard. 1971. *Regulating the Poor: The Function of Public Welfare.* New York: Random House.

President's Commission on Law Enforcement and Administration of Justice. 1968. *The Challenge of Crime in a Free Society.* New York: Avon.

President's Commission on Mental Health. 1978. Task Panel 1, Reports Volume 4. Washington, D.C.: U.S. Government Printing Office.

Prottas, Jeffrey, M. 1979. *People Processing.* Lexington, Mass.: Lexington Books.

Pruger Robert. n.d. "The Good Bureaucrat." Unpublished manuscript.

————. 1973. "The Good Bureaucrat." *Social Work* 18 (4) 26–32.

———. 1978. "Bureaucratic Functioning as a Social Work Skill." In *Educating the Baccalaureate Social Worker.* eds. Betty L. Baer and Ronald Federico. Cambridge, and New York: Ballinger and Council on Social Education.

———. 1979. *Critical Stages in the Bureaucratic Career.* Manpower Monograph 13. Syracuse University, School of Social Work.

"Psychiatric Ghettos, Boarding Homes Get More Dangerous." 1981. *N.Y. Times,* February 8.

Quinnett, Paul. 1981. "The Perfect Out." *N.Y. Times,* August 26.

Rambeck, Roy S. 1976. "Is There a Merger in Your Future?" *Trustee* 29 (7).

Rapoport, Robert. 1960. *Community as a Doctor.* London: Tavistock.

Rapp, C. and J. Poertner. 1978. "Reducing Foster Care." *Administration in Social Work* 2 (3): 335–346.

Reid, William J. 1965. "Inter-Agency Coordination in Delinquency Prevention and Control." In *Social Welfare Institutions,* ed. Mayer N. Zald. New York: Wiley.

Reid, William J., and Christine Beard. 1980. "An Evaluation of In-Service Training in a Public Welfare Setting." *Administration in Social Work* 4 (1): 71–85.

Reid, William J., and Ann Shyne. 1969. *Brief and Extended Casework.* New York: Columbia University Press.

Rein, Martin. 1970. "Social Work in Search of a Radical Perspective." *Social Work* 15 (2): 13–28.

Rein, Martin, and S. M. Miller. 1967. "The Demonstration as a Strategy of Change." In *Organizing for Community Welfare.* ed. Mayer N. Zald. Chicago: Quadrangle Books.

Rein, Martin, and Robert Morris. 1962. "Goals, Structures, and Strategies for Community Change." *Social Work Practice.* New York: Columbia University Press.

Rein, Martin, and Sheldon H. White. 1981. "Knowledge for Practice." *Social Science Review* 55 (1): 1–41.

Reisman, Frank, Jerome Cohen, and Arthur Pearl (eds.). 1964. *Mental Health of the Poor.* New York: Free Press.

Report of the Committee on Local Authority and Allied Personal Social Services. Frederick Seebohm, Chairman. 1968. London: Her Majesty's Stationery Office, Cmmd. 3703.

Report of the National Advisory Commission on Civil Disorders. Otto Kerner, Chairman. 1968. New York: Bantam.

Resnick, Herman, and Rino J. Patti. 1980. *Change from Within.* Philadelphia: Temple University Press.

Richan, Willard C. 1969. "Two Kinds of Social Services in Public Welfare." *Public Welfare* 27 (4): 307–308.

———. 1980. "The Administration as Advocate." In *Leadership in Social Administration,* ed. Felice Perlmutter and Simon Slavin. Philadelphia: Temple University Press.

———. 1983. "Social Work Administration Under Assault." *Administration in Social Work* 7 (314): 9–19.

Richan, Willard C., and Allan Mendelsohn. 1973. *Social Work: The Unloved Profession.* New York: New Viewpoints.

Roberts, Bertram H., and Jerome Myers. 1954. "Religion, National Origin, Immigration and Mental Illness." *American Journal of Psychiatry* 110: 759–764.

Rodman, Hyman. 1965. "The Lower-Class Value Stretch." In *Poverty in America,* ed. Louis A. Ferman. Ann Arbor: University of Michigan Press.

Roethlisberger, F. J., and W. J. Dickson. 1939. *Management and the Worker.* Cambridge, Mass.: Harvard University Press.

Rosenberg, Janet. 1978. "Discovering Natural Types of Role Orientation." *Social Service Review* 52 (1): 85–106.

Rogers, Everett. 1962. *The Diffusion of Innovation.* New York: Free Press.

Romanyshyn, John M. 1971. *Social Welfare.* New York: Random House.

Rosengren, William R. 1967. "Structure, Policy and Style: Strategies for Organizational Control." *Administrative Science Quarterly.* 12: 140–164.

Rosenthal, Seymour, and James Young. 1980. "The Governance of the Social Services." In *Leadership in Social Administration,* ed. Felice Perlmutter and Simon Slavin. Philadelphia: Temple University Press.

Rossens, S. 1977. "Discharge Planning—Social Workers Play an Important Role." *Social Work Administration* 3 (5): 4–5.

Rothman, Jack. 1974. *Planning and Organizing for Social Change.* New York: Columbia University Press.

———. 1978. "Conversion and Design in the Research Utilization Process." *Journal of Social Service Research* 2 (1): 117–131.

———. 1980a. "Harnessing Research to Enhance Practice: A Research and Developmental Model." In *Future of Social Work Research,* ed. David Fanshel. Washington, D.C.: National Association of Social Workers.

———. 1980b. *Social R & D: Research and Developments in the Human Sciences.* Englewood Cliffs, N.J.: Prentice-Hall.

Rothman, Jack, John L. Erlich, and Joseph G. Teresa. 1976. *Promoting Innovation and Change in Organization and Community.* New York: Wiley.

———. 1978. *Fostering Participation and Innovation: A Handbook for Human Service Professionals.* Itasca, Ill.: F. E. Peacock.

Rothman, Jack, and Wyatt Jones. 1971. *A New Look at Field Instruction.* Chicago: Association Press.

Rules and Regulations. 1980. New Jersey Division of Mental Health and Hospitals (September).

Ryan, William. 1971. *Blaming the Victim.* New York: Random House.

Sancier, Betty. 1982. "Case Management-Focus on the Client." *Practice Digest* 4 (4): 3,6.

Sarri, Rosemarie. 1977. "Administration in Social Welfare." In *Encyclopedia of Social Work.* Silver Spring, Md.: National Association of Social Workers.

———. 1982. "Management Trends in the Human Services in the 1980s." *Administration in Social Work* 6 (2 and 3): 19–30.

Sarri, Rosemary, and Yaheskel Hasenfeld (eds.). 1978. *Management of Human Services.* New York: Columbia University Press.

Scheff, Thomas J. 1968. "Societal Reaction to Deviance: Ascriptive Elements in the Psychiatric Screening of Mental Patients in a Midwestern State." In *The Mental Patient: Studies in the Sociology of Deviance,* ed. Stephen P. Spitzer and Norman K. Denzin. New York: McGraw-Hill.

———. 1975. *Labeling Madness.* Englewood Cliffs, N.J.: Prentice-Hall.

Schmidt, Herman, and Charles Fonds. 1956. "Reliability of Psychiatric Diagnosis: A New Look." *Journal of Abnormal Psychology* 52.

Schneider, R. and N. Sharon. 1982. "Representation of Social Agencies: New Definitions, Special Issues and Practice Models." *Administration in Social Work* 6 (1): 59–68.

Schwartz, Edward. 1967. "First Findings from Midway." *Social Science Review* 41 (2): 115–136.

Schwartz, William. 1969. "Private Troubles and Public Issues: One Social Work Job or Two." *Social Welfare Forum.* National Conference on Social Welfare. New York: Columbia University Press.

Segal, Steven P., and Uri Aviram. 1978. *The Mentally Ill in Community Based Sheltered Care.* New York: Wiley.

Selznick, P. 1957. *Leadership in Administration.* Evanston, Ill.: Harper and Row.

Schwartz, Edward. 1977. "Macro Social Work: Practice in Search of Some Theory." *Social Service Review* 51 (2): 209–210.

Shirley, Robert C. 1977. "The Human Side of Merger Planning." *Long Range Planning* 10: 35–39.

Sieverts, Steven. 1972. "Mergers: Elements in a Hospital Marriage." *Hospitals* 46 (22): 16–49.

Simon, Herbert A. 1957. *Administrative Behavior.* New York: Macmillan.

Siporin, Max. 1975. *Introduction to Social Work Practice.* New York: Macmillan.

Slavin, Simon. 1978. *Social Administration.* New York: Haworth Press.

———. 1980. "A Theoretical Framework for Social Administration." In *Leadership in Social Administration,* ed. Felice Perlmutter and Simon Slavin. Philadelphia: Temple University Press.

Social and Economic Conditions of Negroes in the United States. 1967. Washington, D.C.: U.S. Dept. of Commerce and Labor.

Sosin, Michael, and Sharon Caulum. 1983. "Advocacy: A Conceptualization for Social Work Practice" *Social Work* 28 (1): 12–17.

"Sparing of Social Programs: Reagan Bids for a Consensus." 1981 *New York Times,* February 12, p. A24.

Spiegel, John P. 1964. "Some Cultural Aspects of Transference and Countertransference." In *Mental Health and the Poor,* ed. Frank Reissman, Jerome Cohen, and Arthur Pearl. New York: Free Press.

Spitzer, Therese. 1980. *Psychobattery: A Chronicle of Psychotherapeutic Abuse.* Clifton, N.J.: Human Press.

Stanton, A., and M. Schwartz. 1954. *The Mental Hospital: A Study of Institutional Participation in Psychiatric Illness and Treatment.* New York: Basic.

Stein, Leonard I. (ed.). 1979. *Community Support System for the Long Term Patient.* San Francisco: Jossey-Bass.

Stein, Theodore. 1981. "Macro and Micro Level Issues in Case Management." In *Case Management: State of the Art,* Proceedings of the National Case Management Conference on Social Welfare, Indianapolis, Ind. 1980. (Washington, D.C. Administration on Developmental Disabilities).

Steinberg, R., and G. Carter. 1983. *Case Management and the Elderly.* Lexington, Mass.: D.C. Heath.

Steiner, Richard. 1977. *Managing the Human Service Organization.* Beverly Hills, Calif.: Sage.

Stewart, Robert P. 1981. "Watershed Days: How Will Social Work Respond to The Conservative Revolution?" *Social Work* 26 (4): 271–273.

Stoner, Madeleine R. 1983. "Social Service Administration and Practice in a Conservative Welfare Delivery System." *Administration in Social Work* 7 (3,4): 21–31.

Stotland, E., and A. Kobler. 1965. *Life and Death of a Mental Hospital.* Seattle: University of Washington Press.

Strauss, Anselm. 1964. *Psychiatric Ideologies and Institutions.* New York: Free Press.

Street, David, George Martin, Jr., and Laura Gordon Kramer. 1979. *The Welfare Industry.* Beverly Hills, Calif.: Sage.

Sullivan, Ina. 1976. *System Oriented Social Work Administration: Some Effects of Casework vs. Administration Training on Social Work Administration.* Doctoral dissertation. Graduate School of Social Work, Rutgers University.

Sutherland, Edwin, H., and Donald R. Cressey. 1978. *Criminology,* 10th Ed. Philadelphia: J.B. Lippincott.

Sutherland, John W. 1977. *Administrative Decision-Making: Extending the Bounds of Rationality.* New York: Van Nostrand Reinhold.

Szasz, Thomas. 1963. *Law, Liberty and Psychiatry.* New York: Macmillan.

Tabor, Merlin A., and Anthony J. Vattano., 1970. "Clinical and Social Orientations in Social Work." *Social Service Review* 44 (1): 34–41.

Tannenbaum, A. S. 1974. *Hierarchy in Organizations.* San Francisco: Jossey-Bass.

Taylor, F. W. 1923. *The Principles of Scientific Management.* New York: Harper.

Test, Mary Ann. 1975. "The Clinical Rationale for Community Treatment: A Review of Literature." In *Alternative to Mental Hospital Treatment,* ed. Leonard T. Stein and Mary Ann Test. New York: Plenum.

Thomas, Cordell H. 1983. "Social Model." *Social Work* 26 (4): 271–273.

Thomas, Edwin J. 1959. "Role Conceptions and Organizational Size." *American Sociological Review* 24: 30–37.

———. (ed.). 1967. *The Socio-Behavioral Approach and Applications to Social Work.* New York: Council on Social Work Education.

Thompson, James D., and William McEwen. 1958. "Organizational Goals and Environment." *American Sociological Review* 23: 23–31.

Thompson, Victor A. 1961. *Modern Organizations.* New York: Knopf.

———. 1975. *Without Sympathy or Enthusiasm: The Problem of Administrative Compassion.* University: University of Alabama Press.

Thomlinson, Ray J. 1984. "Something Works: Evidence from Practice Effectiveness Studies." *Social Work* 29 (1): 51–56.

Titmus, Richard. 1958. *Essays on the Welfare State.* London: George Allen Unwin.

Torczyner, J., and Arleen Pare. 1979. "The Influence of Environmental Factors on Foster Care." *Social Service Review* 53 (3): 358–377.

Tucker, David J. 1980. "A Quantitative Assessment of the Parallel Bars. Theory of Public—Voluntary Collaboration." *Administration in Social Work* 4 (2): 29–46.

Turner, Judith, 1976. "Comprehensive Community Support Systems and Adults with Seriously Disabling Mental Health Problems." (Summary of Working Conference on Community Support Systems—January.) Washington, D.C.: National Institutes of Mental Health.

Ullman, Leonard. 1967. *Institution and Outcome.* Elmsford, N.Y.: Pergamon.

Vash, C. 1979. *The Burned-out Administrator.* New York: Free Press.

Vail, David. 1966. *Dehumanization and the Institutional Career.* Springfield, Ill.: C.C. Thomas.

Varley, Barbara. 1966. "Are Social Workers Dedicated to Service?" *Social Work* 11 (2) 84–91.

Veninga, R. 1976. "Administrator Burn-out: Causes and Cures." *Hospital Progress* 60: 45–52.

Vinter, Robert. 1959. "Social Structure of Service." In *Issues in American Social Work,* ed. Alfred. J. Kahn. New York: Columbia University Press.

———. 1963. "Analysis of Treatment Organizations." *Social Work.* 8 (3): 3–15.

Wagenfeld, Morton D. 1972. "The Primary Prevention of Mental Illness: A Sociological Perspective." *Journal of Health and Social Behavior* 13 (2): 195–203.

Walden, Theodore. 1979. "The Graduate Admissions Interview: Benefits and Costs." *College and University* 55 (1): 49–50.

Walton, Richard, E. 1969. "Two Strategies of Social Change and Their Dilemmas." *Readings in Community Organization Practice* ed. R. Kramer and H. Specht. Englewood Cliffs, N.J.: Prentice-Hall.

Warfel, David J., Dennis M. Maloney, and Karen Base. 1981. "Consumer Feedback in Human Service Programs." *Social Work* 26 (2): 151–156.

Wasserman, Harry. 1970. 'Early Career of Professional Social Workers in a Public Child Welfare Agency." *Social Work* 15 (3): 93–101.

Weatherly, Richard A. 1983. "Participatory Management in Public Welfare: What Are the Prospects?" *Administration in Social Work* 7 (1): 39–50.

Weatherly, Richard, Claudia Kottwitz, et al. 1980. "Accountability of Social Service Workers at the Front Line." *Social Service Review* 54 (4).

Weber, Max. 1947. *The Theory of Social and Economic Organization,* ed. and trans. A. M. Henderson and T. Parsons. New York: Free Press.

Weich, Ann. 1981. "Reframing the Person-in-Environment Perspective." *Social Work* 26 (2): 140–143.

Weick, Ann. 1983. "Issues in Overturning a Medical Model of Social Work Practice." *Social Work.* 28 (6): 467–471.

Weil, Marie. 1983. "Preparing Women in Administration: A Self-Directed Learning Model." *Administration In Social Work* 7 (3,4): 117–131.

Weiner, Myron E. 1982 *Human Services Management: Analysis and Application.* Homewood, Ill.: Dorsey.

Weissmann, Harold H. 1973. *Overcoming Mismanagement in the Human Service Professions.* San Francisco: Jossey-Bass.

Weissman, Harold H. 1977. "Clients, Staff and Researchers: Their Role in Management Information Systems." *Administration in Social Work* 1 (1): 43–52.

Wiehe, Vernon R. 1980. "Current Practice in Performance Appraisal." *Administration in Social Work* 4 (3): 1–12.

Willetts, Ruth. 1980. "Advocacy and the Mentally Ill" *Social Work* 25: 372–377.

Wilson, Scott M. 1980. "Value and Technology: Foundations for Practice." In *Leadership in Social Administration,* ed. Felice D. Perlmutter and Simon Slavin. Philadelphia: Temple University Press.

Wing, J. 1967. "The Modern Management of Schizophrenia." In *New Aspects of the Mental Health Services,* ed. Hush Freeman and James Farmsdale. Elmsford, N.Y.: Pergamon.

Wing, J. 1978. "Planning and Evaluation Services for Chronically Handicapped Psychiatric Patients in the United Kingdom." In *Alternatives to Mental Hospital Treatment,* ed. Leonard Stein and Mary Test. New York: Plenum.

Wittman, Milton. 1973. "Preventative Social Work." *Encyclopedia of Social Work.* Silver Spring, Md.: National Association of Social Workers.

Wolfensberger, Wolf. 1972. *Normalization.* Toronto: National Institute of Mental Retardation.

Wolock, I., and B. Horowitz. 1979. "Child Maltreatment and Maternal Deprivation among AFDC Recipient Families." *Social Service Review* 53 (2): 175–194.

Wood, Katherine M. 1978. "Casework Effectiveness: A New Look at the Research Evidence." *Social Work* 23 (6): 437–459.

"Working Statement on the Purpose of Social Work." 1981. *Social Work* 26 (1): 6.

Yankey, John A., and Claudia Coulton. 1979. "Promoting Contributions to Organizational Goals: Alternative Models." *Administration in Social Work* 3 (1): 45–55.

Yessian, Mark R., and Anthony Broskowski. 1977. "Generalists in Human-Service Systems: Their Problems and Prospects." *Social Service Review* 51 (2): 265–288.

Yuchtman, E., and S. Seashore. 1967. "A System Resource Approach to Organizational Effectiveness." *American Sociological Review* 32:891–903.

Zaltman, Gerald, Robert Dunca and Jonny Holbech. 1973. *Innovations and Organizations.* New York: Wiley.

AUTHOR INDEX

SUBJECT INDEX